In Conversation with God

Meditations for each day of the year

Francis Fernandez

In Conversation with God

Meditations for each day of the year

Volume Four
Ordinary Time: Weeks 13 – 23

SCEPTER
London   New York

This edition of *In Conversation with God – Volume 4* is published:
in England by Scepter, 1 Leopold Road, London W5 3PB; and
in the United States by Scepter Press Inc., 481 Main Street, New
Rochelle, N.Y. 10801.

This is a translation of *Hablar con Dios – Vol IV*, first published in
1989 by Ediciones Palabra, Madrid, and in 1991 by Scepter, London.

With ecclesiastical approval

© Translation – Scepter, London, 1991
© This edition – Scepter, London, 1991

British Library Cataloguing in Publication Data
Fernandez, Francis
In Conversation with God – Volume 4
Ordinary Time: Weeks 13 – 23
1. Christian life – Daily Readings
I Title   II Hablar con Dios *English*
242'.2

ISBN 0 906138 23 X (Volume 4)
ISBN 0 906138 22 1 (Volume 3)
ISBN 0 906138 21 3 (Volume 2)
ISBN 0 906138 20 5 (Volume 1)
ISBN 0 906138 19 1 (Complete set)

Cover design & typeset in England by KIP Intermedia, and printed in
Singapore.

Contents

Scheduled Use of this Volume

in *Ordinary Time*

Year	Cycle	13th Week begins on Sunday	23rd Week ends on Saturday
1990	A	1 July	15 September
1991	B	30 June	14 September
1992	C	28 June	12 September
1993	A	27 June	11 September
1994	B	26 June	10 September
1995	C	2 July	16 September
1996	A	30 June	14 September
1997	B	29 June	13 September
1998	C	28 June	12 September
1999	A	27 June	11 September
2000	B	2 July	16 September

Thirteenth Sunday: Year A

1. LOVE FOR GOD

1.1 God alone must be loved absolutely and unconditionally. Upright human affections are raised and ennobled when we love God above all other loves.

Over and over again Jesus teaches us that God has to be the principal object of our love. We must love creatures in a secondary, subordinate way. In the Gospel of the Mass[1] He tells us in words that leave no room for doubt: *He who loves father or mother more than me is not worthy of me; and he who loves son or daughter more than me is not worthy of me.* And He continues: *He who finds his life will lose it, and he who loses his life for my sake will find it.*

God alone is to be loved absolutely and unconditionally. Everyone and everything else is to be loved by us in the measure in which they are loved by God. Our Lord teaches us *true* love. He asks us to love family and neighbour, but not even these loves should we put before the love of God, which must always be given an overriding priority. All other earthly loves are enriched, purified and encouraged to grow when we love God. Our heart expands and our capacity for loving increases. We find ourselves able to overcome all the obstacles and limitations of self-centredness that are present in all of us creatures. The pure loves of this life are raised and ennobled still more when we love God first and most of all.

---

1. Matt 10:37-42

To love God the way He wants us to love him, we have to go so far as to *lose* our own life, that of the *old man*. We have to die to those disordered tendencies which incline and induce us to sin. We must die to that sometimes brutal egocentricity which leads man to seek himself in everything he does.[2] God wants us to preserve all that is healthy and upright and truly human in our nature, all that is good and humanly characteristic in each unique individual. Nothing genuinely human, of the positive, of the perfectible, will be lost. The life of grace will permeate the whole of man's nature and elevate it. In this way the personality of the Christian who loves God is richly enhanced. The more a man dies to his selfish *ego*, the more truly human he becomes, and so much the better is he prepared for supernatural life.

The Christian who struggles to deny himself finds he is living a new life, the life of Jesus. Grace respects what is characteristic in each one of us at the same time as it transforms us, so that we come to have the same attitudes and sentiments that Christ himself has concerning men and events. Seeing things as He does, we begin to imitate his deeds. In this way a new, simple, natural behaviour is born in us, encouraging us to be better. We are filled with the same desires as Christ: our one objective becomes that of fulfilling the will of the Father. That, then, is the real expression of love and its clearest manifestation. Remaining what he is, by the help of grace the Christian becomes identified with Jesus in so far, paradoxically, as he divests himself of himself. *My desire is to depart and be with Christ*, says Saint Paul.[3]

Love of God cannot be taken for granted. If we do

---

2. cf R. Garrigou-Lagrange, *Three Ages of the Interior Life*
3. Phil 1:21-23

not nurture and take care of it, it dies. On the other hand, difficulties set it ablaze and confirm us in it if our will holds steadfastly in God. Love of God is nourished in prayer and in the reception of the sacraments, in the constant struggle against our defects, in the unceasing effort to maintain a living presence of God throughout the whole of our working day, in our relations with others, in our times of rest ... The Eucharist above all must be the spring at which our love of God is perpetually refreshed and strengthened. In a way, to love thus is already to possess Heaven on earth.

1.2 There is no limit or measure to the love of God.

The Christian is raised to the order of grace so that he loves with the love of God himself, which is given to him as an ineffable gift.[4] This is the essence of charity. The Christian receives it first at baptism. He can prepare himself for its augmentation through prayer, the sacraments and good deeds.

This love of God is infused in the Christian's soul. It *should be the rule of all his actions. Just as the objects we make are judged to be finished and perfect insofar as they conform to the preconceived plans to which we work, so any human action will be upright and virtuous if it conforms to the divine rule of love. If it departs from it, it will not be good or perfect.*[5] All our deeds can be weighed and measured by this rule because the soul in grace does not receive divine love as something foreign to it. Charity does not destroy. It brings order, imposing on its recipient that unity of love which is so characteristic of the love of God.

---

4. cf 1 John 4:2
5. St Thomas, *On the Double Precept of Charity*, Prologue

Hence it perfects and elevates our will.

Charity, with which we love God, and in God we love our neighbour, comes to fruition precisely to the extent that we use it. The more we love, the greater capacity we have for loving. *And if it (i.e. love) does not possess completely what it loves, it cannot help being weary, in proportion to the absence of that which is not possessed ... Until this possession be achieved, the soul is like an empty vessel waiting to be filled, or like a hungry man craving food, or like a sick person sighing wretchedly for health, or like one suspended in the air with nothing to lean on.*[6]

There is no limit or measure to God's love. He expects us to love him with all our heart, with all our soul and all our mind.[7]

We can always grow in love of God. He tells his children, each one individually, *I have loved you with an everlasting love; therefore I have continued my faithfulness to you.*[8]

We pray to God to convince us that there is only one absolute love, and that this Love is the source of all upright, noble loves. He who loves God will love all of God's creatures more and better. *It is easy to love some; with others it is more difficult. We do not find them attractive, they have offended us or have done us wrong. Only if I love God seriously can I love other creatures as his children, and because He has commanded me. Jesus has also established how we are to love our neighbour – not with feelings alone, but with deeds ... I was hungry in the person of the least of my brothers. Did you give me to eat? Did you visit me when I was sick?*[9] Did you help me to carry the burden

6. St John of the Cross, *Spiritual Canticle*, 9:6
7. cf Matt 22:37-38
8. Jer 31:3
9. John Paul II, *General Audience*, 27 September 1978

when it was too heavy for me to carry it alone?

To love our neighbour in God is not to go about by a long and circuitous route in order to love him. Love of God is a short-cut to our brothers. Only in God can we really understand and love all men, immersed even as they are in their errors and we in ours, and in spite of those things that humanly speaking would tend to separate us from them or lead us to pass them by without a glance in their direction.

1.3 How the love of God is shown.

Our love of God is merely a response to *His* love. *He loved us first.*[10] Ours is the love God places in our souls so that we too are able to love. That is why we ask him, *Lord, give me the love with which you want me to love you.*

We correspond with the love of God when we love others; when we see in them the dignity proper to the human person, made as it has been in the image and likeness of God, created with an immortal soul and called to give glory to God for all eternity. Love is to approach that wounded man we come across on our journey each day; it is to bind up his wounds, restore him to health and take care of him in all things.[11] We must exert ourselves on his behalf, making a serious effort in order to bring him to God. Separation from God is always the greatest of evils, and those thus separated from him are in need of our help and our urgent attention. Apostolate is a wonderful sign of our love for God, and is the way to love him more.

Love is frequently shown by a response of gratitude. To illustrate this, Our Lord relates the parable of the debtors. Having done so, He asks Simon the Pharisee which

---

10. 1 John 4:19
11. cf Luke 10:30-37

of the two debtors He has spoken about would love their generous creditor the more.[12] Jesus uses the verb *to love* here as a synonym for *to be grateful*. In this way He shows us wherein lies the essence of the affection man owes to his principal creditor, God. Etymology also helps to throw light on the deep meaning of the Eucharist; *eucharist* in its derivation is *thanksgiving* for the gift of Love which the Blessed Sacrament itself conveys to us.

We correspond with the love of God when we fight against everything that separates us from him. We need to struggle every day, if only in little things. We shall always come up against obstacles that stand between us and God: defects of character, selfishness, laziness that would prevent us from finishing our work well …

We love God when our whole life is an unceasing search for him. It is sometimes said that not only does God not seek us, but can hide himself from us so that we should seek him. In fact, we have not far to look. We can find him in our work, in our family, in our joys and our sorrows … He asks us for our affection. He places in our heart the desire to seek him, and constantly encourages us in our search. If we could only understand how much God loves us! If we could only say with Saint John: *So we know and believe the love God has for us!*[13] If we could, it would be much simpler and easier for us to love him as we ought.

Our whole life has to become this constant seeking after Jesus, in good times and in those that seem bad, in our work and in our leisure, in the street and in the bosom of the family. This quest is the only one that can give meaning to our lives. We cannot carry out this task of ours alone. Let us go to Mary and beseech her, *Mother, do not*

---

12. cf Luke 7:42
13. 1 John 4:16

leave me! Let me seek your Son, let me find your Son, let me love your Son – with my whole being. Remember me, my Lady, remember me.[14] Teach me to hold fast to him as my first Love, He whom I love for himself, absolutely, above all other loves.

What am I to thee, Lord, that thou should'st command me to love thee; yea, and be angry and threaten to lay huge miseries upon me if I love thee not? Is it perhaps of itself no great misery if I do not love thee?[15]

---

14. J. Escrivá, *The Forge*, 157
15. St Augustine, *The Confessions*, I, 5, 5

THIRTEENTH SUNDAY: YEAR B

2. DEATH AND LIFE

2.1 The death we must avoid and fear.

This Sunday the Liturgy speaks to us about death and life. The First Reading[1] teaches us that death had no place in the initial plan of the Creator: *God did not make death, and he does not take delight in the death of the living.* It is the result of sin.[2] Jesus Christ accepted it *as a necessity of nature, as an inevitable part of man's fate on earth. Jesus Christ accepted it ... in order to overcome sin.*[3] The human heart recoils in anguish from death,[4] but we are comforted by the knowledge that Jesus annihilated it. He has destroyed death.[5] It is no longer the event that man must fear above all else. Rather it is, for the believer, the necessary step from this world to the Father.

The Gospel of the Mass shows us Jesus arriving once more at Capharnaum,[6] where a large crowd had gathered expectantly to meet him. Jairus, one of the rulers of the synagogue, was waiting. His need was great and so was his faith. His daughter was at the point of death. There was also a woman there who had spent every penny she had trying to find a cure for a long illness. Both these people felt an urgent need to meet Jesus. The healing of this woman, who had placed all her hope in him, takes place

---

1. Wis 1:13-15
2. cf Rom 6:23
3. John Paul II, *Homily*, 28 February 1979
4. Heb 2:15
5. 2 Tim 1:10
6. Mark 5:21-43

on the way to Jairus' house.

Jesus has stopped to console the woman. Meanwhile, they inform the ruler of the synagogue: *Your daughter is dead. Why trouble the Master any further?* But Jesus takes Peter, James and John to be witnesses of the miracle He is about to perform. They come to Jairus' house, and He sees the confusion and the people there weeping and wailing. When He enters, He says, *Why do you make a tumult and weep? The child is not dead, but sleeping. And they laugh at him* ... They failed to understand that for God real death is sin, which kills the divine life of the soul. For the believer, bodily death is like a sleep from which we awake in God. That is how the first Christians looked at it.

Saint Paul urged the Christians at Thessalonica not to be of any other mind: *We would not have you ignorant, brethren,* he exhorted them, *concerning those who are asleep, that you may not grieve as others do who have no hope.*[7] We cannot lament like those who expect nothing after this life. For *since we believe that Jesus died and rose again, even so, through Jesus, God will bring with him those who have fallen asleep.*[8] He will do for us what He did for Lazarus: *Our friend Lazarus has fallen asleep, but I go to awake him.* When the disciples thought He meant a natural sleep, Jesus clearly explains: *Lazarus is dead.*[9] When death comes we shall close our eyes on this life and awake in the real Life, a life that lasts for ever. *At night there are tears, but joy comes with dawn,* we pray in the Responsorial Psalm.[10] Sin is real death. It is the dreadful separation of man when he breaks away from God. Compared to this, the other separation, that of the body from

---

7. 1 Thess 4:13
8. 1 Thess 4:14
9. cf John 11:11 ff
10. Ps 29:6

the soul, is temporary and even trivial. *He who believes in me, though he die, yet shall he live, and whoever lives and believes in me shall never die.*[11]

Death, which was to be *the last enemy*[12] is in fact our ally. It has become the last step after which we find ourselves in the definite embrace of Our heavenly Father. He has been waiting for us from all eternity, and has destined us to remain with Him forever. *When you think about death, do not be afraid, in spite of your sins. For He already knows that you love him and what stuff you are made of. If you seek him, He will welcome you as the father welcomed the prodigal son; but you have to seek him.*[13] Lord, you know that I seek you day and night.

2.2 Sin, the death of the soul. Its effects.

The child is not dead but sleeping, Jesus tells Jairus. *For men she was indeed dead. There was no wakening her. For God she was asleep, because her soul lived on under the divine power and her flesh should rest till the resurrection. Thus the custom arose among Christians of calling the dead, whom we know will rise again, by the name of sleepers.*[14]

Bodily death is not an absolute evil. *Don't forget, my son, that for you on earth there is but one evil, which you must fear and avoid with the grace of God – sin.*[15] *The lack of God ... is death to the soul.*[16] When a man falls into grave sin he is lost for himself and for God. It is the greatest tragedy that could befall him.[17] He is radically cut

---

11. John 11:25-26
12. 1 Cor 15:26
13. J. Escrivá, *Furrow*, 880
14. The Venerable Bede, *Commentary on Saint Mark's Gospel*, in loc
15. J. Escrivá, *The Way*
16. St John of the Cross, *Spiritual Canticle*, 2, 7
17. cf Tanquerey, *Compendium of Ascetical and Mystical Theology*, 719-723

off from God by the total loss of divine life in his soul. He loses whatever merits he has acquired throughout his life and is in this state unable to acquire new ones. In some way he is subject to the slavery of the devil, and his natural inclination towards virtue is diminished. This situation is so grave that *by all mortal sins, even those of thought, men are made into 'children of wrath' (Eph 2:3) and enemies of God.*[18] By faith we know that a single sin, even a venial sin, but *a fortiori* a mortal sin, is a disorder greater than the most disastrous catastrophe that could lay waste the whole world, since *the good of grace in a single soul is greater than the natural good of the whole universe.*[19]

Sin not only harms the person who commits it, but harms also his family, his friends, the whole of the Church. *One can speak of 'a communion of sin', whereby a soul that debases itself through sin drags down with itself the Church and, in some way, the whole world. In other words, there is not a single sin, not even the most intimate and secret one, the most strictly personal and individual one, that exclusively concerns the person committing it. With greater or lesser violence, with consequences of greater or lesser harm, every sin has repercussions on the entire ecclesial body and the whole human family.*[20]

We should often ask God never to let us lose the sense of sin and its seriousness. We should never put our soul in danger or get used to seeing sin around us as being of little importance. Let us atone for our own faults and for those of all men. At the end of our lives may God be able to say of us, *he has not died, he is sleeping.* Then He will awaken us to Life.

---

18. Council of Trent, Session 14, Chapter 5
19. St Thomas, *Summa Theologiae,* 1-2, 113, 9, 2
20. John Paul II, *Reconciliatio et Poenitentia,* 2 December 1984, 16

2.3 The life of the soul to be esteemed above all else.

Jesus paid no attention at all to those who laughed at him. On the contrary, *He put them all outside and took the child's father and mother and those who were with him, and went in where the child was. Taking her by the hand He said to her, 'Talitha cumi', which means 'Little girl, I say to you, arise'. And immediately the girl got up and walked; for she was twelve years old. And immediately they were overcome with amazement.*

The evangelists have handed down to us a seemingly small but significantly human touch of Jesus – *and he told them to give her something to eat.* Jesus, perfect God and perfect Man, is also interested in those matters that relate to our life here on earth. But He is far more interested in whatever concerns our eternal destiny. Saint Jerome comments on these words of Our Lord: *The child is not dead, but sleeping.* He points out that *both things are true. It is as though He were saying, 'She is dead for you, but sleeping for me'.*[21] If we love our bodily life, how much more should we esteem the life of the soul!

The Christian who tries to follow Christ closely detests mortal sin and will habitually avoid grave faults, although nobody is confirmed in grace. The recognition of our own weakness will lead us to avoid the occasions of mortal sin, including even remote occasions. The life of the soul is worth a lot! Love for the life of grace will move us to an assiduous mortification of the senses. We shall not trust ourselves, or our experience, or the length of time we have already spent following Christ. We shall love frequent confession and complete sincerity in spiritual direction.

To safeguard the life of the soul we must keep up the

---

21. St Jerome, *Catena Aurea*, vol 4, p.131

struggle at some remove from the borderline between
what is serious and what is less serious, between what is
forbidden and what is permitted. Deliberate venial sins
cause havoc in souls that are not struggling sincerely to
avoid them. They do not, it is true, utterly destroy the life
of grace in the soul, but they certainly weaken it. They
make it more difficult to practise the virtues, and render
the gentle motions of the Holy Spirit less effective. If we
do not react firmly, venial sins make us liable to more
serious falls.

Let us ask our Mother the Blessed Virgin to obtain
for us the gift of esteeming the life of the soul above all
human goods, even that of bodily life itself. She will help
us to react with true contrition against our weaknesses and
errors. We can say with the Psalmist: *Thy eyes shed
streams of tears, because men do not keep thy Law.*[22] Main-
taining and increasing the life of the soul is more important than the death of the body.

---

22. Ps 118:136

THIRTEENTH SUNDAY: YEAR C

3. DON'T LOOK BACK

3.1 The demands of our vocation: promptness in self-giving, detachment, not imposing conditions ...

The Readings of the Mass today help us to meditate on our vocation, as well as on the service to God and men demanded by it. The First Reading[1] tells us how Elijah is sent by God from Horeb to anoint Elisha as a prophet of Yahweh. Elijah left the mountain and found Elisha as he was ploughing; *he passed near to him and threw his cloak over him,* as a sign that God wanted him to dedicate himself to his service. Elisha responded forthwith and wholeheartedly, leaving nothing behind that might cause him to regret his departure. He took the pair of oxen with which he had been ploughing and slaughtered them. He built a fire with the wood of his plough, cooked the oxen and gave the meat to his men, who ate it. He then got up and went after Elijah ...

In the Gospel,[2] Saint Luke tells us of three different men who have it in mind to follow Our Lord. The first approached Jesus as He and his friends are going up on what will be the last long journey to Jerusalem and Calvary. It seems that this new disciple is one who could scarcely be better disposed. *I will follow you wherever you go,* he tells the Master. At this sign of generosity, in order to make sure the newcomer knows what he is letting himself in for, Our Lord points out the kind of life he can

---

1. 1 Kings 19:16; 19:21
2. Luke 9:57-62

expect if he genuinely wants to follow him. The mission of Christ is a constant coming and going, of preaching the gospel in season and out of season, and bringing salvation to all, and the disciple will be following one who himself *has nowhere to lay his head.* Such will be the life of all those who follow him. They will have to be detached from everything that might hold them back, and their dedication will necessarily have to be total.

The second would-be disciple is called directly by Our Lord. *Follow me,* He tells him. This potential disciple welcomes the invitation to follow the Master closely, but not right away. He thinks another time might be better as there is still some family business to be attended to ... He doesn't realise that when God calls, the best time is *now,* notwithstanding the circumstances surrounding a vocation, for they might lead to an all-too-human rationalisation to find grounds for postponing one's dedication. God has higher plans for the disciple as well as for those who would apparently be disadvantaged by his leaving them. From all eternity, everything has been prepared by God so that his choice and his timing is for the good of all concerned. The answer to Christ's call must be prompt, cheerful and unconditional, and be instinctive with a spirit of detachment.[3] When Jesus passes close to us we should not put off our dedication to him. If He passes by, perhaps we will not find him when we try later on to catch up. Our Lord goes on his way. It is a serious matter to succumb to the temptation to put things off, to procrastinate when Christ calls us.[4]

God calls each one of us in special circumstances. In our prayer today let us consider whether we are

3. cf F. Fernandez Carvajal, *St Luke's Gospel*
4. cf F. Suarez, *Mary of Nazareth*

responding promptly, with detachment, unconditionally, to the particular vocation Christ has given to every one of us.

3.2 The proofs of fidelity.

Saint Luke alone mentions the third disciple. He wants to turn back and take his leave of the people at home. Perhaps, since it will be the last opportunity, he wants to spend a little more time with his family. He seems to have *put his hand to the plough* and quite sincerely to want to follow the Master. But Our Lord's call is always urgent. The harvest is great and the labourers few. Some harvests are lost because there is no one to gather them in. To temporise, to look back, to start putting conditions on our proposed commitment, all come to the same thing. Jesus tells this prospective disciple, *Once the hand is laid on the plough, no one who looks back is fit for the Kingdom of God.*

The new task of the one who is called is compared to driving the Palestinian plough. It is an implement not easy to direct, particularly in the hard soil of the fields beside the Sea of Galilee. After having once gripped the handle of the plough there is no looking back. One cannot turn back when God calls. To be faithful, and happy as well, we must have our eyes fixed on Jesus.[5] Once the event has started, the runner doesn't think of other things. His only concern is getting to the tape and winning the race. The ploughman has a fixed point towards which he directs the plough. If he looks back he cannot open up a straight furrow.

At times the temptation to look back comes from our own limitations, or from an environment that is patently hostile to the obligations one has taken on; the temptation

---

5. Heb 12:2

might even be provided by the behaviour of those who should be an example and are anything but. Because of the way they live they seem to tell us that *being faithful* is not one of the basic values. At other times the temptation could spring from a lack of hope, when we see holiness just as far away, as remote an objective as ever, in spite of all our efforts to keep on struggling. *After an initial enthusiasm, the dubieties, hesitations and anxieties have begun to take effect. You are worried about your studies, your family, your financial situation and, above all, by the thought that you are not really up to it, that perhaps you are of no use, that you lack experience in life . . .*

I will give you a sure means of overcoming such fears, which are temptations insinuated by the devil or that come straight from your own lack of generosity! Despise them: eradicate those recollections from your memory. The Master already preached this poignant warning twenty centuries ago: 'No one who looks behind him . . . ' [6] In such situations, instead of allowing ourselves to be filled with unprofitable regrets we must on the contrary resolutely fix our eyes on Christ. *Be faithful,* He tells us. *On you go!* And whenever we look at Jesus we continue to make good progress on our journey. *There is never any real reason for looking back.* [7]

Looking back, Saint Athanasius tells us, *is a sign of our having regrets, and indicates that reawakening of our longings for the things of the world.* [8] It is symptomatic of the lukewarmness that finds its way into the hearts of those who have not set their sights firmly on the Lord. It is the result of our not allowing God and the nobler aspects of our vocation to fill our heart.

---

6. J. Escrivá, *Furrow*, 133
7. cf *ibid*, *Christ is passing by*, 160
8. St Athanasius, *Life of Saint Anthony*, 3

Looking back nostalgically at what we have left behind, vainly imagining *what might have been*, could result in breaking the ploughshare against a stone, or at least making it inevitable that the furrow, the mission entrusted to us, does not come out straight. In the supernatural task to which God is calling all of us, it is souls that are at risk.

We want to have eyes for Christ alone, and for all noble things in him. We can say in the words of this day's Responsorial Psalm: *O Lord, it is you who are my portion and my cup ... You will show me the path of life, the fullness of joy in your presence, at your right hand happiness for ever.*[9] The path of life is our own particular vocation which we must contemplate with love and thanksgiving.

3.3 Virtues which support us in our journey towards God.

Through Saint Luke, the Holy Spirit has willed to transmit to us the words addressed to these three disciples so that we can apply them to the calling we ourselves have received from God.

Man can actually be defined by his vocation. Each human being is and has in himself what God created him for. The meaning and purpose of human life is to know and freely carry out the divine Will. *Man finds his ultimate fulfilment or is lost according to whether he carries out in his life the specific plan God has for him.*[10] We have all of us received a vocation, a call to know God and find in him the source of life. We are invited to a state of intimacy with God, to a personal relationship of prayer. We are asked to make Christ the centre of our life, and to follow him. The decisions we make are to be made while taking

---

9. Ps 15:11
10. J. L. Illanes, *The World and Holiness*

into account his Will. We are called to see our fellow human beings as persons, as God's children. So we are required to overcome selfishness and to live fraternity, carrying out a fruitful apostolate and helping others to find God. Our calling is to do all this in our own lives, in the very conditions and circumstances in which God has placed us, fulfilling in all we do the specific mission which is devised for and corresponds to each individual personally.[11]

Fidelity to our particular vocation means responding to the successive calls God makes on us throughout our life. Normally it is a matter of being faithful in the small things of each day. It is a question of loving God in our work, and in all the joys and sorrows that form part of every life. We must firmly set aside everything that might lead us to where we would be unable to find Christ. Fidelity is based on a number of essential virtues, without which it would be difficult, not to say impossible, to follow the Master. Humility teaches us that we are like the great statue in the Book of Daniel.[12] We too have feet of clay. Prudence and sincerity are the consequences of humility. Charity and fraternity prevent our tendency to egocentricity, from turning us in on ourselves. The spirit of mortification leads us to temperance and sobriety, and helps us to struggle against softness and comfort-seeking. It helps us to avoid being involved in the search for compensations which are bound to turn sour because they lead us away from Christ. The spirit of prayer leads us to look upon and treat God as a friend, our closest Friend of all. *He who never stops walking on, and presses forward all the time*, says Saint Teresa, *may reach his goal late, but gets*

---

11. cf *ibid*
12. cf Dan 2:33

there just the same. Giving up prayer seems to me exactly the same as losing your way and getting lost.[13]

We tell God that we want to be faithful. We want nothing more from life than to follow him in good times and in bad. He is the pivot upon which our whole life turns, the centre upon which all our actions converge. Lord, without you our life would be like a machine that is breaking down, badly off balance and grinding to a halt.

As we finish our prayer, let us turn to the Virgin most faithful, our Mother Mary.

---

13. St Teresa, *Life*, 19:5

THIRTEENTH WEEK: MONDAY

4. THE VALUE OF ONE JUST MAN

4.1 For the sake of ten just men, God would have forgiven thousands of inhabitants of the two cities.

Holy Scripture depicts Abraham, *our father in faith*, as a just man in whom God rejoiced in such a special way that he confided to him the promise of the redemption of all mankind. The *Letter to the Hebrews* speaks with emotion and joy about this holy Patriarch and about all the just men of the Old Testament who died without having received what was promised, but who had *seen it and hailed it from afar.*[1] *This is a comparison*, comments Saint John Chrysostom, *taken from navigators at sea. When they see afar off the city they are making for, although they have not yet entered its harbour, they burst into excited cheers.*[2]

Although in this life the Patriarchs and the just of old times did not come to possess the redemption that had been promised, or to share in the union that we can now enjoy with the Only-begotten Son of God, Yahweh treated them as intimate friends and confided fully in them. Because of their faith and their fidelity He often overlooked the errors made by so many others of their contemporaries. Many men of those generations were saved because they were friends of those *friends of God*. When God proposed the destruction of Sodom and Gomorrah on account of the many sins committed there, He communicated this thought to Abraham.[3] Abraham felt that he shared the

---

1. Heb 11:13
2. St John Chrysostom, *Homilies on the Letter to the Hebrews*, 2:3
3. *First Reading*, Year I. Gen 18:16-33

responsibility of those people: *Then Abraham drew near and said, 'Wilt thou indeed destroy the righteous with the wicked? Suppose there are fifty righteous within the city; wilt thou then destroy the place and not spare it for the sake of the fifty righteous who are in it?'*. Abraham is full of confidence in God. And God replies, *'If I find at Sodom fifty righteous in the city, I will spare the whole place for their sake'*. But it was impossible to find those fifty righteous men. And Abraham had to reduce his original number of just men: *'Suppose five of the fifty righteous are lacking? Suppose forty-five are found there'* ... And God says to him, *'I will not destroy it if I find forty-five there'*. But there were not forty-five either. And Abraham went on interceding with God: 'Suppose forty are found there ... thirty ... twenty ... ?' Finally it was clear that there were not even ten just men in that city. The last time Abraham made his petition God had said : *'For the sake of ten I will not destroy it'*. God would have forgiven everybody in the whole place out of love for ten just men! Such is the value in God's eyes of saintly souls. He is prepared to go to any lengths for them.

Scripture often speaks of solidarity in evil, in the sense that the sins of some can cause harm to the whole community.[4] But Abraham turns the terms the other way round: he asks God who esteems the justice of the saints so highly, that it may be the saints who cause blessings to come down upon everyone, even though many are sinners. And God accepts this approach of the Patriarch's.

We can meditate today on *God's joy and delight* when He sees us struggling to be faithful to him. We can meditate on the value our actions may have when we do them for God. This is true of even our most inconspicuous actions, deeds that we may think nobody sees and that *apparently*

---

4. cf Josh 7:16-26

have little in them of transcendence. God sets great store by those who struggle for sanctity. *God's delight is in the saints*; it is for their sake that He pours out his mercy and his forgiveness on others who may have done nothing themselves to merit it. It is a wonderful but at the same time a real mystery, that God so delights in those who journey towards sanctity.

4.2 Our participation in the infinite merits of Christ.

The prophetic utterance that: *through the death of one man all will be saved*[5] was to be fulfilled with the coming of Jesus Christ. In Christ the mystery of human solidarity attains an undreamt of fullness. Nothing has been or ever will be – the extent of this is infinite – so pleasing to God as the offering – the holocaust – that Jesus made of his life for the salvation of all, and which reached its culmination on Calvary. *For there to take place on earth, within a human soul, an act of love of God of infinite value, it was necessary that that human soul should be the soul of a divine Person. Such was the soul of the Word made flesh; its act of love acquired such a value within the divine Person of the Word, and thus was able to make infinite satisfaction and attain infinite merits.*[6]

Saint Thomas Aquinas teaches that Jesus Christ offered to God more than was demanded as just compensation for the offences committed by the whole of mankind. And this came about through the greatness of the love with which he suffered; through the dignity of the Life that he offered in satisfaction for all men (for it was the life of God-made-Man); through the enormity of the pain that he suffered …[7] *The charity of the suffering Christ was greater*

---

5. Is 55:1 *et seq*
6. R. Garrigou-Lagrange, *The Saviour*
7. cf St Thomas Aquinas, *Summa Theologiae*, 3, 48, 2

than the malice of those who crucified him, and because of it Christ was able, through his Passion, to make satisfaction even greater than the offence of those who crucified him and put him to death. To such an extent was this the case that the Passion of Christ was in itself sufficient and superabundant satisfaction for the sins of those who crucified him.[8] It satisfied too for the sins of the men of all times, for both original sin and the personal sins of all souls, *as though a doctor were to prepare a medicine by which all infirmities could be cured, even those which had still to come.*[9]

Jesus Christ has given full satisfaction to the eternal love of the Father.[10] The Church has always taught this.[11] The love of Christ dying for us on the Cross was more pleasing to God than all the sins of all men together can ever displease him. Insofar as we identify our will with God's Will, we take upon ourselves the merits of Christ. We offer reparation to God by making our own the love and the merits of his Son! The matchless value that a single holy man or woman has in the sight of God is based on this. Although many sins are committed each day, there are at the same time many souls who in spite of their wretchedness desire only to please God with all their strength.

It does not matter if our lives do not cause any outward stir, if we make no apparent mark on the world or its history; what does matter is our decision to be faithful, to turn all the days of our life into an offering made to God. If we know how to set our eyes on God our Father, and to treat him with the same trust and friendship as Abraham did, we will never become pessimistic, even though our constant endeavours to serve God do not show any external results

---

8. *idem*
9. *idem*, 49, 1
10. cf John Paul II, *Redemptor hominis*, 4 March 1979
11. cf Pius XII, *Humani generis*, Denz-Sch 2318/3891

that can win acclaim or that we can pride ourselves on. How astutely cunning the devil is when he tries to fill our souls with pessimism as we regard our apparently scanty achievements. On the other hand, how very happy God is, when He perceives our constant daily struggle, our constant endeavour to begin again!

'Nam, et si ambulavero in medio umbrae mortis, non timebo mala' – though I should walk through the valley of the shadow of death, no evil will I fear. Neither my wretchedness nor the temptations of the enemy will worry me, 'quoniam tu mecum es' – for you, Lord, are with me'.[12] You have always been present in my life, Lord.

4.3 We must be as lights in the world.

For the sake of ten I will not destroy it. Ten just men would have been enough! People who are really holy more than make up for all the crimes, the abuse, envy, lack of loyalty, betrayal, injustice, selfishness ... of all the inhabitants of a great city. If we are united with the redeeming sacrifice of Jesus Christ, God will look with special compassion on our relatives, friends, acquaintances ... who have perhaps strayed from the path out of ignorance, or error, or weakness ... or because they did not receive the graces that we have received. We should try often to carry on the same kind of friendly and pleasant bargaining with Jesus that Abraham carried on with Yahweh! 'Look, Lord' – we will say to him – 'this person is better than he seems. He has good intentions. Help him!' And Jesus, who nevertheless knows the real situation, will move that person with his grace out of regard for our friendship with him.

God pays special attention to the petitions of those who are his own in the world; to the prayers of children,

---

12. J. Escrivá, *The Forge*, 194

who pray with a heart that knows no malice, and the prayers of those who make themselves like children; to the supplications of the sick whom He holds closer to his heart; to the prayers of those who have told him countless times that they have no other will than his, that they want to serve him in the midst of their normal everyday tasks. Those who strive to be united to Christ truly sustain the world. And that union is not generally shown in external deeds that attract attention. *There are incomparably more events than such visible actions whose importance to society remains hidden for the time being. There is, for example, the immense multitude of souls who have spent the whole of their existence giving themselves for others in the anonymity of the home, the factory, the office. There are those who have consumed themselves in anonymity amid the praying society of the cloister; those who have immolated themselves in the daily martyrdom of protracted illness. The day that everything is brought out into the public gaze when the Lord comes again, everyone will see the decisive role that the humble and the inconspicuous have played, in spite of all appearances to the contrary, in the unrolling of the history of the world. And this will also be a cause of joy for the blessed, who will derive from it a theme of everlasting praise of the God who is three times Holy.*[13]

Saint Paul says to the first Christians that they shine *as lights in the world,*[14] enlightening all men with the light of Christ. God looks down from Heaven on our earth and delights in those who live ordinary, normal lives but are conscious of the dignity of their Christian vocation. God is filled with joy as He contemplates our work, which is nearly always small and of little account as the world values it, so long as we try to be faithful.

---

13. John Paul II, *Homily*, 11 February 1981
14. Phil 2:15

THIRTEENTH WEEK: TUESDAY

5. GOD'S SILENCE

5.1 God always listens to those who turn to him for help.

Throughout the Gospels we see Jesus behaving in a way that is both natural and simple. He does not ask for vociferous acclamation from those who follow him. He works miracles without fuss or ostentation, avoiding publicity insofar as He is able. He charges the people He has cured not to go round telling everybody about the grace they have received. He teaches that the Kingdom of God does not come with dramatic display. By the parables of the mustard-seed and the leaven hidden in the dough He makes clear to everyone the mysterious power of his words. We see him also silently listening to pleas for help to which He later accedes. The silence of Jesus during his trial before Herod and again before Pilate is filled with a sublime grandeur. We see him standing in front of a clamorous, excited crowd who bring in false witnesses to try to catch him out in his speech ... We find particularly impressive God's silence as He stands in the midst of the uproar of the milling throng who have been aroused to fury by human passion. That silence of Jesus is neither indifference nor an attitude of disapproval towards some poor creatures who offend him; He is full of mercy and forgiveness. Jesus Christ always hopes for our conversion. God knows how to wait. He has more patience than we have.

His silence on the Cross is not simply a reserving of his ebbing strength, the better to control his anger and utter a final condemnation. It is the ever-forgiving God who hangs there. He opens wide the compassionate channel of a new and definitive era of mercy. God always listens to those who make the decision to follow him, even though sometimes it may appear that He remains silent, that He does not want to listen to us. He is always attentive to and considerate of the weaknesses of his creatures … but it is so that He can forgive them and help them to rise up higher. If at times He keeps silent it is so that our faith, our hope and our love may grow more mature.

In the scene described in the Gospel of today's Mass,[1] we can contemplate Jesus wearied after a day of intense hard work preaching. He got into a boat with his disciples in order to cross to the other side of the lake. When they had been on the water some time, a great storm arose, of such violence that the mounting waves threatened to swamp the boat. Meanwhile, Our Lord, utterly exhausted, had fallen asleep. He was so tired that not even the crashing of the waves against the sides of the boat caused him to wake up. At a moment of such great peril, it seems almost as if Jesus is not there. It is the only passage in the Gospel where we see him asleep.

The Apostles, most of whom were seasoned fishermen, realised immediately that their best efforts could not succeed in holding the boat's head to the wind, and were horribly aware that their lives were in danger. So they went to Jesus and woke him up, shouting: *Save us Lord, we are perishing.*

Jesus tried to reassure them: *Why are you afraid, O men of little faith?* He asked them. It is as if he had said, 'Don't you realise that I am with you, and that this should give you an unwavering steadfastness even though you are

---

1. Matt 8:23-27

surrounded by difficulties?' *Then He rose and rebuked the winds and the sea; and there was a great calm.* The disciples were overcome with amazement, with peace and with joy. They were able to see for themselves yet again that to walk with Christ is to walk safely, even though He may keep silent and seem not to be there at all. And they said: *What sort of man is this, that even the winds and the sea obey him?* He was their Lord and their God. Later on, when the Holy Spirit came into their souls on the day of Pentecost, they realised that they would often have to live in the midst of troubled waters and that Jesus would always be in his boat – the barque of Peter, the Church. At times He would apparently be asleep and silent, and to that extent apparently absent, but He would always be as attentive to them as ever, and at the same time just as powerful. He would never abandon them to their own devices. They understood it well, when soon afterwards, at the beginning of their apostolic mission, they saw themselves beset by persecution and felt the bitterness of being misunderstood by the pagan society in whose midst they carried out their activity. Nevertheless, the Master gave them strength, kept them afloat and encouraged them to embark upon yet more apostolic enterprises. He does the same with us now as He did then with his first followers.

5.2 Trust in God.

Our Lord's being asleep whilst his disciples, struggling with every nerve and sinew, felt themselves about to be overwhelmed by the storm, has often been compared to the silence God maintains as we labour. It will frequently seem that God is paying no heed and is indeed unconcerned about the difficulties that threaten and assail individuals and the Church itself.

When the hurricane rages and we find ourselves faced with similar situations; when all our efforts seem to be achieving nothing, we must follow the example of the Apostles, turn to Jesus and put all our trust in him: *Save, Lord; we are perishing.* Then we will feel the effectiveness of his infinite power and will be filled with confidence and serenity.

Why are you afraid, O men of little faith? He says to his followers, when He sees them overcome with anxiety and convinced that they are sinking. Why are you afraid if I am with you? He is the certainty of certainties. It is enough to be with him in his boat, where He can see us, for us to overcome all the fears we have and the difficulties we may encounter, when we are overwhelmed by meagre results and worry, by trials, by a sense of being misunderstood and by temptations. A lack of trustful certainty only makes its appearance when our faith is weak. Such weakness does bring with it a lack of trust. Precisely at such moments we may forget that the greater the difficulty, the more powerful God's help will be. This will always be the case when we strive to live fully our vocation as Christians, whatever our situation ... in our family life, in our daily work ..., in carrying out our apostolate.

Jesus wants to see us filled with his peace and serenity, at all times and in all circumstances. *Do not be afraid, it is I*, He says to his disciples, who are terrified by huge seas. On another occasion He says: *I tell you, my friends, do not fear.*[2] From the moment of his entry into the world He showed what his presence among men would be like. The message of the Incarnation begins precisely with these words: *Do not be afraid, Mary.*[3] And the Angel of the

---

2. Luke 12:4
3. Luke 1:30

Lord was to say to Joseph: *Joseph, son of David, do not fear.*[4] To the shepherds He would say once again: *Be not afraid.*[5] We cannot be afraid of anything. Even the *holy fear* of God is a form of love; it is nothing but the fear of losing him.

Complete trust in God, using whatever human means are necessary in each situation, gives an incomparable fortitude and a special kind of serenity to the Christian, whatever may happen to him and whatever the tribulations he may have to face up to. The consideration of our divine filiation frequently each day leads us to speak to God, not as if we were speaking to somebody far away who is as indifferent as he is remote, who is cold and inattentive to us, but with the consciousness that we are talking to a father who is concerned about every movement made by his children. We will come to look on him as the Friend who never lets us down and who is always ready to help, and, if necessary, to forgive. Close to him we will learn to understand that every tribulation and all difficulties bring benefits to us men if we know how to accept them with faith, if we do not turn our backs on him. *Blessed be the hardships of this earth! Poverty, tears, hatred, injustice, dishonour ... You can endure all things in him who strengthens you.*[6] And Saint Teresa, with the well-tried experience of the saint, has written for us: *If you have trust in him and are of an encouraging heart – for His Majesty is a great friend of those with such an attitude – do not be afraid that you will want for anything.*[7] the Lord looks after those who are his own, even when He appears to be asleep.

---

4. Matt 1:20

5. Luke 2:10

6. J. Escrivá, *The Way*, 717

7. St Teresa, *The Foundations*, 27, 12

5.3 When God seems to keep silent.

Some Christians who appear to follow Christ so long as everything happens the way they want turn away from him when they have most need of him: when their child, their husband or their wife, their brother or their sister falls sick ...; in times of financial stress; when they are hurt by calumny or defamation and some of their friends turn their backs on them, or if in their own interior life they lose those agreeable feelings that at other moments have made self-surrender and apostolate seem relatively easy. Perhaps now, as a very special grace from God, a grace that purifies their intentions and their hearts, such feelings disappear and give way to dryness and to a certain feeling of sadness. Then, it is possible for them to think that God no longer listens to them, or that He is keeping silent, as though He were neutral as regards their predicament or indifferent to their concerns. It is precisely then that we must say to Jesus even more forcefully: *Lord, save us, we are perishing*! He never fails to respond. He always pays attention to us. Perhaps He is waiting for us to pray with greater intensity and rectitude of intention, and for us to abandon ourselves still more completely into his strong arms.

In every tribulation, in times of difficulty and temptation, we must turn to Jesus immediately. *Seek his face who ever dwells in real and bodily presence in His Church. Do at least as much as the disciples did. They had but little faith; they feared; they had not any great confidence and peace, but at least they did not keep away from Christ ... Do not keep from him, but when you are in trouble, come to him every single day, asking him earnestly and perseveringly for those favours which He alone can give. And as He on the occasion spoken of in the Gospel blamed indeed the disciples but did for them what they asked, so you should 'trust*

*in his great mercy'. Though He discern much infirmity in
you which ought not to be there, yet He will deign to rebuke
the winds and the sea, and will say:*

'Peace, be still' – and there will be a great calm.[8] Our
soul will be filled with serenity even in the midst of tribulation.

With this new peace that Our Lord brings to our
hearts we will set off confidently to fight once again in
those battles of peace – the external battles and those of
the soul. We will joyfully accept those annoying things that
actually serve to purify us, and we will become more
united to him. We should not forget either, in such circumstances, that God has placed an Angel beside us to
look after us, to help us and to carry our prayers the more
easily into his presence. *Whenever you are in need of anything, or are facing difficulties, whether great or small,
invoke your Guardian Angel, asking him to sort the matter
out with Jesus, or to carry out the particular service you may
require.*[9]

---

8. Cardinal J. H. Newman, *Sermon for the Fourth Sunday after
   Epiphany*, 30 January 1848
9. J. Escrivá, *The Forge*, 931

THIRTEENTH WEEK: WEDNESDAY

6. MISSED OPPORTUNITIES

6.1 The Lord sometimes presents himself to us in a way different from what we had expected.

Jesus came to the other side of the lake, *to the country of the Gadarenes*, in the land of the Gentiles.[1] He was looking, perhaps, for a quiet spot in which to rest for a while with his disciples. It was there that Our Lord cured two demoniacs who came out to meet him. There was a herd of swine feeding nearby; the devils begged him, if He cast them out of those tormented men, to send them into the herd of swine. Our Lord permitted just that. *So they came out and went into the swine; and behold, the whole herd rushed down the steep bank into the sea, and perished in the waters. The herdsmen fled, and going into the city they told everything, and what had happened to the demoniacs. And behold, all the city came out to meet Jesus; and when they saw him, they begged him to leave their neighbourhood.*

They begged him to leave that place. It was a great opportunity those people missed; they had God himself among them and were unable to recognise him. Perhaps He never again passed through that region. They had him so close to them! And they asked him, the only One who could give them everything that was good, to leave them! How inhospitable the world sometimes is towards its God! Very often, for many people, it is material goods that

---

1. Matt 8:28-34

matter. It is not unusual to see how people try to build a society in which as far as they are concerned God is not present. They make no room for him. It is *as if God were of no relevance in the sphere of man's joint projects*.[2] The very One who gives meaning to everything is excluded. It is God who throws light upon the meaning of pain, joy, life, death, work ... Without him nothing is worth while.

Exclusion of God, rupture of our union with God, disobedience to God: throughout the history of mankind this has been and still is, in all its various forms, sin. It can go as far as a virtual denial of God and his existence: this is the phenomenon called atheism.[3] At the heart of many attitudes that lead men to reject or exclude supernatural truth can be found a radical and practical materialism, whereby the goods of this world are esteemed above all else. This is what prevents us from seeing God's action in everything around us.

We say to Jesus that we want to place him at the peak of all human activity, through doing our work conscientiously each day. We want him to enter fully into our lives and into the lives of our families. We want him to give meaning to what we are and to what we have: to our intellect, to the love of our hearts, to our friendships, to the clean love of each one in accordance with his particular vocation. We tell him that we want to be ever watchful like the sentry, so that He can enter into our souls, even when He presents himself to us in a way we had not expected.

---

2. John Paul II, Apostolic Exhortation, *Reconciliatio et Paenitentia*, 2 December 1984, 14
3. *idem*

6.2 Detachment if we are to see Jesus and do his Will even when it does not coincide with ours.

In spite of the miracle they had heard of from the swineherds and in spite of having seen those unfortunate men freed and saved from the demons, the Gerasenes still refused to make Jesus welcome. We can imagine what good things would have filled their homes and still more especially their souls! But they were blind to spiritual good. It is just the same with so very many people today. So many people have their own plans for their own well-being that only too often they look on God simply as someone who will help them to carry out those same plans. *The true state of affairs is just the opposite. God has his plans for our happiness, and He is waiting for us to help him accomplish them – and let us be quite clear about it: we cannot improve on God's plans.*[4]

Some Christians, because they are excessively attached to their own ideas and their own whims, more or less tell Jesus to go out of their lives. They may do this precisely at those moments when He is closest to them, and when they need him most. They may do this when they are overtaken by illness or frustrated by setbacks; when they have lost some material things they probably needed to lose so as to be prepared to receive the supreme Good when He comes, very often, along paths quite different from those they were expecting. Perhaps they hoped He would come in triumph, and instead He presents himself to them quietly in the midst of ruin or failure – not' in the type of failure brought about by our own indolence because we have failed to use the right means or to put in the necessary amount of study, (which in any case should lead us to make an act of contrition and

---

4. E. Boylan, *This Tremendous Lover*, p.192

to start again with a firm resolution). It is, rather, the kind of failure that we experience when so far as we can see we have used all the human and supernatural means necessary to produce success. He sometimes comes along totally unexpected paths. How very often does God's logic fail to coincide with man's logic! It is the moment for us to embrace his holy Will: *Is that what you want, Lord? ... Then it's what I want also.*[5] Time and again when confronted with an unexpected reverse we have made this our prayer, repeated in a thousand different ways!

It has been said that God's plan is *all of a piece.* Perhaps the loss of their livestock, the detachment that such material deprivation demanded, could have been the beginning of the conversion of those Gentiles; perhaps they would have been the very first Gentiles to receive Baptism after the dispersion brought about by the first persecution in Judaea. At the end of our lives, and sometimes long before it, we will see how those separate events and fragmented circumstances which seemed to be no more than loose pieces without any particular meaning, dovetail together. *Everything in God works for good with those who love him.*[6]

If we are to discover God's Will in everything that happens in life, even in the least pleasant things – in those things that have harmed us or annoyed us; if we are to follow Christ whatever the circumstances, *we must be thoroughly detached from ourselves, from our intellectual talents, our health, our good name, our noble ambitions, our triumphs and our successes.*

I would also include ... the high ideals that lead us to seek only to give glory to God and to praise him. We can

5. cf J. Escrivá, *The Way*, 762
6. Rom 8:28

ensure our detachment by tailoring our will to this clear and precise rule: 'Lord, I want this or that only if it pleases you, because, if not, I'm not the slightest bit interested.' By acting in this way, we are dealing a mortal blow to the selfishness and vanity that lurk in every conscience. At the same time we will find true peace of soul through this selfless conduct that leads to an ever more intimate and intense possession of God.[7]

We have to purify our hearts of any disordered love (very often a disordered love of self and excessive attachment to the things we have or would like to have, to our own ideas and opinions, to the plans we have made for our own happiness ...) if we are to have more trust in God our Father. Then we will be able to see things clearly and will be able to interpret correctly the things that happen to us and always be able to find God in them.

6.3 Looking at humanly unfavourable circumstances with the eyes of faith, and finding God in them.

If that slaughter of the pigs had not happened, the swineherds would probably not have gone to the town, and its inhabitants would not have learned that Jesus was there, so close to them. If the woman who came across the Master in Capharnaum had not been ill for such a long time and had not spent every penny she had on doctors, perhaps she would never have approached the Master to touch the hem of his garment, and would never have heard Jesus' consoling words – the most important words she was to hear in her life – which were worth far more than all her sufferings and useless expenditure ... What seems a misfortune to us is perhaps not so dreadful; sin is the only absolute evil, and from it – with love, with humility

---

7. J. Escrivá, *Friends of God*, 114

and with contrition – we can draw out the most sweet-tasting effects of a new encounter with Christ,[8] an encounter in which the soul is rejuvenated.

Behind those apparent evils (illness, exhaustion, pain, financial ruin ...) we always find Jesus, smiling at us and holding out his hand to help us bear that situation and grow internally. How grateful that leper must have been for having suffered the sorry burden of his disease, for it was what led him to Christ! The misfortunes of this life are a constant call to our heart, which says to us: *The Teacher is here and is calling for you!*[9] But if we are more attached to our own plans, health, life ... than we are to God's Will – sometimes mysterious and incomprehensible to us at the beginning – we will come to look on misfortune as only the loss of something that, being only partially and relatively good, we have perhaps treated as absolute and definitive. What a great mistake we would make if we failed to see Jesus visiting us at those very moments!

God disposes events with a logic quite different from our own, in such a way that, sometimes with sorrow and at others with delight, we should detach ourselves from everything else so that He may fill our entire existence. We should often think about the inner action of God within us. He disposes even the least of happenings in order to make us happy. He arranges everything in such a way as to make detachment from ourselves and from our future plans easy ..., so that we become saints. In God's eyes *a single soul is of greater value than the whole universe, and the marvels that God works in the secrecy of our lives are, by far, more extraordinary than all the splendid wonders of the material cosmos.*[10] If those Gentiles had understood

---

8. cf St Bernard, *On the Falseness and Brevity of Life*. 6
9. John 11:28
10. M. M. Philipon, *The Gifts of the Holy Spirit*, Madrid, 1983, p.249

who was in their midst, if they had perceived the wonder worked in those two men who were freed from the devil, what would their financial misfortune have mattered if through it they had come to recognise Jesus? They would have been so grateful and would have invited Jesus into their houses and organised a great banquet because the Master was with them and because two lost men had been restored to them.

If we look at the lesser or greater misfortunes of this life with the eyes of faith we will always end up giving thanks for them. For that sickness, for the humiliation we were made to endure when we least looked for it, for hunger, for thirst, for the loss of employment ... 'Thank you, Lord!' we will say to him from the depths of our hearts –'because you have presented yourself to me where I least expected you!'

Let us ask Our Lady, who experienced so many hard-ships, so much anguish, so much sorrow, to teach us not to miss those opportunities of meeting Christ in the midst of the – humanly speaking – most unfavourable cir-cumstances.

THIRTEENTH WEEK: THURSDAY

7. THE INFINITE VALUE OF THE MASS

7.1 The sacrifice of Isaac, an image and figure of the Sacrifice of Christ on Calvary. The infinite value of the Holy Mass.

We read in the Book of Genesis[1] how God wanted to put Abraham's faith to the test. He had been promised that his descendants would be numerous *as the stars of heaven*. The Patriarch had seen time pass him by and was now a great age; his wife was barren. But he nevertheless continued to believe God's word.

Yahweh had announced to him that he would have a son, and Abraham believed *in hope against hope*. When at last the child came into the world, he called him Isaac. And after the boy had grown and become the cherished reward of that trust of his, God, the Lord of life and of death, commanded Abraham to offer him in sacrifice: *Take your son, your only son Isaac, whom you love, and go to the land of Moriah, and offer him there as a burnt offering upon one of the mountains of which I shall tell you*. But at the very moment that he was about to sacrifice his beloved son the Angel of the Lord stopped him. And the Patriarch heard these words filled with abundant blessings: *Because you have done this, and have not withheld your son, your only son, I will indeed bless you, and I will multiply your descendants as the stars of heaven and as the sand which is on the seashore. And your descendants shall possess the gate of their enemies, and by your descendants shall all the nations*

---

1. *First Reading*, Year I: Gen 22:1-19

of the earth bless themselves, because you have obeyed my voice.

The Fathers of the Church have seen in Isaac's sacrifice an announcement of the future sacrifice of Jesus. Isaac, the only son of Abraham, the beloved son, carrying his bundle of wood on his shoulders up the mountain where he is to be sacrificed, is a figure of Christ, the Only-begotten Son of the Father, the Beloved, who carries his Cross on his shoulders up to Calvary, where He offers himself as a sacrifice of infinite value for all men.

In the Mass, after the Consecration, the *Roman Canon* reminds us of this oblation of Abraham's, when he gives up his son. He is *our Father in faith. Look with favour on these offerings*, we say to God the Father, *and accept them as once you accepted the gifts of your servant Abel, the sacrifice of Abraham, our father in faith, and the bread and wine offered by your priest Melchisedech ...* [2]

Abraham's obedience is the greatest expression of his unconditional faith in God. It was because of this faith that he regained Isaac, and after having offered him in sacrifice, received him back as a symbol. He really did consider that God is able to raise men from the dead by his own power; for this reason he received him back and the whole episode is an image of what was to come.[3]

Origen points out that the sacrifice of Isaac makes us more clearly understand the mystery of the Redemption. *The fact that Isaac was compelled to carry the wood for the holocaust is a figure of Christ who was made to carry his cross on his shoulders. But at the same time, carrying the wood for the holocaust is the task of a priest. So Isaac was both victim and priest ... Christ is at one and the same time*

---

2. *Roman Missal, Eucharistic Prayer* I
3. cf Heb 11:19

Victim and High Priest. Indeed, according to the spirit, He offers the victim to his Father; according to the flesh, He himself is offered on the altar of the Cross.[4] For this reason each Mass has an infinite, immense value that we can never fully understand. *It causes the whole heavenly court to rejoice. It alleviates the pain of the souls in purgatory. It draws down all types of blessings upon earth, and gives more glory to God than all the sufferings of all the martyrs together, more glory than the penances of all the saints, than all the tears shed by them since the beginning of the world and all that they may do till the end of time.*[5]

7.2 Adoration and thanksgiving.

Although all of Christ's acts were redeeming acts, there is however in his life an event which is unique and stands out above all others, and to which all other events are directed. It is the moment when the obedience and the love of the Son combine to offer to the Father a sacrifice that knows no bounds; this boundlessness is due to the dignity of the Offering and of the Priest who offers it on Calvary. It is He who remains in the Mass as the principal Priest and as the Victim truly offered and sacramentally immolated.

In the Holy Mass, the effects that relate immediately to God, such as *adoration* and *thanksgiving* are always produced in infinite plenitude. They do not depend on the degree of our attention, or on the fervour of the priest. In each Mass there are infallibly offered to God adoration, reparation and thanksgiving of limitless value, because it is Christ himself who offers the Mass and in it offers himself. Thus it is impossible to adore God in a better way, or to give

---

4. Origen, *Homilies on the Book of Genesis*, 8, 6, 9
5. St Jean Vianney, The Curé d'Ars, *Sermon on the Holy Mass*

greater recognition of his sovereign dominion over all things and all men. It is the most complete fulfilment of the precept: *You shall worship the Lord your God and him only shall you serve.*[6]

It is impossible to make a more perfect reparation to God for the faults that are committed daily than by offering or participating with devotion in the Holy Sacrifice of the Altar.[7] It is impossible to offer him greater thanks for the gifts we have received than through the Holy Mass: *What shall I render to the Lord for all his bounty to me? I will lift up the cup of salvation and call on the name of the Lord.*[8] What a tremendous opportunity the Mass is for us to thank God for all the good things we receive, since we no doubt sometimes forget to thank God for the many, many gifts He has showered upon us; the same may happen to us as happened to those lepers whom Jesus cured . . .

Adoration, reparation and thanksgiving are infallible effects of the sacrifice of the Mass that refer to God himself,[9] for it is He himself who offers and is offered. What a great honour it is for priests to lend Christ their voice and their hands in the Eucharistic sacrifice! What grandeur of privilege is that of the faithful who are able to take part in such a great Mystery!

Tell Our Lord that from now on, every time you celebrate or attend Mass, and every time you administer or receive the Sacrament of the Eucharist, you will do so with greater faith, with a more burning love, just as if it were to be the last time in your life. And be sorry for the carelessness of your past life.[10]

---

6. Matt 4:10
7. Council of Trent, *Session* 22, c.1
8. Ps 115:12
9. R. Garrigou-Lagrange, *The Saviour*
10. J. Escrivá, *The Forge*, 829

7.3 Expiation and atonement for our sins; begging God for all our needs.

On Mount Moriah, Isaac the beloved only son of Abraham, was not in the event sacrificed; on Calvary, Jesus really suffered and died for all of us, *pro peccatis*, on account of our sins. This fruit of *expiation and atonement* also reaches the souls of those who have preceded us and who are being purified in Purgatory, awaiting the award of the *wedding garment*[11] so as to be able to enter into Heaven.

The Eucharistic sacrifice effects, of itself and of its own power, the forgiveness of sins; *but it brings this about in a mediate* way ... For example, a person who without attending the sacrifice, asks God to change his life and to lead him to Confession, will obtain this grace only by virtue of his fervour and his persistence ... but if he hears Mass with this objective, it is certain he will effectively obtain this favour so long as he does not place any obstacles in its way.[12]

When Jesus Christ offers himself to his Father He prays for all men. He *always lives to make intercession for them*.[13] What better moment can we find than during the Holy Mass to approach him and ask for what we so badly need?

Each Mass is offered by the whole Church, who in her turn makes supplication for the whole world. *Each time the Holy Mass is offered it is the blood of the Cross that pours down like rain upon the world*.[14] Together with the Church we pray in a special way for the Pope, for the bishop of the diocese, for our own prelate and for our brothers and sisters, *for all who hold and teach the Catholic faith that comes to us from the Apostles*.[15]

---

11. cf Matt 22:12
12. Anonymous, *The Holy Mass*, Madrid, 1975
13. cf Heb 7:25
14. C. Journet, *The Mass*
15. *Roman Missal*, Eucharistic Prayer I

As well as the general effects of the Mass there are also other particular effects for those who take part in the Holy Sacrifice and for those for whose intention it was celebrated. For the priest there is a very special, irrenounceable effect, as it depends on his meritorious will that the Mass is being said; the servers, the choir ... and all the devout participants who are present at the sacrifice also share in these particular effects, each one according to his or her dispositions. *All of us gathered here before you ... you know how firmly we believe in you and dedicate ourselves to you ... for ourselves and for those who are dear to us. We pray to you, our living and true God, for our well-being and redemption.*[16]

As well as the effects of the *praise* and of the *adoration* that are given to God, the Holy Mass also produces fruits of remission for our sins, and of impetration for all our needs. These are of themselves capable of being infinite and unlimited, but may be finite and limited according to our dispositions. This is why the preparation of our soul to attend and partake of this unique Sacrifice, and the moments of thanksgiving and recollection once the sacred action is over are so very important. *Are you there*, the holy Curé d'Ars asks, *with the same dispositions as Our Lady on Calvary, realising that you are in the presence of God himself and are present at the enactment of that very same sacrifice?*[17]

Let us ask Our Lady to intercede for us so that our celebration of or our participation in the Eucharistic sacrifice may become for us the fountain at which our desires for God are satisfied and ever increased.

---

16. *idem*
17. St Jean Vianney, The Curé d'Ars, *Sermon on Sin*

THIRTEENTH WEEK: FRIDAY

8. HABITUAL MORTIFICATIONS

8.1 Mortifications are the result of love, and in their turn they nourish love.

In the Gospel of today's Mass[1] Saint Matthew tells us that after he had responded to Jesus' call, he prepared a meal for Him in his own house. All the other disciples, and *many tax collectors and sinners* who were perhaps life-long friends of his, came to the meal. When the Pharisees saw this, they said: *Why does your teacher eat with tax collectors and sinners?* Jesus heard what they were saying and He himself answered them. He told them that it is not those who are well who need a physician, but those who are sick. Then He makes his own some words of the Prophet Hosea:[2] *I desire steadfast love and not sacrifice.* Our Lord does not refuse to accept the sacrifices offered to him. He insists, however, that such sacrifices must be accompanied by the love that has its origin in a heart that is good, for it is charity that has to give life to all of a Christian's actions, and particularly to his worship of God.[3]

Those Pharisees, who faithfully fulfilled the Law, did not accompany their sacrifices with the sweet fragrance of charity towards their neighbour or with love of God. Elsewhere Our Lord was to say in the words of the Prophet Isaiah: *These people honour me with their lips, but their heart is far from me.* During that meal in Matthew's house it becomes obvious from their questions that they do not in

---

1. Matt 9:9-13
2. Hos 6:6
3. cf *The Navarre Bible*; cf B. Orchard and others, *Verbum Dei*

the least understand the other guests, and that they make no effort to bring them any closer to God or to the Law which they themselves keep so faithfully. Theirs is a narrow outlook, and there is a lack of love in their way of judging. To use different words, Yahweh had already said to the chosen people, who set too much store upon certain external formalities: *I prefer virtue to austerity*.

That is why we must cultivate penance and mortification as a proof of our true love for God and for our neighbour.[4]

Our love for God is expressed in our acts of worship. But it is also shown in each of our actions throughout the day, particularly in the small mortifications that should inform everything we do, and that carry up to the Lord our desire to forget ourselves and please him in everything.

If, deep down, we do not have this disposition, the mere fact of repeating certain acts will be valueless, because they will be bereft of any real meaning; the little sacrifices we try to offer to the Lord each day have their origin in love, and in their turn nourish this love.

The spirit of mortification that God wants is not something negative or inhuman.[5] It is not an attitude of rejecting what is good and noble in using and enjoying the good things of earth. It is rather a manifestation of supernatural mastery over the body and over all created things – over material things, human relationships, work ...; mortification, whether it is voluntary mortification or whether it is that other type of mortification that comes without our seeking it, is not simply privation: rather is it a manifestation of love, for *to suffer need is something that can happen to anybody, but knowing how to endure it belongs to great souls*.[6] It belongs to souls who have loved much.

---

4. J. Escrivá, *Furrow*, 992
5. cf J. Tissot, *The Interior Life*
6. St Augustine, *On the Good of Matrimony*, 21, 25

Mortification is not simply moderation. It is not just a matter of keeping our senses under control and of avoiding the disequilibrium that follows upon disorder and excess. Rather, it is true self-denial. It makes room in our souls for supernatural life, which is a foretaste of the *glory that is to be revealed to us*.[7]

8.2 Mortifications that make life more pleasant for others.

I desire mercy and not sacrifice ... It is because of this that our mortification should be lived, more than anywhere else, in those things that affect our relationships and dealings with other people. Our attitude should be always one of mercy, just like Our Lord's attitude towards the people He met everywhere He went. Our mortification receives its impulse and direction from the regard we have for those with whom we are in daily contact, whether at home, at work or for any other reason away from home. It leads us to make things in this life more pleasant for them. In particular it leads us to help people who are having to bear even greater physical or moral sufferings; we will do little acts of service for them or deprive ourselves of some small comfort if we can help them in that way.

Our spirit of mortification will lead us to overcome any lack of optimism which would necessarily affect other people. We will endeavour to smile even when we have our own difficulties. We will try to avoid everything, however small, that may annoy those closest to us, to forgive others and to find excuses for them ... In this way we will die to self-love, which is so deeply rooted in our being. We will learn to be humble. This habitual disposition that makes us a cause of joy for others can only be the fruit of a profound spirit of mortification, because *many may not find giving up food and*

---

7. Rom 8:18

drink and a soft bed too difficult ... But bearing an insult, a
wrong, or hurtful words ... this is something to be borne not
by many but by few.[8]

As well as in these mortifications that refer to charity,
God wants us to know how to find him in all those things He
allows to happen, and that can go against our likes and
preferences and upset our plans. These are known as *pas-*
sive mortifications. They can take the form of serious illness; of problems that arise in the family and for which
there seems to be no easy solution; of a major setback at
work ... but perhaps more often, indeed probably every
day, we come up against little things that annoy us and that
we had not expected, whether at work, in our family life or
in the carrying out of the plans we have made for a particular day ... These are opportunities for telling God that we
love him, precisely through accepting those very things we
may have shied away from at the outset. When we accept
that particular reverse – be it great or small – with love,
and offer it to God, we experience peace and joy in the
midst of sorrow. When we do not accept it, our soul
becomes as though out of harmony and sad, or else we
experience an inner rebelliousness that only serves to
separate us from God and from other people.

Another field of mortification in which we can show
our love for God is in the exemplary fulfilment of our duty,
by working intensely, for example; by not leaving unpleasant
tasks for later; by struggling against mental laziness; by taking care of little things – order, punctuality and so on; by
facilitating the task of someone who works alongside us; by
offering up the tiredness that all hard work brings with it. By
these little victories over ourselves, whilst we work and in
our relations with other people – on every possible

---

8. St John Chrysostom, *On the Priesthood*, 3,13

occasion – we are able to show that we love God above all things, and in particular that we love him more than ourselves. By means of these mortifications we raise ourselves up towards him; by not doing them, we remain rooted to the ground. Those little sacrifices we offer up throughout the day prepare our souls for prayer and fill us with joy.

8.3 Other mortifications. A spirit of mortification.

God asks us for sacrifice offered up with love. Mortification is not for the battlefront, where there exists an imminent danger of falling into sin. Mortification belongs rather to the open field of generosity, because it is a matter of knowing how to deprive ourselves of something it would be possible not to deprive ourselves of and still not offend God. The mortified soul is not the soul that does not offend God, but the soul that loves. Saint Paul reminded the first Christians in Corinth that to live like this, with an habitual spirit of mortification *is folly to those who are perishing, but to us who are being saved it is the power of God*.[9]

Our love for God moves us to control our imagination and our memory, and to get rid of useless thoughts and memories. It enables us to control our sensitivity, our tendency to *have a good time* as the foremost reason for being alive. Mortification leads us to overcome our laziness from the moment we get up. It prevents us from allowing our sight and other senses to wander uncontrolled. It leads us to be sober and temperate in matters of food and drink, and to avoid always giving in to our whims and impulses ... It may lead us to practise corporal mortifications, although always with the opportune advice received in spiritual direction or in Confession.

At times we will concentrate on some mortifications

---

9. 1 Cor 1:18

rather than on others. We will always pay special attention to those mortifications that help us improve in the fulfilment of our duties towards God, in our duties of state and in living charity better. We may even find it useful to note down some of the mortifications we propose for ourselves, to look over the list some time during the day, and then to ask our Guardian Angel for help so that we will actually put them into practice. If we bear in mind the tendency every man and every woman has to forget things and to put things off for some time later, we will realise that we need to use the means if we are not just to neglect such resolutions. Those little acts of renunciation throughout the day, many of which we will have foreseen and looked for, bring us close to Christ and constitute a powerful weapon to enable us to acquire, first in one field and then in another, the actual habit of mortification. They are human stratagems that can only be substituted for with difficulty, given our natural tendency to resist the Cross and to try to forget about it.

The promise Jesus made becomes a reality for the mortified soul: *He who loses his life for my sake will find it.*[10] This is the way to find him in the middle of the world, in and through our daily work. *The friend told his Beloved that He should pay him the amount due for the time he had served him. The Beloved took into account the thoughts, desires, tears, dangers and toil that the friend had suffered for love of him. Then the Beloved added eternal bliss to the account, and gave Himself as payment to his friend.*[11]

---

10. Matt 10:39
11. R. Llull, *The Book of the Friend and the Beloved*, 64

THIRTEENTH WEEK: SATURDAY

9. NEW WINE

9.1 Preparing our souls to receive the divine gift of grace. *New wineskins*.

Jesus was teaching, and his listeners well understood what He said. Those people who were the first to hear the words of the Gospel of today's Mass all knew about patching garments; they were all accustomed to work in the country and they knew what happened when new wine, made from recently harvested grapes, was poured into old wineskins. It was through these simple well-known images that Our Lord taught the most profound truths about the Kingdom He had come to bring to souls: *and no one puts a piece of unshrunken cloth on an old garment, for the patch tears away from the garment and a worse tear is made. Neither is new wine put into old wineskins; if it is, the skins burst, and the wine is spilled, and the skins are destroyed; but new wine is put into fresh wineskins , and so both are preserved.*[1]

Jesus makes it clear that we need to receive his teaching with a fresh and youthful spirit: that we have to want to be renewed. Just as the strength of the fermentation of new wine causes old receptacles to burst, so the message that Christ was about to bring to this earth was to break down all types of conventionalism, routine and inertia. Later the apostles were to think back to those days they spent beside Jesus and see them as the starting

---

1. Matt 9:16-16

point of their real life. They did not receive his preaching as just one more interpretation of the Law, but rather as new life which surged up within them with a quite extraordinary impetus and which demanded new dispositions of them.

Throughout these twenty centuries, whenever men have come face to face with Jesus, something has moved within them, and broken down old and worn out attitudes. The Prophet Ezechiel had already announced[2] that God would grant to his followers another heart and He would give them a new spirit. The Venerable Bede, commenting on a certain passage of the Gospel,[3] explains how the apostles would have been transformed at Pentecost and at the same time filled with the fervour of the Holy Spirit. This was to happen later in the Church to every one of her members, once they had received Baptism and Confirmation. Those new wineskins – a clean and purified soul – should always be full; *for empty they are devoured by moth and rust; full of grace they are preserved.*[4]

The new wine of grace needs the soul to possess certain dispositions which are being constantly renewed: determination to start time and again on the path of sanctity, which is a sign of inner youthfulness, of that youthfulness possessed by the saints, who are people in love with God. We dispose our souls to receive God's gift of grace when we respond to the inspirations and suggestions of the Holy Spirit as they prepare us to receive new graces. Then, if we have not been altogether faithful, when we go to Our Lord asking him to cure our souls, we can say with Saint Ambrose, *Remove, Lord Jesus, the rottenness of my sins. Whilst you hold me bound with bonds of love, cure*

---

2. Ezek 36:26
3. St Bede, *Commentary on St Mark's Gospel*, 2,21-22
4. St Ambrose, *Treatise on St Luke's Gospel*, 5, 26

what is sick within me ... I have met a physician who lives in heaven and pours out his medicine on earth. Only He can cure my wounds, for He himself has none; only He can remove sorrow from my heart, wanness from my soul, for He alone knows my innermost secrets.[5]

Only your love, Lord, is able to prepare my soul to receive more love.

9.2 Contrition heals us and prepares us to receive new graces.

The Holy Spirit constantly brings to the soul new wine – sanctifying grace – which has to grow more and more. This *new wine does not grow old, but the wineskins can grow old. Once they tear they are thrown into the rubbish bin and the wine is lost.*[6] This is why it is necessary to constantly restore the soul, to rejuvenate it; there are times when we fail to love, perhaps through venial sins, that render the soul unfit to receive more grace and cause it to grow old. In this life we will always be aware of the scars left by sin – character defects that we are unable to overcome, invitations of grace we do not respond to generously, impatience, routine in our life of piety, failure to show understanding for people ...

It is contrition that disposes us to receive new graces, that increases our hope and enables us to avoid routine. It makes a Christian forget himself and turn to God once again with a still deeper act of love. Contrition brings with it an aversion from sin and conversion to Christ. This heart-felt sorrow is not the same as the state of mind brought about by the unpleasant effects of having sinned – the breakdown of family harmony, the end of a friendship.

---

5. *idem*
6. G. Chevrot, *The Gospel in the Open*

It is not even the same as wishing that we had not done a particular thing ... It is the definite condemnation of an action, the conversion towards what is good, towards God's holiness which is manifested for us in Christ. It is the *irruption of a new life into the soul*,[7] a life filled with love when it finds itself once more with God. This is why a person does not know how to repent, cannot be moved to contrition, if he does not relate his sins, be they large or small, to God.

Before Jesus, all our actions take on their true dimension. If we were simply to stop at our faults, without any reference to the person who has been offended, we would probably seek to justify our faults and sins and give little importance to them. On the other hand we might find ourselves filled with discouragement and despair in the face of so much error and omission. God teaches us to acknowledge the truth of our lives, and in spite of all our wretchedness and defects, He fills us with peace and the desire to improve and to start again.

The humble soul feels the need to ask God for forgiveness many times each day. Each time she separates herself from what God has expected of her, she sees the need to return, like the prodigal son, with true sorrow: *Father, I have sinned against heaven and before you; I am no longer worthy to be called your son; treat me as one of your hired servants*.[8] And Our Lord, *who is close to those of contrite heart*[9] will hear our prayer. With this spirit of contrition the soul is constantly prepared to receive the *new wine* of grace.

---

7. cf M. Schmaus, *Dogmatic Theology*, Madrid, 1963
8. Luke 15:18-19
9. St Augustine, *Commentary on St John's Gospel*, 15, 25

9.3 Sacramental Confession: a means of growing in interior life.

Our Lord, knowing that we were fragile, left us the sacrament of Penance, where the soul not only comes away healed, but, if it has lost grace, rises with a new life. We must go to receive this sacrament with a sincerity that is complete, humble, contrite and with the desire of reparation. A well-made Confession presupposes a deep examination of conscience – deep does not necessarily mean long in a time sense, especially if we go to Confession frequently – if possible in front of the tabernacle, and always in the presence of God. In his examination of conscience, the Christian sees what God has expected his life to be and what in reality it has been. He sees the goodness or the malice of his actions, the omissions, the opportunities he has let slip ..., the gravity of the fault committed, the length of time he has remained in it before asking for forgiveness.[10]

The Christian who wants to have a refined conscience, and so goes to Confession frequently, *will not be content with a Confession that is simply valid, but he will aspire to a good Confession* which is an effective help to the soul in its aspiration towards God. For frequent Confession to achieve this end we need to take this principle in all seriousness: without repentance there is no forgiveness of sin. This gives rise to the fundamental norm of anyone who goes to confession frequently – not to confess any venial sin without first seriously and sincerely repenting of it.

There is a 'general repentance'. This is pain and detestation for all the sins committed in one's past life. This general repentance is of exceptional importance for frequent

---

10. cf St Francis de Sales, *Introduction to the Devout Life*, II, 19

confession,[11] since it helps to heal the wounds that our weaknesses left behind them, purifies our soul and makes it grow in love of God.

Whenever necessary, sincerity will lead us to get down to those little details that enable us to acknowledge our weaknesses better: how? when? why? for how long? We have to avoid insubstantial and prolific detail just as much as generalisation. We need to say simply and delicately what has happened, what is the true state of our soul. We have to flee from digressions such as *I wasn't humble, I was lazy, I lacked charity*: things that are applicable to almost every human being. When we practise frequent confession, we have to make sure that it is always a *personal act* in which we ask God's forgiveness for very real specific weaknesses, and not generalisations.

This sacrament of mercy is a sure refuge: in it our wounds are cured. What was already worn and growing old is rejuvenated. All our errors, large or small, are cured, because Confession is not only a judgement in which our transgressions are forgiven, but also a medicine for the soul.

Confession that is impersonal often hides a point of pride and of self-love that seeks to camouflage or to find justification for anything that is humiliating and leaves us, humanly speaking, looking bad. Perhaps it can help us to make this act of penance more personal, if we are careful about the very way we make our confession: *I accuse myself of ...*, for this sacrament is not to woefully relate things that have happened; it is humbly and simply to accuse oneself of one's errors and weaknesses before God himself, who will forgive us through the priest and will inundate us with his grace.

---

11. B. Baur, *Frequent Confession*

'Blessed be God' you said to yourself after having finished your sacramental Confession. And you thought: it is as if I had just been born again.

You then continued calmly: 'Domine, quid me vis facere? – Lord, what would you have me do?'

And you yourself came up with the reply: 'By the help of your grace I will let nothing and no one come between me and the fulfilment of your most Holy Will: Serviam – I will serve you unconditionally!'[12] I will serve you, Lord, as you have always wanted me to: with simplicity, in the midst of all the ordinary, everyday events of my life.

---

12. J. Escrivá, *The Forge*, 238

FOURTEENTH SUNDAY: YEAR A

10. HELPING OTHERS TO CARRY THEIR BURDENS

10.1 Christ's example.

Jesus behaved towards people in a way very different from the way many of the Pharisees behaved towards them. He came to free men from the heaviest of their burdens by taking them upon himself. *Come to me, all who labour and are heavy laden, and I will give you rest. Take my yoke upon you, and learn from me; for I am gentle and lowly in heart, and you will find rest for your souls. For my yoke is easy, and my burden is light.*[1]

Close to Christ, all our efforts and indeed all those things we find most difficult to bear if we are to fulfil God's Will become even pleasant. Sacrifice offered with Christ does not bring with it a feeling of harsh rebelliousness, but rather one of joyful giving. He bore upon himself our sorrows and our weightiest burdens. The Gospels give us a constant example of his concern for all men. Saint Gregory the Great writes that *everywhere He left examples of his mercy.*[2] He raises the dead, cures the blind, the lepers, the dumb, and frees those possessed by the devil … There are occasions when He does not even wait for the sick person to be brought to him, but says: *I will come and heal him.*[3] Even at the moment of his own death He shows his concern for the people around him.

---

1. Matt 11:28-30
2. St Gregory the Great, *Homilies on the Gospels*, 25, 6
3. Matt 7:7

He gives himself up to death lovingly; *He is the expiation for our sins, and not for our sins only, but also for the sins of the whole world.*[4]

We must imitate Our Lord not only by avoiding causing unnecessary worries to others, but by helping people to bear the worries they already have. Whenever possible we will help others to fulfil their human task. We will help them to carry the burdens that life itself imposes on them: *When you have finished your work, do your brother's, helping him, for Christ's sake, so tactfully and so naturally that no one – not even he – will realise that you are doing more than what in justice you ought.*

This, indeed, is virtue befitting a son of God![5]

We should never think that any act of self-denial or sacrifice offered for the good of another is more than we should do. Charity should stimulate us to show our regard for others in very specific ways. It should lead us to look for opportunities of making ourselves useful, of lightening the burdens of others and of giving joy to all those we are able to help in any way, even though we know that we will never do as much as we should.

We should always try to relieve others from whatever seems to weigh them down, just as Christ would have done in our place. Sometimes this will mean our doing some small act of service. At times it will mean giving a word of encouragement or of hope. At others we will help someone to glance up at the Master so that he comes to see his situation in a more positive light; it may be a situation which had seemed to overwhelm him simply because up till then he had felt he must face it alone. We should think too of those aspects of our behaviour with which

---

4. 1 John 2:2
5. J. Escrivá, *The Way*, 440

sometimes, without really meaning to, we make life a little harder for others ... our whims and fancies, our rash judgements, negative criticism, a lack of consideration for others, an unkind word ...

10.2 We should be compassionate and merciful. The burden of sin and of ignorance.

Love enables us to discover in others the divine image in whose likeness we have all been made. We should recognise in everyone the tremendous price paid for his ransom – the pricelessness of his redemption – the very Blood of Christ.[6] The greater our love, the more we are able to appreciate our neighbour and, as a consequence, show concern for his needs and sorrows. Then we see not only another human being who is suffering or having a hard time, we see Christ in that person, Christ, who identified himself with all men: *Truly I say to you, as you did it to one of the least of these my brethren, you did it to me.*[7] Christ makes himself present to us through charity. He acts in the world at every moment through the members of his Mystical Body. It is for this reason that our constant union with Jesus enables us also to say: *Come to me all who labour and are heavy laden , and I will give you rest.* Charity is the full realisation of the Kingdom of God in the world.

If we are to be faithful followers of Christ we have to ask him unceasingly to give us a heart like his, capable of feeling sorrow for all the evil that man drags along behind him. We should be particularly sorry about the evil that is sin, which, more than any other evil, drags man down and overwhelms him. Jesus always responded with compassion

---

6. cf 1 Pet 1:18
7. Matt 25:40

when He saw all the limitations and the weaknesses of men: *I have compassion on the crowd ...,*[8] the evangelists record in their different ways. Christ was moved by all the kinds of misfortune He encountered during his time on this earth. We know that He always looks with mercy on the mass of human wretchedness that has been accumulated throughout the centuries. If we are to call ourselves followers of Christ we must bear in our hearts the same feelings of mercy as the Master had.

In our personal prayer, let us ask Our Lord to help us with his grace to feel true compassion, above all for those who suffer the immeasurable evil of sin, for those who are far from God. Then we will be able to understand how it is that the apostolate of Confession is the greatest of the works of mercy. It is by doing this apostolate that we give God the opportunity to pour out his generous forgiveness on that prodigal son who has left his father's house. Of what a great burden do we relieve the person who was burdened by sin and now goes to Confession! What a true relief! Today could be a good time to ask ourselves: how many people have I helped to make a good Confession. Who else can I help?

We should try especially to lighten the burdens of people more closely connected to us because they share the same faith, the same spirit, the same ties of blood, the same work ... Saint Leo the Great said emphatically: *Certainly look on everyone who suffers with a general benevolence, but be especially concerned about those who are members of Christ's Body and are united to us through the Catholic Faith. For we owe more to those who belong to us through the union of grace than to strangers through the community of nature.*[9]

---

8. Mark 8:2
9. St Leo the Great, *Sermon 89*

As far as we can, let us relieve all those who carry the heavy burden of ignorance, especially ignorance of their religion, which *today reaches levels never before descended to in certain countries of Christian tradition. Perhaps because of the impositions of a secular state or because of lamentable disorientation and negligence, crowds of children who have been baptised are reaching adolescence with a total lack of the most elementary notions of the Faith and morals and even of the rudiments of piety. Today, to teach the unlearned means above all to teach those who know nothing about Religion; it means 'to evangelise them' – that is to say, to speak to them about God and about the Christian life.*[10] What a great weight has to be borne by those who do not know Christ, by those who have been deprived of Christian doctrine or who are imbued with error!

10.3 We should turn to Christ when life becomes difficult for us, and learn from Our Lady how to forget ourselves.

We will find that no way leads more certainly to Christ and happiness than that of a sincere concern to free those who are weary and heavy-laden from whatever weighs them down. God has disposed things in such a way that *we should learn to bear one another's burdens: because there is nobody without any defect; nobody who is sufficient unto himself; indeed nobody who is sufficiently wise unto himself.*[11] We all need one another. Living with other people requires that mutual help without which we would find it difficult to keep going.

If at some time we should find ourselves wrestling with a burden that is beyond our strength, we should not fail to listen to Our Lord's words: *Come to me.* Only

10. J. Orlandis, *The Eight Beatitudes*
11. Thomas à Kempis, *Imitation of Christ*, I, 16, 4

He can restore our strength, only He can quench our thirst. *Jesus says now and always: 'Come to me, all who are weary and heavy laden, and I will give you rest'. We can be sure that Jesus constantly invites us to come to him, sees our difficulties and has compassion on us. Still more does He offer us his promises, his friendship, the hope of goodness, of a healing remedy for our ills, of comfort; and still more does He offer us nourishment, bread, the very source of energy and life.*[12] Christ is our repose.

Our continuous conversation with Our Mother Mary teaches us to be understanding with our neighbour in his time of need. There was nothing that she failed to notice, because even the smallest of cares were important to the love that always filled her Heart. She will help us to follow the way that leads to Christ at those very times when our need to unburden ourselves on him is even greater: *You will draw strength from it to put the Will of God fully into practice, and you will be filled with desires of serving all men. You will be the Christian you have sometimes dreamed of being: full of works of charity and justice, happy and strong, understanding towards others and demanding on yourself.*[13]

---

12. Paul VI, *Homily*, 12 June 1977
13. J. Escrivá, *Friends of God*, 293

FOURTEENTH SUNDAY: YEAR B

11. *MY GRACE IS SUFFICIENT FOR YOU*

11.1 God gives us his help to enable us to overcome all obstacles, temptations and difficulties.

In the *Second Reading*[1] of today's Mass, Saint Paul lets us see the depths of his humility. After speaking to the Corinthians about his labours for Christ and the visions and revelations he had received from the Lord, he goes on to tell them of his weakness: *to keep me from being too elated by the abundance of revelations, a thorn was given me in the flesh, a messenger of Satan to harass me, to keep me from being too elated.*

We do not know with any certainty what Saint Paul is referring to when he speaks of this *thorn in the flesh*. Some Fathers of the Church, (e.g. Saint Augustine) think it is a particularly painful physical affliction; others, (e.g. Saint John Chrysostom) think that he is referring to the tribulations caused him by the continuous persecutions of which he is the victim; and some, (e.g. Saint Gregory the Great) are of the opinion that he is referring to temptations that he finds particularly difficult to resist.[2] Whatever it is, it is something that humiliates the Apostle, and that in some way hinders his work as a bearer of the Gospel.

Saint Paul had asked God three times to remove this obstacle from him. He received this sublime reply: *My grace is sufficient for you, for my power is made perfect in weakness.* God's help is sufficient for him to overcome

---

1. 2 Cor 12:7-10
2. *The Navarre Bible*, St Paul's Epistles to the Corinthians, *in loc*

that difficulty; at the same time we are given to know about the divine power that enabled him to overcome it. He becomes stronger when he relies on God's help, and this causes him to exclaim: *For the sake of Christ, then, I am content with weaknesses, insults, hardships, persecution, and calamities; for when I am weak, then I am strong*. In our own weakness we too constantly experience the need to turn towards God and draw on the strength that comes to us from him. How often God has said to us deep in our hearts: *My grace is sufficient for you*, you have my help to enable you to overcome all trials and difficulties.

Perhaps we sometimes have a particularly vivid experience of loneliness, weakness or tribulation: *If so, seek the support of him who died and rose again. Find yourself a shelter in the wounds in his hands, in his feet, in his side. And your willingness to start again will revive, and you will take up your journey again with greater determination and effectiveness*.[3]

Even our frailty and our weaknesses can be turned to good account. In his commentary on this passage, Saint Thomas Aquinas explains that God can sometimes allow certain evils of a physical or moral order precisely so as to draw from them a greater, more necessary good.[4] God will never abandon us in the midst of temptation. Our very weakness helps us to have greater trust, to seek refuge in God more urgently, to ask him for greater strength and to be more humble: *'Lord, put not your trust in me. But I, I put my trust in you'. Then, as we sense in our hearts the love, the compassion, the tenderness of Christ's gaze upon us – for He never abandons us – we shall come to understand the full meaning of those words of Saint Paul: 'Virtus*

---

3. J. Escrivá, *The Way of the Cross*, Twelfth Station, 2
4. St Thomas, *Commentary on 2 Corinthians, in loc*

in infirmitate perficitur' (2 Cor 12:9). If we have faith in Our Lord, in spite of our failings – or, rather, with our failings – we shall be faithful to our Father, God; his divine power will shine forth in us, sustaining us in our weakness.[5]

11.2 *If you want to, you can.*

A thorn was given me in the flesh, a messenger of Satan, to harass me ... It seems here as if Saint Paul senses his limitations in a very vivid way, and at the same time relives the occasions when he contemplated the greatness of God and the greatness of his own mission as an Apostle. Sometimes in the course of our lives we too have caught glimpses of *generous aims, aims of sincerity, of perseverance ..., and yet, it seems as though we have, in the very depths of our soul, a sort of radical infirmity, a lack of strength, an obscure impotence ..., and this sometimes makes us feel sad and we say 'I can't'.*[6] We can see what Our Lord wants of us in this or that situation, but perhaps we feel weakened and exhausted by the trials and difficulties facing us. *Your intelligence – enlightened by faith – shows you the way clearly. It can also point out the difference between following that way heroically or stupidly. Above all, it places before you the divine greatness and beauty of the undertakings the Trinity leaves in our hands.*

Your feelings, on the other hand, become attached to everything you despise, even while you consider it despicable. It seems as if a thousand trifles were awaiting the least opportunity, and as soon as your poor will is weakened through physical tiredness or lack of supernatural outlook, those little things flock together and pile up in your imagination, until they form a mountain that oppresses and

---

5. J. Escrivá, *Friends of God*, 194
6. A. G. Dorronsoro, *Time to Hope*

discourages you. Things such as the rough edges of your work; your resistance to obedience; the lack of proper means; the false attractions of an easy life; greater or smaller but repugnant temptations; bouts of sensuality; tiredness; the bitter taste of spiritual mediocrity ... and sometimes also fear – fear because you know God wants you to be a saint, and you are not a saint.

Allow me to talk to you bluntly. You have more than enough 'reasons' to turn back, and you lack the resolution to correspond to the grace that He grants you, since He has called you to be another Christ, 'ipse Christus'! – Christ himself. You have forgotten the Lord's admonition to the Apostle: 'My grace is enough for you', which is confirmation that, if you want to, you can.[7]

My grace is sufficient for you. Our Lord says these words directly to each one of us so that we should be filled with fortitude and with hope when we see the trials that await us. Our very weakness will help us to rejoice at Christ's power; it will teach us to love and to feel the need to be always very close to Jesus. Our very failures, our unfulfilled plans, will lead us to exclaim: *When I am weak, then I am strong,* for Christ is with me.

Whenever we are beset by greater temptations, set-backs or weariness, the devil will try to make us stray from the path by causing a lack of trust and discouragement to creep into our soul. This is why today we must learn the lesson Saint Paul wants to teach us: it is at such times that Christ is especially present to us and ready to help us; we have just to turn to him. Then we too will be able to say with the Apostle: *For the sake of Christ, then, I am content to put up with weaknesses, insults, hardships, persecutions, and calamities.*

---

7. J. Escrivá, *Furrow*, 166

11.3 Means we should use in times of temptation.

It would be rash to desire temptation or to provoke it, but it would also be wrong to be afraid of temptation, as though Our Lord were not going to give us his help to overcome it. We can confidently apply to ourselves the words of the Psalm: *For he will give his angels charge of you, to guard you in all your ways. On their hands they will bear you up, lest you dash your foot against a stone. You will tread on the lion and the adder, the young lion and the serpent you will trample under foot. Because he cleaves to me in love, I will deliver him; I will protect him, because he knows my name. When he calls to me, I will answer him; I will be with him in trouble, I will rescue him and honour him. With long life I will satisfy him, and show him my salvation.*[8]

At the same time, Our Lord asks us to be prepared for temptation and to use all the means at our disposal to overcome it: prayer and voluntary mortifications; fleeing from the occasions of sin, for *whoever loves danger will perish by it*;[9] leading a life of hard and constant work, carrying out the duties of our work in an exemplary manner and simply changing our activity in order to rest; fostering a great horror for every sin, however small it may seem; and, above all, making a real effort to increase within ourselves our love for Christ and for Our Lady.

We are putting up an effective struggle when we open our soul in spiritual direction whenever we are tempted to be unfaithful. *To speak about it is already almost to overcome it. He who reveals his own temptations to his spiritual director can be certain that God grants his director the grace he needs to direct him well* ...

---

8. Psalm 91:11 *et seq*
9. Sir 3:26

We should never think that temptation is overcome by settling down to argue with it, or even by attacking it head-on ... As soon as it presents itself to us we should turn away from it and direct our glance towards Our Lord, who lives within us and fights at our side, who himself has conquered sin; let us embrace him in an act of humble submission to his Will, of accepting that cross of temptation ..., of trust in him and of faith in his closeness to us, at the same time making an act of supplication that He may transmit his strength to us. In this way temptation will lead us to prayer, to union with God and with Christ; it will not be loss, but rather gain. In everything God works for good with those who love him (Rom 8:28). [10]

From our trials, our tribulations and temptations we can draw out much good, for in undergoing them we will show Our Lord that we need him and that we love him. They will set us on fire with love and increase all the virtues within us, for a bird flies not only by the impulse of its wings, but also by the lift and resistance of the air: in some way we have need of obstacles and setbacks in order that our love may grow. The greater the resistance to any progress along our way provided by our surroundings or by our own weakness, the more help and grace God will give us. And our Mother in Heaven will always be particularly close to us at those moments of greatest need: we should not fail to seek her motherly protection.

---

10. B. Baur, *In Silence with God*

FOURTEENTH SUNDAY: YEAR C

12. AS A RIVER OF PEACE

12.1 Our Lord comes to bring peace to a world that lacks peace.

This Sunday's Liturgy centres in a special way on peace as being of great benefit for the individual soul and for society. In the *First Reading*,[1] the Prophet Isaiah announces that the era of the Messiah will be characterised by its abundance of this divine gift; it will be like *a torrent of peace*, like *an overflowing stream*. It is to be an era that will gather together everything that is good: joy, happiness, consolation and the prosperity promised by God when Jerusalem was restored after the Babylonian exile. *As one whom his mother comforts, so will I comfort you*. Isaiah refers in these words to the Messiah, the bearer of that peace which is, at one and the same time, grace and eternal salvation for each individual and for the whole people of God. The new Jerusalem is an image of the Church and of each one of us.

The Gospel of today's Mass[2] tells how Our Lord sent the disciples out to announce the coming of the Kingdom of God. Wherever they went miracles occurred time and again: blind men recovered their sight, lepers were cleansed, sinners were moved to repentance. Wherever they went they carried with them the peace of Christ. Before sending them out on that apostolic mission, Our Lord himself had charged them: *Whatever house you enter,*

---

1. Is 66:10-14
2. Luke 10:1-12; 17-20

*first say, 'Peace be to this house'. And if a son of peace is
there, your peace shall rest upon him* ... The Church will
repeat this message until the end of the world.

Nevertheless, after so many years, we can still see
that the world is not at peace; it desires peace and
clamours for it, but it does not find it. There are few ages
when the word 'peace' has been pronounced so often, and
there are perhaps few ages when peace has been further
away from the world. Even, it has been said, *in many
nations and countries, the general situation has little to do
with peace. Not that there is war, or at least what we generally understand by war, but there is certainly a lack of
peace. Race struggles. Class struggles. The struggle between
ideologies and political parties. Terrorism. Guerrilla warfare.
Kidnap and assassination attempts. Insecurity. Riots.
Disputes. Violence. Hatred which brings resentment, accusations and recriminations.*[3] *'Peace, peace', they say, when
there is no peace.*[4] There is no peace in society, or in the
family or within souls. What is happening for there to be
no peace? Why is there so much tension and so much
violence? Why are our souls beset by so much anxiety and
so much sadness, if what everyone wants is peace?

Perhaps the world is looking for peace where peace
cannot be found; perhaps we are confusing peace with a
quiet life. Quite possibly we think peace depends on external circumstances that have nothing to do with man himself. Peace comes from God and it is a gift of God *that
passes all understanding.*[5] It is granted only to men of good
will[6] – to those who strive with the whole of their strength
to live their lives in accordance with God's Will. *Peace,*

---

3. F. Suarez, *When the Son of Man comes*
4. cf Jer 6:14
5. Phil 4:7
6. cf Luke 2:14

and the joy that comes with it, cannot be given by the world.

Men are forever 'making peace' and forever getting entangled in wars. This is because they have forgotten the advice to struggle inside themselves and to go to God for help. He will then conquer, and we will obtain peace for ourselves and for our own homes, for society and for the world.

If we do things in this way, you and I will have joy, because it is the possession of those who conquer. And with the grace of God – who never loses battles – we will be able to count ourselves conquerors as long as we are humble.[7] Then we will be the bearers of true peace, and we will carry it wherever we go as an invaluable treasure. We will take it to our families, to our place of work, to our friends … to the whole world.

12.2 Violence and anxiety have their roots in men's hearts; they are consequences of sin.

In the beginning, before original sin had been committed, everything was ordered so as to give glory to God and happiness to men. There were no such things as wars, hatred, anger, lack of understanding, injustice … Through that first sin, to which personal sins were subsequently added, man turned into a being who was selfish, proud, mean, avaricious … If we look at sin we will detect in it the cause of all the failings we see around us. John Paul II has pointed out that *violence and injustice have their roots deep in the hearts of each individual, of each one of us.*[8] It is from the heart that come *all the disorders that men are capable of committing against God, against their brothers and against themselves, provoking far down in their consciences a rent, a deep bitterness, a lack of peace that is*

---

7. J. Escrivá, *The Forge*, 102
8. John Paul II, *Message for World Day of Peace*, 8 December 1984

necessarily reflected in the network of social life. But it is also from the human heart, from its great capacity to love, from its generosity in being willing to undergo sacrifice, that there can arise – made fruitful by Christ's grace – feelings of fraternity and works of service to men who 'like a stream of peace' (Is 66:12) work together for the construction of a more just world, in which peace brings with it the badge of citizenship and impregnates all structures of society.[9] Peace is the consequence of sanctifying grace, just as violence, in any one of its manifestations, is the consequence of sin.

The whole future of peace is in our hearts,[10] for sin has not been so powerful that it could completely obliterate the image of God in man, but only *soil it, deform it and weaken it. It was able to wound his soul but not annihilate it. It was able to darken his intellect, but not destroy it. Sin managed to open a way for hatred, but not to eliminate man's capacity for loving. It twisted man's will, but not to such an extent as to make rectification impossible.*[11] This is why, although man tends towards evil when he lets himself be led by his fallen nature, he can nevertheless, with the help of grace, overcome those disordered passions and possess and communicate to others the peace Christ won for us. It is then that the life of a Christian becomes a cheerful struggle to overcome evil and to reach Christ. In that struggle he finds safety which is filled with optimism. If ever he forms a pact with sin and with his own wretchedness, he loses that feeling of certainty and becomes a source of unease and even of violence for himself and for others.

As one whom his mother comforts, so will I comfort you. It is only in Christ that we will find the peace that we

---

9. A. del Portillo, *Homily*, 30 March 1985
10. Cf John Paul II, *op cit*, 3
11. F. Suarez, *op cit*

so much want for ourselves and for those closest to us. Let us go to him when the difficulties of life threaten the serenity of our soul. Let us go to the Sacrament of Penance and to spiritual direction if, because we have not struggled hard enough, worry and anxiety have entered into our hearts.

12.3 Peace begins in the soul when we acknowledge all that separates us from God with a heartfelt act of contrition. Spreading peace throughout the world by starting with the people closest to us.

Christ's presence in the hearts of his followers is the beginning of true peace. Such peace brings with it rich fulfilment; it is not mere ease of life or absence of struggle. Saint Paul affirms that Christ himself is our peace;[12] to possess him and to love him is the origin of all true serenity.

This stream of peace in our soul, an *overflowing stream*. begins with the acknowledgement of our sins, faults, negligences and errors. Then if we are humble and we look at Christ, he will disclose to us his great mercy, *as though he were hidden behind a veil saying to us: 'Those are the shortcomings I have taken upon myself in order to show you the Father's love in a very personal way, through this loneliness and sorrow. His love is the only love capable of freeing us from our wretchedness, of turning it around, so to speak, and using it towards your salvation'. Then there will resound in the ear of our hearts, the words: 'Your faith has saved you and has cured you. Go in peace'[13]* There is no peace without contrition. There is no peace unless we are deeply sincere with ourselves and acknowledge those

---

12. Eph 2:14
13. S. Pinckaers, *In Search of Happiness*

things in our lives that separate us from God and our fellow men. There is no peace without deep, undiluted sincerity in Confession.

With this interior calm, we will find that by beginning over and over again and never complying with our defects and our shortcomings we will be able to go out into the world, to that space in which we spend each day of our lives, and spread around us that peace that the world does not have and consequently cannot give.

Whatever house you enter, first say, 'Peace be to this house' ... It is not simply a greeting – it is Christ's peace that his followers have to take out into all the paths of the world. We will say to everyone that true peace *is founded on justice, on the sense of the inviolable dignity of man, on the acceptance of an indelible and desirable equality of man, on the basic principle of human brotherhood, that is to say, on the respect and love due to each man.*[14] The peace of the world begins within the heart of each individual.

The Christian who lives by faith is a man of peace who spreads serenity around him; people feel at ease with him and others will seek his company. Let us ask Our Lady, as we finish these moments of prayer, to teach us to go humbly to the source of peace (the tabernacle, Confession, spiritual direction) if ever we see that anxiety, fear, sadness or worry are seeking a way of entering into our hearts. *Regina pacis, ora pro nobis ... ora pro me.*

---

14. Paul VI, *Message for World Day of Peace*, 1971

Fourteenth Week: Monday

13. FINDING CHRIST IN THE CHURCH

13.1 It is not possible to love, follow or listen to Christ without loving, following and listening to the Church.

Everyone looks for Jesus. Everyone needs Jesus, and He in turn is always ready to have compassion on all who approach him with faith. His most Sacred Humanity was like a channel through which all graces flowed, for as long as He remained among men. This is why the crowds tried to touch him, *for there flowed out of him a power that cured all*.

The woman we hear about in the Gospel of today's Mass[1] also felt moved to approach Christ. To her physical sufferings – which had already lasted for twelve years – was added the shame of feeling herself impure according to the law. The Jews at that time considered not only the woman affected by a sickness of this type to be impure, but also everything she touched. This is why she approached Jesus from behind and touched just his cloak, so that people would not notice her. *She delicately touched the hem of his cloak, she approached with faith, she believed and she knew she had been cured ...*[2]

These miracles – cures and the casting out of – devils that Christ worked whilst He lived on this earth were a proof that the Redemption was already a reality, not merely a hope. The people we see coming up to the Master foretell, as it were, the devotion Christians would later have to the Most Sacred Humanity of Christ. Later, when He was about to go up to Heaven and take his place

---

1. Matt 9:20-22
2. St Ambrose, *Commentary on St Luke's Gospel*, VI, 56

beside his Father, knowing that we would always have need of him, He established the means by which, at any time or in any place, we would be able to receive the infinite riches of the Redemption: He founded the Church, in such a way that we would easily see it or find it. When we look for the Church we are like those those people who looked for the Son of Mary. *To be in the Church is to be with Jesus*; to unite oneself to this flock is to unite oneself to Jesus. To belong to this society is to be a member of his Body. It is only in the Church that we can find Christ – Christ himself – the very same Christ that the chosen people waited so long for.

Those people who claim to approach Christ whilst leaving his Church to one side, and even causing her harm, may one day get the same surprise as Saint Paul did when he was on his way to Damascus: *I am Jesus whom you are persecuting.*[3] And, the Venerable Bede reflects that *He does not say 'why are you persecuting my members, but why are you persecuting me?' For He is still affronted in his Body, which is the Church.*[4] Paul did not know until that moment that *to persecute the Church was to persecute Jesus himself.* When he speaks about the Church later on, he does so in words that describe her as the Body of Christ,[5] or simply as Christ;[6] and he describes the faithful as members of Christ's Body.[7] It is not possible to love, follow or listen to Christ, without loving, following or listening to the Church, because she is the presence, at once sacramental and mysterious, of Our Lord, who prolongs his saving mission in the world to the very end of time.

3. Acts 9:5
4. St Bede, *Commentary on the Acts of the Apostles*, in loc
5. 1 Cor 12:27
6. 1 Cor 1:13
7. Rom 12:5

13.2 In the Church we share in Christ's Life.

Nobody can say that he loves God if he does not choose the way to him – Jesus – laid down by God himself. *This is my beloved Son ... listen to him.*[8] We act illogically if we claim to be Christ's friends and at the same time spurn his words and his wishes.

Those crowds of people from many different places all find in Jesus someone who speaks to them with authority, who speaks to them about God. He himself is the divine Word made flesh – they come face to face with Jesus the Master. And we in our day attach ourselves to him when we accept the teaching of the Church: *He who hears you hears me, and he who rejects you rejects me.*[9]

Moreover, Jesus is our Redeemer. He is the Priest; He fully possesses the one and only priesthood and He offered himself as the propitiatory victim for sin. *So also Christ did not exalt himself to be made a high priest, but was appointed by him who said to him 'Thou art my Son' ...*[10] We unite ourselves to Jesus, at once priest and victim, who gives honour to God the Father and sanctifies us when we take part in the life of the Church; we do so particularly when we partake of her sacraments, which are like divine channels through which grace flows until it reaches our souls. Each time we receive the sacraments we come into contact with Christ himself, the fountain of all grace. Through the sacraments the infinite merits that Christ gained for us reach men of all times and are, for all, the firm hope of eternal life. In the Holy Eucharist that Christ commanded the Church to celebrate, we renew his oblation and immolation. *This is my body which is given for you. Do this in remembrance of me.*[11] And only the Holy Eucharist

---

8. Matt 17:5
9. Luke 10:16
10. Heb 5:5
11. Luke 22:19

guarantees to us the Life that He has gained for us: *Whoever shall eat of this bread shall live for ever, and the bread that I shall give is my flesh which is the life of the world ...* [12]

The condition for sharing in this sacrifice and banquet stems from another of the sacraments Christ conferred on his Church – Baptism. *Go therefore and make disciples of all nations, baptising them in the name of the Father and of the Son and of the Holy Spirit.*[13] *He who believes and is baptised will be saved ...* [14] And if our sins have caused us to be separated from God, the Church is also the means by which our condition as living members of the Lord is restored: *If you forgive the sins of any, they are forgiven; if you retain the sins of any, they are retained.*[15] Christ laid it down that this strong link with him should be brought about by those visible signs that are the sacramental life of his Church. Through the sacraments we also find Christ.

Although there may sometimes be dissensions within the Church, it will not be difficult for us to find Christ. Majorities and minorities do not matter much when it is a question of finding Jesus: on Calvary there stood only his Mother with a few women and an adolescent, but there, a few yards away, was Jesus! In the Church we too know where our Lord is: *I will give you the keys of the kingdom of heaven,* He declared to Peter, *and whatever you bind on earth shall be bound in heaven, and whatever you loose on earth shall be loosed in heaven.*[16] Not even Simon's denials of him were sufficient for him to revoke those powers. Our Lord, once He had risen from the dead, confirmed those powers in a solemn way: *Feed my lambs ... Feed my*

---

12. Luke 6:51
13. Matt 28:19
14. Mark 16:16
15. John 20:23
16. Matt 16:19

sheep.[17] The Church is where Peter and his successors – and the bishops in communion with him – are.

13.3 Faith, hope and love for the Church.

In the Church we see Jesus, the same Jesus the crowds wanted so much to touch *for there flowed out of him a power that cured all*. Anybody who binds himself to Christ the Teacher, the Priest and the King by accepting the doctrine, the sacraments and the authority of the Church, belongs to the Church. In a certain way we maintain the same relationship with the Church as we do with Christ – by means of faith, hope and charity.

First of all *faith*, which means believing what on so many occasions is not so obvious. The contemporaries of Jesus too saw a man who worked, who grew tired, who needed food, who felt pain, cold and fear ..., but that Man was God. In the Church we have seen holy people who often pass unnoticed, hidden as they have been by a very ordinary life. We also see weak people like ourselves, small-minded, lazy, self-interested. But if they have been baptised and remain in a state of grace, despite all their defects, they are in Christ, they share in his very life. If they are sinners, the Church welcomes them too into her midst as members who need her still more.

Our attitude towards the Church also has to be one of *hope*. Christ himself assured us: *On this rock I will build my church, and the powers of death shall not prevail against it*.[18] She will be the *firm rock* where we can seek safety against the erratic lurches the world seems to make. She can never fail us, because in her we will always find Christ.

And if we owe God *charity*, love; that is, we must have

---

17. John 21:15-17
18. Matt 16:18

this same sentiment towards our Mother the Church, for *no-one can have God for his Father who does not have the Church for his Mother.*[19] She is the Mother who gives life to us – that life of Christ's by which we are children of the Father. A mother is to be loved. Only bad children remain indifferent, sometimes hostile, towards the person who gave them their very being. We have a good mother: this is why we are so hurt by the wounds that are caused her by some outside and by some inside the Church, and by the sicknesses that others of her members can sometimes undergo. This is why, as good sons and daughters of the Church, we try hard not to talk about the weaknesses of individuals, past or present, of this or that Christian, whether or not they have been placed in positions of authority. We try never to criticise the Church who is Holy and so merciful that she does not deny her motherly care even to sinners. How can we ever speak about her coldly, harshly or insolently? How can we remain *indifferent* to our mother? We are not and we do not want to be indifferent. Whatever is hers is ours, and we cannot be expected to take a neutral stance, like a judge who will impartially hear a case against someone. Such can never be the attitude of a child in relation to his mother.

We belong to Christ when we belong to the Church. In her we become members of the body of him whom Our Lady conceived, gestated, and brought into the world. This is why the Blessed Virgin is *Mother of the Church, that is to say, Mother of the whole people of God, both faithful and pastors.*[20] The latest jewel that filial piety has set in the litany of Our Lady, the most recent compliment to the *Mother of Christ* is almost synonymous: *Mother of the Church* we say.

---

19. St Cyprian, *On Unity*, 6, 8
20. Paul VI, *Address*, 21 November 1964

FOURTEENTH WEEK: TUESDAY

14. THE ASCETICAL STRUGGLE

14.1 Many battles are waged each day in men's hearts. Our Lord's constant help in the struggle.

Jacob's mysterious wrestling-match with the angel in human form on the banks of the River Jabbok marks a pivotal turning point in the Patriarch's life. Up till then Jacob had behaved in an all too human way, relying on purely natural means. From that moment on he would put his trust above all else in God, who reaffirmed in him his Covenant with the chosen people.

Jacob was able to win in that contest only through the strength that God gave him, and the lesson to be learned from this event was that God's blessing and protection would never be wanting in any of the difficulties that were to come.[1] The Book of Wisdom expresses it thus: *In his arduous contest she gave him the victory, so that he might learn that godliness is more powerful than anything.*[2]

For the Fathers of the Church this scene from the Old Testament is an image of the spiritual struggle the Christian has to sustain against forces very superior to himself, and against his own passions and tendencies, which have inclined mankind towards evil ever since original sin was committed. Saint Paul warns us that *we are not contending against flesh and blood, but against the principalities, against the powers, against the world rulers of this present darkness, against the spiritual hosts of*

---

1. *First Reading*, Year I: Gen 32:22-32
2. Wis 10:12

wickedness in the heavenly places.[3] These are the rebel angels, who have already been vanquished by Christ, but who will not cease to incite man towards evil until the very end of his life on earth. Every day there are contests within our hearts, Saint Augustine teaches. Each man fights against a whole army within his soul. The enemies are pride, avarice, gluttony, sensuality, laziness … And, the saint adds, it is difficult to prevent those attacks from wounding us.[4] Nevertheless we can be certain of victory if we make use of the resources that God has given us, namely prayer, mortification, complete sincerity in spiritual direction, the help of our guardian angel and, above all, of our Mother, Mary. Moreover, *if He who has given his very life for us is the Judge in this contest, how can we fail to be rightfully proud and confident?*

In the Olympic games, the referee stations himself between the two adversaries without favouring either one or the other, awaiting the outcome. If the referee places himself equidistant from the two contenders, it is because his attitude is neutral. In the struggle where we come face to face with the devil, Christ does not remain impartial; He is entirely on our side. How can this be? 'You can see that from the moment we entered the lists' – these are words spoken by Saint John Chrysostom to some Christians on the day of their Baptism – *'He anointed us whilst at the same time He bound the other in chains. Us He has annointed with the oil of gladness, and the devil He has bound with unbreakable fetters so as to bring his assaults to nothing. If I stumble He holds out his hand to me: He raises me from my fall and He sets me on my feet again.*[5]

However many temptations, difficulties or

---

3. Eph 6:12
4. St Augustine, *Homily on Psalm 99*
5. St John Chrysostom, *Baptismal Catechesis*, 3:9-10

tribulations may assail us, Christ is forever our safeguard. He does not leave us. *He is not neutral*! He is always on our side. We can all say with Saint Paul: *Omnia possum in eo qui me confortat* ... , I can do everything in Christ who strengthens me, who gives me the help I need if only I turn to him and use the means He has established.

14.2 Daily effort which is both cheerful and humble is necessary if we are to follow Christ.

A mountaineer was climbing towards a shelter high up on the mountain. The path became steeper and steeper and at times it was difficult for him to take the next step forward; the icy wind whipped against his face, but he was oblivious to this owing to the impression made on him by the great silence that reigned all around and by the beauty of the landscape.

The refuge, which was simple and rough-hewn, was very welcoming. Very soon he noticed some words written above the fireplace, words that he felt completely identified with. *My place is at the summit*, they said. That is our place also: at the summit, next to Christ, with a constant desire of aspiring to sanctity in the place where we are, even though we are only too well aware of the poor clay of which we are made, of our shortcomings and failings. But we know too that God asks us to make a small effort every day. He asks us to struggle without respite against the passions that tend to pull us down. He asks us never to form a pact with our defects or mistakes. What will make us persevere in this struggle is love, a deep love for Christ, whom we seek unceasingly.[6]

The Christian's ascetical struggle has to be positive, cheerful, constant, and be carried on with a *sporting spirit*,

---

6. A. Tanquerey, *The Spiritual Life*, 193 *et seq*

a spirit of energetic contest. *Sanctity has the flexibility of supple muscles. Whoever wishes to be a saint should know how to behave in such a way that while he does something that involves a mortification for him, he omits doing something else – as long as this does not offend God – which he would also find difficult, and thanks the Lord for this comfort. If we Christians were to act otherwise we would run the risk of becoming stiff and lifeless, like a rag doll.*

Sanctity is not rigid like cardboard; it knows how to smile, to give way to others and to hope. It is life – a supernatural life.[7]

In the interior struggle we will also meet with failures. Many such failures will be unimportant; others will be more serious, but our atonement and our contrition will bring us even closer to God. And if ever we smash into small pieces what we felt was most precious in our life, God will be able to mend that very thing if we are humble. He always forgives us and helps us when we turn to him with a contrite heart. We must learn to begin again many times; with new joy, with new humility, for even if we have caused serious offence to God and have done much harm to other people, we can still later come very close to God in this life and be happy with him in the next, as long as there is true repentance, as long as we make room in our lives for penance, humility, sincerity and repentance – and begin again.

God allows for our weakness and always forgives us, but we need to be sincere, to repent, and to struggle to rise up again. There is incomparable joy in heaven each time we begin again. Throughout our journey on earth we will have to do so many times, because there will always be faults, shortcomings, weaknesses and sins for us to recover

---

7. J. Escrivá, *The Forge*, 156

from. May we never lack the straightforwardness to acknowledge this and to open our souls to Our Lord in the Tabernacle and in spiritual direction.

14.3 Beginning again many times. Recourse to the Blessed Virgin, our Mother.

The Christian's daily struggle will generally be specific and will entail fighting on very minor matters. Fortitude will be necessary in order to fulfil with sincere effort our acts of piety towards God, without abandoning them no matter what presents itself during the course of the day, and so as not to let ourselves be carried away by our state of mind at the time. The way we live charity, overcoming sudden ill-temper, making an effort to be warm, good-natured and considerate towards others – these will be important, as will our efforts to finish off the work we have offered to God, without skimping or taking any shortcuts, doing it as well as we possibly can and using the means to receive the formation we need ...

There will be moments of victory and of defeat, of falling and of rising again. We must always begin again ...; it is what God asks of all of us. The struggle demands a love that is vigilant and an effective desire to seek God throughout the day. This cheerful struggle is the exact opposite of lukewarmness, which is characterised by carelessness, a lack of interest in seeking God, laziness and sadness in fulfilling our obligations towards God and other people.

In this struggle we can always count on the help of Mary our Mother, who follows step by step our journey towards her Son. In *the Divine Office*, the Church commends every day to her priests this Antiphon of the Virgin: *Hail, loving Mother of the Redeemer, gate of Heaven ever open, star of the sea; assist your people who have fallen yet strive to rise again* ... [8]

This people that falls and struggles to rise up again is ourselves, is each one of us. The change that occurs each time we begin again, even though it may be in aspects that appear to be of little importance – the particular examination of conscience, the advice received in spiritual direction, the resolutions resulting from our self-examination – is greater than we can ever imagine. Think how much greater it will be when it is a matter of passing from the death of sin to the life of grace! *Mankind has made wonderful discoveries and achieved extraordinary results in the fields of science and technology. It has made great advances along the path of progress and civilisation, and in recent times one could say that it has succeeded in speeding up the pace of history. But the fundamental transformation, the one which can be called 'original', constantly accompanies man's journey, and through all the events of history accompanies each and every individual. It is the transformation from 'falling' to 'rising', from death to life.*[9]

Each time we begin again, each time we decide to struggle once more, we receive the help of Our Lady, *Mediatrix of all graces*. We must turn to her with complete abandonment whenever temptations become stronger. *My Mother! Mothers on earth look with greater love upon the weakest of their children, the one with the worst health, or who is the least intelligent, or is a poor cripple.*

Sweet Lady, I know that you are more of a Mother than all other mothers put together. And, since I am your son, since I am weak, and ill, and crippled, and ugly ... [10]

---

8. *Divine Office*, Antiphon, *Alma Redemptoris Mater*
9. John Paul II, *Redemptoris Mater*, 25 March 1987, 52
10. J. Escrivá, *op cit*, 234

FOURTEENTH WEEK: WEDNESDAY

15. *GO TO JOSEPH*

15.1 Jacob's son – a figure of Saint Joseph.

Many Christians, conscious of the exceptional mission of Saint Joseph in the life of Jesus and Mary, since the Old Testament is the forerunner of the New Testament, have tried throughout the centuries to find in the history of the Hebrew people deeds and images that prefigure the man who was to be the virginal spouse of Mary. Many Fathers of the Church have seen in the person of the same name, Joseph, son of Jacob the Patriarch, a prophetic announcement. When Pope Pius IX proclaimed Saint Joseph patron of the universal Church he gathered together those ancient insights. The Liturgy also gives witness to this same parallelism. Not only did these two men share the same name, but there are also to be found in their lives, interwoven in both cases with trials and joys, certain virtues and attitudes which are similar and coincide in many instances.

Joseph the son of Jacob and Joseph the virginal spouse of Mary both went to Egypt as the result of whole series of providential circumstances. The first Joseph went there because he was pursued by his brothers and handed over to strangers out of envy, circumstances that prefigure the betrayal that Christ would have to undergo. The second Joseph went to Egypt having fled from Herod in order to save the Child who was to bring salvation to the world.[1]

---

1. cf M. Gasnier, *The Silences of Joseph*

Joseph the son of Jacob received from God the gift of being able to interpret Pharaoh's dreams, and was thus himself forewarned as to what would happen later. The other and greater Joseph also received God's messages in dreams. Saint Bernard observes that the former was given to understand the mysteries of dreams; the latter deserved to know and to share in the most supreme mysteries.[2]

It is as if the dreams of the first Joseph, although experienced in his person, were in fact fulfilled in the second Joseph. Now Joseph had a dream, and when he told it to his brothers ... he said to them ... behold, we were binding sheaves in the field, and lo, my sheaf arose and stood upright; and behold, your sheaves gathered round it, and bowed down to my sheaf ... Then he dreamed another dream, and told it to his brothers, and said ... and behold, the sun, the moon and eleven stars were bowing down to me ...,[3] These dreams became a reality when his father Jacob went down to Egypt with the whole family and did indeed kneel before Joseph, who was by then governor of that land. But at the same time we can see his dream prefiguring the mystery of the Holy Family of Nazareth, that mystery in which Jesus, The Sun of Justice and Mary, praised in the Liturgy as shining Star, all bright and beautiful, both submitted to the authority of the head of the household. We can think of it as prefiguring the many devout Christians who turn to this great saint and ask for his help in so many ways.

The first Joseph won the confidence and the favour of Pharaoh and became the overseer of the granaries of Egypt. When famine ravaged the lands of neighbouring peoples and they came to Pharaoh to beg for wheat in

---

2. cf St Bernard, *Homily on the Virgin Mother*, 2
3. cf Gen 37:5-10

order to stay alive, he said to them: *Go to Joseph; and what he says to you, do*.[4] When the whole of those regions were famished, *Joseph opened all the storehouses, and sold to all comers from Egypt's empire ... Moreover, all the earth came to Egypt to Joseph to buy grain, because the famine was severe over all the earth.*

Now too the entire world is ravaged by hunger, a hunger for doctrine, for piety and love. The Church bids us: *Go to Joseph*. In the face of all the necessities that we personally suffer, she says to us: Go to the Holy Patriarch of Nazareth.

There are moments of great indecision in our lives, moments of uncertainty and urgent need. *Go to Joseph*, Jesus says to us. He who during his life was entrusted with the great mission of caring for Me and my Mother in our bodily needs, he who guarded our very lives at so many times of crisis, will continue to care for Me in my members, who are all those who suffer and are in any kind of want. *Go to Joseph*; he will give you whatever you need.

15.2 Saint Joseph's patronage over the universal Church and over each one of us. We should turn to him in any necessity.

He is the prudent and trusted servant whom the Lord placed over his household.[5] The Liturgy applies these words to Saint Joseph, a faithful and wise father, who promptly attends to the needs of the Church, that great family of the Lord.

It is very pleasing to Jesus that we should get to know Joseph and ask for his help. He is the one Jesus loved so much whilst he was on earth and loves so much now in

---

4. *First Reading*, Year I: Gen 41:55
5. Roman Missal, *Mass for the Solemnity of St Joseph, Entrance Antiphon*, Luke 12:42

Heaven. He is the one from whom He learned so much and to whom He talked from the moment He could lisp his first words.

Joseph governed the house of Nazareth with a father's authority. The Holy Family was not only a symbol of the Church, but in a certain way contained the Church within itself as a seed contains the tree, and a spring contains the river. The holy house of Nazareth contained the foundations of the nascent Church. This is why the holy Patriarch *considers specially entrusted to him the crowds of Christians who go to make up the Church, that is to say, this immense family spread throughout the earth, over which – because he is Spouse of Mary and Father of Jesus Christ – he possesses, so to speak, a father's authority. Thus is it something natural and most worthy of the blessed Joseph, that, as once he succoured all the needs of the family of Nazareth and surrounded it in a holy fashion with his protection, so now he should emcompass the Church of Jesus Christ with his heavenly protection and defence.*[6]

This patronage of the holy Patriarch over the universal Church is principally of a spiritual order; but it also extends to the temporal order, as did that of the other Joseph, son of Jacob, who was called by the king of Egypt *saviour of the world.*

Saints and good Christians of all centuries have had recourse to him. Saint Teresa tells of the great devotion she had to Saint Joseph, and of her own experience of his patronage: *I do not remember even now that I have ever asked anything of him which he has failed to grant. I am astonished at the great favours God has bestowed on me through this blessed saint, and at the perils from which he has freed me, both in body and in soul. To other saints the*

---

6. Leo XIII, *Quamquam pluries*, 15 August 1889

Lord seems to have given grace to succour us in some of our necessities, but of this glorious saint my experience is that he succours us in them all, and that the Lord wishes to teach us that as He was himself subject to him on earth, (for, being his guardian and being called his father, he could command him) just so in Heaven He still does all that he asks ...

If I were a person writing with authority, I would gladly describe at length and in the minutest detail, the favours which this glorious saint has granted to me and to others ...
I only beg, for the love of God, that anyone who does not believe me will put what I say to the test, and he will see by experience what great advantages come from his commending himself to this glorious patriarch and having devotion to him. Those who practise prayer should have a special affection for him always. I do not know how anyone can think of the Queen of the Angels, during the time she suffered so much with the Child Jesus, without giving thanks to Saint Joseph for the way he helped them.[7]

15.3 *Ite ad Ioseph* ... Go to Joseph.

We must turn to Saint Joseph and ask him to guard and protect the Church, since he is her defender and protector. We must ask him to help our families in their necessities, and to help us in our own spiritual and material needs: *Sancte Ioseph, ora pro eis, ora pro me ...* Pray for them, pray for me.

For the men and women of today, just as for those of any other age, Saint Joseph represents a dearly loved and venerable figure, whose vocation and dignity we all admire, and for whose faithfulness in the service of Jesus and Mary we thank him. *Through Saint Joseph we go*

---

7. St Teresa, *Life*, 6

straight to Mary, and through Mary, to the source of all holiness, Jesus Christ.[8] He teaches us to speak to Jesus with piety, respect and love: *Joseph, blessed and happy man,* we say to him in the words of an ancient prayer of the Church, *who was permitted to see and hear the God whom many kings wished in vain to see and hear, and not only to see and hear him, but to carry him in your arms, kiss him, clothe him and care for him ...* , teach us to receive him with love and reverence in Holy Communion; give us a greater sensitivity and finesse of soul. *Saint Joseph, our Father and Lord: most chaste, most pure ... You were found worthy to carry the Child Jesus in your arms, to wash him, to embrace him. Teach us to get to know God, and to be pure, to be worthy of being other Christs.*

And help us to do and to teach, as Christ did. Help us to open up the divine paths of the earth, which are both hidden and bright; and help us to show them to mankind, telling our fellow men that their lives on earth can be of an extraordinary and continual supernatural effectiveness.[9]

Moreover, Saint Joseph provides us with a model whose silent teaching we can and should strive to follow. *In human life, Joseph was Jesus' master in their daily contact, full of refined affection, glad to deny himself the better to take care of Jesus. Isn't that reason enough for us to consider this just man, this holy Patriarch, in whom the faith of the old covenant bears fruit, as a master of the interior life? Interior life is nothing but continual and direct conversation with Christ, so that we may become one with him. And Joseph can tell us many things about Jesus. Therefore, let us never neglect devotion to him – 'Ite ad Ioseph': 'Go to Joseph' – as Christian tradition puts it in the words of the*

---

8. Benedict XV, *Bonum sane et salutare*, 25 July 1920
9. J. Escrivá, *The Forge*, 553

Old Testament (Gen 41:55).

A master of interior life, a worker deeply involved in his job, God's servant in continual contact with Jesus – that is Joseph. 'Ite ad Ioseph.' With Saint Joseph, the Christian learns what it means to belong to God and fully to assume one's place among men, sanctifying the world. Get to know Joseph and you will find Jesus. Talk to Joseph and you will find Mary, who always sheds peace about her in that attractive workshop in Nazareth.[10]

---

10. *idem, Christ is passing by,* 56

FOURTEENTH WEEK: THURSDAY

16. THE SUPERNATURAL MISSION OF THE CHURCH

16.1 The Church proclaims the message of Christ and carries on his work in the world.

Jesus consummates the work of Redemption through his Passion, Death and Resurrection. After his Ascension into Heaven He sends the Holy Spirit so that his disciples may be able to announce the Gospel and to make the whole of mankind sharers in salvation. In this way the Apostles are the labourers sent into the harvest by the owner, the servants sent to call those who have been invited to the marriage feast, the servants who are charged with filling the wedding hall.[1]

But as well as having this mission the Apostles represent Christ and the Father himself: *He who hears you hears me, and he who rejects you rejects me, and he who rejects me rejects him who sent me.*[2] The mission of the Apostles is to become intimately united to that of Christ: *As the Father has sent me, even so I send you.*[3] It will be precisely through them that Christ's mission will be extended to all nations and to all ages. The Church, founded by Christ and built on the Apostles, continues to proclaim the Lord's own message and carries on his work in the world.[4]

---

1. cf Matt 9:38, John 4:38, Matt 22:3
2. Luke 10:16
3. John 20:21
4. cf Second Vatican Council, *Lumen gentium*, 3

The Gospel of today's Mass[5] tells us how Jesus urges the *Twelve* whom He has just chosen to go out to fulfil their new task. This first errand is a preparation and a figure of the definitve sending that will take place after the Resurrection. Then He will say to them: *Go ... Preach the gospel to the whole creation. Make disciples of all nations. Lo, I am with you always, to the close of the age.*[6]

Until the coming of Jesus, the Prophets had foretold to the chosen people of the Old Testament all the benefits the Messiah would bring with him. Sometimes they had employed an imagery adapted to the mentality of people who were not yet mature enough to understand fully the reality that was to be accomplished. Now, in this first apostolic mission, Jesus sends his Apostles to announce that the Kingdom of God, so long promised, is imminent, and to manifest its spiritual aspects. Our Lord tells them exactly what they have to preach: *The Kingdom of Heaven is at hand*. He does not say anything about freedom from the Roman yoke under which the nation was suffering. He does not speak about what kind of social or political system they were to live under, nor, indeed, about any other exclusively worldly matter. Christ did not come for such a purpose, and they have not been chosen to concern themselves with such things.

They will live to bear witness to Christ, to spread his teaching and to make all men sharers in his salvation. Saint Paul followed along the same path. *If we were to ask him about his preaching he himself would summarise it thus: 'I decided to know nothing among you except Jesus Christ and him crucified' (1 Cor 2:2). To enable men to know Jesus Christ better and better; to enable them to have*

---

5. Matt 10:7-15
6. cf Mark 16:15, Matt 28:18-20

a knowledge of him that would not stop at faith alone, but would be translated into real deeds, is what the Apostle strove for with the whole of his strength.[7]

The Church, which continues in time the work of Jesus Christ, has the same supernatural mission that her Divine Founder transmitted to the Apostles. *The Church was founded to spread the kingdom of Christ over all the earth for the glory of God the Father and to make all men partakers in redemption and salvation so that they may lay the entire world at the feet of Christ.*[8] Her mission transcends all social movements and ideologies or the claims made by various groups ...; at the same time, with ever-renewed solicitude, she shows her concern for all human problems and tries to direct her social teaching towards the supernatural and truly human end of man.

16.2 The Church's mission is of a supernatural order, but she is not indifferent to undertakings that affect human dignity.

Go and preach, saying that the Kingdom of Heaven is at hand. The mission of our Mother the Church is to give men the most sublime treasure that we can ever imagine. Her mission is to lead all men to their supernatural and eternal destiny mainly through preaching and the sacraments: *This and no other is the end of the Church: the salvation of souls, one by one. For this the Father sent the Son. And, Jesus said, 'even so I send you' (John 20:21). From this arises the command to make his doctrine known and to baptize, so that the Most Blessed Trinity may reside in the soul, through grace.*[9] Jesus Christ has told us himself: *I came that they may have life, and have it abundantly.*[10] Our

---

7. Benedict XV, *Humani generis Redemptionem*, 15 June 1917
8. Second Vatican Council, *Apostolicam actuositatem*, 2
9. J. Escrivá, *In Love with the Church*, 49
10. John 10:10

Lord was not referring to an easy and comfortable earthly life, but rather to eternal life. He came to free us mainly from everything that prevents us from reaching the life we were destined for – to liberate us from sin, which is the only absolute evil. Thus He also gives us the possibility of overcoming the numerous consequences of sin in this world, such as anxiety, injustice, loneliness … He shows us how to bear them cheerfully for God when we cannot avoid them, and how to turn sorrow into fruitful suffering which wins eternity.

Like her Master, the Church does not take sides in particular temporal options. Those who without faith saw him almost completely deserted on the Cross might have thought He had failed. *Precisely because He did not opt for any one human solution, He was followed by neither Jews nor Romans. But no. It is precisely the opposite: Jews and Romans, Greeks and Barbarians, freemen and slaves, men and women, the healthy and people in poor health, all follow after this God-made-man who has freed us from sin, in order to set us on the path towards our eternal destination. It is only there that our true fulfilment will be achieved; this will be no less than the freedom and perfected humanity of man, made in the image and likeness of God, and whose deepest aspirations far exceed any mere transient ambitions and endeavours, however noble they may be.*[11]

The Church has as her mission the charge to lead her children to God, to their eternal destination. However, she is not indifferent to human endeavour. By the very nature of her spiritual mission she moves her children and all men to become aware of the root from which all evils spring, and urges them to find solutions for so much injustice, for the deplorable conditions in which so many

---

11. J. M. Casciaro, *Jesus and Politics*

people live, and which are an offence against the Creator and against human dignity. *The hope of heaven does not weaken commitment to the progress of the earthly city, but rather gives it meaning and strength. It is of course important to make a careful distinction between earthly progress and the growth of the Kingdom, which do not belong to the same order. Nonetheless, this distinction is not a separation, for man's vocation to eternal life does not suppress but rather confirms his task of using the energies and means which he has received from the Creator for developing his temporal life.*[12]

We are co-redeemers with Christ, and we must ask ourselves to what extent we pass on to our family and friends the most precious gift that we have – our faith in Christ. When we contemplate this incomparable gift we should feel moved to act, for *caritas Christi urget nos*,[13] the charity of Christ urges us on to help build up around us a world which is more just and more human.

16.3 Christians manifest their unity of life by encouraging works of justice and mercy.

Heal the sick, raise the dead, cleanse the lepers ...

From the Church's earliest days faithful Christians spread the Faith to all parts of the world. From those first years too, vast numbers of Christians have *committed their powers and their lives to liberation from every form of oppression and to the promotion of human dignity. The experience of the saints and the example of so many works of service to one's neighbour are an incentive and a beacon for the liberating undertakings that are needed today.*[14] They

---

12. Sacred Congregation for the Doctrine of the Faith, *Instruction on Christian Freedom and Liberation*, 22 March 1986, 60
13. 2 Cor 5:14
14. Sacred Congregation for the Doctrine of the Faith, *op cit*, 57

are needed perhaps with an even greater urgency than in other periods of history.

Our faith in Christ moves us to be aware of our common involvement with the problems and shortages that other men experience, and often with their ignorance and their lack of economic resources. This solidarity with our fellow-man is not a *superficial sentiment about the evils that beset so many people, whether close to us or far away,* but *a firm and persevering determination to strive for the common good; that is to say, for the good of all and of individuals, so that we may all be truly responsible for all men.*[15] Faith leads us to feel a deep respect for others, for each individual person, and never to remain indifferent to other people's needs: *heal the sick, raise the dead, cleanse the lepers, cast out demons ...* Following Christ will manifest itself in deeds of justice and mercy; it will show itself too in our determination to get to know the principles of the social doctrine of the Church and to carry them out, first of all in our own surroundings, right there where we live.

It should be possible to say of each one of us at the end of our lives, as it was said of Jesus, *He went about doing good.*[16] We have to *do good* within our own families, among our colleagues at work and among our friends, and even with those people we just chance to come across. *As disciples of Christ we have to be sowers of fraternity whatever occasions and circumstances life brings with it. When a man or a woman lives the Christian spirit in all its intensity, all his or her activities and relationships reflect and communicate God's love and the surpassing goods of the Kingdom. As Christians we need to know how to make fast and strengthen our relationships each day with our families, our*

---

15. John Paul II, *Sollicitudo rei socialis*, 3 December 1987, 38
16. cf Acts 10:38

friends and our neighbours, whether we are at work or at lei-sure, sealing them with the seal of Christian love, which is simplicity, truthfulness, faithfulness, meekness, generosity, solidarity and joy.[17]

---

17. Spanish Episcopal Conference, *Catholics in Public Life*, 22 April
     1986, III

FOURTEENTH WEEK: FRIDAY

17. PRUDENT AND SIMPLE

17.1 Our Lord's example of two virtues − prudence and simplicity − which mutually perfect each other.

Jesus sends *the Twelve* out all over Israel to announce that *the Kingdom of God is at hand*, that it is now very close. And the Master gives them some very precise instructions about what they have to do and to say, making no secret about the difficulties they will encounter. We read then in the Gospel of today's Mass: *Behold, I send you out as sheep in the midst of wolves; so be wise as serpents and innocent as doves*.[1] They must be vigilant so as not to be taken unawares by evil, so that they will recognise the wolves disguised as lambs and be able to distinguish the false from the true prophets.[2] In this way they will not miss a single opportunity of proclaiming the Gospel and of doing good. They have to be at the same time simple, for it is only in this way that they can win over the hearts of all. Without simplicity, prudence would easily become cunning.

As Christians we have to both live and propagate these two virtues, which strengthen and complement each other. Simplicity means having rectitude of intention and behaving with firmness and consistency. Prudence always points out to us the most appropriate means of achieving our end. Saint Augustine teaches that prudence is *the love that distinguishes what helps us to go towards God from*

---

1. Matt 10:16
2. Matt 7:15

what hinders us.[3] This virtue enables us to *know objectively* the reality of things, according to their ultimate end; *to judge with certainty* concerning the right way to follow, and to act in consequence. *The prudent person is not, as is so often believed, the man who shrewdly knows how to make his way in the world and make the most of it for himself. He is, rather, the one who manages to construct the whole of his life in accordance with the voice of a right conscience and the demands of sound morals.*

We can then see that prudence is the keystone by which we each accomplish the fundamental task we have been given by God. This task is the perfection of man himself,[4] – holiness.

Our Lord taught us by his words and by his example to be prudent. The first time He spoke, at twelve years of age, in the portico of the Temple *all were amazed at his understanding.*[5] Later on, during his public life, his words and his conduct were as clear as they were prudent, being such that his enemies could not *find fault with him*. Our Lord does not seek subterfuges, but keeps in mind who it is He is talking to. It is for this reason that He makes it known only gradually that He is the Messiah. He announces his death on the Cross in accordance with the degree of preparation and knowledge of those to whom he is speaking. We too must learn from Christ.

17.2 Seeking advice.

In order to be prudent we have to have light in our understanding; then we will be able to judge events and circumstances correctly.[6] It is only with good doctrinal,

---

3. St Augustine, *On the Customs of the Catholic Church*, 25, 46
4. John Paul II, *Address*, 25 October 1978
5. Luke 2:47
6. cf R. Garrigou-Lagrange, *The Three Ages of the Interior Life*, vol.II

religious and ascetical formation, and with the help of grace, that we will discover the ways that truly lead to God and know what decisions to make ... Nevertheless there are many occasions when we need to ask for advice. *To be prudent the first step is to acknowledge our own limitations. This is the virtue of humility. Through it, we admit that in certain matters we cannot cover everything, that in many cases we cannot take in all the circumstances that have to be borne in mind in order to make a fair judgement. So we look for advice – but not advice from just anyone. We go to someone who has the right qualities, to someone who wants to love God as sincerely as we do and who tries to follow him faithfully. It is not enough to ask just anyone for his opinion. We must go to somebody who can give us sound and disinterested advice.*[7]

Saint Thomas points out that, generally, before making any decision that may have serious consequences for oneself or for others, we must seek advice.[8] But it is not only in these extreme cases that we must look for it. Sometimes people, both young and old, are in urgent need of guidance as to their reading – books, magazines and newspapers. They need to know whether to go to performances that, sometimes quite blatantly and sometimes in a less obvious but subtle way, may undermine our faith or create an evil compost in our hearts in which afterwards all sorts of doubts or temptations may take root. Such doubts and temptations could have been avoided with just a little more humility and prudence. There is no justification for not giving a wide berth to a situation which could be the beginning of our straying from the right path.

---

7. J. Escrivá, *Friends of God*, 86
8. St Thomas, *Summa Theologiae*, 2-2, q.49, a.3

Simplicity moves us to put things right when we have made a mistake, or when new facts come to light that put an entirely different complexion on a problem. In the supernatural life, simplicity, so close to humility, leads us to ask for forgiveness many times in our lives, for we succumb to so many weaknesses and errors.

Pope John Paul II, speaking about prudence, invited his listeners to make an examination of conscience as to their own behaviour. We can too can examine ourselves today. *Am I really prudent? Do I live in a consistent and responsible fashion? Does the programme I am following help me towards the true good? Does it help to bring about the salvation that Christ and the Church want for me?*[9] Am I going straight towards achieving my supernatural end – sanctity – to which Our Lord has called me? Do I put aside anything that might hamper my progress? Do I seek advice in matters relating to my soul? Do I put things right when I make a mistake?

17.3 False prudence.

Prudence would not be true prudence if, having given due consideration to the facts, it chose the cowardly way of not making a decision that involved risk, or caused us to avoid facing up squarely to a problem. The attitude of the person who allows himself to be led by human respect in the apostolate and lets opportunities slip, while he waits for other opportunities that may never arise, is not a prudent attitude. Saint Paul calls this false virtue *prudence of the flesh*.[10] It is a false virtue that asks for more reasons and considerations before giving God what He asks of us personally. It is what causes us to worry excessively about

9. John Paul II, *loc cit*
10. cf Rom 8:6

the future, and gives us a reason for not being generous here and now. It is what always makes us find some excuse for not deciding to commit ourselves fully.

Prudence means not shunning the boldness of giving oneself and daring to become involved in God's work. It is not the ability to find lukewarm compromises or to justify a remiss and negligent attitude by giving it the name of some acceptable theory. That is not how the Apostles went about things. Despite their weaknesses and at times their fear, they constantly sought the quickest way of spreading the Master's teaching, even though those ways sometimes led them into a plenty of trouble and caused them count-less tribulations – and even martyrdom.

Following Our Lord means living a life of small and great acts of madness, as is always the case where true love is concerned. When Our Lord asks more of us – and He always asks for more – we cannot draw back with a false prudence, the prudence of the world. We must not be swayed by the judgement of those who do not feel them-selves called, and who see everything through merely human eyes, and sometimes with eyes that are not even human, because they have what is no more than an earthly outlook, an outlook that prevents them ever getting off the ground. No man and no woman would ever have given themselves to God or ever have initiated any supernatural undertaking if they had followed that 'prudence of the flesh'. They would always have found more or less con-vincing reasons for refusing to procee – or for deferring their response till a more convenient time, which often boils down to the same thing.

It was said of Jesus, *He is beside himself.*[11] It seems that the most elementary precautions would have enabled

---

11. Matt 3:21

him to escape death. Just a few formulae would have been
sufficient to mitigate the rigour of his teaching and for him
to arrive at a compromise with the Pharisees. He could
have presented in some other way his teaching on the
Eucharist in the synagogue at Capharnaum,[12] where many
left him. Just a few words would have been sufficient for
him, who was eternal Wisdom, to obtain his freedom at
Pilate's hands. Jesus was not 'prudent' according to the
world, but he was more prudent than serpents, than men,
or than his enemies. His was a different type of prudence.
This has to be our type of prudence even if, because we
imitate him, men may sometimes call us mad and 'impru-
dent.' Supernatural prudence shows us at each moment
the quickest and most direct way to reach Christ ... bringing with us many friends, relatives and colleagues.

*Do you want to be daring in a holy way, so that God
may act through you? Have recourse to Mary, and she will
accompany you along the path of humility so that, when
faced by what to the human mind is impossible, you may be
able to answer with a resounding 'fiat' – be it done!, which
unites the earth to Heaven.*[13]

---

12. cf John 6:1 *et seq*
13. J. Escrivá, *Furrow*, 124

FOURTEENTH WEEK: SATURDAY

18. LOVE FOR TRUTH

18.1 We should talk about God and God's teaching clearly, firmly and fearlessly.

The Gospel of today's Mass[1] is yet another invitation from Our Lord for us to lead a life that is essentially truthful, the result of the faith we bear in our hearts. We should not be afraid of the unpleasantness or gossip that the following of Christ closely sometimes brings with it. *It is enough for the disciple to be like his teacher, and the servant like his master. If they have called the master of the house Beelzebul, how much more will they malign those of his household? So have no fear of them ...*

It may happen that in a given situation we are made to suffer calumny or slander – or quite simply some vexation – because we have spoken truthfully, because we have adhered to the truth. Perhaps there will be times when our words or our actions are wrongly interpreted. Our Lord wants his disciples, which means us, always to speak clearly and openly: *What I tell you in the dark, utter in the light; and what you hear whispered, proclaim upon the housetops.* With divine pedagogy, Jesus had spoken to the crowds in parables and, little by little, He had revealed to them his true personality and the truths of the Kingdom. He never concealed his teaching. Since the coming of the Holy Spirit, those who follow him have to proclaim the truth in the full light of day, from the

---

1. Matt 10:24-33

housetops, without fear that the doctrine they preach may conflict with the teachings currently in vogue or happen to be most prevalent. How else are we going to convert the world in which we are so deeply immersed?

Some people think, either as a matter of tactics or out of diffidence, that the lives of Christians and the conception they have of the world, of man and of society, should not be unduly or conspicuously pressed when circumstances are against them or when their reputation might be jeopardised. If they were to do this, Christians would be as though *caught in an ambush* in the midst of a society that seems to see its objectives as being situated in a radically different direction; then the fact of being men and women who look on Christ as their supreme ideal would have no outward resonance. That is not what Our Lord taught. *'Ego palam locutus sum mundo.' I have preached openly before the whole world, was the answer Jesus gave to Caiphas when the time had come for him to give up his Life for us.*

And yet there are Christians who are afraid to show 'palam' – openly – veneration for Our Lord.[2]

In the society in which we live we will have to speak out with the certainty and firmness that truth unfailingly gives. We will have to talk about many subjects which are of transcendent importance for the family, for society and for the dignity of the human person. Take the indissolubility of marriage. Freedom in education. The Church's teaching on the transmission of human life. The dignity and beauty of purity. The excellence of virginity and celibacy for love of Christ. The consequences of social justice in relation to thoughtless spending or unjust wages ... There may be occasions when out of prudence or charity

---

2. J. Escrivá, *Furrow*, 50

we should keep quiet. But prudence and charity are not the result of cowardice or self-comfort. It will never be prudent to keep quiet when keeping quiet may cause scandal or confusion, or when such behaviour may have an adverse effect on the faith of others.

What I tell you in the dark, utter in the light ... Our Lord is speaking to us, for there are today many enemies of God and of truth who do not want Christians to be *salt* and *light* within secular undertakings. Such people use all sorts of means to achieve their results.

18.2 Acting according to one's conscience. Sincerity with oneself.

There is an episode in the Gospel[3] that shows us the behaviour of some Pharisees, who were not known for their love for truth. Whilst Our Lord was walking in the Temple, the chief priests, the Scribes and the elders came up to him and asked him: *By what authority are you doing these things, or who gave you authority to do them*? Our Lord is prepared to answer their question if they show sincerity of heart. He asks them their opinion about the baptism of John: whether it was from Heaven, and thus enjoyed divine approbation, or whether it was only from men, and as such did not merit any further consideration. But they do not tell him their true opinion, their opinion in all conscience. They do not go into the truth of the matter, they do not seek to form the heartfelt judgement the question deserves. Instead, they analyse the consequences of their possible answers, and choose the reply that suits them best in this particular situation: *If we say 'From heaven' He will say, 'Why then did you not believe him?'* But if they say the baptism of the Precursor was from

---

3. Mark 11:27-33

men, the people might lay hands on them, for *all held that John was a real prophet'*.

In spite of being religious leaders, they do not have the strong principles that could give meaning to their words and their deeds. *They are 'practical' men, who dedicate themselves to 'politics'. In all that concerns their own interest or comfort, their reasoning is intelligent. But they are not prepared to go any further in their reasoning: they are men for whom comfort has taken the place of conscience.*[4] Their norm of conduct is to follow whatever course of action is most opportune or most convenient on each occasion. They do not act in accordance with the truth. This is why they say: *We do not know*. It was not in their interest to know, much less to say so. Christ's reaction is very significant: *Neither will I tell you by what authority I do these things*. It is as if He were saying to them: if you are not prepared to be sincere, to look into your hearts and face up to the truth, any dialogue between us is useless. I cannot talk to you, and you cannot talk to me. We would not understand each other. The same thing happens every day. *The person whose life is not guided by sincerity, by an habitual disposition to face up to the truth or to the demands of his conscience – however uncomfortable or hard they may be – flatly separates himself from any possibility of communicating with God. Anyone who is afraid of looking into his conscience is afraid of looking at God. Only those who can look God in the face can really get to know him.*[5] It is not possible to find God without this radical love of truth. Neither is it possible to get on well with the people around us.

Love for the truth will lead us first of all to be sincere

---

4. C. Burke, *Conscience and Freedom*
5. *idem*

with ourselves, to keep a clear conscience and not deceive ourselves. We will not allow our conscience to become dulled by allowing errors or culpable ignorance to creep in. We will not be afraid of going deeper into those personal demands that truth brings with it. If, with the help of grace, we are sincere with ourselves, we will be sincere with God. Our life will then be filled with light, peace and fortitude. *You were reading in that dictionary the synonyms for 'insincere': 'two-faced, surreptitious, evasive, disingenuous, sly'. As you closed the book, you asked the Lord that nobody should ever be able to apply those adjectives to you, and you resolved to improve much more in this supernatural and human virtue of sincerity.*[6]

18.3 Always tell the truth – in what is important and in what seems a small matter.

In a world where so many people habitually think little of a lie and indulge in pretences, we, as Christians must be men and women of truth who always flee from even the smallest falsehood. This is how people should know us – as men and women who never tell lies even in matters of little importance, as men and women who shut out of their lives anything that smacks of dissimulation, hypocrisy and duplicity, and who know how to put matters right if they make a mistake. Then our lives will be filled with a great apostolic fruitfulness, for people always trust an upright person, one who knows how to speak the truth with charity and understanding towards all and without hurting people.

How many weaknesses, how much opportunism, how much conformity, how much vileness![7] said Pope Paul VI

---

6. J. Escrivá, *op cit*, 337
7. Paul VI, *Address*, 17 February 1965

referring to *those good people who forget the beauty and the seriousness of the commitments that unite them to the Church*. That same situation, which has perhaps become more apparent in recent years, will lead us to hate any falseness, however trivial it may seem to us, because *lying opposes truth just as light opposes darkness, as piety opposes impiety, as justice opposes iniquity, as goodness opposes sin, as health opposes sickness and life opposes death. This being so, the more we love truth, the more we must abhor lying.*[8] It is not a matter of knowing just how far we can go in saying things that are untrue before we incur a grave fault. It is a matter of hating lying in all its forms. It is a matter of telling the whole truth, and, when out of prudence or charity this cannot be done, then we will hold our tongue and not invent little 'white lies' that falsely ease our consciences.[9] We must love the truth in itself and for itself, not only in those things that can harm or benefit ourselves, or other people in a personal way. We must abhor lying as something stupid and despicable, for whatever reason it is resorted to. We must hate it because it is an offence against God, who is supreme Truth.

We easily believe what we want to believe. This is why, for example, many of her enemies are always inclined to regard any injurious rumours about the Church as true, and to pass judgement without having sufficient facts. They will even seek to influence public opinion on such a basis. This is really the same as lying, because of where the rumour comes from and what it leads to. In direct opposition to lying, which is so often resorted to in cold blood, we have truth, light and sincerity which are

---

8. St Augustine, *Against Lying*, 3, 4
9. cf St Francis de Sales, *Introduction to the Devout Life*, III, 30

unambiguous and cannot be mistaken. We must firmly practise truthfulness in our everyday relations with other people, in our business affairs, in our family life, in our study and, whenever we have access to them, through the organs of public opinion. We should be resolutely opposed to matching one lie with another.

The prayer of the Liturgy on this day invites us to exclaim: *Lord, may our voices, our spirits and the whole of our lives be a continual praise in your honour ...* [10] May our conversations be always truthful, proper to a child of God.

---

10. *Divine Office, Prayer for Lauds, 2nd Week*

FIFTEENTH SUNDAY: YEAR A

19. THE PARABLE OF THE SOWER

19.1 The seed and the path. Lack of interior recollection prevents union with God.

Saint Matthew tells us in the Gospel of today's Mass[1] that Jesus sat beside the sea and that such great crowds gathered about him to hear his words that He had to get into a boat so that they could listen to him from the shore. Sitting now in a small fishing-vessel, Our Lord began to teach them: *A sower went out to sow*. And the seed He spoke about fell on very different types of soil.

In Galilee, where the terrain tended to be very uneven and hilly, it was only the narrow strips of land in the valleys and skirting the river banks that were sown with seed. The parable faithfully records for us the agricultural situation of that particular area. The sower scattered his seed broadcast, which is why some of it would fall onto the path. The seed that fell on those paths would soon be eaten up by birds or trodden underfoot by passers-by. The detail of the rocky soil, covered perhaps by only a thin layer of earth, was also true to reality. Because of the lack of soil-depth, the seed shoots up more rapidly, but only to have the heat dry it up just as quickly, since it has no depth of root.

The soil on which the good seed falls is the whole world; it represents each individual person. We too are soil for the divine seed. Even though the sowing is carried

---

1. Matt 13:1-23

out with great love – it is God who pours himself into our souls – the results depend largely on the condition of the soil on which it falls. Christ's words tell us forcefully about the responsibility man has to prepare himself to receive God's grace and to correspond with it.

Some seeds fell along the path, and the birds came and devoured them. When anyone hears the word of the kingdom and does not understand it the evil one comes and snatches away what is sown in his heart. The path is soil that has been trodden on until it has become hard. These compacted areas are dissipated, empty souls, prepared to accept only external things. Such souls are incapable of recollecting their thoughts and guarding their senses. They have no order in their affections and are not particularly watchful over their feelings, so that they frequently allow their imagination to engage in useless thoughts. These souls are like ground that has never been tilled or cultivated, having always turned their face away from God. Their hearts are hardened, like those constantly trodden pathways. They hear God's word, but the devil easily snatches it away from them. *He is not idle; rather, he has his eyes always wide open and is always ready to spring and snatch away the gift that you do not use.*[2]

We must ask Our Lord for fortitude so that we never become like those *who are like the path on which the seed fell – negligent, lukewarm and full of scorn*.[3] Negligence and lukewarmness are manifestations of a lack of contrition and repentance, and of our failure to put up a determined struggle against venial sins. The first time the divine Sower scattered his seed onto the soil of our soul was in Baptism. How often since then has He given us an

---

2. Cardinal J. H. Newman, *Sermon for Sexagesima Sunday: Calls to Grace*
3. St John Chrysostom, *Homilies on St Matthew's Gospel*, 44, 3

abundance of his grace! How often has He passed close beside us, helping, encouraging and forgiving us! At this moment, in the intimacy of our prayer, we can say to him quietly: *O Jesus! If in spite of the poor way I have behaved, you have done for me what you have done, what more would you do if I were to respond well?*

This truth will lead you to be generous without measure.

Weep and show with sorrow and love how much it pains you, for Our Lord and his Blessed Mother deserve from you a different kind of treatment.[4]

19.2 The rocky ground and the thorns. The need for sacrifice and detachment in the supernatural life.

Other seeds fell on rocky ground, where they had not much soil, and immediately they sprang up, since they had no depth of soil; but when the sun rose they were scorched, and since they had no root they withered away. This stony ground represents superficial souls with little inner depth, souls that are inconstant and incapable of persevering. They have good dispositions; they even receive grace with joy, but when the moment comes to confront difficulties they turn back. They are not capable of sacrificing themselves in order to fulfil the resolutions they have made so their resolutions die without bearing fruit.

Saint Teresa taught that there are some people who, having overcome the first enemies of the interior life, *cease to make any effort; they lose heart,* and give up the struggle when they are only *a couple of steps away from the fountain of living water* – the water concerning which Our Lord told the Samaritan woman that whoever drank of it *would never thirst.*[5] We must ask Our Lord for constancy in

---

4. J. Escrivá, *The Forge*, 388
5. St Teresa, *The Way of Perfection*, 19, 2

our resolutions, and for a spirit of sacrifice so that we do not give up when faced with difficulties – as we surely will be. We have to begin time and again, with holy stubbornness, and we have to strive always to reach the sanctity that Jesus calls us to, and for the attainment of which He gives us all the graces we need. Saint John of the Cross taught that *the soul that truly loves God never allows laziness to prevent it from doing everything in its power to find the Son of God, its Beloved. And after having done all it can, it is still not satisfied and considers it has done nothing.*[6]

Other seeds fell upon thorns, and the thorns grew up and choked them. This is the one who hears the word, but the cares of the world and the delight in riches stifle it, and it proves unfruitful.

Love of riches, a disordered ambition to gain influence or power, and excessive concern for well-being and a comfortable way of life are like sharp thorns that prevent any union with God. The souls of people who seek only such things are souls immersed in material things, being wrapped in a *deep-seated avarice that leads us to appreciate only what we can touch. Such eyes are firmly fixed on earthly things and consequently are blind to supernatural realities.*[7] It is as though they were blind to all that really matters.

If we allow our hearts to become attached to money, influence or praise; if we set our hearts on the ultimate comfort we see advertised; if we give in to our own whims and seek so many things that are quite unnecessary, we are allowing a serious obstacle to God's love to become embedded in our hearts. It is difficult for anyone obsessed

---

6. St John of the Cross, *Spiritual Canticle*, 3, 1

7. J. Escrivá, *Christ is passing by*, 6

by the thought of owning more and more possessions, and by the constant determination to seek out what is most comfortable, not to fall into other sins. In connection with such things, Saint John of the Cross comments: *This is why Our Lord called them 'thorns' in the Gospel, so that we should understand that anyone who fondly caresses such things with his will, will be wounded by some sin.*[8]

Saint Paul teaches that anyone who puts his heart on earthly things, as though they were the absolute good, commits a type of idolatry.[9] This disorder in the soul often leads to a lack of mortification and to sensuality, so that we give up looking at supernatural things. Those words of our Lord's are always fulfilled: *For where your treasure is, there will your heart be also.*[10] The seed of grace will be choked without any doubt in this bad soil.

19.3 Correspondence to grace. Bearing fruit.

As for what was sown on good soil, here we have the man who hears the word and understands it; he indeed bears fruit, and yields in one case a hundredfold, in another sixty, and in another thirty.

God hopes we will be good soil that will receive his grace and bear fruit. The greater our generosity towards God the better and more abundant will be the fruit we produce. *The only thing that matters*, comments Saint John Chrysostom, *is that we should not be a beaten-down thoroughfare, or rocky ground, or thorns, but that we should be good soil ... Our hearts must not be that path from which the enemy, like the birds, snatches the seed trodden underfoot by passers-by. Our hearts must not be the rocky ground where the shallowness of the soil causes the seed to*

---

8. St John of the Cross, *The Ascent of Mount Carmel*, 3, 18, 1
9. cf Col 3:5
10. Luke 12:34

germinate immediately so that it is scorched by the sun. Our hearts must not be a thistle-bed of human passions strangled by the cares of this world.[11]

All men, whatever their lives may have been in the past, are able to become soil that is prepared to receive God's grace. God pours himself into our souls in accordance with the degree of welcome He finds there. God gives us so many graces because He trusts each one of us; there is no soil that is too impervious or too uncultivated for him, so long as it is prepared to change and to respond to him. Any soul can become rich pasture land, although previously it has been nothing but desert, because God's grace never fails us, and his care is greater than that of the most expert husbandman. Once grace has been given, the results depend only on man, who is free to correspond or not. *The ground is good, the sower is the same and the seeds are the same in each case. Nevertheless, how is it that one gives a hundredfold, another sixtyfold and another thirtyfold? We can see that the difference depends on the person receiving it, for even where the soil is good there is a great deal of difference between one patch of ground and another. You can see that neither the farmer nor the seed is at fault, but the soil on which the sowing was done. This is not a result of nature, but of the disposition of the will.*[12]

Let us consider in our prayer today whether we correspond with the graces God gives us, and whether we apply the *particular examination of conscience* to those harmful roots in our soul that prevent the growth of the good seed. Do we we get rid of any noxious weeds through frequent Confession? Do we try to increase the number of acts of Contrition that prepare our soul so well to receive

---

11. St John Chrysostom, *Sermon*, 101, 3
12. St John Chrysostom, *loc cit*

God's inspirations? *We can never be content with what we are doing to serve our God, just as an artist is never satisfied with the painting or statue he is working on. Everyone tells him how marvellous it is, but he thinks: 'No. It isn't quite right. I wanted it to be better.'* This is how we should feel.

Moreover, the Lord has given us so much. *He has a right to the very best from us – and we must go at his pace.*[13] Don't let us fall behind.

---

13. J. Escrivá, *The Forge*, 385

FIFTEENTH SUNDAY: YEAR B

20. LOVE AND VENERATION FOR THE PRIESTHOOD

20.1 The priest's identity and mission.

All baptised persons can apply to themselves Saint Paul's words to the Christians of Ephesus which we find in the Second Reading of today's Mass: *He chose us in him before the foundation of the world, that we should be holy and blameless before him.*[1] Through Baptism and Confirmation all the Christian faithful belong to *a chosen race, a royal priesthood, a holy nation, God's own people.*[2] *The baptised*, says the Second Vatican Council, *by regeneration and the anointing of the Holy Spirit, are consecrated to be a spiritual house and a holy priesthood, that through all the works of Christian men they may offer spiritual sacrifices.*[3] By their sharing in the priesthood of Christ, the faithful take an active part in the celebration of the Sacrifice of the Altar. They sanctify the world through their secular tasks, sharing in the one mission of the Church by means of the different vocations they have received from God. Housewives, for example, sanctify the various aspects of motherhood and related duties; sick people are called to offer up their suffering lovingly to God; each one makes a pleasing offering to God of his daily tasks and circumstances.

From the ranks of the faithful, all of whom have this

---

1. Eph 1:3-14
2. 1 Pet 2:9
3. Second Vatican Council, *Lumen gentium*, 10

common priesthood, some are called by God, through the Sacrament of Holy Orders, to exercise the ministerial priesthood. This second priesthood builds upon the first one, but they are essentially different. By means of the consecration received in Holy Orders, the priest becomes an instrument of Jesus Christ, to whom he offers his entire being, in order to bring the grace of Redemption to all mankind. He is a man *chosen from among men and appointed to act on behalf of men in relation to God, to offer gifts and sacrifices for sins*.[4] What then is the priest's identity? *That of Christ. Each one of us Christians can and should be not just any other Christ, 'alter Christus', but Christ himself, 'ipse Christus!' But in the priest this happens in a direct way, by virtue of the sacrament*.[5]

Our Lord, who is present among us in many ways, is so particularly in the person of the priest. Every priest is a great gift of God to the world. He is Jesus who goes about *doing good*; he cures illnesses, he brings peace and joy to men's minds; he is the *living instrument of Christ* in the world.[6] He offers Our Lord *his voice, his hands, his whole being*.[7] At Mass, he renews *in persona Christi* the redemptive Sacrifice of Calvary itself. He makes Christ's Redemption present and effective within history. Pope John Paul II reminded the clergy of Brazil that *Jesus identifies himself with us in such a way in carrying out the powers he conferred upon us, that it is as if our personality disappears before his, since it is He himself who acts through us*.[8] It is Christ who changes the substance of bread and wine into his Body and Blood at Mass. And *it is*

---

4. cf Heb 5:1
5. J. Escrivá, *In Love with the Church*, 38
6. cf Second Vatican Council, *Presbyterorum ordinis*, 12
7. J. Escrivá, *In Love with the Church*, 39
8. John Paul II, *Homily*, 2 July 1980

Jesus himself who, in the sacrament of Penance, utters the authoritative and fatherly words 'your sins are forgiven.' It is He who speaks when the priest, carrying out his ministry in the name and in the spirit of the Church, announces the Word of God. It is Christ himself who cares for the sick, for children and sinners, when he enfolds them with the love and pastoral care of the sacred ministries.[9]

A priest is of more value to mankind than the entire material universe. We must pray constantly for the holiness of priests, helping them and sustaining them with our prayer and our affection. We must see Christ himself in them.

20.2 The priest, a steward of the mysteries of God.

Jesus selects the Apostles, not only as messengers, prophets and witnesses, but also as his own representatives.

This new identity, to act *in persona Christi*, must be expressed in a life which is simple and austere, a holiness which inspires a wholehearted dedication to the welfare of others. The Gospel of today's Mass tells us that Jesus sent his disciples and *gave them authority over the unclean spirits.*[10] He told them to take a staff for their journey, but nothing else: no bread, no haversack, and no money in their wallets.

God takes possession of the man He calls to the priesthood and consecrates him to the service of his fellow men, and bestows upon him a new personality. And once he has been chosen and consecrated to the service of God and others he is not just a priest at certain moments only, for example while he is carrying out sacred functions. *He is a priest always and at every moment, whether he is*

---

9. *ibid*
10. Mark 6:7-13

performing the highest and most sublime office or the most vulgar and humble action of his ordinary life. Just as a Christian cannot leave aside the fact that he is a new man, that Baptism has given him a particular character, and act 'as if' he were just a man purely and simply, neither can the priest leave aside his priestly character and behave 'as if' he were not a priest. Whatever he does, whatever attitude he adopts, whether he likes it or not, it will always be the action or the attitude of a priest, because he is a priest always and at all times down to the very depths of his being, whatever he may do or whatever he may think.[11]

The priest is a messenger from God to the world, sent to announce to mankind its salvation, and is constituted a steward of the mysteries of God.[12] These mysteries include the Body and Blood of Christ, which he offers the faithful at Mass and Holy Communion; the grace of God in the sacraments; and the divine word which he utters in preaching, in catechesis and in confession. To the priest has been confided *the most divine of divine works*, the salvation of souls. He has been made an ambassador and a mediator between God and men.

It warms my heart to think of the quiet human and supernatural dignity of those brothers of mine, scattered throughout the world. It is only right that they should now feel themselves surrounded by the friendship, help and affection of many Christians. And when the moment comes for them to enter God's presence, Jesus will go out to meet them. He will glorify forever those who have acted on earth in his Person and in his name. He will shower them with that grace of which they have been ministers.[13]

Let us meditate now in the presence of God on how

---

11. F. Suárez, *About Being a Priest*, p.8
12. cf 1 Cor 4:1
13. J. Escrivá, *In Love with the Church*, 49

well we pray for priests, how we treat them, how grateful we ought to be to them for having responded positively to our Lord's call, how to help them persevere and be saints. Let us ask *God our Lord to give all of us priests the grace to perform holy things in a holy way, to reflect in every aspect of our lives the wonders of the greatness of God.*[14]

20.3 How to help priests. Praying for them. Respect for the priestly state.

So they went out and preached that men should repent. And they cast out many demons, and anointed with oil many that were sick and healed them. Priests are, as it were, an extension of Our Lord's Sacred Humanity, because they continue to perform in souls the same miracles which He himself did while He was on earth: the blind see, people who can scarcely walk recover their strength, and those who have died through mortal sin recover the life of grace through the sacrament of Confession.

The priest does not seek worldly compensations or the enhancement of his reputation, nor does he measure his task according to this world's scale of values. His task is not that of an arbitrator of differences[15] nor of caring for people's material welfare: that is a job for every Christian, and for all men of good will, whereas the priest's rôle is to bring people eternal life. That is what he has to offer. It is also what the world needs most. That is why we must pray to God that the Church will always have enough priests, priests who are really trying to be holy. We must ask for and encourage priestly vocations, if possible, among the members of our own families, children, brothers and cousins. It is indeed a great joy for a family if God blesses

---

14. *ibid*, 39
15. cf Luke 12:13

them with the gift of a vocation.

The laity have the very pleasant duty to help priests, especially with their prayer, so that they celebrate Mass with dignity and spend many hours hearing confessions, eager to administer the sacraments to the sick and the elderly, and particularly keen to teach catechism. We pray that priests will always be very concerned for the upkeep of God's House, and cheerful, patient, generous, friendly and indefatigable workers in spreading the kingdom of Christ. We have to be generous in contributing financially and helping their work in whatever way we can. And we should never speak badly of them: *One should speak about Christ's priests only in order to praise them.*[16]

If we sometimes see faults and defects in our priests, we have to make excuses for them and behave like the good sons of Noah, covering over their failings with the cloak of charity.[17] That can be yet another reason to help them with our good example and our prayer, and – whenever it is opportune – with a correction which will be fraternal and filial at the same time.

To help us grow in love and veneration for priests, we can meditate on these words which Saint Catherine of Siena places on Our Lord's lips: *I do not want the respect which priests should be given to be in any way diminished, for the reverence and respect which is shown them is not referred to them, but to Me, by virtue of the Blood which I have given to them to administer. Were it not for this, you should render them the same reverence as lay people, and no more ... You must not offend them; by offending them you offend Me and not them. Therefore I forbid it and I have laid it down that you shall not touch my Christs.*[18]

---

16. cf J. Escrivá, *Furrow*, 904
17. cf J. Escrivá, *The Way*, 75
18. St Catherine of Siena, *Dialogue*, ch. 116, quoted in J. Escrivá, *In Love with the Church*, 38

FIFTEENTH SUNDAY: YEAR C

21. THE GOOD SAMARITAN

21.1 The first expression of charity is to bring our neighbour closer to the Faith.

You shall love your neighbour as yourself. The doctor of the Law gave the right answer. Jesus confirms it: *You have answered right; do this, and you will live.* The story is told in the Gospel of today's Mass.[1]

This precept already existed in the Jewish Law, which even specified it in practical details. We read for example in Leviticus: *When you reap the harvest of your land, you shall not reap your field to its very border, neither shall you gather the gleanings after your harvest. And you shall not strip your vineyard bare, neither shall you gather the fallen grapes of your vineyard; you shall leave them for the poor and for the sojourner.*[2] And after specifying other expressions of mercy, Scripture continues: *You shall not take vengeance or bear any grudge against the sons of your own people, but you shall love your neighbour as yourself.*[3]

Here we have a distant foreshadowing of what was to be Our Lord's *new commandment*. But among the Jews there was a certain vagueness about the word 'neighbour': it wasn't clear whether it included only the members of one's own clan, or one's friends, or the entire chosen people. Opinions varied on the subject, and that was why the doctor of the Law asked Our Lord, *Who is my*

1. cf Luke 10:27
2. Lev 19:9-10
3. Lev 19:18

neighbour? To whom should I show all this love and mercy?

Jesus answers with a very beautiful parable, which we find in the Gospel of Saint Luke: *A man was going down from Jerusalem to Jericho, and he fell among robbers, who stripped him and beat him, and departed, leaving him half-dead.*[4] This is my neighbour: he is a man, any man who-ever who has need of me. Our Lord makes no specific reference to race, friendship or blood connections. Our neighbour is anyone who is close to us and has need of help. Nothing is said of his country, or of his background or social condition: *homo quidam,* just a man, a human being.

As we go through life we come across many cases of people who have been similarly injured and left destitute and half-dead in body and soul. Our concern to help them, which springs from our closeness to Jesus, broadens our heart and prevents us from falling into narrow-mindedness and selfishness. One discovers people who have been hurt by misunderstanding and loneliness, or by the absence of the most basic human necessities; people humiliated in their dignity as persons; people who have been shamefully robbed of their most elementary rights in ways which cry to heaven for vengeance. Christian men and women can never pass by on the other side, as some of the individuals in the parable did.

Every day we also meet the man who was left half dead, either because he has not been taught the elementary truths of the Faith, or because they have been stolen from him by the effects of others' bad example, or by media-conditioning. We can never forget that the Faith is the greatest treasure man has, much more important than

---

4. Luke 10:25-37

all material and human values. *At times, before preaching the Faith, we may first have to approach the man lying at the roadside and tend to his injuries. But as Christians we can never overlook the need to spread the Faith and to help people understand it better, and to propagate the Christian meaning of life.*[5] At the same time, we try to provide other good things as well – education, culture, personal betterment, an appreciation of the value of work, honesty in personal relationships, and a desire for social justice. All these things are living expressions of what charity really means in practice.

A Christian cannot be uninvolved in the human and social progress of mankind, *but the over-riding concern to enlighten men's minds in regard to faith and the religious life cannot ever be relegated to second place.*[6]

21.2 Sins of omission in the area of charity. Jesus is the object of our charity.

The parable goes on: *Now by chance a priest was going down that road; and when he saw him he passed by on the other side.*

Here Our Lord is speaking to us about sins of omission. Those who passed by on the other side did not inflict any fresh injuries on the abandoned and badly-wounded wayfarer; they did not steal whatever he had left, or insult him. They had worries of their own, they didn't want any complications, they had important things to do. They gave greater importance to their own business than to the man in need. Therein lay their sin: they *passed by on the other side.*

That service which they omitted to offer the injured

---

5. Cardinal M. González Martín, *Free, in Charity*, p.58
6. *ibid*, p.59

wayfarer would have merited the same praise Our Lord gave to Mary Magdalen – *she has done a beautiful thing to me*[7] – since anything we do for others we do for God. Christ himself awaits us in the person of that needy individual. Saint John Chrysostom puts on Our Lord's lips these words: *I am not saying to you: solve all my problems for me, give me everything you have, even though I am poor for love of you. I only ask for some bread and clothes, some relief from my hunger. I am in prison. I do not ask you to free me. I only wish, that for your own good, you pay me a visit. That will be enough for me, and in return I will make you a gift of heaven. I have freed you from a prison a thousand times more harsh. But I am happy if you come and visit me from time to time.*

I could in fact present you with your crown without asking any of this. But I do want to be grateful to you, so that afterwards you can come and receive your reward with confidence. That is why I, who am quite capable of feeding myself, prefer to dog your steps, asking, and to stretch out my hand at your door. My love is so great that I want you to feed me. That is why, as a friend, I prefer to sit at your table. I glory in that, and I can show you off to the whole world as the one who does good to me.[8]

The secret of overcoming differences of race or culture, or even of age or character, is to realize that the object of our charity is Jesus himself. When we look upon our fellow men, it is He whom we see: *It is as if Christ himself were crying out through the mouths of these poor people to the charity of his disciples.*[9]

---

7. Mark 14:6
8. St John Chrysostom, *Homilies on Romans*, 15
9. Second Vatican Council, *Gaudium et spes*, 88

21.3 Practical and real charity. Our own needs have to take second place to those of others.

The Gospel goes on: *But a Samaritan, as he journeyed, came to where he was; and when he saw him, he had compassion, and went to him and bound up his wounds, pouring on oil and wine; then he set him on his own beast and brought him to an inn, and took care of him. And the next day he took out two denarii and gave them to the innkeeper, saying, 'Take care of him; and whatever more you spend, I will repay you when I come back.'*

The Samaritan, in spite of the gulf between Jews and Samaritans, immediately felt sorry for the man's misfortune: *he had compassion.* There are people who are blind to anything that would put them out, and there are people who have a quick intuition for the sorrow in another's heart. What we need first of all is a readiness to see the misfortunes of others, and not hurry through life so much that, when we meet with need and suffering, we easily find an excuse for passing by on the other side.

The Samaritan's compassion was not a purely theoretical and ineffective one. On the contrary, he managed to offer the man practical assistance. What he did was not perhaps very heroic in itself, but it was what the circumstances called for. Firstly, *he went up to him.* This is the first thing to be done whenever we encounter misfortune or need: we have to get up close, we cannot just observe the situation from a distance. The Samaritan next did what had to be done: *he took care of him.* The charity Our Lord asks of us is shown in deeds; it consists in doing whatever needs to be done in each individual case.

God places our neighbour, and his needs, along the road of our life. Love is always ready to do whatever the immediate situation demands. It may not be anything particularly heroic or difficult; indeed, what is called for is very often something small and simple: *This love is not something reserved for important matters, but must be exercised above all in the ordinary circumstances of daily life.*[10] It may require offering some small service, perhaps trying to cheer someone up when we find him gloomy; or maybe a word of appreciation and thanks, or smiling, or giving a stranger directions courteously, or listening with interest to what someone has to say.

The business the good Samaritan had in hand was left to wait, and the urgent things he had to do were no longer all that important. He gave his time unstintingly to help the man in need. It is not only a question of time, though. Our interests, the things we like doing – not to mention any self-indulgence – must all take second place to the needs of others.

Jesus concludes the lesson with a friendly word to the doctor of the Law: *Go and do likewise*, He says to him: be understanding, involved and compassionate with whoever needs you. And now, as we come to the end of our meditation, we hear those words as spoken to each of us too. To put them into practice we need to have recourse to the Blessed Virgin. *There is no heart more human than that of a person overflowing with supernatural sense. Think of our Mother Mary, who is full of grace, Daughter of God the Father, Mother of God the Son, Spouse of God the Holy Spirit. Her Heart has room for all humanity and makes no distinction or discrimination. Every person is her son or her daughter.*[11]

---

10. *ibid*, 38
11. J. Escrivá, *Furrow*, 801

FIFTEENTH WEEK: MONDAY

22. PARENTS AND THEIR CHILDREN'S VOCATION

22.1 Complete freedom to follow Christ. A vocation is a great honour.

He who loves father or mother more than me is not worthy of me; and he who loves son or daughter more than me is not worthy of me, we read in the Gospel of today's Mass.[1] When one freely decides to follow Christ completely it takes preference over other plans: one's father or mother, one's boy-friend or girl-friend. God's call comes first, and everything else has to take second place to this.

Christ's words don't create any incompatibility between the First and Fourth Commandments, but rather highlight their mutual relationship. We should love God with all our strength, according to the vocation we have received. We should also love and respect the parents God has given us, both in theory and in practice, since we owe them so much. But love for our parents cannot take precedence over love for God. Ordinarily there will be little reason for conflict to arise, but should it ever happen, that would be the moment to recall the words of the adolescent Jesus in the Temple of Jerusalem: *How is it that you sought me? Did you not know that I must be in my Father's house?*[2] Jesus' reply to Mary and Joseph, who had

---

1. Matt 10:34 - 11:1
2. Luke 2:49

sought him anxiously, is a very good example for both children and parents: for children it teaches them that they shouldn't put affection for their family before love for God, especially when Our Lord asks them to follow him with a total self-giving; for parents, it helps them see that their children belong above all to God, and that He has a right to do with them as He wishes, even though in certain circumstances it may require considerable sacrifice on their part.[3]

It would be very sad if someone were to turn a deaf ear to God's call so as not to upset his or her parents. And even worse would be the situation of the parents, for, as Saint Bernard says, *the source of their consolation is the death of their child.*[4] It would be difficult to cause that son or daughter greater harm.

To follow Our Lord properly calls for a completely unfettered detachment, a freedom of heart that is not hampered by sadness or regret, which would only lead to a half-hearted self-giving; the person concerned also needs to have the necessary autonomy to fulfil God's will. Nothing is gained by half measures, by a decision made with a divided heart. It could happen that in some cases a life of total dedication to Our Lord is not accepted by one's own relations: having dreamed of other plans, quite reasonable in themselves, they do not understand this new development, or maybe they do not wish to be part of the renunciation it involves. We have to take this into account and realize that fidelity to Christ, even at the cost of causing sorrow for our parents, is in the long run much better both for ourselves and for our family. In all circumstances, we have to be very firm in following our vocation, and at the

---

3. cf *The Navarre Bible*, notes to Matt 10:34-37 and Luke 2:49
4. St Bernard, *Letters*, 3, 2

same time we have to love our parents even more than before. We have to pray a lot that they come to understand that *it is no 'sacrifice' for parents when God asks them for their children. Neither, for those whom He calls, is it a sacrifice to follow him.*

It is, on the contrary, an immense honour, a motive for a great and holy pride, a mark of predilection, a very special affection that God has shown at a particular time, but which has been in his mind from all eternity.[5] It is indeed a great honour and a great blessing from God to that family.

22.2 There comes a time for everyone when they have to leave home and parents.

When someone gives their heart completely to God, it is returned more youthful and enlarged, with a greater capacity to love others. Love for one's parents, brothers and sisters is then enriched by being passed through the Heart of Christ. Saint Thomas Aquinas points out that James and John, in following Our Lord and abandoning their father, were praised. They were not praised because he had incited them to do something evil, but because *they realised that their father would be able to spend his life some other way, while they followed Christ.*[6] The Master passed by and called them, and from that moment, on everything else paled into insignificance. In heaven their parents will surely have received a special reward, in large measure due to their sons' response to the divine call: vocation is a blessing and a great good for all concerned.

Vocation is God's initiative; He knows well what is best for the person called, and for the family. Many parents accept God's will for their children joyfully and

---

5. J. Escrivá, *The Forge*, 18
6. St Thomas, *Summa Theologiae*, 2-2, 101, 4, 1

unconditionally and are happy when one of them is called
to follow Christ. There are some, though, who react quite
differently, for various reasons, some logical and under-
standable and others tainted by selfishness. With the
excuse that their children are too young to answer God's
call – though not too young to undertake other commitments – or that they lack the necessary experience, they
allow themselves to succumb to the temptation alluded to
by Pope Pius XII: *Even among those who boast of the
Catholic faith, there are not lacking parents who do not
resign themselves to the vocation of their children and fight
without scruple the divine call, eliciting every type of argument. They may even use means that put in danger not only
the vocation to a more perfect state, but conscience itself
and the eternal salvation of those who ought to be their most
dearly beloved.*[7] They forget that they are God's 'collabora-
tors', and that it is inevitable that sooner or later their children will leave home anyway, either to form a family of
their own, or for work or study reasons. Very often when
young people leave home no great catastrophe occurs; at
times indeed, it is the parents themselves who, for their
children's own good, are the prime movers in causing it to
happen. Why then, in the case of someone seeking to follow Christ, should they create difficulties for them? *Christ
never separates souls.*[8]

22.3 Wanting the best for one's children.

Good parents always want the best for their children.
Since they are capable of making great sacrifices for their
material welfare, why not too in the case of their supernatural well-being? They sacrifice themselves so that their

---

7. Pius XI, *Ad catholici sacerdotii*, 20 December 1935
8. cf J. Escrivá, *Furrow*, 23

children grow up healthy, and do well at their studies, and have good friends; and likewise so that they live as God wants them to, leading a life that is Christian and honourable. This is the mission that God has called parents to in matrimony – the education of their children. It is the express will of God for them, and a consequence of the Natural Law.

In the Gospel we find many petitions in favour of children: the woman who follows Jesus perseveringly until she obtains a cure for her daughter;[9] the father who asks that the devil which torments his son be cast out;[10] Jairus, the ruler of the Capharnaum synagogue, who anxiously awaits Our Lord because his twelve year old daughter is at the point of death.[11] We admire the determination of the mother of James and John, who approached Our Lord to ask him for something that they themselves would not dare to request. Without thinking about herself, she approached Jesus, *and kneeling before him she asked him for something*.[12] How many are the fathers and mothers who down through the ages have asked for their children special favours which they would never have dreamed of asking for themselves? Our Lord, understanding this motherly demonstration of affection, does not reject it, but instead turns to the two sons and promises them the greatest honour a person could receive: the invitation to share with him his own cup, his own destiny, his own mission.

Parents ought to ask for the best for their children, and the best is for them to follow the vocation that God has foreseen for them. This is the great secret of being

---

9. cf Matt 15:21-28
10. cf Matt 17:14-20
11. cf Matt 9:18-26
12. Matt 20:20

happy on earth and of attaining the boundless joy of
Heaven. However, considering each calling in itself, the
most elevated of all is the vocation to celibate chastity for
the love of God. *The Church, throughout her history, has
always defended the superiority of this charism to that of
marriage, by reason of the wholly singular link which it has
with the Kingdom of God.*[13] How many are the vocations to
a complete self-giving that God has given to children
because of the generosity and prayer of their parents! In
fact Our Lord ordinarily makes use of parents to create a
suitable climate in which the seed of vocation may develop
and flourish. *Christian couples are, for each other, for their
children and their relatives, cooperators of grace and
witnesses of the Faith. They are the first to pass on the Faith
to their children and to educate them in it. By word and
example they form them to a Christian and apostolic life;
they offer them wise guidance in the choice of vocation, and
if they discover in them a sacred vocation they encourage it
with all care.*[14] More they cannot do, for it is not within
their competence to discern whether or not their children
have a vocation. Their task is to help them form their consciences well and enable them to discover their own path
without pressurizing them.

A vocation in a family is a special sign of God's love
and confidence for all its members. It is a privilege and a
great treasure that ought to be protected, especially with
prayer. God blesses the place where a faithful vocation is
born: *giving up one's children to the service of God is not a
sacrifice: it is an honour and a joy.*[15]

---

13. John Paul II, *Familiaris consortio*, 16
14. Second Vatican Council, *Apostolicam actuositatem*, 11
15. J. Escrivá, *Furrow*, 22

FIFTEENTH WEEK: TUESDAY

23. SORROW FOR SIN

23.1 In spite of all Christ's miracles, some Jewish towns didn't do penance. We too are visited by Our Lord just as they were.

On leaving Nazareth, Jesus chose Capharnaum as his place of residence. At times the gospels refer to it as *his city*. From there his preaching spread to the whole of Galilee and all of Palestine. It is possible that Jesus stayed in Peter's house and made it the base for his apostolic trips to the surrounding countryside. No other place in the gospel narrative witnessed as many of Christ's miracles as did Capharnaum.

On the north shore of Lake Gennesareth, not far from Capharnaum, there were two flourishing towns – Chorazin and Bethsaida – where Jesus also did *very many miracles*; yet, in spite of all the signs and blessings, all those acts of mercy, the local inhabitants were not converted by Jesus' presence among them. The Gospel of today's Mass recalls the harsh words Our Lord had for those towns which weren't prepared to do penance and repent of their sins: *Woe to you, Chorazin! Woe to you, Bethsaida! For if the mighty works done in you had been done in Tyre and Sidon, they would have repented long ago ... And you, Capharnaum, will you be exalted to heaven? You shall be brought down to Hades. For if the mighty works done in you had been done in Sodom, it would have remained until this day.*[1]

So many graces, so many miracles! And yet many of the inhabitants didn't change and didn't repent of their sins. In fact, they actually rebelled against Christ: *Dirumpamus vincula eorum, et proiciamus a nobis iugum ipsorum:*[2] Let us break the commandments of the Lord and throw off his sweet yoke! How often have those words of Psalm 2 been repeated since!

Look now at Jesus as he passes by, pouring out upon us his grace and his compassion. How often it has been so! Think of the countless times and occasions Our Lord has stopped to cure us, to bless us, to encourage us to do good. He has given us so much care and attention. And, since he has lavished so much grace upon us, he expects us to respond in kind – with sincere repentance of our faults, total hatred of deliberate venial sin and of all that could in any way separate us from him. Jesus always listens to us, but particularly when we go to him completely ready to change, to rediscover our way and to begin once more with *a broken and contrite heart.*[3] This ought to be so always, because there are lots of occasions when, deliberately or otherwise, we reject his grace; and the offence we cause him is in proportion to the love He has shown us. Can anyone be so blind as to fail to recognize Christ in these repeated encounters of his with our fallen nature?

23.2 The fruits of sorrow.

A broken and contrite heart, O God, thou wilt not despise. The word 'contrition' comes from the Latin *contritus* – smashed in pieces, as of a rock, and has come to mean sorrow for one's faults and sins in the sense that the

---

1. Matt 11:20-24
2. Ps 2:3
3. Ps 51:17

heart hardened by sin can be said to shatter when stricken by sorrow at having offended God.[4] In everyday language we use the term 'heartbroken' to describe our reaction to some great tragedy that affects us to the depths of our being. Something similar should happen on contemplating our sins in the light of God's holiness and the great love He has for us. In the soul that genuinely seeks God this reaction is attributable not so much to the sensation of failure produced by sin as to the remorse at having cut itself off from God to even the tiniest extent. This sorrow for sin – contrition – consists essentially in a sense of remorse and a sincere detestation of the offence against God, and a firm resolution of not sinning again;[5] it is a turning towards the good, which causes life to blossom anew in the soul.[6]

It is love, above all, that should lead us to ask God very often for forgiveness for the countless times we don't respond as we ought to the graces we receive. *The friend recalled his sins, and through fear of hell he tried to weep but found he could not. He besought Love for tears, and Wisdom answered him that he ought to weep more out of reverence for his Beloved than for fear of the pains of hell, because tears shed for love please him more than those shed through fear.*[7] It is love that should lead us to the sacrament of Penance.

Contrition gives the Christian soul a special strength: it gives it back hope, peace and happiness, and makes it forget about itself and abandon itself in the Lord with greater interior refinement and sensitivity. To approach God with a contrite heart we need to acknowledge our

---

4. cf *Catechism of St Pius X*, 684-685
5. cf Council of Trent, *Session XIV*, chap. 4, Dz 987
6. cf M. Schmaus, *Dogmatic Theology*, VI, *The Sacraments*, p.562
7. R. Lull, *The Book of the Friend and the Beloved*, p.341

faults and sins as they are, without making any lame excuses, and not be surprised and shocked on discovering defects and failings we thought had already been overcome. If we were to blame our failings on the environment or other such circumstances, we would forsake the path of humility and would not encounter God, who is so close to us precisely when we abandon him. On considering our faults in our daily examination of conscience, we have to see them primarily as offences against God rather than as personality defects. If we don't measure them against the background of God's love we will easily tend to find excuses for them and will eventually lose the good dispositions of contrition, repentance and atonement we need to have for our sins. With God we can never be 'in the clear': our condition is rather that of the debtor who *could not pay;*[8] we will always be in need of his infinite mercy. *God, be merciful to me a sinner,*[9] we say to him in the words of the tax-collector who, in all humility, recognized his own unworthiness when face to face with the holiness of God.

One thing we can't do as regards our sins and failings is to accept them as something inevitable and natural, and 'come to terms' with them. What we have to do is always to ask for pardon, and begin again as often as necessary, saying to God Our Lord: *Father, I have sinned against heaven and before you; I am no longer worthy to be called your son; treat me as one of your hired servants.*[10] And God, who *is close to the contrite of heart,*[11] always hears our prayer.

Again and again in life we meet Jesus passing by, as he did of old in those towns of Galilee, inviting us to come

8. cf Matt 18:25
9. Luke 18:13
10. Luke 15:18-19
11. St Augustine, *Commentary on St John's Gospel*, 15, 25

out to meet him and leave our sins behind. Let us not postpone this loving encounter. *Nunc coepi*: Now I begin, once more, with your help, O Lord.

23.3 Sorrow is a gift we must ask for. The works of penance.

Woe to you, Chorazin! Woe to you, Bethsaida! We can imagine the disillusionment in Our Lord's voice as he uttered those words, realizing that the grace he lavished so bountifully on his listeners was not taking root in their souls. From time to time they may have followed him all right, full of enthusiasm and expressing their appreciation on witnessing a cure, but at the bottom of their hearts they were never really with him.

We for our part have to ask the Holy Spirit for the marvellous gift of contrition. We should try to make many acts of love-sorrow, especially if we have offended Our Lord in something serious, and also whenever we go to Confession, when examining our conscience, and throughout the day. It can help a lot if we do the Stations of the Cross or meditate on Our Lord's Passion. We should never tire of considering Jesus' infinite love for us, and the insult and indignity that sin represents for him.

Sincere sorrow for sin does not necessarily require having to *feel* sorry. Just like love, sorrow is an act of the will, not a feeling. And in the same way as one can love God deeply without any emotional reaction, one can also be truly sorry for sin without experiencing anything sentimental. Real sorrow is seen principally in the way one unhesitatingly avoids all occasions of offending God and is ready to do specific acts of penance for any infidelities committed. These are the things to help us atone for the punishment our sins deserve, to overcome bad inclinations, and to strengthen us in doing good.

What are the acts of penance that are pleasing to God? They are: prayer, fasting, almsgiving, small mortifications, putting up patiently with the disappointments and difficulties of life, being ready to accept the monotonous aspects of our job and the tiredness that is part and parcel of work. In particular, we should always be ready and eager to go to Confession well, truly sorry for our faults and sins. *Turn to Our Lady and ask her – as a token of her love for you – for the gift of contrition. Ask that you may be sorry, with the sorrow of Love, for all your sins and for the sins of all men and women throughout the ages.*

And with that same disposition, be bold enough to add: 'Mother, my life, my hope, lead me by the hand. And if there is anything in me which is displeasing to my Father God grant that I may see it, so that, between you and me, the two of us, we may uproot it.'

Do not be afraid to continue, saying to her: 'O clement, O loving, O sweet Virgin Mary, pray for me, that by fulfilling the most lovable Will of your Son, I may be worthy to obtain and enjoy what Our Lord Jesus has promised.'[12]

---

12. J. Escrivá, *The Forge*, 161

FIFTEENTH WEEK: WEDNESDAY

24. OUR FATHER GOD

24.1 God is always by our side.

As Moses tended the flock of his father-in-law Jethro near Mount Horeb, the holy mountain, God appeared to him in a burning bush. There Moses was given the extraordinary task – his life's work – of leading the chosen people out of the slavery of Egypt into the Promised Land. God confirmed him in his mission with these words: *I will be with you.*[1] Moses little imagined how closely God would be accompanying him and the people in the midst of the trials and tribulations that awaited them.

In our lives too, God's presence at every moment is something we can scarcely fathom. It takes on even greater definition when God sees us on the road to holiness. He is like a father minding a toddler. Jesus Christ, true God and true Man, is always reminding us in the Gospel of God's paternal concern. He alone can do this, since *no one knows the Father except the Son and any one to whom the Son chooses to reveal him,*[2] as He tells us in today's gospel. The Son knows the Father in the very knowledge by which the Father knows him. There is no greater intimacy than that. This identity of knowing and knowledge bespeaks the unity of the divine nature. In claiming it, Jesus revealed that He was God.

As the Son, one in substance with the Father, He is

---

1. *First Reading*, Year I: Ex 3:1-6, 9-12
2. Matt 11:27

also able to reveal the Father's relationship with and attitude towards us, and in particular his goodness in granting us the gift of the Holy Spirit. The mystery of the Blessed Trinity is at the heart of what He had to reveal to us, and with it and in it we find the wonder of God's fatherhood. During that last evening in the upper room, when He seemed to be summing up those years of self-giving and trusting revelation, He said: *I have manifested your name to the men whom you gave me.*[3]

To manifest someone's name really meant to reveal his mode of being. Our Lord has revealed to us the depths of the trinitarian mystery: the fact that God is a father, so close to us men. Jesus is always using the title 'Father', both in private conversations and in his preaching. He dwells on the goodness of the Father, who rewards our slightest action and recognises our good deeds, even the ones that no one sees,[4] who bestows his bounty upon the just and the unjust,[5] and who is always aware of and concerned about what we need.[6] The word 'Father' is like a constant refrain on Our Lord's lips. This Father is never far away, no more than would be a father who sees his little toddler alone and in danger. If we try to please him we will find him by our side. *When you really come to love God's Will you will never, even in the worst state of agitation, lose sight of the fact that our Father in Heaven is always close to you, very close, right next to you, with his everlasting Love and with his unbounded affection.*[7]

---

3. John 17:6
4. cf Matt 6:3-4, 17-18
5. cf Matt 5:44-46
6. cf Matt 7:7-8, 6:25-33
7. J. Escrivá, *The Forge*, 240

24.2 Imitating Christ is the way to be true children of God the Father.

God didn't just make us and then leave us, like a painter with his painting. He is a father to us, and has even brought us to be *partakers of the divine nature*.[8] The Father's desire was *that we should be called children of God; and so we are*.[9] Being children of God is not something we achieve on our own; it is a gift from God. Pondering this will make us thank him often every day. The sense of our divine filiation will be at the root of our joy and confidence in carrying out the mission God has given us. In it we find assurance in the face of difficulty and anguish. Father, my Father, we will find ourselves saying, savouring that gentle but strong word 'Father', be it at times of joy or of danger. *Call him 'Father' many times a day and tell him – alone, in your heart – that you love him, that you adore him, that you feel proud and strong because you are his son*.[10]

It is through Christ that we share in this divine sonship, as we try to resemble him, the first-born among many brethren and the Only-begotten of the Father.

The more like Jesus we become, the more God the Father will see us as his children, if we try to work as He did, if we too have pity on the people we meet each day, if we make reparation for sin and show our thanks, as Jesus did. But we achieve this above all by imitating Christ's prayer to his Father. This means bursting into praise and thanksgiving for the many expressions of God's love we meet. *I thank you, Father, Lord of heaven and earth*, we read in today's Gospel.[11] Thank you, we will say, for

---

8. 2 Pet 1:4
9. 1 John 3:1
10. J. Escrivá, *Friends of God*, 150
11. Matt 11:25

bringing that friend of mine back to the sacraments, for helping me with my family, for the chance I get to open my heart in spiritual direction, indeed for everything. If our minds and hearts turn to God often, in good times and in bad, then we are living as good sons and daughters of God should.

> My soul, give thanks to the Lord,
> all my being, bless his holy name.
> My soul, give thanks to the Lord,
> and never forget all his blessings.
> It is he who forgives all your guilt,
> who heals every one of your ills,
> who redeems your life from the grave,
> who crowns you with love and compassion.[12]

Let's try to see people as Christ saw them. The world looks so different through his eyes! It is the Holy Spirit who configures us to the Master. *For all who are led by the spirit of God are sons of God.*[13] Saint John Chrysostom explains that it is *through the spirit that we belong to Christ, we possess him, and we vie with the angels. Through the spirit we crucify the flesh, we taste the joy of eternal life, we possess the pledge of the resurrection and make sure progress on the path of virtue.*[14] Divine filiation is the easiest way to reach the Blessed Trinity.

24.3 Union with Christ, a consequence of divine filiation.

How often we have reflected on God's mercy, how He chose to become man so that man could, in a sense, become God,[15] sharing in God's very life. The sanctifying grace which we receive in the sacraments and as a reward

---

12. *Responsorial Psalm*, Year I: Ps 102:1-4
13. Rom 8:14
14. St John Chrysostom, *Homilies on Romans*, 13
15. cf St Irenaeus, *Against heresies*, 5, Preface

for our good works identifies us with Christ and makes us 'sons in the Son,' since God the Father has only one Son and it is only 'in Christ' that we can attain to this divine filiation. We become united and identified with him, as members of his Mystical Body, as Saint Paul wrote to the Galatians: *It is no longer I who live, but Christ who lives in me.*[16]

So when we turn to the Father it is really Christ who is praying in us. When we deny ourselves something for him, He it is who inspired this detachment of spirit. When we try to bring someone back to the sacraments, our apostolic spirit is a reflection of Jesus' zeal for souls. Our work and our sufferings complete the works and sufferings which Our Lord took on for his Mystical Body the Church. Think of the value which our daily work and our sorrows assume in this light.

The interior struggle which brings us, with the help of grace, to be conformed to Christ, also moves us to *have this mind among yourselves, which was in Christ Jesus;*[17] and this in turn makes us 'more' children of God, so to speak. In the ordinary way one can not be more or less the son of one's father, though one could be a better or worse one. In the supernatural sphere, the holier one is, the more one is a son or daughter of God, not just a better one. This is the real goal of the Christian life: a constant growth in divine filiation.

Our mother Mary is the perfect example of what divine grace can achieve when it is fully availed of. No one, excepting the sacred Humanity of Our Lord, was ever closer to God, and no created being could ever become the Daughter of God the Father that she was.

---

16. Gal 2:20
17. Phil 2:5

Let us ask her to make us seek the counsel of the Holy Spirit, who will get us to imitate Jesus. Under his influence we will feel the pressing need to turn to the Father at all times, but particularly at Mass, when we address him as *clementissime Pater* – 'most merciful Father',[18] in union with the sacrifice of his Son. We will think of him as our Father, calling him *Abba*, anointed as we are by the spirit of his Son who cries out *Abba, Father*.[19] He will also make us feel the hunger and thirst for God and for his glory which were so apparent in his Incarnate Son. The Father also receives glory from our growing more like his Only-begotten Son, *who by the power at work within us is able to do far more abundantly than all that we ask or think.*[20] [21]

---

18. *Roman Missal, Eucharistic Prayer I*
19. Gal 4:6
20. Eph 3:20
21. cf B. Perquin, *Abba, Father*, London 1990, p.119

FIFTEENTH WEEK: THURSDAY

25. OUR LORD'S YOKE IS LIGHT

25.1 Jesus Christ frees us from the heaviest burdens.

Come to me, all who labour and are heavy laden, Jesus declares to us in today's Gospel,[1] *and I will give you rest.* He is speaking to the crowds following him, harassed and downtrodden, like sheep without a shepherd,[2] lifting the loads that oppressed them. The Pharisees were crushing them with a series of minute rules[3] which never brought peace to their hearts.

The heaviest weights that men carry are their sins, as Saint Augustine pointed out. *Jesus tells people who are sweating under heavy and useless burdens, 'Come to me ... and I will give you rest.' How could He relieve those weighed down by sin except by forgiving them?*[4] Every confession is a liberation, for sins – even venial ones – are a wearisome oppression. We come away from this sacrament at peace, ready to struggle afresh. It is as though He said: *All you who are tormented and afflicted, labouring beneath the burden of anxiety and desire, cast it aside by coming unto Me, and I will refresh you; and your souls shall find that rest of which your desires rob you.*[5]

Our Lord invites us to exchange his yoke for the burden of sin, pride and selfishness: *Take my yoke upon*

---

1. Matt 11:28-30
2. Matt 9:36
3. cf Acts 15:10
4. St Augustine, *Sermon 164*, 4
5. St John of the Cross, *The Ascent of Mount Carmel*, 1, 7, 4

you, and learn from me; for I am gentle and lowly in heart, and you will find rest for your souls. For my yoke is easy, and my burden is light. Saint Augustine remarks: *This burden is not a weight at all, it is wings to fly with.*[6] The commitments of our vocation and the share of the Cross we are asked to bear are a blessed weight which allows us to soar to God.

In any case, if we keep close to Christ we will find that the inevitable hitches and problems we encounter take on a different meaning. Instead of being our cross they become Christ's, bringing us to co-redeem with him as we purify our evil inclinations and grow in virtue. But we will still hear the voices of those who see no need for sacrifice. They are good-living people, no doubt, but their faith is dead. *He told you that this way is very hard. And, on hearing it, you heartily agreed, remembering that bit about the Cross being a sure sign of the true way ... But your friend noticed only the rough part of the road, without bringing to mind Jesus' promise: 'My yoke is sweet.'*

Remind him about it, because – perhaps when he realises it – he will give himself,[7] and realise that he too has been called to holiness.

We must shout to the four winds that following Christ is a joyful road and even when it passes under the Cross it is marked with optimism and peace. The trials are the most fruitful stretches of all. *Bees live and feed on bitter food when making their honey; in the same way, we can never practise gentleness and patience or produce honey from such excellent virtues more surely than when eating the bread of bitterness and living in the midst of afflictions.*[8]

---

6. St Augustine, *Sermons 164*, 7
7. J. Escrivá, *Furrow*, 198
8. St Francis de Sales, *Introduction to the Devout Life*, III, 3

25.2 We have to be ready for sorrow, for difficulties and obstacles.

Nobody can expect to go through life without sorrow, pain or worry. A Christian cannot make the mistake which Saint Gregory the Great described as follows: *There are some who wish to be humble, but without being despised, who wish to be happy with their lot, but without being needy, who wish to be chaste, without mortifying the body, to be patient without suffering. They want both to acquire virtues and to avoid the sacrifices those virtues involve: they are like soldiers who flee the battlefield and try to win the war from the comfort of the city.*[9] Virtues cannot be had without effort and trials.

So there will always be problems, worries and sorrows. Sometimes they will seem easy and other times hard to bear; but if we keep close to Our Lord we will always manage. Whether they are big or small, if we accept them and offer them to God they will not be a weight; in fact they will enable our soul to pray and to see God in everything that happens. Any problem that God permits can be solved and its burden borne if we turn to him for help. If a particularly serious difficulty should arise, God will provide more grace. *If it is God who lays the burden upon you, God will also give you the strength to bear it.*[10]

In this life trials and tribulations are the normal thing. This was what Saint Peter warned the early Christians: *Beloved, do not be surprised at the fiery ordeal which comes upon you to prove you, as though something strange were happening to you.*[11] So we should not be surprised either, especially knowing that the Cross is the right road to happiness and effectiveness. God often permits

---

9. St Gregory the Great, *Moralia*, 7, 28, 34
10. J. Escrivá, *The Forge*, 325
11. 1 Pet 4:12

tribulations to afflict those He loves to make them more fruitful. If a branch is joined to the vine and is giving fruit, that branch *He prunes that it may bear more fruit*.[12] But He never leaves us to face it on our own, and he stays close to his friends when they feel themselves to be under pressure.

25.3 Facing adversity in a sensible and realistic way, with joyful courage. We are to flee from discouragement.

God gives only good gifts. If he permits pain or sorrow, financial or family problems, all this is for the sake of something better.

We often find that God blesses his favourites with the Cross and with the grace to carry it with spirit, from both the human and supernatural points of view. Towards the end of her life, when Saint Teresa was on her way to make a new foundation, she found the road blocked by extensive flooding. Having spent a night in an inn which offered such poor hospitality that there were no proper beds,[13] she set off again the next morning, for this was the Lord's will. He had told her: *Make no account of the cold, for I am true heat. The devil is making every effort to hinder this foundation. Do thou make every effort in its favour, and go in person without fail, for it will bring thee great advantage*.[14] So when next day she decided to cross the river Arlanzon she found it was just an enormous sea of water, with the wooden pontoons scarcely visible.[15] Those watching from the river-bank saw the carriage she was in swaying on the brink of the torrent. She jumped out awkwardly, up to her knees in water, and hurt herself in the process. Wryly she

---

12. cf John 15:2
13. St Teresa, *The Foundations*, 27, 12
14. *ibid*, 31, 11, p.188
15. cf M. Auclair, *Life of St Teresa*, pp.422-423

complained: *So much to put up with and you send me this*!
Jesus replied: *Teresa, that's how I treat my friends*. She was
not lost for an answer: *Small wonder you have so few!*[16]
Soon her good humour and that of her travelling-
companions returned, for *once the danger was passed, they
enjoyed talking about it.*[17]

God wants us to bear difficulties peacefully and
firmly, being happy to place our trust in him. He never lets
his friends down, especially when their only care is to do
his will. When we kneel before the tabernacle, perhaps
uttering the words *Adoro te devote, latens deitas* – God-
head here in hiding, whom I do adore – we realise that as
long as we are with Christ the yoke is easy and the most
awkward burden is light. He it is who helps us to bear up
and tackle problems with spirit and confidence and with
the good humour of the saints. This attitude does a great
deal of good both to ourselves and our neighbour.

It is a matter of facing things which are unpleasant or
painful, and which go against our plans, in a cheerful way,
like an athlete. We also need a straightforward attitude
which doesn't invent imaginary problems and sorrows for
us, or make us start suspecting the arrival of all sorts of
complicated scenarios. For even when the problems are
real enough we can find ourselves giving too much importance to them. We begin to think we are doing nothing
right, that things are going from bad to worse, that our
apostolate is getting nowhere and that we are unable to
swim against the current. This kind of attitude can creep in
because we forget about the surest fact of all, that we are
sons and daughters of God, and that from the difficulties
of these situations his grace will always draw a greater

---

16. *ibid*, p.423
17. St Teresa, *The Foundations*, 31, 17, p.191

good.

With his presence and the protection of Our Lady, *refugium nostrum et virtus* – our refuge and our strength – we will weigh up the problems and seek help in spiritual direction, and we will often find that what had seemed so difficult can easily be coped with. That sort of optimistic and cheerful spirit is absolutely essential for growing in God's love and doing apostolate, and a soul which has faced adversity thereby becomes strong, generous and long-suffering. Such trials are our great opportunity to toughen ourselves up and to deepen our love.

FIFTEENTH WEEK: FRIDAY

26. OUR LORD'S PASSOVER

26.1 The Jewish Passover.

The Passover was the most solemn feast of the Jewish year; it had been instituted by God to commemorate the exodus of the Hebrew people from Egypt and to recall annually their liberation from the slavery to which they had been subjected. The Lord established[1] that on the eve of the feast every family would sacrifice a lamb: it had to be one year old and with no blemish or disfigurement. The whole family would gather to eat the animal roasted on an open fire, along with bread that had not been leavened, and with bitter herbs. The unleavened bread symbolized the haste of their exodus from Egypt, fleeing from Pharaoh's armies; the bitter herbs represented the bitterness of the many years of slavery. They had to eat it hurriedly, with their feet shod and with staves in their hands, like people ready to depart on a journey.

The feast began with the paschal meal shortly after sunset on the evening of the 14th of Nisan, the first month of the Hebrew year, and went on for a further seven days; during this time no yeast was used in baking bread, whence it became known as the Azymes, or Days of Unleavened Bread. All yeast was removed from the houses in the evening of the 14th; in this way the Hebrew people recalled that sudden exodus from the land in which they had suffered so much.

---

1. *First Reading*, Year I: Ex 12:1-14

All this was a figure and image of the renewal which Christ would bring about in their souls, and of their liberation from the slavery of sin. *Cleanse out the old leaven that you may be a new lump, as you really are unleavened. For Christ, our paschal lamb has been sacrificed. Let us, therefore, celebrate the festival, not with the old leaven, the leaven of malice and evil, but with the unleavened bread of sincerity and truth.*[2] The paschal lamb of the Jewish feast was a promise and figure of the true Lamb, Jesus Christ, immolated in the sacrifice of Calvary on behalf of the whole human race.[3] He is the true Lamb who took away the sin of the world; by dying He destroyed our death, by rising He restored our life.[4] He is the Lamb who, by his voluntary sacrifice, really obtains what the sacrifices of the Old Law merely symbolized, namely, satisfaction to God for the sins of mankind.

Christ's sacrifice on the Cross, renewed each time Mass is celebrated, enables us to live in a continuous state of celebration. For that reason Saint Paul exhorted the Corinthians to cleanse out the old leaven, a symbol of all that is old and impure, so that they might lead an authentic Christian life.[5] The Mass, which we can also make present throughout our day, is a foretaste of heavenly glory. Having received so many benefits, *is it possible not to be in a state of continuous celebration during your earthly life?* asks Saint John Chrysostom. *Far from us be any flagging of spirit because of poverty, sickness or the persecutions which oppress us. The present life is a time for celebrating,*[6] a foretaste of everlasting glory and happiness.

---

2. 1 Cor 5:7-8

3. cf St Thomas, *Summa Theologiae*, 3, 73, 6

4. *Roman Missal, Easter Preface I*

5. cf *The Navarre Bible, Corinthians, in loc*

6. St John Chrysostom, *Homilies on 1 Corinthians*, 5:7-8

26.2 Our Lord's Last Supper with his disciples. The true Paschal Lamb.

Jesus signalled in advance, and with special emphasis, the last Passover He was to eat with his disciples;[7] and made them see how earnestly He desired to eat it with them.[8]

John and Peter prepared everything necessary – the unleavened bread, the bitter herbs, the cups for the wine, and the lamb, which had to be sacrificed that afternoon in the atrium of the Temple. That evening, probably in the house of Mary the mother of Mark, the institution of the Holy Eucharist took place, and the New Covenant, which was to be fulfilled the following day, was brought forward sacramentally. *At one table two Passovers are celebrated, that of the figure and that of the reality. Just as a painter, on the same surface, first traces the outline and then adds the colours, so too does Christ.*[9] Using the old rite, He established the true Passover, the feast *par excellence*, of which the former was only a figure. The bitter herbs now have a close link with the bitterness of the Passion which was about to take place.

The paschal meal was a sacrifice, the sacrifice of the Lord's Passover.[10] The Mass is also a sacrifice, being the unbloody but real renewal of the sacrifice of the Cross. At the Last Supper Jesus brought forward in a sacramental form – *my body which wll be given up for you, my blood shed for you* – the sacrifice which he was to accomplish the following day on Calvary. Once and for all Jesus replaced the old rite with his redeeming sacrifice. That night in the Cenacle was fulfilled the event from which countless

---

7. cf John 2:13-23; 6:4; 11:55; 12:1
8. cf Luke 22:15
9. St John Chrysostom, *The Betrayal by Judas*, 1, 4
10. Ex 12:27

generations of people have obtained life, and which is the centre of our very existence. O happy place, exclaims Saint Ephraem, *in which the paschal lamb comes out to meet the Lamb of Truth! ... O happy place! Never was there prepared a table like yours, neither in the house of kings, nor in the Tabernacle, nor in the Holy of Holies.*[11]

With the words *Do this in memory of me* Our Lord made it possible for this mystery of love to be repeated until the end of time, granting the Apostles and their successors the power of performing it.[12] How thankful we should be for this share in the countless benefits we receive in Holy Communion! How close to us is that same Jesus who gave himself up completely to his disciples and all mankind on that memorable night. We can now tell him, in the intimacy of our heart: *I love you, Lord Jesus, with my whole heart, my whole soul and my whole strength; and if you see that I don't love you as I ought, I desire at least to love you so; and if I don't desire it sufficiently, I want at least to desire it in this way ... O most sacred Body torn open by five wounds, put yourself as a seal upon my heart and impress your charity upon it! Seal my feet, that I may follow your steps; seal my hands, that they may always do good works; seal my side that it may ever burn in fervent acts of love for you. O most precious Blood that washes clean and purifies all men! Wash my soul and put a sign on my face so that I may never love any one else but Thee.*[13]

---

11. St Ephraem, *Hymn*, 3
12. cf 1 Cor 11:24-25; Luke 22:19
13. Cardinal J. Bona, *The Sacrifice of the Mass*

26.3 The Mass, centre of the interior life.

At that last Passover Jesus offered himself to his Father as a victim to be immolated, as the most pure Lamb. And both that Supper and the Mass constitute one single and perfect sacrifice with the oblation offered on Calvary, because in all three cases the victim offered and the priest who offers is the same, namely, Christ.[14]

We have to make the Mass the centre of our whole life. *Keep trying, so that the Holy Sacrifice of the Altar really becomes the centre and the root of your interior life, and so your whole day will turn into an act of worship – an extension of the Mass you have attended and a preparation for the next. Your whole day will then be an act of worship that overflows in aspirations, visits to the Blessed Sacrament and the offering up to God of your daily work and your family life.*[15]

Let us prepare ourselves for Mass as if Our Lord had invited us personally to that last Passover which He ate with his closest friends. Every day we have to hear in our heart, as if addressed to us, those words of Our Lord: *Desiderio desideravi hoc Pascha manducare vobiscum*, I have earnestly desired to eat this passover with you.[16] Great is Jesus' desire, many are the graces He is preparing for us.

The story is told of Saint John of the Cross that, on receiving the news of the death of a priest who had just been ordained, he asked if he had managed to say Mass at all before he died, and on hearing that he had only been able to do so once, the saint is said to have remarked: 'How much he will have to account to God for.' Let us consider now during this period of prayer how well we

---

14. cf C. Journet, *The Mass*
15. J. Escrivá, *The Forge*, 69
16. cf Luke 22:15

celebrate or take part in the Holy Sacrifice of the Altar; and what can we say of our desires, our preparation, our efforts to prevent other matters occupying our mind, our acts of faith and of love, during that all too brief period of time we devote to hearing Mass and to making our thanksgiving after Holy Communion?

If, with the help of grace, we really work at it, the Mass will truly be for us the centre to which we refer all our practices of piety, our family and social duties, our work and our apostolate; it will also become the fountain where we recover our strength to begin again each day; the summit towards which we direct our steps, our works, our apostolic desires and the most intimate longings of our soul; it will also be the heart whence we learn to love others who have defects just like our own, and who like ourselves have their own less attractive features. If we manage to love the Mass a little more each day, we will be able to say to Our Lord during the thanksgiving after Holy Communion; *I'm leaving you now for a while, Lord Jesus, but I'm not going without you, who are my consolation, my joy and all the good of my soul ... From now on, whatever I do, I will do for you and through you, and nothing will be the object of all my words and actions save you, my love.*[17]

17. Cardinal J. Bona, *The Sacrifice of the Mass*

FIFTEENTH WEEK: SATURDAY

27. HE WILL NOT CRUSH THE BRUISED REED

27.1 The gentleness and mercy of Christ.

The Gospel of today's Mass shows us Jesus drawing away from the Pharisees because they *held counsel ... how to destroy him.*[1] Although he withdrew to a safer place – perhaps in Galilee – *many followed him, and he healed them all, and ordered them not to make him known.*[2] This is the occasion which Saint Matthew, moved by the Holy Spirit, identifies as the fulfilment of Isaiah's prophecy about the Servant of Yahweh, in which the Messiah – Jesus – is prefigured in very clear terms. *Behold my servant, whom I uphold, my chosen in whom my soul delights; I have put my Spirit upon him, he will bring forth justice to the nations. He will not cry or lift up his voice, or make it heard in the street; a bruised reed he will not break, and a dimly burning wick he will not quench.*[3]

The Messiah had been foreseen in his prophecy by Isaiah, not as a conquering king, but as serving and healing mankind. His mission is characterized by gentleness, faithfulness and mercy. The evangelist points out that this prophecy was being fulfilled in the person of Jesus.[4] By means of two very beautiful images the prophet describes the gentleness, sweetness and mercy of the Messiah. The *bruised reed*, the *dimly burning wick*, represent all types of

---

1. cf Mark 3:6
2. Matt 12:15-16
3. Is 42:1-4
4. cf *A Catholic Commentary on Holy Scripture*, London 1953, 696d

miseries, sufferings and punishments which mankind suffers. He does not finally snap the broken reed; on the contrary, he bends over it, straightens it with exquisite care and gives it the strength and life it needs. Likewise he does not snuff out the wick of a lamp which is on the point of going out, but rather does all he can to restore its flame to burn brightly once more. This is Jesus' way of dealing with people.

In everyday life we sometimes say that 'there is no known cure' for a particular disease, and healing is assumed to be out of the question. It is not like that in the spiritual life. Jesus is the Doctor who never considers those who are sick in soul to be irretrievably lost. For him nobody is a hopeless case. The most hardened criminal, the most inveterate sinner, is never abandoned by the Master; He comes to the rescue with a medicine that can heal. Christ can sense the openness to conversion which lies hidden in the soul of every individual. In his patience and love He never writes anybody off; we, for our part, could ask ourselves now if we ever think of anybody as being 'beyond redemption'? If we ourselves are ever unfortunate enough to find we are apparently lost, are we going to abandon our confidence in the One who said He had come to seek and save what was lost?

Mary Magdalen was like the bruised reed, and so was the good thief, and the woman taken in adultery. Peter is won back when he is distraught by the denials of that unhappy night, and he is not even made to promise that he won't deny Our Lord again. He is only asked: *Simon, son of John, do you love me?* That is the question we are all asked whenever we haven't been faithful: *Do you love me?* Each Confession is also, and above all, an act of love. Today let us think about how we love, and how we respond to that question of Our Lord's.

27.2 Jesus gives no one up for lost.

A bruised reed he will not break, and a dimly burning wick he will not quench.

Jesus' mercy for people never faltered for a moment, despite all the ingratitude, difficulties and hatred he encountered. His love for men is so great because He is concerned above all for their souls, and to bring them with his powerful help to eternal life; at the same time, it knows no bounds and extends to all mankind. He is the Good Shepherd of our souls, who knows us all and calls each one of us by our name,[5] and leaves none abandoned on the mountainside. He has given his life for each man and woman. When a soul strays, Christ's immediate reaction is to do all He can to help it return, and we can visualize him watching daily to catch a glimpse of it in the distance. Whenever someone offends him grievously, He tries to draw him to his merciful Heart. He doesn't break the bruised reed, he doesn't finally snap it off and throw it away. Instead, he mends it very carefully, giving it all the attention it needs.

What does He say to those who are devastated by sin, or who no longer give any light because the divine fire in their soul has gone out? *Come to me, all who labour and are heavy laden, and I will give you rest.*[6] *He has pity on the great misfortune they have suffered on account of sin, and leads them to repentance without judging them harshly. He is the father who embraces his prodigal son after he has fallen into disgrace through his own fault. He it is who pardons the adulterous woman who is being threatened with stoning. He receives the repentant Magdalen and immediately opens to her the mystery of his intimate life. He speaks about eternal*

---

5. Matt 11:5
6. Matt 11:28

*life to the Samaritan woman in spite of her waywardness; He
promises heaven to the good thief. Truly in him are fulfilled
the words of the prophet Isaiah: 'A bruised reed he will not
break, and a dimly-burning wick he will not quench'.*[7]

No one ever loved us, or will love us, as Christ does;
no one understands us better than He. When the faithful
of Corinth went about, divided, saying to one another: 'I
belong to Paul, I belong to Apollos, I belong to Cephas, I
belong to Christ,' Saint Paul writes to them: *Was Paul
crucified for you?*[8] That is the ultimate argument.

We can never lose hope. God wants us to be saints,
and puts his power and his providence at the service of his
mercy. Therefore, we cannot pass the time dwelling on our
evil fortune, losing sight of God, getting discouraged by
our failures, feeling tempted to say: 'What's the use of trying, considering how much I have sinned, how much I have
failed my Lord?' No, we must trust in the love and power
of Our Father God, and in his Son, sent into the world to
redeem and strengthen us.[9]

It is very good for our soul to see ourselves, in Our
Lord's sight, like *a bruised reed* which needs a lot of care,
like a flickering wick which needs the oil of divine love in
order to burn as God wants! We never lose hope as long
as we realize that we are weak, full of defects and dirt.
Our Lord never leaves us; we just need to use the means
and not reject the hand that He offers us.

**27.3 Our behaviour towards others has to be full of com-
passion, understanding and mercy.**

Jesus' meekness and mercy for the weak are for us a
pointer to the path we should follow in order to bring our

---

7. R. Garrigou-Lagrange, *The Saviour*
8. 1 Cor 1:13
9. cf B. Perquin, *Abba, Father*

friends to him, for *in his name will the Gentiles hope*.[10]
Christ is the saving hope of the world.

We cannot be surprised by the ignorance, the errors,
hard-heartedness and resistance which characterize so
many people's journey towards God. Our attitude towards
them has to be one of sincere esteem, understanding and
patience. Because *he breaks the bruised reed who does not
give a hand to the sinner, nor carries his brother's burden;
and he puts out the smouldering torch who despises, in
those who still believe but little, the tiny spark of the faith*.[11]

Our friends, all the different people we come across,
have to discover in our friendship or our attitude a firm
support for their faith. If we want to be for them a source
of strength, then we have to be close to them in their
weakness. We have to look upon them with eyes of mercy,
as Christ does, with genuine esteem, accepting the *chiaros-
curo* – the interplay of light and shadow – of their
strengths and weaknesses. On the one hand, we should
bear in mind that *if we are to serve others, for Christ's sake,
we need to be very human ... We have to understand everyone; we must live peaceably with everyone; we must forgive
everyone*.[12] On the other hand, *we shall not call injustice,
justice; we shall not say that an offence against God is not
an offence against God, or that evil is good. When confronted by evil we shall not reply with another evil, but rather
with sound doctrine and good actions: drowning evil in an
abundance of good* (cf Rom 12:21). *That's how Christ will
reign in our souls and in the souls of the people around us*.[13]

The fruits of this attitude of ours towards all the people we meet – very understanding, and at the same time

---

10. Matt 12:21
11. St Jerome, in *Catena Aurea*
12. J. Escrivá, *Christ is passing by*), 182
13. ibid

very highly motivated – are so rewarding, both for us personally as well as for them, that they make it easy to see them as souls, when we find them so much in need, as Our Lord did.

It is not sufficient, writes a contemporary author, to value brilliant men because they are brilliant, or good men because they are good.[14] We must value each man because he is man, whether he be ignorant, or uneducated, or insignificant. And we will not be able to do that unless our conception of what man is makes him the object of our esteem. The Christian knows that every man is the image of God, that he has an immortal spirit and that Christ died for him. Frequent consideration of this truth will help us not to cut ourselves off from others, especially when their defects, their lack of good upbringing and their bad behaviour are more apparent. Following Our Lord's example, we will never crush the bruised reed. Like the good Samaritan in the parable, we will approach the wounded wayfarer and bandage his wounds, and alleviate his sufferings with the balm of our charity. And one day we will hear these sweet words from Our Lord's lips: *As you did it to one of these the least of my brethren, you did it to me.*[15]

Nobody knows the mystery of divine mercy as Mary does. She knows the price of it and how great it is. In that sense, we also call her *Mother of mercy ... Mother of divine mercy*.[16] We go to her now as we come to the end of our meditation, in the certainty that she always leads us to Jesus and urges us to be understanding and merciful, as her Son is.

---

14. cf F. J. Sheed, *Society and Sanity*, pp.30-31
15. cf Matt 25:40
16. cf John Paul II, *Dives in misericordia*, 9

SIXTEENTH SUNDAY: YEAR A

28. THE COCKLE OF FALSE DOCTRINE

28.1 The relevance of the parable of the weeds.

In the Gospel of today's Mass Our Lord teaches us the parable of the wheat and the cockle.[1] The world is like a field where God is continually sowing the seed of his grace; this divine seed takes root in the soul and produces fruits of holiness. Jesus offers us his grace with such wonderful love! For him each of us is unique, and in order to redeem us He did not hesitate to assume our human nature. He prepared us like good soil and bestowed upon us his saving doctrine. *But while men were sleeping, his enemy came and sowed weeds among the wheat, and went away*.

The weed in question – cockle-seed – is a plant that is often found growing in cereal crops in the Middle East. It resembles wheat so closely that even to the farmer's practised eye it is impossible to tell the two plants apart until the stalks begin to mature, at which stage the cockle can be recognized by its slender ear and emaciated grain; it is quite toxic to humans, and if mixed with flour will ruin bread.[2] Sowing cockle among the wheat was a form of revenge not unheard of in those countries. Periodic plagues of cockle were very much feared by the peasants, because they could cause them to lose their entire harvest.

The Fathers of the Church have understood the cockle to be a metaphor for false doctrine,[3] which is not

---

1. Matt 13:24-43
2. cf F. Prat, *Jesus Christ*
3. cf St John Chrysostom, *Homilies on St Matthew*, 47; St Augustine, in *Catena Aurea*

easy to distinguish from the truth, above all at the beginning, *because it is proper to the devil to mix falsehood with truth*;[4] and if error is allowed to flourish it always has catastrophic effects on the people of God.

This parable has lost none of its relevance nowadays: we can see that many Christians have fallen asleep and have allowed the enemy to sow bad seed with total impunity. There is practically no truth of the Catholic Faith which hasn't been called into question. We have to be very careful indeed, both with ourselves and with anybody we are responsible for, in the whole area of magazines, television, books and newspapers, all of which can be a real source of false doctrine and which require us to make a special effort to look after our on-going formation in the doctrinal area.

If we are to be faithful to all the requirements of the Christian vocation we have to be constantly watchful and not let ourselves be caught off guard, because once false doctrine manages to take root in the soul it quickly gives rise to sterility and to estrangement from God. We need to be watchful too in the area of our affections, and not fool ourselves with excuses about how at our time of life 'things don't affect us'; and we should be careful also about the effect of such false ideas on those whom God has entrusted to our care.

28.2 We have to give doctrine by every available means.

Error and ignorance have been the cause of many disasters. The prophet Hosea, on seeing the Chosen People far from the happiness to which they had been called, wrote: *My people are destroyed for lack of knowledge*.[5] We

---

4. St John Chrysostom, in *Catena Aurea*
5. Hos 4:6

too can see great masses of our fellow men steeped in sin and misery, distraught and totally confused because they are bereft of divine truth. Many people are carried along by the latest fashions and by ideas dictated by a few very influential individuals, or let themselves be led astray by false logic, almost always with the connivance of their own lower nature.

The enemy of God and of souls makes use of every trick known to man. We hear about news reports being totally distorted, or even about certain major events that never get reported at all. Television series watched by huge audiences night after night portray totally pagan lifestyles, ridiculing chastity and celibacy, promoting the notion that abortion and euthanasia are somehow acceptable, casting doubt on the value of the sacraments, and in general presenting an idea of life wholly incompatible with Christianity, as if Christ had never come to redeem us and remind us that our homeland is in Heaven. And all this is done with an astonishing energy and persistence. The 'enemy' never lets up.

If we want to follow in the Master's footsteps we can't stand idly by as if everything were irredeemably lost and as if nothing can be done about it. History is not in any way predetermined, certainly not in the direction of evil, and God has made us free in order that we may direct the world to him. This is a task for everyone: every single Christian is duty bound to dispel ignorance from men's minds. And even though some professions have a greater influence than others in public life, all of us can and ought to sow the seed of good doctrine attractively and congenially at every opportunity, in the circle of our family or friends and among our colleagues at work: letting them see for themselves the attractiveness of truth; being ready to unmask falsehood; getting people to attend formative activities like retreats, circles and spiritual direction; recommending them good books on doctrinal topics; and inspiring them by our example to behave as good Christians. Thanks to our steady and unwavering attitude, many people will feel encouraged to tackle this avalanche of false doctrine that pours down around us, and they in turn will become an inspiration for others who are still in darkness. And we will experience the truth of that phrase of Tertullian's in which he describes the pagan world which rejected Christ: *they cease to hate who cease to be ignorant.*[6]

We have to take advantage of the thousand and one opportunities we get in daily life to sow the good seed of Christ – when, for example, travelling, or reading a newspaper, or chatting with friends, or attending to our children's education, or taking part in the activity of a professional association, or voting in an election. Many such opportunities will arise spontaneously, like life itself; and others we will create deliberately, with the help of grace and our native ability, all in the service of Christ: we are his voice in the world.

28.3 We have to smother the cockle in good seed, and not miss a single opportunity.

The spread of the cockle can only be countered by an even greater abundance of good doctrine: we have to overcome evil with good,[7] living out our convictions in daily life, which is the essence of naturalness. We are called to seek holiness in the middle of the world, in the fulfilment of ordinary duties; and this requires us to be actively present in the whole range of human experience. It is not

---

6. Tertullian, *Ad nationes*, 1, 1
7. cf Rom 12:21

enough to bemoan the evils of our time and all their powerful allies, above all at a time *when a subtle persecution condemns the Church to die of starvation, putting it outside the sphere of public life, and above all obstructing its part in education, culture and family life.*

These are not our rights; they are God's rights. He has entrusted them to us Catholics so that we may exercise them.[8]

It is time to come out boldly with all the means at our disposal, plentiful or not, and not to waste a single opportunity, as well as telling those friends of ours who have started to follow the Master's footsteps that he needs them to help many people learn to know and love him. We can ask ourselves now in our prayer: What can I do – in my family, at work, in school, in the societies or sports clubs which I belong to, with my neighbours – to make Christ really present with his grace and his teaching? What formative activities are most suitable for my particular situation?

Fashions come and go, and, through our effort, our optimism, our holy human and supernatural stubbornness, we Christians will manage to change all the things that are steadfastly opposed to Christ's doctrine. The First Reading of today's Mass encourages us to trust in God's power: *You show your strength when men doubt the completeness of your power, and you rebuke any insolence among those who know it.*[9] Nothing is inevitable, everything can be changed, provided there are men and women who love Christ enough and are determined to make their surroundings conform to the will of God. For this we need the help of grace, which is not lacking, and to have each

---

8. J. Escrivá, *Furrow*, 310
9. Wis 12:17

man and woman really to want to be God's instrument in his or her place in society, and show with their word and example that Christ's teaching is the only way to bring joy and happiness to the world. *That is why you have to ... carry your own environment about with you in a natural manner, and so give your own 'tone' to the society in which you live.*

And then, if you have acquired this spirit, I am sure you will tell me with the amazement of the disciples as they contemplated the first-fruits of the miracles being worked at their hands in Christ's name: 'There's no denying our influence on the environment!'[10]

---

10. J. Escrivá, *The Way*, 376

SIXTEENTH SUNDAY: YEAR B

29. REST AND RECREATION

29.1 Sanctifying rest and recreation.

In the First Reading[1] the prophet Jeremiah tells us: *I will gather the remnant of my flock ... and I will bring them back to their fold, and they shall be fruitful and multiply.* The prophecy is referring to the Messiah's careful attention to every member of the human race. *Near restful waters he leads me, to revive my drooping spirit,* we read in the Responsorial Psalm.[2]

The Gospel[3] on this Sunday shows us Jesus' solicitude for his disciples, tired out as they are after an apostolic mission to the neighbouring towns and villages. *Come away by yourselves to a lonely place, and rest awhile,* He says to them. And the Evangelist explains that there were so many people coming and going at that time that *they had no leisure even to eat. And they went away in the boat to a lonely place by themselves. What marvellous things Jesus must have asked them and told them!*[4]

Our life, like theirs, is one of service to Christ, to our family and to society; it is a life of work and of dedication to souls. And so we shouldn't be surprised if we sometimes feel tired and need a rest. In our free time we need to recuperate our energies if we are to serve better and also avoid injuring our health. If this latter were to

---

1. Jer 23:1-6
2. Ps 22:1-6
3. Mark 6:30-34
4. J. Escrivá, *Furrow*, 470

happen it would, among other considerations, have repercussions on the people around us, on the quality of what
we offer to God and and on our apostolic task; it would
affect the proper attention to children, to husband or wife,
to our brothers or sisters, to our friends; our apostolate,
and the attention and formation of the people whom Our
Lord has placed under our care, would all suffer as a
result.

On occasion we may be seriously obliged to take a
rest. Saint Gregory Nazianzen comments that *a cord cannot endure constant tension, and an archer needs to loosen
the ends of a bow if he wants to be able to draw it again
later on.*[5] God wills that as far as we ourselves are concerned we should take care to be in good physical condition, because He expects a lot of us. *See how much God
loves us, my brethren*, says Saint Augustine, *because when
we rest, it is really He who rests!*[6] But we have to rest like
good Christians, in the first place by sanctifying our loss of
energy and loving God in our tiredness when circumstances force us to work without a break for a long
period. In situations of this sort we can draw special comfort from having recourse to Jesus Our Lord, who himself
so often ended his day exhausted. He understands us well.

29.2 The Christian attitude to recreation.

Very often, perhaps for long stretches at a time, we
may not feel in great form and yet have to soldier on at
our business, housework or study. This shouldn't upset us:
it is part of the human condition and very often simply a
sign that we are working hard. *There come days*, says Saint
Teresa in all simplicity, *when a single word distresses me*

---

5. St Gregory Nazianzen, *Prayer 26*
6. St Augustine, *Commentary on the Psalms*, 131, 12

and I long to leave the world altogether, for everything in it seems to weary me.[7] Moments like these are for turning to God, because it means that Our Lord is very close to us and wants us to take the appropriate remedy: to go to the doctor perhaps, and do what he tells us; to get a little more sleep; to go for a walk or maybe read a good book. God allows things like this to happen to us to make us more detached from our health, or to get us to grow in charity, to make the effort to smile even though it may be hard – perhaps very hard. Offering this situation to God can be extremely meritorious, even though we may feel totally dry and with no appetite for devotional practices.

Come away ... and rest awhile, says the Master. Far from being an excuse to get wrapped up in ourselves, relaxation is an occasion to seek Christ, because there are no holidays in Love. Saint Augustine tells us that *whichever way the soul of man turns, if it be not towards thee it encounters pain*[8] – at the very least, the pain of having pushed God aside.

Holiday time isn't meant to be a time for doing nothing. *Rest means recuperation – to gain strength, to form ideals and make plans. In other words, it means a change of occupation, so that you can come back later to your daily job with a renewed energy.*[9] It has to be a time of interior enrichment, a time when love of God is given a chance to grow in a climate of careful attention to our devotional practices and self-effacing acts of service, and when we try in a special way to make life more pleasant for the people around us; their contentment and happiness can contribute greatly to our own relaxation.

Nowadays one gets the impression that many people

---

7. St Teresa, *The Way of Perfection*, 38, 6
8. St Augustine, *Confessions*, 4, 10, 15
9. cf J. Escrivá, *Furrow*, 514

leave their supernatural life totally to one side when planning where to go for their holidays: they often choose resorts which are so paganized that no good-living Christian should be seen there. It would be very silly of someone who normally tries to live in the presence of God, to tacitly endorse that sort of environment by holidaying there, not to mention the danger of leaving themselves open to offending God grievously. It would be even worse in the case of parents allowing their children and other dependants to do so, and as a result suffering what will possibly be irreparable damage to their souls: they would then have on their consciences their own sins and the sins of their children.

For situations like these one could quote the words of Saint Augustine: *What mean you thus to travail and trudge on through these hard and painful ways? There is no rest where you are seeking it. Seek still that which you seek, but seek it not there where you seek it. You seek for a happy life in the very region of death. Not there is it to be found. For how can a happy life be found there, where there is not so much as any life at all?*[10]

In some environments people seem to be totally unaware of the morality of cooperation in evil, and so if we want to live like good Christians, and to have others do so too, we need to refresh their minds about it as the occasion arises, always putting things to them very positively. We shouldn't forget that the obligation to rest is not something absolute, because our spiritual welfare – and our neighbour's – comes before bodily well-being. The unity that there should be in a Christian's life between faith and behaviour demands that the time spent recovering physical

---

10. St Augustine, *Confessions*, 4, 12, 18; cf *Commentary on the Psalms*, 33, 2

energies should not cause the soul to become sick and paralyzed, or at least enfeebled. Moreover, with a little bit of good will it is always possible to find or to set up ways and means of taking a break while having God very close to us in our soul in grace, and to make good use of the time to deepen friendships and to do a fruitful apostolate.

29.3 Observance of Holy Days.

Christians ... should cooperate in the cultural frame-work and collective activity characteristic of our times, to humanize them and imbue them with a Christian spirit.[11] In present-day society many people enjoy more free time thanks to the tendency to shorten the working week with longer weekends and holiday periods, and it is up to us to offer them upright and attractive alternatives in the use of such additional leisure. We also have to get across to them the essentially religious nature of Holy Days of obligation, without which those very special times would lose their meaning – Christmas, Holy Week, Sundays and the other feasts of Our Lord and the Blessed Virgin. This is an urgent apostolate, because as time goes on more and more people are making use of these days to take a break from their daily duties, and perhaps also from God.

Holy Days have a decisive rôle in helping *Christians receive better the action of divine grace and in enabling them to respond to it more generously.*[12] The Mass is *the heart of the Christian feast,*[13] and in it we offer Our Lord everything that makes up our day. Nothing else can have any meaning if we neglect this, our first duty to God, or if it is left to be 'fitted in' at some spare moment, and the rest of the

---

11. Second Vatican Council, *Gaudium et spes*, 61
12. Spanish Episcopal Conference, *Holy Days of Obligation*, 13 December 1982, 1, 5
13. *ibid*

day filled with things which are reckoned to be more important. In a Christian who wants God to be the centre of his or her life, to behave like this would, at the very least, be a sign of lukewarmness. We have to give Him the best we have, especially on feast days, even if to do so means having to make some changes in our plans. If we are generous, we will experience the deep joy that always comes from responding to the love of our Father God.

When Jesus headed off in the boat with his disciples to get away from it all, the Gospel of the Mass continues to tell us that many saw where they were making for and went there on foot *and got there ahead of them*. When Jesus landed He saw a great throng, and He had compassion on them *because they were like sheep without a shepherd; and He began to teach them many things*. That day neither Jesus nor his disciples managed to get any rest. Our Lord's example teaches us here that the needs of others come before our own. On many occasions we too have to forgo our rest, postponing it till later because of people who are expecting care and attention from us. Let us do it as as readily as Our Lord looked after that multitude who needed him, putting to one side the plans He had made. It is a good example of detachment for us to apply to our own situation.

Sixteenth Sunday: Year C

30. MARTHA'S WORK

30.1 The Lord is well taken care of in Bethany. Friendship with Jesus.

My lord, if I have found favour in your sight, do not pass by your servant. Let a little water be brought, and wash your feet, and rest yourselves under the tree, while I fetch a morsel of bread, that you may refresh yourselves, and after that you may pass on – since you have come to your servant.[1] When the Lord appeared as a pilgrim to Abraham by the oaks of Mamre, this is how Abraham gave him welcome. God never forgot Abraham's hospitality.

Today's Gospel recounts the arrival of Jesus and his disciples at the house of their friends Martha, Mary and Lazarus in Bethany.[2] (On a later occasion, Jesus wept when he learned that Lazarus had died. He then brought him back to life). Bethany lies about two miles from Jerusalem. Jesus would stop there to rest in the home of his friends before going on up to the holy city. He felt at home in that place, surrounded as he was by joy and affection. This is how we ought to welcome Jesus, who is in the Tabernacle. We have no more faithful friend than He. He deserves our loving attention more than anyone else.

In this warm family environment the sisters behaved with naturalness and simplicity, even as they revealed

---

1. *First Reading*: Gen 18:1-5
2. Luke 10:38-42

different attitudes. *Martha was distracted with much serv-ing*. She seems to have been the elder of the two – Saint Luke says, *a woman named Martha received him into her house*. She was completely taken up with the work of tend-ing to the Lord and his disciples. Certainly, there would have been plenty to keep her occupied. To receive such a numerous group was no easy task, especially since they had arrived so unexpectedly. Understandably, Martha wants to welcome the Lord in an appropriate manner. We know that at a certain point she lost her equanimity and became frustrated due to her misreading of the situation. Mary, on the other hand, *sat at the Lord's feet and listened to his teaching*. Martha was distracted from her task of preparing the meal. *In her eagerness to get the meal ready for the Lord, Martha becomes preoccupied by a million little details. Her sister Mary prefers instead to devote herself to their guest. She forgets about her sister and sits before him, doing nothing else but listen to his word.*[3] With the help of divine grace, we have to learn how to live a unity of life, which consists of the union of Martha's and Mary's atti-tudes. Our love of God should be inseparable from our apostolic zeal, and our work be well done for the glory of God.

30.2 Working with the knowledge that the Lord is by our side. Presence of God in the workplace.

Showing a real sense of trust in her guest, the elder sister complained to Jesus, *Lord, do you not care that my sister has left me to serve alone? Tell her then to help me*.

For many centuries these two sisters have been held to represent two rival lifestyles. According to this tradi-tional interpretation Mary exemplifies the way of

---

3. St Augustine, *Sermon 103*, 3

contemplation, the life of union with God. Similarly, Martha is seen as the personification of an active life of work. *But the contemplative life does not consist in simply being at the feet of Jesus doing nothing. That would be a disorder, if not pure and simple indolence.*[4] For we must find God in our daily job, transforming *our professional work into the hinge on which our calling to sanctity rests and turns.*[5] We show our love for God through the exercise of the human as well as the supernatural virtues. It is very difficult, perhaps impossible, to have a deep interior life and at the same time live a vibrant apostolate if we lack a serious commitment to our daily work.

For too long a time there has been a mistaken insistence on the supposed incompatibility between secular work and the interior life. Nevertheless, it is there *in the midst of daily work* and by means of it, *not in spite of it,* that God wants to call most Christians to lives of holiness. We are to sanctify the world and sanctify ourselves with a life of prayer that gives divine meaning to earthly tasks.[6] This was the constant message of the Founder of Opus Dei, who taught thousands to find God in their ordinary lives. On one occasion, while speaking to a large number of people, he said, *You must understand now more clearly that God is calling you to serve him 'in and from' the ordinary, material and secular activities of human life. He waits for us every day, in the laboratory, in the operating theatre, in the army barracks, in the university lecture room, in the factory, in the workshop, in the fields, in the home and in all the immense panorama of work. Understand this well: there is something holy, something divine hidden in the most ordinary situations, and it is up to each one of you to discover it.*

---

4. A. del Portillo, *Homily,* 20 July 1986

5. J. Escrivá, *Friends of God,* 62

6. cf J. L. Illanes, *On the Theology of Work*

There is no other way. Either we learn to find our Lord in ordinary, everyday life, or else we shall never find him. That is why I can tell you that our age needs to give back to matter and to the most trivial occurrences and situations their noble and original meaning. It needs to restore them to the service of the Kingdom of God, to spiritualize them, turning them into a means and an occasion for a continuous meeting with Jesus Christ.[7] This involves combining the love of Mary with the 'work ethic' of Martha.

Jesus responds to Martha with that affectionate counsel, *Martha, Martha, you are anxious and troubled about many things; one thing is needful. Mary has chosen the good portion, which shall not be taken away from her.*

It is as if He had said, 'Martha, you are worried about worldly affairs, but you are forgetting about me. You are deeply concerned about important tasks, but you are neglecting the most important one of all, which is union with God, personal sanctity. If your worries lead you to lose presence of God while you work, those worries are not good for you, even though your work itself be good and necessary.'

Jesus does not pass sweeping judgment upon Martha or Mary. He responds to Martha's question with profundity by pointing to what is most important in life, that being the presence of Christ in the house. How often might not the Lord make the same reproach to us? Nothing can justify forgetting Jesus in our daily work, not even the most important of concerns. We cannot put him who is *the Lord of all things* aside for the sake of *the things of the Lord*. We certainly cannot minimize the importance of prayer with the excuse that we are too busy with apostolate, with activities of formation, with works of charity, etc.[8]

---

7. *Conversations with Monsignor Escrivá*, 114
8. cf John Paul II, *Address*, 20 June 1986

30.3 Work and prayer.

We need to have a *unity of life* which is so vibrantly integral that work itself will lead us to be in the presence of God. At the same time, those periods we devote to prayer will help us to work better. *We cannot expect to reach an 'armistice' of some kind between temporal occupations and the spiritual life, between work and prayer. Work feeds prayer and prayer feeds work. This is true even to the point where work in and of itself, as a service done in a professional manner for man and society, becomes an acceptable offering to God.*[9]

To maintain the presence of God while we work we need to resort to simple reminders, little things that will help us remember that our work is for God. He is there next to us as our companion, watching us as we work. It may help us to recall that he is physically quite close to us in the nearest oratory or church. *From there, where you are working, let your heart escape to the Lord, right close to the Tabernacle, to tell him, without doing anything odd, 'My Jesus, I love You'. Don't be afraid to call him so – my Jesus – and to say it to him often.*[10]

All worldly occupations, when engaged in with the right intention, allow us the opportunity to put into practice charity, mortification, a spirit of service to others, joy and optimism, understanding and an apostolate of friendship and confidence. We sanctify ourselves through our work. This is what really matters – to find Jesus in the midst of our daily concerns, not to forget about *the Lord of all things*. And when our daily tasks are in some way directly related to him, we should make an even greater effort to live this *unity of life*. Otherwise, we will end up

9. A. del Portillo, *Work and Prayer*, in *Palabra*, May 1986
10. J. Escrivá, *The Forge*, 746

doing what is, in fact, his work for ourselves, thereby neglecting the Master.

As we finish this time of prayer, we ask the Virgin to give us the diligence of Martha as well as the presence of God of Mary.

SIXTEENTH WEEK: MONDAY

31. FAITH AND MIRACLES

31.1 The need for good dispositions in order to receive Christ's message.

We read in today's Gospel that certain of the Scribes and Pharisees asked Jesus to work a miracle so as to prove that He was the long-awaited Messiah.[1] They wanted Jesus to confirm with dramatic display what he was preaching with simplicity. Instead of serving them up a miracle, the Lord tells his critics that they will have their proof in his death and Resurrection. Drawing upon the figure of Jonah, he affirms that *an evil and adulterous generation seeks for a sign; but no sign shall be given to it except the sign of the prophet Jonah*. With this reference to the three days which Jonah spent in the belly of the whale Christ makes clear that the definitive proof of his divine Sonship will occur with his glorious Resurrection on the third day.[2]

Jonah was sent by God to convert the city of Nineveh. Moved by the preaching of the prophet, the city's inhabitants did penance for their sins.[3] Yet when Jesus tried to win over Jerusalem, the city would not accept his message. Jesus recalls how when the Queen of Sheba visited King Solomon she was amazed at the extent of his wisdom. Like Jonah, Solomon is a figure of Christ. By alluding to the example of these pagans who had become

---

1. Matt 12:38-42
2. cf *The Navarre Bible*, St Matthew, *in loc*
3. John 3:6-9

converted, Christ makes his reproach all the more force-ful: *Something greater than Jonah is here ... something greater than Solomon is here*. This *something greater* is, in fact, infinitely greater, but Jesus seems intent on making his point by understatement.[4]

For the time being, Jesus will not give his critics any more signs and miracles. These people are not disposed to believe, no matter how many sermons or signs they receive from God's Son. Despite the great lessons con-tained in the miracles, if people lack good dispositions those miracles are capable of being misinterpreted. As the old adage goes, lessons are received *ad modum recipientis recipitur*, according to the nature of the recipient. In his Gospel, Saint John teaches us that *though he had done so many signs before them, yet they did not believe in him*.[5] Miracles can help our human reason to believe. But if a person lacks good dispositions and is full of prejudices, then that person will see only darkness.

We ask Jesus in our prayer to give us a clean heart so that we may see him in the midst of our daily concerns. We ask him for a clear mind free of prejudice so that we may better understand other people, ever mindful of avoiding negative judgments.

31.2 Wanting to know the truth.

To hear the word of Christ one has to be listening to him. One has to draw near to him with a clean mind and heart, being totally open to God's message.

One example of bad dispositions is the case of the Pharisees who questioned the man born blind after Jesus had miraculously healed him. *What did he do to you? How*

---

4. cf *The Navarre Bible, ibid*
5. John 12:37

did he open your eyes? The man blind from birth *sees* that his interrogators are deaf to his explanations. *I have told you already, and you would not listen. Why do you want to hear it again?*[6]

The same thing happens with Pilate. Jesus says to him, *For this I was born, and for this I have come into the world, to bear witness to the truth. Every one who is of the truth hears my voice.* The Roman Procurator then utters his famous response, *What is truth?* Having asked the question he does not bother to wait for a reply: *After he had said this, he went out to the Jews again.*[7] He turns his back on the answer to his question. He turns his back on Truth. Without a doubt, Pilate had no interest in an answer because he had no interest in the truth. He is only interested in his own interests, in making the best of a bad situation.

If we are well disposed the Lord will give us abundant light to help us persevere on our journey to him. We will have the joy of contemplating him in the created things around us. There he has left his signature as Creator. We will see him in our work, in joy, in sickness … The history of every person is full of these signs. There will be many times when we shall receive the grace to see him in the intimacy of our prayer. At other times we will see him by means of our spiritual director.

As for those who did not want to see, the majority of the Pharisees, we know that they did not change. They did not convert to the Messiah despite the fact that they had been eyewitnesses to so many of his miracles. Their pride blinded them to what is most essential. They went so far as to claim that *He casts out demons by the prince of demons.*

---

6. John 9:26-27
7. John 18:38

In today's world, many people are blind to the supernatural because of pride, because of prejudice, because of
attachment to earthly things, because of inordinate desires
for comfort and security, because of hedonism and sensuality. *I heard some people I knew talking about their radio
sets. Almost without realising it, I brought the subject round
to the spiritual area: we have got a strong earth, too strong,
and we have forgotten to put up the aerial of the interior life.
That is why there are so few souls who keep in touch with
God. May we never be without our supernatural aerial.*[8]

31.3 Purifying the heart so as to see clearly. Allowing our-selves to be led in moments of obscurity.

*Something greater than Jonah is here ... something
greater than Solomon is here.* Christ himself is at our side!
He beckons to man not as a stranger, but as a friend eager
to share his thoughts, even his life. He wants to give us the
divine solution to those problems which worry us and
sometimes tear us to pieces.

Yet much as sound-waves can interfere with good
reception, so it is with obstacles to our life of faith. These
obstacles can affect even those who have spent many years
in Christ's service, to the extent that they can become
disconcerted and disoriented, unable to see the beauty of
their self-giving. Here are some questions for the examination of conscience of someone in this situation: Do I truly
want to see? Am I fully disposed to want to see, to affirm
at the very least that God's presence can be found in the
circumstances of my life? Do I allow myself to be helped?
Do I explain my situation clearly? Do I reveal my inmost
self without any hesitation?

Pride is the principle obstacle in our struggle. But

---

8. J. Escrivá, *The Forge*, 510

there are other obstacles such as a comfort-seeking environment with its instinctive aversion to sacrifice and the Cross. This environment brings with it subtle tempting attachments which will provide plenty of human reasons for not doing the will of God. Following God's will is a joyful way, but it also requires constant effort and self-surrender. It means being 'savagely sincere' in spiritual direction. It means keeping a lock on our heart and a brake on our will. We need to purify the heart from its wayward affections so that it can be filled with the true love of Christ. It is indeed very hard to appreciate the light when one's vision is clouded.

Laziness and love of comfort are two other obstacles which can affect our struggle. As in the case of every true love, a personal commitment to the faith and to a vocation involves a complete self-giving. Laziness and love of comfort tend to compromise and weaken our commitment of love.

We may experience times when the Lord seems hidden from our view. He probably wants us to look for him with greater love, with greater humility, with greater abandonment to the counsels of our spiritual director. If we make the effort required we will always come to discover the most lovable face of Christ.

The word 'faith' has its roots in the notion of a person's placing himself in the care of someone who is stronger, trusting in this other person's assistance.[9] We put our trust in God. But He wants us to rely on those He has put by our side to help us see. God frequently gives light through his creatures.

The Lord passes by so close to us that we should be able to find him and follow him. Frequent recourse to the

---

9. cf J. Dheilly, *Biblical Dictionary*, Barcelona

sacrament of Penance is an excellent way to ensure that we see God more clearly in ourselves and in those around us. We ask the Blessed Virgin to help us purify our mind and heart so that we can find God in the circumstances of every day.

Lord, I believe in you: increase my faith. I trust in you: strengthen my trust. I love you: let me love you more and more.[10]

---

10. *The Universal Prayer* (Attributed to Pope Clement XI)

SIXTEENTH WEEK: TUESDAY

32. THE NEW FAMILY OF JESUS

32.1 Our union with Christ is stronger than any human bond. The bonds we have uniting us to our Lord are stronger than those we have to our natural family.

In today's Gospel we find Jesus preaching in a house so full of people that even his Mother and other relatives cannot manage to get in. So they send him a message. *While He was still speaking to the people, behold, his mother and his brethren stood outside, asking to speak to him. But He replied to the man who told him, 'Who is my mother, and who are my brethren?' And stretching out his hand toward his disciples He said, 'Here are my mother and my brethren! For whoever does the will of my Father in heaven is my brother, and sister, and mother.'*[1]

On another occasion a peasant woman commented on the teachings of Jesus with words of praise for Mary, *Blessed is the womb that bore you, and the breasts that you sucked!* But the Lord gives the impression of rejecting these words when he replies, *Blessed, rather, are those who hear the word of God and keep it!*[2]

Pope John Paul II analyses the meaning of these words in relation to what Jesus said to Mary and Joseph when they found him in the Temple after their three-day search. Jesus tells them with an infinite love and total clarity, *How is it that you sought me? Did you not know that*

---

1. Matt 12:46-50
2. Luke 11:27-28

I must be in my Father's house?[3] From his earliest days
Jesus was dedicated to his relationship with his Father. *He
announced the Kingdom: the 'Kingdom of God' and 'his
Father's business', which add a new dimension and meaning to everything human, and therefore to every human
bond, insofar as these things relate to the goals and tasks
assigned to every human being. Within this new dimension,
a bond such as that of 'brotherhood' also means something
different from 'brotherhood according to the flesh' deriving
from a common origin from the same set of parents.
'Motherhood', too, in the dimension of the Kingdom of God
and in the radius of the fatherhood of God himself, takes on
another meaning.*[4]

The Lord teaches us repeatedly that doing the Will of
God transcends the demands of every human bond or
authority, even that of the family. Jesus tells us that as we
follow him the more closely in our vocation we will find
that our bonds to him are indeed stronger than those to
our natural family.[5] Saint Thomas explains that *everyone
who does the Will of the Father becomes like unto a brother
to Christ, He who did the will of his Father. He who not
only obeys Christ but works to convert others, to beget Christ
in them, becomes like unto the Mother of Christ.*[6] The
bonds of blood are certainly strong, but stronger still are
the bonds originating in a deep love for Christ. There is no
human relationship, no matter how close it might be, that
is stronger than our union with Jesus and with those who
follow him.

---

3. Luke 2:49
4. John Paul II, Encyclical, *Redemptoris Mater*, 20
5. *The Navarre Bible*, note to Mark 4:31-35
6. St Thomas, *Commentary on St Matthew's Gospel*, 12, pp 49-50

32.2 We need to have a sense of detachment and personal responsibility in order to fulfil the demands of our vocation.

'Who is my mother?' Is Jesus thereby distancing himself from his mother according to the flesh? Does he perhaps wish to leave her in the hidden obscurity which she herself has chosen? If this seems to be the case from the tone of those words, one must nevertheless note that the new and different motherhood which Jesus speaks of to his disciples refers precisely to Mary in a very special way.[7] She is loved by Jesus in a singular way since she is indeed his Mother according to the flesh. But Jesus loves her even more and is more intimately united with her because of her faithfulness to her vocation, to the Will of the Father. For this reason the Church reminds us that the Blessed Virgin Mary *received the words whereby, in extolling a kingdom beyond the calculations and bonds of flesh and blood, He declared blessed those who heard and kept the word of God, as she was faithfully doing.*[8]

In living out our vocation we should find that we are developing an even greater love for our parents, our children, our brothers and sisters. God expands and refines the heart even as He requires our detachment from the things of this world. We need this bigger heart so as to fulfil our vocation, although we should be forewarned that our vocation can provoke suffering in those we love the most. So it was that Mary and Joseph went three days looking for him, *anxiously*. Mary, she who was *full of grace*, and Joseph, the *just man*, did not understand Christ's words to them, in spite of all their holiness. Later on, they understood more while witnessing the events of Christ's

---

7. John Paul II, *loc cit*
8. Second Vatican Council, *Lumen gentium*, 58

life, with Mary enjoying a deeper understanding than Joseph. It should not surprise us, then, when at times our relatives do not understand our vocation.

What a joy it is to take part ourselves in those strong bonds of union with the new family of Jesus! How we have to love and help those who are united with us in the bonds of faith and vocation! It is then that we will understand those words of Holy Scripture: *Frater qui adiuvatur a fratre quasi civitas firma.*[9] A brother helped by his brother is like a strong city. Nothing can overcome a charity and a fraternity which are well lived. *The power of charity! If you live that blessed brotherly spirit, your mutual weakness will also be a support to keep you upright in the fulfilment of duty – just as in a house of cards, one card supports the other.*[10]

32.3 Mary, the Mother of the new family of Jesus – the Church – is also the Mother of each one of us.

For whoever does the Will of my Father in heaven is my brother, and sister, and mother. Perhaps the Blessed Mother actually heard him say these words or some one may have repeated them to her. She knew very well the strong bonds which united her Son and herself. They were bonds of nature and, even more, they were bonds predicated on her perfect union with the Holy Trinity. She knew in an ever more perfect manner that she had been called from all eternity to be the Mother of this new family of Jesus. As Pope John Paul II has written, *If 'through faith' Mary became the bearer of the Son given to her by the Father through the power of the Holy Spirit, while preserving her virginity intact, in that same faith she 'discovered and accepted the other dimension of motherhood' revealed by*

9. Prov 18:19
10. J. Escrivá, *The Way*, 462

Jesus during his messianic mission. One can say that this dimension of motherhood belonged to Mary from the beginning, that is to say from the moment of the conception and birth of her Son. From that time she was 'the one who believed'. But as the messianic mission of her Son grew clearer to her eyes and spirit, she herself as a mother became ever more open 'to that new dimension of motherhood' which was to constitute her 'part' beside her Son.[11]

Much later, at Calvary, Christ reveals to Mary the totality of her spiritual motherhood for all centuries to come: *Woman, behold, your son!*[12] Jesus points to John, the one who is a representative for all mankind. Mary's maternity extends in a particular way to all those who are baptized and to those who are en route to the fullness of the faith. This is because Mary is the Mother of the whole Church, the great family of the Lord which will continue until the end of time.[13]

There is a correlation between the moment of the Incarnation and the moment of the birth of the Church at Pentecost. *The person who links these two moments is Mary: 'Mary at Nazareth' and 'Mary in the Upper Room at Jerusalem'. In both cases her discreet yet essential presence indicates the path of 'birth from the Holy Spirit'. Thus she who is present in the mystery of Christ as Mother becomes – by the will of the Son and the power of the Holy Spirit – present in the mystery of the Church.*[14] The presence of Mary in the Church is a maternal presence. Just as in a family the relation of motherhood and sonship is unique and unrepeatable, so is the relationship of Mary to each Christian unique and unrepeatable. In imitation of John,

---

11. John Paul II, *loc cit*
12. John 19:26
13. cf C. Pozo, *Mary in the work of Salvation*, Madrid
14. John Paul II, *op cit*, 24

who *'took her to his own home', the Christian seeks to be taken into that 'maternal charity' with which the Redeemer's Mother 'cares for the brethren of her Son ... '*[15]

She cares for each one of us as if we were her only child. She watches out for our sanctity and our salvation as if she had no other children on earth. We have to call to her many times a day. Mother! As we finish this time of prayer, we must say to her from the bottom of our heart, 'Mother of mine, don't leave my side! Help me to be always near your Son.'

---

15. *ibid*, 45

SIXTEENTH WEEK: WEDNESDAY

33. HUMAN VIRTUES

33.1 Human virtues act as the foundation for the supernatural virtues.

In today's Gospel we learn how the seed of divine grace falls upon different types of terrain – among thorns, on the roadway worn down by many travellers, on rocky ground and on good soil.[1] God wants us to be like good soil which receives the seed and in due time brings forth much fruit. The human virtues can be thought of as the terrain in each person. If the land is well worked, if a person is well disposed, then the action of divine grace can foster the development of the supernatural virtues. Many virtuous persons who perhaps through ignorance have lived apart from God do have the capacity to receive the grace of faith. Noble human conduct is the foundation for the supernatural edifice. Grace builds on nature.

The life of grace in each Christian is not superimposed on human reality. On the contrary, grace penetrates, enriches and perfects human nature. *That is why the Church requires its saints to be heroic in practising not only the theological virtues but also the moral or human ones; and it is why people who are truly united to God through the theological virtues of faith, hope and love also perfect themselves humanly: they are refined in their relationships with others; they are loyal, affable, well-mannered, generous, sincere, precisely because they have*

---

1. Matt 13:1-9

placed all their affections in God.[2]

The supernatural order does not overwhelm or destroy the natural order. *The supernatural order lifts up and perfects the natural order, working in a manner which is suitable to its proper dignity and nature. This is so because both orders proceed from God, who cannot be at odds with himself.*[3]

Although grace in and of itself can transform people, God normally prefers to have grace work in concert with human virtues. How is the cardinal virtue of fortitude to be sown in a Christian who will not struggle against small habits of laziness or comfort-seeking, who is unduly preoccupied with the outside temperature, who habitually gives in to his moods, who is completely taken up with his own plans and belongings? How is a person supposed to face life's difficulties with optimism, with eyes of faith, when that person behaves like a grouchy pessimist in ordinary life? *None of the essentials, none of the good qualities in human nature must be changed. To suppress any of the good qualities in a man – and there are many – is the worst thing a Christian can do. Develop your character, your human faculties: develop them to the utmost degree. Everything which curtails your expansion, which limits your development, which makes you narrow-minded, which you back for fear of something, is not in any way Christian. The complete purification from sin and evil inclinations which, with the help of God, man has to accomplish, is a very different process from suppressing any part of his true personality.*[4] The Lord wants each of us to have a unique and well-developed personality. Our personality will be the result of our understanding and appreciation for the

---

2. A. del Portillo, *On Priesthood*, 15
3. Pius XI, Encyclical, *Divini illius Magistri*, 31 December 1929
4. J. Urteaga, *Man the Saint*, 41

talents God has given to us, as well as of our effort to bring those talents to fruition.

It is the good soil (these human virtues) that allows the divine seed to take root, to grow and develop unhindered. The work of grace acts to improve the soil itself. The practice of Christian life perfects human conditions because it gives them a greater finality. Man is more human insofar as he is the more Christian.

33.2 Jesus Christ possessed all the virtues in a perfect way.

The Lord wants us to practise all the human virtues – optimism, generosity, order, fortitude, cheerfulness, cordiality, sincerity, honesty. Christ wants us to imitate him, perfect God and perfect Man. The human virtues find their plenitude in his person. When God became Man, He did so in a most perfect way. *He dressed according to the fashion of his age, he ate as everybody else did, he behaved according to the customs of the time, place and nation to which he belonged. He imposed hands, he ordained, got angry, smiled, wept, talked, became tired, was sleepy and exhausted, felt hunger and thirst, grief and joy. And the union, the fusion, of the divine and human was so complete and so perfect that every one of his actions was both divine and human. He was God, yet he liked to call himself the Son of Man.*[5] Christ taught his disciples to aim for human perfection according to the natural law.[6] He formed his disciples not only in the supernatural virtues but also in social decorum, in sincerity, in human elegance.[7] He urged them to be men of good judgment.[8]

---

5. F. Suarez, *About being a Priest*, 87
6. Matt 5:21 ss
7. Matt 5:37
8. John 9:1-3

Christ himself showed regret at the lack of gratitude in those lepers he had cured.[9] He reacted to bad manners and to any lack of hospitality on the part of educated people.[10] Jesus attached so much importance to the human virtues that he went so far as to tell his disciples, *If I have told you earthly things and you do not believe, how can you believe if I tell you heavenly things?*[11]

Whenever we make an effort to be sincere, loyal, hard-working, compassionate, even-tempered, we are imitating Christ, the perfect Model for our behaviour. We thereby make ourselves into good soil which the supernatural virtues can take root in. We should often contemplate the Master and observe in him the fullness of everything human. We have in Jesus our human and divine ideal.

33.3 The need for human virtues in the apostolate.

The Christian in the middle of the world is like a light shining out from a lampstand, like a city set on top of a hill. The first thing one notices is the humanity of the Christian – the good example of integrity, loyalty, decency, bravery. This is what gets people's attention. The human virtues thus serve as instruments in the apostolate of bringing others closer to God. One's professional prestige, friendliness, sincerity, can prepare souls to listen to the message of Christ. The human virtues are necessary in the apostolate. If our friends are unable to see our virtues as reality, much less will they be able to discern supernatural truths. If a Christian were not honest, why would his friends trust him? How can we introduce others to the most lovable face of Christ if we do not follow him in the

---

9. Luke 17:17-18
10. Luke 7:44-46
11. John 3:12

basics? The human virtues may be thought of as the lamp-stand, as the hill upon which the city is set. Many people will appreciate supernatural life once they see it made real in normal human conduct.

We have to let others know that Christ is alive by our sense of peace and joy in the midst of difficult and even painful circumstances, by our work well done, by our sobriety and temperance, by our human warmth extended to everyone. When lived to the full, the Christian vocation should affect every aspect of our existence. All the people who deal with us or know us in one way or another should be able to sense the joy within our heart. *We have to act in such a way that others will be able to say, when they meet us: this man is a Christian, because he does not hate, because he is willing to understand, because he is not a fanatic, because he is willing to make sacrifices, because he shows that he is a man of peace, because he knows how to love,*[12] because he is generous with his time, because he doesn't complain, because he knows how to overlook what is superfluous ...

The world desperately needs the testimony of out-standing men and women who carry Christ in their hearts. There has perhaps been no other time when there has been so much talk about the rights of man and human achievements. Humanity has rarely been so conscious of its own accomplishments. Yet, at the same time, never have the rights of the individual been more brutally pushed aside than today. Those rights derive from the fact that man has been made in the image of God.

Humanity is waiting for Christians to proclaim once again that most fundamental teaching – that we are all called to be children of God. To reach that goal we first

---

12. J. Escrivá, *Christ is passing by*, 122

have to develop our God-given human nature. We must become very human so as to become very Christ-like. Grace will never be lacking to those men and women who prove by their lives that they want to be children of God.

SIXTEENTH WEEK: THURSDAY

34. BROKEN CISTERNS.
THE EFFECTS OF SIN

34.1 Sin is the greatest deception to which man can fall prey.

After their long and difficult experience in the desert the Jewish people were well aware of the importance of water. To discover water in the desert was to come across a great treasure. Wells were guarded more closely than jewels. Lives depended upon their security. It is fitting, therefore, that Holy Scripture should refer to God as *a fountain of living waters*. The just man is described as *a tree planted by streams of water*,[1] which bears fruit *in the year of drought*.[2]

In his conversation with the Samaritan woman Jesus reveals that He is capable of giving souls *living water*.[3] During the feast of the *Tabernacles* or *Tents*, when the Jews commemorated their passage through the desert, Jesus once again spoke of himself as water. *On the last day of the feast, the great day, Jesus stood up and proclaimed, 'If any one thirst, let him come to me and drink. He who believes in me, as the scripture has said, Out of his heart shall flow rivers of living water'.*[4] Only Christ can satisfy man's thirst for eternity, a thirst which God has placed in our heart. Only Christ can give fulfilment to our life. Many

---

1. Ps 1:3
2. Jer 17:5-8
3. John 4:10-15
4. John 7:37-38

of the Fathers of the Church considered the open side of
Christ, that gave forth blood and water, as the origin of the
sacraments which impart supernatural life.[5]

It is in this context that the words of the Prophet
Jeremiah carry a special force in today's prayer. The Prophet laments how the chosen people have abandoned their
Lord. In a more symbolic reading, he is speaking about
sin, about the effect of our sins. *Be appalled, O heavens, at
this, be shocked, be utterly desolate, says the Lord, for my
people have committed two evils: they have forsaken me, the
fountain of living waters, and hewed out cisterns for themselves, broken cisterns, that can hold no water.*[6]

Every sinful act involves a separation from God. Sin
means making a choice between nothing and the living
water that springs up to eternal life. This is the greatest
deception a man can fall prey to. This is true evil. Sin takes
away sanctifying grace, the life of God in the soul, that
which is the most precious gift we possess. Sin always
entails *the squandering of our most precious values. This is
the hard reality, even though sin may occasionally allow us to
achieve successes. Our distancing ourselves from the Father
brings with it great harm to those involved, to those who give
their consent. Sin leads to the dissipation of our inheritance,
which is the dignity proper to each human person, the inheritance of grace.*[7] Sin converts the soul into stony ground
where it is impossible for grace to take root or human virtues to develop. This is the parched ground, the beaten-
down ground full of thorns which we heard about in
yesterday's Gospel, which we shall consider again tomorrow. Sin constitutes the ruin of man, the abandonment of
the *fountain of living waters* for the sake of *broken cisterns*.

---

5. cf *Roman Missal, Preface to the Mass of the Sacred Heart of Jesus*
6. *First Reading*, Year II, Jer 2:12-13
7. John Paul II, *Homily*, 16 March 1980

34.2 The effects of sin.

Apart from God, man will find only unhappiness and death. Sin is the vain attempt to hold water in broken cisterns. *Help me repeat in the ear of this person and of that other one ... and of everyone: a sinner who has faith, even if he were to obtain all the blessings of this earth, will necessarily be unhappy and wretched. It is true that the motive that leads us (and should lead everyone) to hate sin, even venial sin, ought to be a supernatural one: that God abhors sin from the depths of his infiniteness, with a supreme, eternal and necessary hatred, as an evil opposed to the infinite good. But the first reason I mentioned to you can lead us to this other one.*[8] The solitude sin leaves in the soul should be enough to lead us away from it. The road to hell is itself a living hell.

Sin separates the soul from the things of God. In today's Gospel Jesus quotes the Prophet Isaiah, *You shall indeed hear but never understand, and you shall indeed see but never perceive. For this people's heart has grown dull, and their ears are heavy of hearing, and their eyes they have closed, lest they should perceive with their eyes, and hear with their ears, and understand with their heart ...* [9] We need only look round about us to see the reality of these words of the Lord. So many people have lost their sense of sin and have become indifferent to supernatural realities.

Mortal sin causes a radical break between God and man because it deprives the soul of sanctifying grace. The sinner loses all the merit previously acquired by his good works. The soul is unable to receive any new merit. In a certain sense the soul falls under the power of the devil. The sinner's natural inclination to do good is diminished in

---

8. J. Escrivá, *The Forge*, 1024
9. Matt 13:10-17

such a way that it becomes increasingly difficult to perform good works. Sometimes a person who falls into mortal sin will suffer physical effects – discontent, bad humour, indolence, a weak will. This state of soul leads to disorder in the sentiments. It produces harm to the whole Church and to all men, even though externally it may go undetected. Just as every just man who does his best to love God and his fellow man elevates the world, *every sin drags down with itself the Church and, in some way, the whole world. In other words, there is no sin, not even the most intimate and secret one, the most strictly individual one, that exclusively concerns the person committing it. With greater or lesser violence, with greater or lesser harm, every sin has repercussions on the entire ecclesial body and the whole human family.*[10]

Every sin is intimately and mysteriously related to the Passion of Christ. Our sins were present and were the cause of that suffering. We have the power to crucify the Son of God all over again.[11] *How much must He have loved us! What did it cost him to save us? What message for us have the sorrowful mysteries of the rosary, the stations of the cross, the crucifix, the nails, the lance, the corpse in the lap of the Mother? All this for us – suffered for every one of us. All this simply to bestow upon us the grace of being God's children, with all the accompanying graces we require. We sin. What does the price He paid matter to us? That was his most bitter reflection on the Mount of Olives. With divine clarity He foresaw all our ingratitude.*[12]

With the help of divine mercy, because there is no right to grace, the Christian who follows Christ closely will not fall habitually into grave faults. But the knowledge of

10. John Paul II, Apostolic Exhortation, *Reconciliatio et Poenitentia*,16
11. cf Heb 6:6
12. B. Baur, *In Silence with God*, 50

our weakness should lead us to avoid any occasion of sin, even the most remote. We do so by mortifying our senses, by not trusting in our own judgment or our years of faithfulness or our excellent formation. We have to ask the Lord to make us abhor every sin and every deliberate fault, to give us a conscience sensitive enough to detect the smallest sins. We need to purify our soul with frequent Confession so that we do not lose our sense of sin, that sense which seems so absent from our society.

We will tell Jesus, *Help us to conquer our indifference and our sloth! Give us a sense of sin. Create in us, O Lord, a pure heart, and renew a willing spirit in our minds.*[13]

34.3 The struggle against venial sins. Love for Confession.

In order to begin well a serious struggle against sin, we have to face up to our daily faults without excuses, without seeking justifications that would weaken our sorrow and contrition. These faults include omissions in fulfilling our professional responsibilities, lack of fraternity, neglect in our dealings with God, negative judgments towards others, envy, mistreatment of others, neglect of family, our more ignoble and disordered ambitions to be the centre of attention, to be supreme, to have more than we need. These are authentic venial sins because they are moments when the will refuses to follow the will of God, even though this refusal does not constitute a complete separation from him. Our desire to be every day closer to Jesus is incompatible with actions or desires that separate us from him. Every deliberate venial sin is a step backwards on our way to God. Venial sin hinders the action of

---

13. John Paul II, *Homily at Opening of the Holy Year of Redemption*, 25 March 1983

the Holy Spirit in our soul.

Knowing our desire to abhor mortal sin and avoid all venial sin, Jesus gives us this invitation: *If any one thirst, let him come to me and drink.*

The Lord promises to give us *living water*. We certainly cannot keep it in *broken cisterns*. The sacrament of Penance restores the soul, purifies it and fills it with grace. Let us go to this sacrament with real contrition. Then we will be able to say with the Psalmist, *My eyes shed streams of tears, because men do not keep thy law.*[14]

We go to Our Mother Mary, *Refuge of sinners*, to ask that she win us the grace to detest every venial sin. We also ask her for a great love for the sacrament of divine Mercy. Let us examine ourselves as we end this time of prayer to see how often we receive this sacrament, with what love and with what purpose of amendment.

---

14. Ps 118:136

SIXTEENTH WEEK: FRIDAY

35. THE VIRTUE OF TEMPERANCE

35.1 The dignity of the body and all created things. The need for this virtue.

The Church has always recognized the dignity of the body and of all created things. In the Creation narrative, the inspired author points out how God was pleased with his work.[1] Following the creation of man, *God saw everything that he had made, and behold, it was very good.*[2] God honoured man by placing him at the head of all creation. The dignity of man was further enhanced when the Second Person of the Holy Trinity took to himself a human nature and accomplished his task of redemption. No teaching could be further from Christian doctrine than the notion of a radical opposition between the soul and the body. For it is the human person in his entirety, soul and body, who is called to attain eternal life. The Church has been a constant and preeminent witness to the dignity and respect due to the human body. As Saint Paul writes, *Do you not know that your body is a temple of the Holy Spirit within you, which you have from God? You are not your own; you were bought with a price. So glorify God in your body.*[3]

Notwithstanding his God-given prestige, man has constantly to struggle to avoid falling prisoner to the things of this world which God created for his legitimate use.

---

1. cf Gen 1:25
2. *ibid*, 1:31
3. 1 Cor 19-20

This is because of the disorder in creation caused by sin. It seems characteristic of our age that there are many who would treat created things, their acquisition and enjoyment, as man's final end, when their true purpose is to serve as a means to man's final end, which is God. As a result of this mistaken view of reality, many people choose to set aside God's laws, and in doing so contradict the nature of man and human dignity itself. Regrettably, this process of so-called 'liberation' inevitably leads people to degradation and enslavement. To counteract this threat to human dignity we need to exercise the virtue of temperance. Temperance *ensures that the body and the senses fulfil their proper function in our human nature,*[4] a function which has been ordained by God.

He who will not struggle to achieve unity within himself will have a hard time achieving unity with God. Whoever makes easy concessions to his feelings or whims, who has no self-control, turns himself into ground where the divine seed cannot take root. Such a person may even become incapable of making progress in human virtues. As the Lord teaches us in today's Gospel, *As for what was sown among thorns, this is he who hears the word, but the cares of the world and the delight in riches choke the word, and it proves unfruitful.*[5] The Christian life will not flourish among people who worship their bodies, their health, their appearance. God's goods have been converted into *thorns* which suffocate what is most noble in man and obstruct his salvation. *When the body becomes heavy and satiated, the soul finds its mount in poor condition for the ride to heaven.*[6]

We need to be vigilant that we not be carried away by

---

4. John Paul II, *On Temperance*, 22 November 1988
5. Matt 13:22
6. St Peter of Alcantara, *Treatise on prayer and meditation*, II, 3

the siren song of our 'consumer culture'. Many people in today's world believe that the highest aim in life is to have more than others, while making sure they let these others know that this is the case. Yet true success lies in being faithful to God and to his plans for us to be with him forever in Heaven. We know that our hearts can only be filled by God. Temporal goods will always leave us empty and forlorn.

35.2 Through the exercise of temperance man becomes more human. Detachment from worldly goods. Giving good example.

Our Mother the Church has always taught her children the need for temperance. Temperance requires self-control, sacrifice and mortification. By practising temperance we ensure that the divine seed will take root in our soul, that it will not be suffocated. We have to be everwatchful, since *the orientation of modern culture is tending towards a kind of hedonism, a headlong pursuit of the easy life, marked by a desire to erase the cross from the aspirations of peoples*.[7] This phenomenon threatens many of our contemporaries.

Through the exercise of temperance man becomes more human. He who abandons himself to the satisfaction of his instincts becomes not unlike a runaway train. It hurries along out of control, jumps the tracks and ends up wrecked, unable to proceed ahead. In this sad state man's noblest attributes, his intelligence and will, are swamped by his animal powers of instinct and his passions. One acquires the virtue of temperance by performing many small actions which moderate our desires and direct our senses towards man's final end. The person who lives this

---

7. Paul VI, *Address*, 8 April 1966

virtue *knows how to do without those things that may harm his soul, and also comes to realise that his sacrifice is more apparent than real; for living this way, with a spirit of sacrifice, means freeing oneself from many kinds of slavery, savouring instead, in the depths of one's heart, the fullness of God's love.*

Life then takes on again shades and tones which intemperance had tended to blur. We find ourselves able to care for the needs of others, to share what is ours with everyone, to devote our energies to great causes.[8]

To live temperance well means to be detached from earthly things, to give them the importance which they merit and nothing more, to avoid creating personal needs, to exercise moderation with regard to food and drink, to rein in our whims and passions ...

The Lord asks us to give testimony of temperance in the middle of the world. If we were to compromise in this area, we would find it more difficult to follow Christ as one of his apostles. With the example of our lives we have to teach many people that *man is more precious for what he is than for what he has.*[9] In a special way, parents have to instruct their children to believe *in the essential values of human life. Children must grow up with a correct attitude of freedom with regard to material goods, by adopting a simple and austere life style.*[10] And everyone has to make an effort to exercise self-control over the senses.

35.3 Some manifestations of temperance.

The virtue of temperance ought to inform and impregnate every aspect of our Christian life – from our

---

8. J. Escrivá, *Friends of God*, 84
9. Second Vatican Council, *Gaudium et spes*, 35
10. John Paul II, Apostolic Exhortation, *Familiaris Consortio*, 22 November 1981, 37

conveniences at home to the instruments of our work and relaxation. For example, when we rest we usually do not need to run up unnecessary expense or allocate to our leisure an inordinate amount of time. One area where we can give good example in this virtue relates to our use of television and all the other means of comfortable pastime offered by modern technology.

It is unfortunate that so many people have come to live their lives strictly for the sake of 'having a good time'. Specifically, it can be said of many of our contemporaries that *their god is the belly*.[11] The person who lives temperance will try to avoid eating between meals, will not yearn for rare delicacies and expensive repasts, will not consume excessive quantities ... *Ordinarily you eat more than you need. And the natural result, a heavy fullness and discomfort, benumbs your mind and renders you unfit to savour supernatural treasures. What a fine virtue temperance is, even by earthly standards!*[12]

Although most of these manifestations of gluttony are not serious sins, they are, nevertheless, offences against God which weaken the will. Such behaviour can lead us away from the austere, joyful and detached way of life required of Christ's followers. It can act as the *thorns* that suffocate the divine seed, leaving us to wallow in lives of lukewarmness and regret.

To grow in this virtue we have to practise mortification in eating and drinking. Sometimes we will find it necessary to deny ourselves in the matter of desires which are completely licit. The Church gives sobriety a higher meaning when she reminds us that food is a gift of God which should be blessed by him. The Church

---

11. Phil 3:19
12. J. Escrivá, *The Way*, 682

recommends that Christians pray before and after meals. Saint Thomas teaches that although sobriety and temperance are necessary for everyone, these virtues are especially important for the young (who are the most inclined to err in this realm), for women, for the elderly (that they give good example), for the ministers of the Church and public officials (so that they carry out their duties with wisdom).[13]

Temperance also has to do with the moderation of our curiosity, of our sense of humour, of our fondness for hearing the sound of our own voice ... Pope John Paul II has said, *I think that this virtue requires of each person a specific humility with regard to the gifts which God has given to us in human nature. I would recommend a 'humility of the body' and a 'humility of the heart'*.[14] We should put aside temptations related in any such way to ostentation and vanity.

Temperance is an excellent defence in the face of the aggressive tactics of our 'consumer culture'. Temperance prepares us to be *good soil* ready to receive the divine seed, the action of the Holy Spirit. This virtue is an indispensable means towards our realizing an effective apostolate in the middle of the world.

13. St Thomas, *Summa Theologiae*, 2-2, 149, 4
14. John Paul II, *On Temperance*, 22 November 1988

SIXTEENTH WEEK: SATURDAY

36. THE NEW COVENANT

36.1 The covenant of Sinai and the New Covenant of Christ on the Cross.

We read in the first book of *Exodus* that when Moses came down from Mount Sinai he gave God's commandments to the chosen people.[1] The Israelites were obliged to obey the commandments, and Moses put them into writing. On the following morning the people built an altar at the base of the mountain and raised twelve stones to symbolize the twelve tribes of Israel. The Jews offered sacrifice to Yahweh to ratify the covenant. Through this pact the Israelites pledged themselves to comply with the Ten Commandments and Yahweh promised to exercise paternal care over his chosen people. The sacrificial rite was confirmed in blood, symbol of the source of life. The blood was spilt upon the altar, which symbolized God. After Moses had read from *the book of the covenant*, he sprinkled the blood upon those who were present, thereby confirming the special union between Yahweh and his people.[2]

This event was of such great importance that it had to be recalled and renewed on many occasions.[3] The chosen people would time and time again break the covenant, but God never wearied of pardoning them and loving them. What is more, He not only pardoned them, but He

---

1. *First Reading*, Year I: Ex 24:3-8
2. cf B. Orchard and others, *Verbum Dei*, vol I, *in loc*
3. cf 2 Sam 7:13-16, 28:69; Jos 24:19-28

promised to make them a more perfect gift of himself. Over and over again, God speaks through his Prophets of a 'new Covenant' which would express his infinite mercy.[4] This Covenant was sealed by the Blood of Christ hanging upon the Cross. The New Covenant unites God with his new people, all mankind, who are called to become part of the Church. The sacrifice of Calvary was one of infinite merit, opening up a new and definitive relationship between God and man.

Do you wish to know … the value of that blood? asks Saint John Chrysostom. *See from where it springs and who is its source. It flowed from the Cross itself. Its source was the open side of the Lord. The Gospel says, 'When they came to Jesus and saw that he was already dead, they did not break his legs. But one of the soldiers pierced his side with a spear, and at once there came out blood and water.' Water is the symbol of Baptism. Blood is the symbol of the Eucharist. The soldier who pierced his side opened up a breach in the wall of the holy temple. I have found a hidden treasure there and I rejoice at my newfound wealth.*[5] We encounter this wealth every day at Holy Mass, where, before the astonished gaze of the angels themselves, heaven seems to come down to earth. In this sacrifice we are closely united with Christ. The chosen people could never have imagined anything so tremendous. The words of a traditional prayer of thanksgiving after Mass are here appropriate: *I beg of you, Sweet Jesus, that your Passion be my strength and deliverance, that your wounds be my food and drink, that the sprinkling of your blood be purification for my sins, that your death be my life eternal, that your Cross be my everlasting glory …*[6]

---

4. cf Jer 31:31-34; Ez 16:60; Is 42:6

5. St John Chrysostom, *Teachings on baptism*, III, 19

6. *A Selection of Prayers*, Cologne, 1987

36.2 The Holy Mass as renewal of the Covenant.

'Behold, the days are coming', says the Lord, 'when I will make a new covenant with the house of Israel and the house of Judah, not like the covenant which I made with their fathers when I took them by the hand to bring them out of the land of Egypt ... '[7] During the Last Supper, Jesus anticipated what shortly thereafter he was to accomplish in his death. He showed his disciples what he was anxious to do, what he was soon to carry out – the sacrifice of his Body and Blood for everyone. The Last Supper is an anticipation of the sacrifice of the Cross.[8] Twenty-seven years later, Saint Paul would quote these words of Jesus in the First Letter to the Corinthians: *This cup is the new covenant in my blood. Do this, as often as you drink it, in remembrance of me.*[9]

The word *commemoration* harkens back to the Hebrew word which signifies the Jewish feast recalling the flight from Egypt and the Covenant made on Mount Sinai.[10] During this feast the Jews not only remember the past event but they continually renew it, generation after generation. When the Lord commands the Apostles, *Do this in remembrance of me*, he is not just asking them to remember a single moment. He is asking them to renew the sacrifice of Calvary.

This Covenant is renewed each and every day throughout the entire world whenever the Holy Mass is celebrated. The priest performing each Mass *re-presents*, that is to say, he *makes present once again*, in a mysterious manner, the same sacrifice which Christ offered on Calvary. The work of our Redemption takes place *here and*

---

7. Jer 31:31
8. cf M. Schmaus, *Dogmatic Theology*, VI, 244
9. 1 Cor 11:25
10. cf *The Navarre Bible*, note to 1 Cor 11:24

now. It is as if the twenty centuries separating us from Calvary had disappeared. The New Covenant of the Eucharistic Sacrifice becomes especially manifest in the moment of Consecration.[11] It is at this moment that we should make heartfelt acts of faith and love.

Let us take advantage of some guidelines given to priests on how to celebrate the Mass, in order to help us live the sacrifice with ever greater devotion: After uttering the words which bring Christ down upon the altar, *look at the sacramental species with the eyes of faith. As you kneel, see the legions of angels which surround Christ and adore him with profound reverence. This sight should make you exceedingly humble. In the elevation, contemplate Christ elevated on the Cross. Ask Him to bring all things to Himself. Make fervent acts of faith, hope, love, adoration, humility, saying with the mind, 'Jesus, Son of God, have mercy on me! My Lord and my God. I love you, my God. I adore you with my whole heart and soul'. You may also renew the intention of the Mass which you are celebrating, offering up the Eucharist according to its four ends. But when you lift up the chalice, make sure to remember in a very contrite way that the blood of Christ has been shed for you, even though you have oftentimes despised it. Adore him so as to make up for your past neglect.*[12]

We have to fortify our faith and love in these moments of the Consecration.

36.3 Love for the Holy Sacrifice.

How lovely is thy dwelling place, O Lord of hosts! My soul longs, yea, faints for the courts of the Lord; my heart and flesh sing for joy to the living God.[13] With what love

---

11. cf B. Orchard and others, *loc cit*
12. Cardinal J. Bona, *The Sacrifice of the Mass*
13. *Responsorial Psalm*, Year II: Ps 83:1-3

and reverence we should approach Holy Mass! There, in this Holy Sacrifice, is to be found the sublime spring of grace to which every generation will repair for strength as man makes his way towards eternity.[14] There we will find not only grace, but the Author of all grace.[15]

Whenever we prepare to celebrate or participate in the Holy Sacrifice of the altar, we have to do so with an intensity that binds us closer and closer to Jesus Christ, the High Priest. As Saint Paul tells us: *Have this mind among yourselves, which was in Christ Jesus*.[16] We offer the Supreme Sacrifice through him and with him and in him. We offer up ourselves.[17] One detail which will help us foster this union with Jesus Christ in the Mass has to do with our manner of participating in the Liturgy. We need to be *serious, pious and active*, recollected in spirit, our soul united with our body in prayerful harmony.[18] We have to give our full attention to the readings and the acclamations. During the times reserved for silent prayer, we ought to make acts of faith and love. We should ask the Blessed Virgin to teach us how to be lovingly attentive at the moment of Consecration, when we receive Jesus in Communion ... Other details to keep in mind relate to our punctuality and the way we dress. *A man who fails to love the Mass fails to love Christ. We must make an effort to 'live' the Mass with calm and serenity, with devotion and affection. Those who love acquire a finesse, a sensitivity of soul that makes them notice details that are sometimes very small, but that are important because they express the love of a passionate heart. This is how we should attend the Holy*

---

14. cf R. Garrigou-Lagrange, *The Three Ages of the Interior Life*
15. cf Paul VI, Instruction, *Eucaristicum Mysterium*, 25 March 1967, 4
16. cf Phil 2:5
17. cf Pius XII, Encyclical *Mediator Dei*, 20 November 1947
18. cf Second Vatican Council, *Sacrosanctum Concilium*, 11 and 48

Mass. And this is why I have always suspected that those who want the Mass to be over quickly show, with this insensitive attitude, that they have not yet realized what the sacrifice of the altar means.[19]

Our time of thanksgiving after Mass sums up these very special moments of the day which can have such a decisive influence on our work, on our family life, on our cheerful dealings with others, on our peace and joy. Lived in this fashion, the Mass will never be an isolated event, but instead will serve us as real spiritual nourishment. The Mass will give to our actions an eternal meaning. The Mass will help us to live as children of God and co-Redeemers with Christ.

We should try to be at the side of Our Lady during the holy Mass, just as she stood by her Son on Calvary. As we offer up Jesus to the Father, we offer ourselves with him through the intercession of Mary. *Most holy Father! Through the Immaculate Heart of Mary I offer you Jesus, your beloved Son. I offer myself through him, with him and in him for all his intentions, in the name of all creatures.*[20]

---

19. J. Escrivá, *Christ is passing by*, 92
20. P. M. Sulamitis, *Prayer of Offering to the Merciful Love*, Madrid

SEVENTEENTH SUNDAY: YEAR A

37. THE GREAT NET

37.1 The net is an image of the Church, containing as it does both the just and sinners.

Today's Gospel contains a number of parables concerning the Kingdom of Heaven – the hidden treasure, the pearl of great value found by an enterprising merchant, the great net thrown into the sea which brings in all kinds of fish, some good and others bad.[1] The fishermen throw the good fish into vessels. The bad fish are discarded. The net thrown into the sea is an image of the Church which holds both the just and sinners. The Lord teaches this same idea on other occasions. His Church contains saints as well as sinners, his friends and those others who abandon the house of the Father to waste the inheritance received in Baptism. Yet all belong to the Church, though in different ways.

Christ 'holy, innocent and undefiled' (Heb 7:26) knew nothing of sin (2 Cor 5:21), but came only to expiate the sins of the people (cf Heb 2:17). The Church, however, clasping sinners to her bosom, at once holy and always in need of purification, follows constantly the path of penance and renewal.[2] No matter what sins they commit, sinners continue to belong to the Church since spiritual goods still subsist in them – goods such as the indelible character received in Baptism and Confirmation, the theological virtues of faith and hope ... along with the charity that

---

1. Matt 13:44-52
2. Second Vatican Council, *Lumen gentium*, 8

reaches them by reason of all the Christians struggling to be saints. Just as a sick or paralysed part of the body receives assistance from the rest of the body, so it is with the Mystical Body of Christ.

The Church *continues to live in her children who are not in the state of grace. The Church seeks to work against the evil that corrupts their souls. She struggles to keep them in her fold, to bring them back to life with her love. She conserves them as one conserves a treasure not easily parted from. And it is not because she wants to carry around dead weight. She only hopes that through the power of patience, gentleness and pardon the sinner will make his return to her. It is like the withered branch which for lack of sap is allowed time to regain health and flower once more.*[3] The Church does not forget for one single day that she is a Mother. She continually prays for her children who are ill. She waits with infinite patience. She seeks to help them with abundant charity. We ought to bring to the Lord our prayers, works, joys and sufferings for the sake of those who belong to the Church but who do not participate fully in the life of grace. We should especially keep in mind those we happen to know personally who may need to return to the fullness of spiritual life.

37.2 The Church is made up of sinners, but it is without sin. The Church ought not to be judged on the basis of those who have not lived up to their Christian vocation.

The Church is made up of sinners, in some cases great sinners, yet she herself is free from sin. Just as one can say of Christ that he came from above and not from below, so also does the Church have a divine origin. Christ *joined her to himself as his body and endowed her with the*

---

3. C. Journet, *Theology of the Church*, Bilbao

gift of the Holy Spirit for the glory of God ... This holiness of the Church is constantly shown forth in the fruits of grace which the Spirit produces in the faithful and so it must be; it is expressed in many ways by the individuals who, each in his own state of life, tend to the perfection of love, thus sanctifying others.[4] The Church knows that she is not a creature of this world. She is not a cultural phenomenon, nor a political institution, nor a scientific school, but a creation of the heavenly Father by means of Jesus Christ. *Christ has given the Church his words and works, his life and salvation. She has been entrusted with this treasure for all generations to come.*[5]

Sinners belong to the Church, despite their sins. They still can return to the house of their Father, even if it be at the last moment of life. Having received Baptism, they carry within themselves the hope of reconciliation which not even the most grievous of sins can erase. The sin which the Church finds in her children does not belong to her. It belongs to her enemy. It would be a shame if we allowed people to judge the Church on the basis of what she is not.

According to John Paul II, the Church *is a Mother, through whom we are born to a new life in God. A mother should be loved. She is holy with regard to her Founder, her works and her doctrine, but she is, nevertheless, composed of sinful men. It is our duty to make a positive contribution to the life of the Church, to help her progress along the way of faithful renewal. This is not accomplished by negative criticisms.*[6]

When people speak of the so-called defects of the Church in days gone by or in the present, they betray a

---

4. Second Vatican Council, *loc cit*, 39
5. M. Schmaus, *Dogmatic Theology*, vol IV, 603
6. John Paul II, *Homily in Barcelona*, 7 November 1982

mistaken understanding of the nature of this supernatural institution. *Take heed to yourselves and to all the flock, in which the Holy Spirit has made you guardians, to feed the church of the Lord which he obtained with his own blood.*[7] Christ has watched over the Church from its foundation, *having cleansed her by the washing of water with the word, that he might present the church to himself in splendour, without spot or wrinkle or any such thing, that she might be holy and without blemish.*[8] As Saint Paul writes to Timothy, the Church is *the household of God ... the pillar and bulwark of the truth.*[9]

If we love the Church, there will never arise in us a morbid interest in airing, as the faults of the Mother, the weaknesses of some of her children. The Church, the spouse of Christ, does not have to intone any 'mea culpa'. But we do: 'mea culpa, mea culpa, mea maxima culpa'. The only true 'mea culpa' is a personal one, not the one which attacks the Church, pointing out and exaggerating the human defects which, in this holy mother, result from the presence in her of men whose actions can go far astray, but which can never destroy – nor even touch – that which we call the original and constitutive holiness of the Church.[10]

37.3 The fruits of sanctity.

The Church is the source of sanctity in the world. She continually offers to men the means for drawing close to God. *Certainly our Holy Mother shines out spotless in her sacraments by means of which she brings forth her children and nourishes them; in her faith, which has never suffered contamination; in her most holy laws, by which she*

---

7. Acts 20:28
8. Eph 5:27
9. 1 Tim 3:15
10. J. Escrivá, *In Love with the Church*, 7

*commands all men; and in her evangelical counsels which
she proposes to all men; finally, in her heavenly gifts and
charisms, by means of which, with inexhaustible fecundity,
she brings forth armies of martyrs and virgins and confes-
sors.*[11]

As the fountain of sanctity, the Church has produced
many saints down through the centuries. First there were
the martyrs who gave their lives for the faith. Later, history records the testimony of innumerable men and
women who have spent their lives for the love of God to
help others in need. Has there ever been a human want
for which the Church has not shown a maternal solicitude?
Countless parents have led heroic lives of silent sacrifice
while faithfully fulfilling the demands of their divine vocation. Similarly, there are those many men and women who
strive to achieve holiness in the middle of the world by living apostolic celibacy. In sum, the Church is holy because
*all in the Church, whether they belong to the hierarchy or are
cared for by it, are called to holiness.*[12]

By virtue of the holiness of her Founder, the Church,
the Bride of Christ, is forever young and beautiful, *without
spot or ... blemish.*[13] She is always worthy of divine
favour. The holiness of the Church is an inherent characteristic, part of her nature which does not depend upon the
number of Christians nor upon the depth of their commitment to her. The Church is holy due to the constant action
of the Holy Spirit and not because of the behaviour of her
human members. *I would also like you to consider that
even if human failings were to outnumber acts of valour, the
clear undeniable mystical reality of the Church, though
unperceived by the senses, would still remain. The Church*

---

11. Pius XII, Encyclical, *Mystici Corporis*, 29 June 1943, 30
12. Second Vatican Council, *loc cit*, 39
13. Eph 5:25-27

*would still be the Body of Christ, Our Lord himself, the
action of the Holy Spirit and the loving presence of the
Father.*[14]

As devout members of the People of God, we ask the
Lord to increase our desire for *personal sanctity* so that we
might be worthy sons of his Church. *For this sublime mission aimed at the flowering of a new age of evangelization in
Europe, evangelizers with a special preparation are required
today. There is a need for heralds of the Gospel who are
experts in humanity, who have a profound knowledge of the
heart of present-day man, participating in his joys and
hopes, anguish and sadness, and who are at the same time
contemplatives in love with God. For this we need new
saints. 'The great evangelizers of Europe have been the
saints'. We must supplicate the Lord to increase the
Church's spirit of holiness and send us new saints to
evangelize today's world.*[15]

---

14. J. Escrivá, *op cit*, 22
15. John Paul II, *Address to the Symposium of Council of European
    Episcopal Conferences*, 11 October 1985

Seventeenth Sunday: Year B

38. FAITHFULNESS IN LITTLE THINGS

38.1 Jesus is always attentive to our needs. He teaches us to sanctify temporal realities.

Along the shores of the Sea of Galilee people from the surrounding villages gathered to hear the Lord. While Jesus was speaking, no one had given a thought to their weariness, to the hours they had been without food, to their lack of provisions and to the impossibility of procuring any. The people had become captivated by the words of the Lord. They had forgotten their hunger as well as their travel plans. Nevertheless, Jesus had the material needs of his audience in mind. He took pity on those exhausted people who had been following him for a number of days. So, he worked the splendid miracle of the multiplication of the loaves and fishes.[1]

After everyone had eaten, Jesus took advantage of the opportunity to teach a lesson to his Apostles – and to us – about the importance of little things. *And when they had eaten their fill, he told his disciples, 'Gather up the fragments left over, that nothing may be lost'. So they gathered up and filled twelve baskets with fragments from the five barley loaves, left by those who had eaten.* Jesus shows us his magnanimity in two ways: first by giving to the people *as much as they wanted* and secondly by making sure that no food was wasted. He educates by means of dramatic action as well as through insignificant detail.

The grandeur of the heart of Christ is revealed in

---

1. John 6:1-15

both the large and small happenings of each day. *The col-
lecting of the left-overs is a way of showing us the value of
little things done out of love for God – orderliness, cleanli-
ness, finishing things completely.*[2] Christ spent the better
part of thirty years immersed in ordinary, everyday life.
While He occupied himself in a simple workshop, the Son
of Man was engaged in the Redemption of humanity.

According to the Gospels, during the years of his public life Jesus remained in continual conversation with his
heavenly Father. Yet Jesus was fully aware of what was
going on all around him. Having brought the daughter of
Jairus back to life, He asked that she be given something to
eat. Right after performing the miracle of the resurrection
of Lazarus, He told the bewildered spectators: *Unbind
him, and let him go.*[3] Jesus sensed when it was time for his
disciples to get some rest.[4] He teaches us to treat human
situations according to their proper importance. We have
to sanctify our daily concerns. We cannot live in the clouds.
We should be actively involved in the lives of others.

In the Second Reading of the Mass, Saint Paul reminds us of how we should behave towards the people
around us: *with all lowliness and meekness, with patience,
forbearing one another in love.*[5] The Lord is calling us to
live those virtues which make life pleasant for others. This
is how we will demonstrate our love of God.

**38.2 Drawing close to the Lord through the faithful
fulfilment of our duties. The value of little things.**

Gather up the fragments left over ... This would seem
to be a detail of little importance in comparison with the

2. *The Navarre Bible;* note to Mark 6:42
3. John 11:44
4. Mark 6:31
5. Eph 4:16

spectacular miracle, but it is the Lord who makes the request. Our entire life is made up of many things which are very simple and mundane. We develop virtues by our habitual, day-to-day struggle. It is in this struggle that we forge our sanctity. *'Love means deeds and not sweet words.' Deeds, deeds! And a resolution: I will continue to tell you often, Lord, that I love you. How often have I repeated this today! But, with your grace, it will be my conduct above all that shows it. It will be the little things of each day which, with silent eloquence, will cry out before you, showing you my Love.*[6]

The Lord values order, punctuality, care for the books we use and the instruments we work with, our friendliness towards colleagues, our dedication to spouse, children, friends. We have to fight against any sense of routine in our relationships or in our work. We have to want to give new meaning to each day and each hour, even though we may have been doing the same thing for years on end. Life becomes a bore when we give in to any sense of routine. We can find a broad field for living mortification in our daily work – not putting people down, working with intensity, carrying out our tasks with a spirit of service ...

It is possible that we might some day be challenged to save someone else's life at the risk of our own. It's possible, but not very likely. Yet we do find opportunities virtually every single day to give of ourselves for others. This may involve having a smile for someone we don't really like, giving a word of encouragement to a member of the family who seems tired or out of sorts, a willingness to withhold our opinion for the sake of avoiding an argument, a conscious effort to listen with interest to someone we

---

6. J. Escrivá, *The Forge*, 498

don't find very interesting. It can happen that an action of little consequence (a friendly greeting, a tiny favour, a thank-you note) can produce in others a good result out of all proportion to what we might have expected. These simple courtesies help others to feel wanted and appreciated. Social life thus becomes a reflection of God himself. This is in marked contrast to those situations where people treat one another as mere objects, with careless disregard for the most fundamental aspects of human dignity.

Little things are essential to our struggle to live all of the virtues. Faith can be expressed with a momentary act of love when we pass by a Tabernacle in the middle of a city. Fortitude can be lived whenever we interrupt an impure conversation, whenever we take a stand for our beliefs, for Jesus Christ and his Church.

Christ awaits us in everyday life. This is the 'real world' to which we belong, which we need to sanctify by our diligence and 'sporting spirit'. It is here that we will learn to appreciate what He appreciates – those treasures which last on into eternal life. Our hope is that we will be fortunate enough to win the Master's praise: *Well done, good and faithful servant; you have been faithful over a little, I will set you over much.*[7]

38.3 Whatever God may ask of us is within our reach. We need to be faithful even in those areas that seem of little importance.

Our life is made up of many small actions. If we channel all these actions in the direction of God's Will, they will carry us very far. Many small steps will take us to the end of our journey. Faithfulness in little things will steel us in the face of any great temptation.[8] As we read in

---

7. Matt 25:21
8. cf Luke 16:10

the book of Sirach: *A workman who is a drunkard will not become rich; he who despises small things will fail little by little.*[9]

God is asking something of us at every moment, and that something is always well within our reach. As a consequence of our initial correspondence to grace, there follow more graces for the second challenge. If we are faithful, one grace succeeds upon another.

By focussing on little things, we enjoy the added advantage of diminishing our vanity. Who will honour us for giving up our seat on the bus? What testimonial will we receive for having kept order in our work area? Who will build a statue to the mother who smiles, to the professor who carefully prepares each lecture, to the student who really studies for an exam, to the doctor who treats a patient with respect for his dignity?

When we offer up our work we transform little things into big things, human details into supernatural events. Every morning we should make our *morning offering* with greater and greater devotion. We will see the human and divine come together in a unity of life which will allow us to win Heaven little by little. To be faithful in little things we need to have a great love for the Lord. We have to foster an ardent desire to be united with him, to find him in the normal circumstances of daily life. This constant care for little things will nourish our love for God.

Our Blessed Mother will teach us to appreciate what seems to be of little importance, to care for details. This should be our approach in family life, in social relations, in the fulfilment of our duties and in our dealings with God.

---

9. Sir 19:1

SEVENTEENTH SUNDAY: YEAR C

39. LEARNING TO ASK

39.1 We should pray frequently about our divine filiation.

Jesus had the habit of praying early in the morning in out-of-the-way places.[1] His disciples would often find the Lord thoroughly absorbed in conversation with his heavenly Father. *He was praying in a certain place, and when he ceased, one of his disciples said to him, 'Lord, teach us to pray ...* [2] We ought to make the same request: Jesus, teach me how to deal with you, tell me what I should ask you for ... We should do this because we can frequently find ourselves in front of God without knowing what to say to him or how we should speak to him.

The Lord answered his disciple's request with the perfect prayer, the *Our Father*. He pronounced every word with care. He taught them how to put all their trust in prayer to their Father God. *Which of you who has a friend will go to him at midnight and say to him, 'Friend, lend me three loaves; for a friend of mine has arrived on a journey, and I have nothing to set before him' ... I tell you, though he will not get up and give him anything because he is his friend, yet because of his importunity he will rise and give him whatever he needs.* Whenever we talk to God we are most probably asking him for something. This is because we are children of God, children in need. For his part, God wants only to spend himself on us. *What father among you, if his son asks for a fish, will instead of a fish give him a serpent; or if he asks for an egg, will give him a scorpion?*

---

1. cf Matt 14:23; Mark 1:35; Luke 5:16; 9:18
2. Luke 11:1-13

The Lord solemnly promises to be attentive to our requests: *For every one who asks receives, and he who seeks finds, and to him who knocks it will be opened.* Jesus cannot be more emphatic. We are simply deluding ourselves if we think that we have no need of God, having grown accustomed to our faults and failures. *He has filled the hungry with good things, and the rich he has sent empty away.*[3] We should go to the Tabernacle exactly as the sick and the suffering used to go to Jesus in the New Testament. In the words of John Paul II, *What does praying mean? Prayer means feeling one's own insufficiency through the various necessities which man has to face, necessities that are part of his life. Such as, for example, the need for bread to which Christ refers in the example of that man who wakes up his friend at midnight to ask him for bread. Similar necessities are numerous. The need for bread is, in a way, a symbol of all material necessities, the necessities of the human body, the necessities of this existence which springs from the fact that man is a body. But the range of these necessities is wider.*[4]

Humility is a prerequisite to confident conversation with God. We need to realise our limitations before we can appreciate how much we depend on our Father God. Again, from the Pope, *To learn to pray means 'to learn the Father'. If we learn the 'Father' reality in the full sense of the word, in its full dimension, we have learned everything ... To learn who the Father is means learning what absolute trust is. To learn the Father means acquiring the certainty that he absolutely cannot refuse anything. This is all said in today's Gospel. He does not refuse you even when everything, materially and psychologically, seems to indicate refusal. He never refuses you.*[5] He will never abandon us. In our conversation

3. Luke 1:53
4. John Paul II, *Homily*, 27 July 1980
5. *ibid*

with God we have to keep in mind our divine filiation and
our human limitations.

39.2 We should ask for spiritual and material goods insofar as they bring us closer to God.

*For everyone who asks receives, and he who seeks finds,
and to him who knocks it will be opened.*

In our prayer to God, the first things we should seek
from him are spiritual goods – the grace to love him more
each day, to have an authentic desire for sanctity. We
should also ask God for material goods insofar as they
serve to bring us closer to him. These goods can include
good health, economic well-being, getting a job …

Saint Augustine advises us: *Pray for temporal goods in
private, and rest in the knowledge that they come to us from
him who knows what is best for us. Did you ask and not get
what you wanted? Trust in your Father. If it would have been
good for you, you would have received it. Before God, you
are much as a little child is before you. All day long, the child
cries his eyes out so that you will give him a knife to play with.
You wisely refuse his plea and pay no attention to his wailing.
When the child demands to ride your horse, you won't let
him. The child doesn't know how to ride, and may get injured
or even killed as a result. You deny him in little things so as to
preserve more important things. You want the child to grow
up safely and possess all his own goods without danger.*[6]
This is how the Lord is with us. So many times we are like
the child who doesn't realise what it is he is asking for.

God always wants what is best for us. Man's happiness, therefore, is always to be found in his full
identification with the Divine Will. Even though what God
wills may sometimes not seem so appealing from a human

---

6. St Augustine, *Sermon 80*, 2, 7-8

point of view, it necessarily leads to what is in our best interests. Pope John Paul II once recalled how impressed he was by the cheerfulness of a man he met in a hospital during the Warsaw Uprising. *This man achieved happiness by some other way because visibly, judging his physical state from the medical point of view, there was no reason to be so happy, to feel so well, and to consider himself heard by God. Yet he was heard in another aspect of his humanity.*[7] This aspect was the identification of his human will with the Divine Will. We have to want the Will of God: *thy Will be done on earth as it is in heaven.* This is the best path to follow. It is the one prepared for us by the Lord. *Tell him: Lord, I want nothing other than what You want. Even those things I am asking you for at present, if they take me an inch away from your Will, don't give them to me.*[8] If you don't want these things, why should I? *You know best.* Your Will be done.

39.3 The prayer of Abraham.

The First Reading in today's Mass presents us with a moving example – the prayer of Abraham, *the friend of God,* for those cities which had offended God. *Wilt thou indeed destroy the righteous with the wicked? Suppose there are fifty righteous within the city; wilt thou then destroy the place and not spare it for the fifty righteous who are in it?* Abraham tries to save the cities from destruction by giving his beloved God a hard time. He makes his case to God that even a small number of holy people are an *immense treasure*.

The Lord takes such great pleasure in those who love him that He is ready to forgive thousands of sinners for the

---

7. John Paul II, *loc cit*

8. J. Escrivá, *The Forge*, 512

sake of a handful of just men. God is willing to forget the sins and iniquities of entire cities for the sake of the love and adoration of ten people. This is an unmistakable teaching for all of us who seek to follow the Lord closely. We may at times be tempted to question the merit of our struggle when there are so many people around us who live without a care for God and his rights. One day the Lord will show us the enormous efficacy of our humble prayers, of the sacrifices made by a mother for her family's welfare, of the suffering offered up by a sick person for the Church, of the merit of an hour of study or work converted into prayer …

Yahweh was willing to save Sodom and Gomorrah for the sake of only ten just men. According to divine logic, the good works of a few people can outweigh in value the sins of thousands. When we struggle to be faithful to the Lord we are bound to experience the joy of knowing that we are pleasing him. For God listens attentively to our prayer. We ought to pray every day for our society, a society which seems to be moving farther and farther away from its Creator. As Pope John Paul II has pointed out in this regard, *I think that Abraham's prayer and its content is very relevant in the times in which we live. Such a prayer is so necessary, to negotiate with God for every just man, to redeem the world from injustice.*[9]

We finish today's prayer with this resolve, that we must learn to pray as sons of the Father. We have to go to the Lord frequently each day. Truly, like those many sick people in the Gospels, we need to be brought to Jesus to be cured. The Blessed Virgin will teach us how to be daring in our petitions. We ask her to help us do an effective apostolate where we live and work.

---

9. John Paul II, *loc cit*

40. LEAVEN IN THE DOUGH

40.1 Christians, like leaven in dough, are called to transform the world from within.

The Lord teaches us in today's Gospel that *the kingdom of heaven is like leaven which a woman took and hid in three measures of meal, till it was all leavened.*[1] The people listening to our Lord were quite familiar with this phenomenon. They had witnessed it many times in their own homes. By mixing a tiny quantity of yeast into a mass of dough, one would soon have a good loaf of bread.

In reflecting upon this comparison, we should first consider how little leaven is needed in order to transform the mass of dough. Despite outside appearances, the effect of the small portion of yeast is surprisingly great. This thought should lead us to be daring in the apostolate, since the power behind the Christian ferment is not merely human; it is the power of the Holy Spirit acting in the Church. In addition, the Lord takes our limitations and frailties into account. *Is yeast, by its nature, better than dough? No. But it is what makes the dough rise and become good and nourishing food. Reflect a moment, even if only in general terms, on the way yeast works in the making of bread – that simple, staple food which is available to everyone. In many places (you yourselves may have seen it done) the baking process is like a real ceremonial, ending up with a splendid product that you can almost taste with your*

---

1. Matt 13:31-35

eyes. They start with good flour, of top quality if possible. Then the dough is worked in the kneading-trough and the yeast is mixed in. It is a long and patient job. The dough must now be left to rest; this is essential for the leaven to do its work and make the dough rise. Meanwhile, the oven is made ready, its temperature rising as the logs of wood burn bright. The risen dough is placed in the glowing oven and turns into high quality bread, wonderfully light and fresh. This result would never have been possible had it not been for the small amount of leaven, which dissolved and dis-appeared among the other ingredients, working effectively and passing unnoticed.[2] Without this little bit of leavening yeast, the mass of dough would have been something use-less and inedible. In the course of our daily lives we can be the cause of light or darkness, joy or sadness, peace or anxiety. We can be a dead weight holding people back or the ferment that transforms the mass of dough. Our life-time on earth is not something indifferent. We can bring others closer to Christ. We can also drive people away from him.

The Lord sends us out to proclaim his message to the ends of the earth. We are to bring it to those who do not know him personally, on a one-to-one basis, just as the first Christians did with their families, their colleagues and their neighbours. To do this apostolate, we need not resort to strange behaviour. *And when they see that we live the same life as they do, they will ask us, 'Why are you so happy? How do you manage to overcome selfishness and comfort-seeking? Who has taught you to understand others, to live well and to spend yourself in the service of others?' Then we must disclose to them the divine secret of Christian existence. We must speak to them about God, Christ, the*

---

2. J. Escrivá, *Friends of God*, 257

Holy Spirit, Mary. The time has come for us to use our poor words to communicate the depth of God's love which grace has poured into our souls.[3]

Are we leaven in our family, in our place of work or study? Do we show by our spirit of peace and joy that Christ is alive?

40.2 Good example.

We should also consider the fact that the leaven has an effect only when it is in contact with the dough. Without being distinguishable from the dough, but working from within, the leaven does the work of transformation. *The woman not only inserts the leaven, but she also kneads it into the mass and hides its presence. In like manner, you have to mix in with other people and become identified with them ... Just as the leaven is hidden but does not disappear, so, little by little, all of the mass is transformed to the proper degree.*[4] Only in the middle of the world can we bring all things to be renewed by God. It is for this task that we have been called by divine vocation.

The first Christians acted as a fermenting yeast in a world that was in decay. In a short space of time they were able to spread the faith to their families, to the Senate, to the army and even to the Imperial Palace itself. *We started only a short while ago and now we fill the world and everything that belongs to it – houses, cities, islands, towns, assemblies, even unto the army barracks, the clans and the classrooms, the palaces, the Senate, the Forum.*[5]

Without eccentricities, as ordinary faithful, we can show what it means to follow Christ closely. We should be known as persons who are loyal, sincere, cheerful and

---

3. *idem*, *Christ is passing by*, 148
4. St John Chrysostom, *Homilies on St Matthew's Gospel*, 46, 2
5. Tertullian, *Apologetics*, 37

hard-working. We should behave in an exemplary manner in family and social life, fulfilling our duties with the serenity befitting sons and daughters of God. Our life, with all our weaknesses, should be a sign that brings people to Christ. Our example should lead people to think, 'This is the way to reach God'.

Ordinary customs and courtesies, for example, can be the first steps towards intimacy with God for many persons. These customs make life in society more amenable, but they frequently represent only the appearance of friendship. Christians should practise these customs as the fruit of true charity, as manifestations of a deep concern for the welfare of others. They should be the external reflection of an intimate union with God.

One of the most convincing and attractive aspects of a Christian's life is to be found in the practice of temperance. No matter where we find ourselves, we ought always to give good example in this virtue. It should be shown in our sincerity. Genuine sincerity has attracted many people to begin their encounter with God. Our temperance should be apparent at meals, in the way we spend our money, in the way we choose to relax and find entertainment. *Christ has put us on earth to act as beacons that give light, as doctors who teach, so that we might fulfil our duty as leaven ... It would certainly not be necessary to preach doctrine if your lives were so radiant, nor would it be necessary to have recourse to words if your works gave testimony. There would not be a single pagan if we conducted ourselves like true Christians.*[6]

With this focus on our good example of peace and joy, of small but frequent acts of service, of work well done, it will be easier to bring those who live and work

6. St John Chrysostom, *Homily on the First Epistle to Timothy*

around us to the Lord. This is especially true with regard to our apostolate of Confession, which the Church says is so urgently needed in these times. *All one's cares and efforts are of little value compared to the interests of a single soul. He who brings back a lost sheep to the fold has won for himself a powerful intercessor before God.*[7] We should seek to gain many such 'powerful intercessors' by means of our patient and constant labours.

40.3 Union with Christ makes us apostles.

To be vibrant, to act as ferment, we need to be united to Christ. We cannot afford to allow our love for the Lord to weaken, since it is the interior strength which drives our apostolate. Without this union, all of our work and effort will be without fruit. There have always been those who believed they could transform the world by their own efforts. How quickly have their hopes been dashed to the ground! It is as if to fulfil the words of the Lord: *Apart from me you can do nothing.*[8]

If leaven is not used for fermenting, it rots. There are two ways leaven can disappear, either by giving life to dough, or by being wasted, a perfect tribute to selfishness and barrenness.[9] The Christian wastes away when he gives in to lukewarmness, that being a distaste for the things of God and a preoccupation with self. A Christian acts as leaven when his faith is proved by deeds. Love for Christ is the source of all apostolate; it is what makes the Christian into leaven. We have to foster this love continually through personal prayer and the frequent reception of the sacraments. *It is necessary that you be a 'man of God', a man of*

---

7. St Thomas de Villanueva, *Homily on Sunday 'in albis'*, 1, c, pp. 900-901
8. John 15:5
9. J. Escrivá, *Friends of God*, 258

*interior life, a man of prayer and of sacrifice. Your aposto-
late must be the overflow of your life 'within'.*[10]

We might measure our love for God by the amount of
effort we put into influencing others at work, at home, and
all around us.

If we want to become daring in our ordinary life we
need only look to Our Lady. *The perfect example of this
type of spiritual and apostolic life is the most Blessed Virgin
Mary, Queen of Apostles, who while leading the life common to all here on earth, one filled with family concerns
and labours, was always intimately united with her Son and
in an entirely unique way cooperated in the work of the
Saviour.*[11]

---

10. *idem, The Way*, 961
11. Second Vatican Council, Decree, *Apostolicam actuositatem*, 4

SEVENTEENTH WEEK: TUESDAY

41. THE FRIENDS OF GOD

41.1 Friendship with Jesus.

During their long journey through the desert, the chosen people would set up the *tent of meeting* outside of their camp. It was a holy site, away from the business of the world. To visit the Lord one had to leave the camp. It was there that Moses went to plead for his people before the Lord: *Thus the Lord used to speak to Moses face to face, as a man speaks to his friend.*[1]

There are a number of occasions when Holy Scripture reveals God to be a friend of men. Through the Prophet Isaiah God speaks of *Abraham, my friend.*[2] The chosen people rely on this friendship to obtain pardon and divine protection. Even more, all of Revelation tends towards the formation of a people who are friends with God, bound to him by an intimate Covenant which is continually renewed. *Through this revelation, therefore, the invisible God out of the abundance of his love speaks to men as friends and lives among them, so that He may invite and take them into fellowship with himself.*[3] This divine plan came to fruition in the fullness of time when the Son of God, the Second Person of the Holy Trinity, became man. Friendship presupposes a certain equality and personal contact,[4] but the distance between God and man

---
1. *First Reading*, Year I: Ex 33:11
2. cf Is 41:8
3. Second Vatican Council, *Dei Verbum*, 2
4. cf St Thomas, *Summa Theologiae*, 2-2, q 23, a 1

is infinite. God took on a human nature so that man could take a part in his divinity by means of sanctifying grace.[5]

Friendship requires mutual love. God reached out to us, and, thus, we were able to correspond. We love him because *he first loved us*.[6] Man corresponds by accepting God's love, opening his soul to him, allowing himself to be loved and expressing his own love in deeds.

The essence of the friendship between God and men is to be found in the nature of charity, which is a supernatural gift. *God's love has been poured into our hearts*.[7] This gift allows us to love God with the same love by which he loves us. Jesus says to us, *As the Father has loved me, so have I loved you; abide in my love*.[8] Jesus prays to his Father: *That the love with which thou hast loved me may be in them, and I in them*.[9] The Christian's joy is rooted in the sure knowledge that God loves him. For God said: *You are my friends* ... [10] What a great joy it is to be able to call ourselves 'friends of God'!

In the course of his earthly life Our Lord was always open to friendship with those who approached him. On some occasions it was He who took the initiative to bring people to himself, as in the cases of Zacchaeus and that of the Samaritan woman. He was a friend to his disciples, and they were quite aware of his concern. When they didn't understand something, they would draw close to him with confidence, as is shown in today's Gospel. They ask the Lord: *Explain to us the parable* ... [11] So the Lord takes them apart and reveals to them the meaning of his teachings. The

---

5. *ibid*
6. 1 John 4:19
7. cf Rom 5:5
8. John 15:9
9. John 17:26
10. John 15:13-14
11. Matt 13:36-43

disciples joined in Christ's happiness and in Christ's worries. Christ encouraged them whenever necessary.

In a like manner the Lord now offers his friendship to us from the Tabernacle. There He will console us, encourage us, pardon us. From the Tabernacle, as in the *tent of meeting*, the Lord speaks with everyone *face to face, as a man speaks to his friend*. Here there is the great difference that our temples house the God made Man, Jesus, the same one who was born of the Blessed Virgin Mary; he who was to die for us on a cross.

41.2 Jesus Christ, the perfect model of true friendship.

Jesus enjoyed speaking with everyone who came to see him, and with those he met along the road. He took advantage of those moments to enter into souls, to raise up hearts to a higher plane. If the person concerned was well disposed, Jesus would give him or her the grace to be converted and make a commitment to his service. He also wants to speak with us in the time of prayer. For this to happen, we have to be willing to talk and be open to real friendship. *He himself has changed us from being servants to being friends, as he clearly stated: 'You are my friends if you do what I command you' (John 15:14). He has given us a model which we should imitate. As a result, we have to give our willingness as a friend, telling him what we have in our soul and paying close attention to what He carries in his heart. Once we open up our soul, He will reveal his own. The Lord has declared: 'I have called you friends, for all that I have heard from my Father I have made known to you' (John 15:14). The true friend hides nothing from his friend. He reveals all of his spirit, just as Jesus poured into the hearts of the Apostles the mysteries of the Father.*[12]

---

12. St Ambrose, *About the work of ministers*, 3, 135

Christians should be men and women with a great capacity for friendship, because close contact with Jesus Christ prepares us to put aside our egoism, our excessive preoccupation with personal problems. We can thus be open to all those who meet us along the way, even though they be of different ages, interests, cultures or positions. Real friendship is not born of a mere occasional meeting, or simply from mutual need of assistance. Not even camaraderie, a shared task or the same roof will necessarily lead to friendship. Two people who cross paths every day on the same escalator or the same bus, or in the same office, are not thought to be friends. Neither is mutual sympathy, in itself, a proof of genuine friendship.

According to Saint Thomas,[13] not all love equals friendship, but only that love which involves benevolence. This is the attitude where we care for someone in such a way that we want that person's good. There is a greater possibility of friendship when there is a greater reason to share the good which one possesses. *True friends are those who have something to give and, at the same time, have sufficient humility to receive. This behaviour is proper to virtuous men. When vice is shared it does not produce friendship, but complicity, which is not the same thing. Evil can never be legitimized by a fake friendship.*[14] Sin never joins people together in friendship or love.

We Christians should give our friends understanding, attention, encouragement, consolation, optimism and joy, along with many acts of service. But, above all, we should give them the greatest good we have, which is Christ himself, the 'Best Friend' of all. True friendship leads to apostolate, we share the wonderful goods of the faith.

---

13. St Thomas, *loc cit*
14. J. Abad, *Faithfulness*, Madrid 1987

41.3 Fostering friendship with the people around us. Apostolate and friendship.

Thus the Lord used to speak to Moses face to face, as a man speaks to his friend. He who lives in friendship with God will understand more readily the value of friendship in itself, and, without instrumentalizing it, will be the cause of a vibrant apostolate.

A faithful friend is a sturdy shelter – he that has found one has found a treasure. There is nothing so precious as a faithful friend, and no scales can measure his excellence.[15] Friendship has to be protected and defended against the forgetfulness which comes with the passage of time. It also has to be safeguarded from envy, which is usually what is the most corruptive force.[16] Hopefully, we will one day be able to echo those words at the close of one man's autobiography, *Of one thing I can boast. I believe that I have never lost a single friend.*

Friends are expected to be loyal, to be faithful in difficulties, to overcome the test of time and contradictions, to come to the defence of one another in the hour of need. As Saint Ambrose counsels, *Be steadfast in true friendship, because there is nothing so precious in human relations. It is a great consolation in this life to have a friend to whom we can open our heart. It helps a lot to have a friend to share our joys and sorrows, and to sustain us in hard times.*[17]

We should foster sincere friendships with our neighbours, with our partners at work, with those persons we run into on a frequent basis. We should strive to be friends with our Guardian Angel. *We all need a lot of company, company from Heaven and company on earth. Have great*

---

15. Sir 6:14-17
16. cf St Basil, *Homily on envy*
17. St Ambrose, *op cit*, 3, 134

devotion to the Holy Angels! Friendship is a very human thing, but it is also very much a thing of God; just as our life is both human and divine.[18] Our Guardian Angel will not be put off by our moods and defects. He knows our weaknesses, and in spite of them he loves us very much.[19]

Over and above all friendships we must work to strengthen our bonds with *that great friend, who will never fail you.*[20] We can find him with ease. He is always ready to receive us, to stay with us as long as we desire. *Go about the world as you will, change your home as often as you will, in the nearest Catholic Church your Friend is always there, and day by day He is at home to you.*[21] There we can speak with him face to face, as a man speaks to his friend. He is forever waiting for us. He wants us to come and visit him … and listen to him. In him we will truly learn how to be friends of our friends. We will be open to every sincere friendship, knowing that this is the natural road for Christ, our Friend, to enter into souls.

18. J. Escrivá, *Friends of God*, 315
19. cf A. Vazquez de Prada, *On Friendship*, Madrid 1956
20. cf J. Escrivá, *The Way*, 88
21. R. A. Knox, *Pastoral Sermons*, 280

42. THE TREASURE AND THE PEARL OF GREAT VALUE

42.1 A divine vocation is something of immense value and a proof of special love by God.

The kingdom of heaven is like treasure hidden in a field, which a man found and covered up; then in his joy he goes and sells all that he has and buys that field. Again, the kingdom of heaven is like a merchant in search of fine pearls, who, on finding one pearl of great value, went and sold all that he had and bought it.[1]

With these two parables from today's Gospel Jesus describes the great worth of the Kingdom of Heaven, as well as how people should pursue it. The treasure and the pearl are images which have been traditionally used to express the grandeur of divine vocation, the way to follow Christ in this life so as to be with him forever in the next.

The treasure signifies that abundance of gifts which one receives with a vocation – grace to overcome obstacles, to grow in fidelity day by day, to do apostolate. The pearl represents the beauty and splendour of the call. Not only is it something of great worth, but it is also the most perfect ideal which a person can follow.

There is a key difference between the two parables with respect to the prizes. The discovery of the pearl presupposes a great amount of effort, a search, while the

---

1. Matt 13:44-45

treasure buried in the field seems to have been discovered almost by accident.[2] This is how it is with Jesus and the way He calls people. Many find their vocation almost without looking. Other people are restless in their hearts until they find the pearl of great value. In the latter case, it is God who sows the restlessness in the soul. Many have said to our Lord in the intimacy of their souls, *All these I have observed; what do I still lack?*[3] Whether the search has been a rapid one or long-drawn-out, the prize is of enormous worth. *It is ... an immense honour, a motive for a great and holy pride, a mark of predilection, a very special affection that God has shown at a particular time, but which has been in his mind from all eternity.*[4]

Once a person has discovered his vocation he has to make an effort to live up to it. The Lord calls and invites, but He will not force our will.

After the pearl has been discovered or the treasure found, one more step is required. It is the personal response – which is identical in both parables. The man *went and sold all that he had and bought it*. Generosity and detachment are indispensable conditions for perseverance in a vocation. *You wrote ... This passage from the Gospel has taken root in my soul. I had read it so many times before, without grasping its meaning, its divine flavour. Yes, 'everything'. The prudent man has to sell everything to obtain the treasure – the precious pearl of Glory.*[5] There is nothing in the whole wide world of such great value!

---

2. F. M. Moschner, *Parables of the Kingdom of Heaven*, Madrid, 1957
3. Matt 19:20
4. J. Escrivá, *The Forge*, 18
5. *ibid*, 993

42.2 God plays a part in the life of every person. He beckons to everyone.

As soon as someone has discovered his divine vocation, the disparate pieces of his past life seem to come together. What had previously been a riddle or a mystery is now clearly understood – why we got to know a certain person, the special helps we experienced at different moments ... The vocation also casts its light upon our future life, which we now see to be full of meaning.[6]

Neither of the protagonists in the parables showed hesitation or regret at the thought of selling all that they possessed. Their new wealth was so tremendous that nothing could put it in the shade. The same reaction holds true for those who give all of their love to Christ. They give all and they get all. The Lord makes a point in order to emphasise the joy that accompanies the sale of the goods. We might wonder what these men were selling – a house, furniture, ornaments ... things that represented years of work. But they sold everything, without haggling, without a lot of 'hemming and hawing', with joy. They sold everything because they knew very well the worth of the treasure they would be getting in exchange. Beside this wealth, all things pale in importance.

God plays a part in the life of every person, and does so in a concrete way, at a certain age, in a special situation ... He challenges us according to the nature of these circumstances, foreseen by him from all eternity. Jesus passes by and beckons. To some, He calls *at the first hour*,[7] when they are young. He asks them for their ambitions, their hopes and dreams, all of which seem so full of promise. Others are called when they have reached an age of

_____

6. cf F. Suarez, *Mary of Nazareth*, 89
7. cf Matt 20:1 ss

maturity. Still others are called in their final years. The Lord finds the majority of these men and women immersed in the middle of the world. He prefers them to remain in the world, that they may sanctify the world through the exercise of their professional work. The Lord finds others who are married. He asks them to sanctify the family, with all its joys and sorrows.

Regardless of what our age happens to be when we receive our vocation, we will find that the Lord will give it to us along with a wonderful interior youthfulness. *Ecce nova facio omnia*,[8] says the Lord. I can renew all things. I can teach you to throw off routine in your life, to raise your vision to a higher plane. What, then, is the best age at which to give oneself to the Lord? The age when God calls. The most important thing is to be generous with him, without questioning God's timetable. It is never too late to follow him. And it is never too soon.

42.3 Generosity in response to God's call.

... *the kingdom of heaven is like a merchant in search of fine pearls, who, on finding one pearl of great value, went and sold all that he had and bought it.* Saint Gregory the Great has written that nothing has the slightest value compared to that one pearl. The soul gives up everything for the sake of that treasure, forsaking all that it had found beautiful in the world. The splendour of that finest of pearls has captured the soul's complete attention.[9]

Whoever is called, no matter what his or her personal circumstances, ought to give the Lord all He asks for. Since circumstances vary, giving everything often does not mean that everyone gives in the same way. For example, a

---

8. Rev 2:2-6
9. cf St Gregory the Great, *Homilies on the Gospels*, 11

married person cannot abandon what belongs to his family – love for the spouse, dedication to the welfare and the education of the children ... On the contrary, giving everything for this person entails living the same life in *an entirely new manner*, which means doing a better job of fulfilling one's ordinary duties. *In the real world of the husband and wife who belatedly discover the vocational meaning of matrimony, this 'discovery' always appears as part of their Christian vocation. Their response is an important aspect of their total obedience in faith.*[10]

To follow our Lord more closely we cannot be content to remain in our own little world. There should be no doubt in our minds that clarity has to be brought to souls. It is necessary that we enter into our environment so as to transform it from within. We should increase the number of our friendships, giving light to many souls.

The greatest event of our life is our receiving the calling from our Lord, just as it was for those he called on the shores of the lake. Yet to follow Christ wholeheartedly is never easy. The person who enjoys a more or less steady job, who thinks that the pattern of his life is 'set', should recognize the danger lurking in this false tranquillity, which may even be considered one's rightful due. Christ asks us to break with routine, to cast aside the mediocre, to go beyond a life of compromise. With the divine vocation Christ challenges us to undergo a profound change in our daily conduct. God asks for everything, including whatever we may have been reserving for ourselves. He gives us light to see our failings, which we may have up till now looked upon as beyond reforming, but which turn out to be the price for securing the pearl of great value. It is Christ himself who seeks us out, saying, *You did not*

---

10. P. Rodriguez, *Vocation, Work, Contemplation*, Pamplona, 1986

choose me, but I chose you.[11] And when Christ calls, He gives at the same time the graces we will need to follow him, from the beginning of the way and throughout the rest of our life.

Saint Joseph, our Father and Lord, found the treasure of his life and the *pearl of great value* in his mission of watching over Jesus and Mary here on earth. Today we ask him to help us to live up to whatever God wants of us, and that we do so with generosity and joy. We rest in the knowledge that nothing is so worthwhile as the fulfilment of one's proper vocation.

---

11. John 15:16

SEVENTEENTH WEEK: THURSDAY

43. CHRIST'S PRESENCE
IN THE TABERNACLE

43.1 God lives in our midst.

Throughout the Old Testament God makes known his intention of having an ongoing presence among men. The *tent of meeting* was the first temple to God in the desert. Upon the tent there came to rest a cloud which symbolized the glory of God and his presence. *Then the cloud covered the tent of meeting, and the glory of the Lord filled the tabernacle.*[1] The cloud was a sign of the divine presence.[2]

Much later, the Temple of Jerusalem was the place where the Israelites worshipped God.[3] It was the place they had been longing for while they were in the desert. They would recall the enthusiasm of old when they would go to the house of the Lord singing songs of joy and praise: *How lovely is thy dwelling place, O Lord of hosts! My soul longs, yea, faints for the courts of the Lord; my heart and flesh sing for joy to the living God.*[4] To be far from the sanctuary was to be deprived of true happiness. *My soul thirsts for God, for the living God. When shall I come and behold the face of God?*[5]

In the fullness of time, the Word became flesh. In the

---

1. *First Reading*, Year I: Ex 40:34
2. cf Num 12:5; 1 Kings 8:10-11
3. cf Is 1:12; Ex 23:15-17
4. *Responsorial Psalm*, Year I: Ps 83:1-3
5. Ps 42:3

moment of the Incarnation the power of the Most High overshadowed Our Lady.[6] This is an expression of the omnipotence of God. Following upon the Incarnation, the Virgin became the Tabernacle of God. The Word of God *dwelt among us*.[7] *Saint John uses a Greek verb for 'dwelt' which originally meant 'to pitch one's tent', hence, to live in a place. The careful reader of Scripture will immediately think of the tabernacle, or tent, in the period of the exodus from Egypt, where God showed his presence before all the people of Israel through certain signs of his glory such as the cloud covering the tent … In many passages of the Old Testament it is announced that God 'will dwell in the midst of the people' (cf for example, Jer 7:3; Ezek 43:9; Sir 24:8). These signs of God's presence, first in the pilgrim Tent of the Ark in the desert and then in the Temple of Jerusalem, are followed by the most wonderful form of God's presence among us – Jesus Christ, perfect God and perfect Man, in whom the ancient promise is fulfilled in a way that far exceeded men's greatest expectations. Also the promise made through Isaiah about the 'Emmanuel' or 'God-with-us' (Is 7:14; cf Matt 1:23) is completely fulfilled through this dwelling of the Incarnate Son of God among us.*[8] From that time onwards, we can say with exactitude that God lives among us. We can be next to him every day, closer to him than anyone might imagine possible. God truly dwells among us!

43.2 Christ is present in the Tabernacle.

From the moment of the Incarnation we can affirm that God is with us in the personal presence of Jesus Christ. As both true God and true Man, Jesus is closer to

---

6. cf Luke 1:35
7. John 1:14
8. *The Navarre Bible*, St John, 50

us than any other being. Jesus is *God-with-us*. In earlier times the Israelites would say that God was 'with them'. Now we can say this in a very literal sense. When Christ travelled about Palestine, He made an effort to preach in many towns. *And when Jesus had finished these parables, he went away from there,*[9] we read in today's Gospel. God left one town to go and meet other people. When the priest consecrates the host during Holy Mass, he brings Christ to the altar with his Holy Humanity. He is there in the Eucharist with a special presence for as long as the sacramental species last. This presence affects the Body of Christ in a direct way and the Three Persons of the Holy Trinity in an indirect way. The Word is tied to Christ's Humanity, while the Father and the Holy Spirit are related by the mutual immanence of their divine Persons.[10] Christ is really present in the Tabernacle with his Body, Blood, Soul and Divinity. It can be said quite literally that 'God is here', close to me. *My Lord and my God, I firmly believe that you are here, that you see me, that you hear me ...*

Down through the centuries the Church has developed a precise way of describing this eucharistic presence, often requiring such exact definition to counter erroneous beliefs. The eucharistic presence is a *real* presence. It is not symbolic, nor does it signify or insinuate any image. The eucharistic presence is a *true* presence. It is not fictitious or merely the product of the imagination or the will. It is *substantial*, because the words of the consecration spoken by the priest change the substance of the bread and the wine into the Body and Blood of Christ. *Every theological explanation which seeks some understanding of this mystery must, in order to be in accord with*

---

9. Matt 13:53
10. cf Council of Trent, Decree, *De Sanctissima Eucharistia*, ch. 11

*Catholic faith, maintain that in the reality itself, indepen-
dently of our mind, the bread and wine have ceased to exist
after the Consecration, so that it is the adorable Body and
Blood of the Lord Jesus that from then on are really before
us under the sacramental species of bread and wine ...* [11] *As
a result of transubstantiation, the species of bread and wine
... contain a new 'reality' which we may justly term 'onto-
logical'. Not that there lies under those species what was
already there before, but something quite different; and that
not only because of the faith of the Church, but in objective
reality ...* [12]

Jesus is present in our Tabernacles whether or not we
take advantage of this ineffable wonder. He is there, with
his Body, his Blood, his Soul and his Divinity. God made
Man. He could not be closer. The Church possesses the
Author of all grace and the cause of our sanctification. We
may venture to say that the eucharistic presence of Christ
is the sacramental prolongation of the Incarnation.

From the Tabernacle Jesus invites us to bring to him
our concerns and our petitions. In the visit to the Blessed
Sacrament and other acts of worship offered to the Holy
Eucharist we give thanks for this gift. There we can repair
to find new strength, to tell Jesus that we miss him, to tell
him that we need him very much. *... the Eucharist is
reserved in the churches and oratories as in the spiritual centre of a religious community or of a parish, yes, of the
universal Church and of all of humanity, since beneath the
appearance of the species, Christ is contained, the invisible
Head of the Church, the Redeemer of the World, the Centre
of all hearts, 'by whom all things are and by whom we exist'*
(*1 Cor 8:6*).[13]

---

11. Paul VI, *Creed of the People of God*, 28
12. *idem*, Encyclical, *Mysterium Fidei*, 3 September 1965
13. *ibid*, 69

43.3 Devotion to the Blessed Sacrament. The hymn *Adoro te devote*.

It has been the constant practice of the Church to adore Christ present in the Tabernacle. If we recall how much reverence the Israelites had for their *tent of meeting* in the desert and for the Temple at Jerusalem, which were figures or images of reality, how much more reverence should we have for Christ truly present in the Tabernacle? In the first centuries of the Church the main reason for reserving the Sacred Species was for the sake of those who were not able to get to Holy Mass, especially the sick and the dying, and for those in prison due to religious persecution. The Sacrament of the Lord was brought with piety and fervour so that these Christians might also receive communion. Later, faith in the presence of Christ led to the cult of the Blessed Sacrament. The Church has authoritatively approved these practices. The Council of Trent declared, *There is, therefore, no room left for doubt that all the faithful of Christ in accordance with a custom always received in the Catholic Church offer in veneration the worship of 'latria' which is due to the true God, to this most Holy Sacrament.*[14]

In the thirteenth century Saint Thomas Aquinas composed a eucharistic hymn which embodies the faith of the Church in a faithful and pious manner. We should make this hymn our own so as to nourish our piety and give honour to the Blessed Sacrament. *Adoro te devote latens deitas* ...

> O Godhead hid, devoutly I adore thee,
> Who truly art within the forms before me;
> To thee my heart I bow with bended knee,
> As failing quite in contemplating Thee.

---

14. Council of Trent, Session XIII, can. 5; Dz 1643

Here we have all the truths of the Faith. We have understanding with humility and thanksgiving, amazement
before the power of God, surprise at the extent of his
mercy. With the confidence gained by having him so close
by, we ask the Lord for his grace to unite ourselves to his
most holy Will.

Next to the Tabernacle we will learn how to love.
There we will draw the strength necessary to remain faithful. There we will find consolation in times of sorrow. He
waits for us always and He rejoices when we are next to
him, even if only for a short while. There Jesus waits for
his people who suffer the contradictions of this life. He
comforts them with the warmth of his understanding and
his love. It is in the Tabernacle that those words of our
Lord come to life: *Come to me, all who labour and are
heavy laden, and I will give you rest.*[15] We will not fail to
visit him. He is waiting for us. How many are the gifts He
has prepared for us!

---

15. Matt 11:28

SEVENTEENTH WEEK: FRIDAY

44. WITHOUT HUMAN RESPECT

44.1 Having the courage to follow Christ in whatever environment we are in.

When Jesus began his public life many of his neighbours and relatives took him for a madman.[1] On his first visit to Nazareth, which we read about in today's Gospel, his relatives deny seeing in him anything supernatural or extraordinary.[2] In their comments, one can see that their envy is barely concealed. *Where did this man get this wisdom and these mighty works? Is not this the carpenter's son? ... And they took offence at him.*

Right from the start, Jesus faced a steady stream of insults and abuse born of cowardly egoism, because He proclaimed the Word without human respect. This ill-treatment increased steadily with time, until it broke out into calumny and open persecution, culminating in the death sentence. Christ's fortitude was recognized even by his enemies, who said, *Teacher, we know that you are true, and teach the way of God truthfully, and care for no man; for you do not regard the position of men.*[3]

Christ asks his disciples to imitate him in this practice. Christians should foster and defend their well-earned professional, moral and social prestige, since it belongs to the essence of human dignity. This prestige is also an important component of our personal apostolate.

---

1. Mark 3:21
2. Matt 13:54-58
3. Matt 22:16

Yet we should not forget that our conduct will meet with opposition from those who openly oppose Christian morality and those who practise a watered-down version of the Faith. It is possible that the Lord will ask of us the sacrifice of our good name, and even of life itself. With the help of his grace we will struggle to do his Will. Everything we have belongs to the Lord.

Each Christian has to put aside any fears of 'rocking the boat' should his upright conduct provoke criticism or rejection. Whoever out of human respect would hide his Christian identity in the midst of a pagan environment would merit this denunciation of Jesus: *Whoever denies me before men, I also will deny before my Father who is in heaven.*[4] Our Lord teaches us that confessing our faith is a requirement for being his disciple, no matter what the consequences may be.

This is the way many of Christ's first disciples conducted themselves. Joseph of Arimathea and Nicodemus were hidden disciples of the Lord, but they stepped forward as Christians at the hour when all seemed lost. Unlike many others, *they are courageous in the face of authority, declaring their love for Christ 'audacter' – 'boldly' – in the hour of cowardice.*[5] This is how the Apostles behaved before the Sanhedrin and the pagan persecutions. *For the word of the cross is folly to those who are perishing, but to us who are being saved it is the power of God.*[6] As the dauntless Saint Paul wrote to his disciple Timothy, *for God did not give us a spirit of timidity but a spirit of power and love and self-control. Do not be ashamed then of testifying to our Lord ...*[7] These are words which are directed

---

4. Matt 10:32
5. J. Escrivá, *The Way*, 841
6. 1 Cor 1:18
7. 2 Tim 1:7-8

at us today, as we seek to be faithful to the Master even though the environment may seem to be against us.

44.2 Overcoming human respect is part of the virtue of fortitude.

The life of a Christian should develop in a fairly ordinary manner in normal circumstances. Yet frequently this way of life will stand in stark contrast to other 'lifestyles' more or less Christian, as well as to a kind of behaviour which is beneath human dignity and is therefore anti-Christian. In these latter cases it is not surprising that the contrast will be striking. We should not be surprised that non-believers or the indifferent may unjustly criticize a follower of Christ, perhaps even to the extent of resorting to ridicule. The same thing happened to Our Lord.

In the course of day-to-day living, we are probably not talking about suffering physical harm for the sake of the Gospel. What a Christian may well have to put up with are rumours and calumnies, mockery, discrimination at work, the loss of economic opportunities or superficial friendships ... At times, perhaps in our family or among friends, it may be necessary to exercise supernatural fortitude in order to be consistent with our beliefs. In these uncomfortable circumstances it may be tempting to take the easy way out and 'give in'. By such means we could avoid rejection, misunderstanding and ridicule. We could become concerned at the thought of losing friends, of 'closing doors' which we will later be unable to re-open. This is the temptation to be influenced by human respect, hiding one's true identity and forsaking our commitment to live as disciples of Christ.

In such difficult circumstances the Christian ought not to wonder which path is the most opportune to follow, but, rather, which path is the most faithful to Christ. Certainly, our desire for popularity is the direct consequence of self-love. It may be that the Lord is waiting for us in just this kind of sacrifice, and this is the time we must choose between his way and our own. This choice may ultimately be expressed by our silence, by a few words, by a gesture or an attitude ... Our behaviour will be the proving-ground of our deepest convictions. This firmness in the Faith is often an excellent testimony to the beliefs of the Christian. In some cases it can cause people to begin their return to the House of the Father.

For many who begin to follow Christ, the necessity for this sacrifice is one of the major obstacles in their path. According to the saintly Curé d'Ars there is no doubt about it: *Do you know what the Devil's first temptation is to the person who wants to serve God with dedication? It is human respect*.[8] We all have an inner aversion from being put to shame before others. But this sacrifice, if we make it, will be the cause of our greatest joy – to take a stand for Jesus Christ, whenever and wherever the circumstances require it. We can be assured that we will never regret being true to our Christian beliefs.

44.3 Many people are in need of our good example in this area.

There are many people around us who are waiting for clear testimony to the Christian Faith. How much we can accomplish by our good example! How much is the world in need of Christian workers who are friendly, cordial and firm in the Faith! Occasionally we hear of a 'daring' article in which somebody attacks the teaching of the Pope or defends abortion or artificial contraception ... Nevertheless, the real daring in our age is to defend the

---

8. St Jean Vianney, (The Curé d'Ars), *Sermon on Temptations*

teaching authority of the Roman Pontiff in what pertains to faith and morals, to defend the right to life of every person, to have a large family if that be God's Will, to defend the indissolubility of marriage. How many wavering hearts have been fortified by one person's loyalty to principle!

In order to have the courage necessary to overcome our fears we need to rely on God's help. We cannot allow that God be removed from society or 'put into a parenthesis', that misguided men relegate the universal moral law to the closet of individual 'conscience'.

It should not surprise us that we may be tempted to pass unnoticed in certain disagreeable situations. Saint Peter himself, after having been confirmed as the Head of the Church, after having received the Holy Spirit, gave in to the human respect of his Jewish brethren. It took no less a man than Saint Paul to correct him in the matter.[9] This famous confrontation, far from disproving the holiness and unity of the Church, in fact demonstrates the perfect unity of the Apostles, the respect that Saint Paul had for the visible Head of the Church and the great humility of Saint Peter in changing his position. We can help one another in similar circumstances by practising fraternal correction with our fellow Christians, as was done in the earliest days of the Church.

The Lord gives us good example on how we should conduct ourselves. From that sad day in Nazareth He knew that many people were not in agreement with him. Yet He never based his actions upon the opinions of men. Only one thing matters to Jesus – the Will of his Father. For example, He never gave up curing people on the Sabbath even though spies were watching him.[10] Jesus knew

---

9. cf Gal 2:11-14
10. cf Mark 3:2

what He wanted to do, and He knew that from the start. We never see him have second thoughts or hesitate, much less reverse a decision. Christ asks us to follow him with the same kind of fortitude. *It is his own method quite personal to himself that he here enjoins on his disciples. Unconsidered, over-hasty action, vacillation, any coming to terms or compromising, these are not for him. His whole life and being are a Yea and Nay, nothing else. Jesus is always the complete man, always prepared, for he never speaks or acts except out of his whole clear consciousness and his own firm will.*[11]

We ask Jesus for the strength to guide us at all times to do God's unchanging Will rather than the fickle will of men.

---

11. K. Adam, *The Son of God*, 80

45. KNOWING WHEN TO SPEAK

45.1 The silence of Jesus.

For thirty years Jesus lived a life of silence. Mary and Joseph were the only people who knew the mystery of the Son of God. During his public life, when He returned to his home town his relatives were disconcerted by his wisdom and his miracles. They had known him solely from his exemplary life of work.

During the three years of his public life we see how He retreats into the silence of prayer, to be alone with his Father God. He withdraws from the superficial clamour of the multitude that wants to make him their king. He performs his miracles without ostentation, asking the people He cures to refrain from publicising his powers.

The silence of Jesus before his enemies in the Passion is very moving: *But he was silent and made no answer.*[1] In the face of so many false accusations He makes no defence. As Saint Jerome comments, *Our God and Saviour, who because of his mercy had redeemed the world, allows himself to be led to his death like a lamb, without a word of complaint or self-defence. The silence of Jesus obtains pardon for the protest and excuse of Adam.*[2] Jesus says nothing during the hearings before Herod and Pilate. We see him standing silent at their preference for Barabbas in front of his hate-filled enemies: *But when he was accused by the chief priests and elders, he made no*

---

1. Mark 14:61
2. St Jerome, *Commentary on the St Mark's Gospel, in loc*

answer. Then Pilate said to him, 'Do you not hear how many things they testify against you?' But he gave him no answer, not even to a single charge; so that the governor wondered greatly.[3]

The silence of God in the face of human passions, before the sins which are committed every day by humanity, is not a silence of anger. It is a silence full of patience and love. The silence of Calvary is that of a God who comes to redeem all men by his indescribable agony on the Cross. The silence of Jesus in the Tabernacle is that of a love which waits for a response. It is the patient silence of One who treasures our attentions.

Christ's silence during his earthly life represents interior strength and sense of purpose. Those who complain continually about their misfortunes or their 'bad luck' should look to the example of Our Lord. Those who proclaim their problems to the four winds should consider the behaviour of Christ. Those who feel compelled to explain and excuse their actions, who wait anxiously for praise or approval, should take note of Christ, who says nothing. We will imitate him when we learn to accept life's duties and worries without sterile complaints, when we confront our personal problems without dumping them in someone else's lap, when we face squarely the consequences of our actions, when we do our work for the glory of God without looking for earthly praise ...[4]

Iesus autem tacebat. Jesus says nothing. And we have to learn to say nothing on many occasions. At times, vanity will have us say things which should have been kept locked in the soul. The silent figure of Christ is the ever-present Model to reproach empty or useless words. His example

---

3. Matt 27:12-14
4. cf F. Suarez, *The Two Faces of Silence, Nuestro Tiempo,* 297 and 298

will lead us to remain silent before calumny and rumour. *In silentio et in spe erit fortitudo vestra*. Through the Prophet Isaiah, the Holy Spirit advises us that our fortitude is grounded in silence and in hope.[5]

45.2 Speaking out when necessary, with charity and fortitude. Avoiding the silence of consent.

Yet Jesus does not always remain silent. For there is a silence which can collaborate with lying, a silence which can cooperate with cowardice, a silence which springs from the love of comfort and the fear of complicating one's life. You can close your eyes to what is disagreeable. You can put off making a fraternal correction that ought to be made at home or at work. These are forms of silence too.

The word of Jesus is full of authority as He faces injustice and abuse: *Woe to you, scribes and Pharisees, hypocrites! For you devour widows' houses and for a pretence you make long prayers* ...[6]

Saint John the Baptist, whose martyrdom is recounted in today's Gospel,[7] was *the voice of one crying in the wilderness*. He teaches us to say everything that must be said, even though it may seem as if we too are crying in the wilderness. Our Lord will not allow our words to be wasted. It is important that we say what has to be said, without worrying ourselves about the immediate consequences. If each Christian were to speak in conformity with the Faith, we would surely change the world. We cannot sit by silently in the face of such crimes as abortion and the degradation of marriage and the family. Nor can we surrender to those forces that would seek to remove

---

5. Is 30:15
6. Matt 23:14
7. Matt 14:1-12

God from the formation of the young. We cannot be silent at attacks upon the Pope and Our Lady, or upon institutions of the Church. To be silent when we should be speaking out can be a way of collaborating with evil, because others may think that our silence implies consent. If Catholics were to speak out when there is need, if they were to boycott anti-Catholic publications or literature, it would be more difficult for these enterprises to prosper.

We should speak out when necessary. At times, the occasion will be when we are with a little group of our friends, coming or going to school or work. In letters to the editor, we can write in praise of a good article or to criticise a bad one. We should always act with charity. It is worth while to remember that true charity goes hand in hand with fortitude. We need to exercise good manners, always working with the intention of bringing souls to Jesus Christ. Yet we should act at the same time with the fortitude of the Lord.

45.3 Courage and strength in ordinary life. Living up to the full the demands of the Faith and of our vocation.

If, upon realising that his life was in danger, the Baptist had remained silent or retired to the sidelines of public affairs, he would not have been beheaded by Herod. But John was not that kind of man. He was not like *a reed shaken by the wind*. He was true to his vocation and his principles to the end. If he had remained silent, he could have lived a few more years, but his disciples would not have been the first to follow Our Lord. He would not have prepared and made straight the way of the Lord, as prophesied by Isaiah. He would not have lived up to his vocation. His life would have been bereft of meaning.

Jesus is probably not asking us to suffer a martyr's death for him. But He is asking us for courage and fortitude in facing up to the demands of ordinary life – to stop watching a bad television show, to cease putting off an apostolic conversation ... We cannot allow ourselves to hide behind excuses when there is so much apostolic work to be done. We have to act with optimism, loving the world and the good that is in it while seeking to increase that goodness. We can do this with the example of a joyful family and of the youthful love that is born of holy purity.

There are other kinds of cowardly silence which we have to struggle against. There is the silence we maintain with the person next to us. God has put him there so that we might be a beacon of light for him or her. In addition, it is hard to imagine that we can be courageous at all in this life if we are not first courageous with ourselves, especially when talking with our spiritual director.

Many of our friends, on seeing that we truly practise what we preach, will be attracted to the Faith. Centuries ago, many people converted after witnessing the martyrdom of the first Christians.

We dedicate this day to Our Lady. We ask her to teach us when to be silent and when to speak out.

EIGHTEENTH SUNDAY: YEAR A

46. THE MESSIANIC GOODS

46.1 The multiplication of the loaves. Jesus cares for his followers.

Why do you spend your money for that which is not bread, and your labour for that which does not satisfy? Hearken diligently to me, and eat what is good, and delight yourselves in fatness.[1]

The Gospel of today's Mass recounts how the Lord went off on a boat alone to a deserted place.[2] But when the people found out where He was going, they followed him on foot from their towns. Upon disembarking, He saw before him a great multitude *and he had compassion on them, and healed their sick*. He cured them without being asked. After all, the fact that they had come so far bringing their sick with them was sufficient proof of a great faith. With regard to this passage, Saint Mark points out that Jesus spent a lot of time teaching this crowd because *they were like sheep without a shepherd.*[3] So it grew quite late. The disciples were somewhat anxious at the thought of their being in a deserted place at such a late hour. *Send the crowds away*, they urged the Master, *to go into the villages and buy food for themselves*. Jesus surprised them with his answer: *They need not go away; you give them something to eat*. The Apostles obeyed. They did what they could, finding five loaves and two fishes. It is worth noting

---

1. Is 55:2-3
2. Matt 14:13-21
3. Mark 6:33-44

that those present included *about five thousand men, besides women and children*. Jesus works the miracle with a few loaves and fishes, and with the obedience of his followers.

After telling the crowd to sit down upon the grass, Jesus, *taking the five loaves and the two fish ... looked up to heaven, and blessed, and broke and gave the loaves to the disciples, and the disciples gave them to the crowds. And they all ate and were satisfied*. The Lord takes care of his own, even in material necessities, but He counts on our cooperation, even though our contribution will be of comparatively minor importance. *If you help him, even with a trifle, as the Apostles did, He is ready to work miracles; to multiply the bread, to reform wills, to give light to the most benighted minds, to enable those who have never been upright to be so, with an extraordinary grace. All this he will do ... and more, if you will help him with what you have.*[4] Then we will better understand what Saint Paul writes in today's Second Reading: *Who shall separate us from the love of Christ? Shall tribulation, or distress, or persecution, or famine, or nakedness, or peril, or sword? ... No, in all these things we are more than conquerors through him who loved us. For I am sure that neither death, nor life, nor angels, nor principalities, nor things present, nor things to come, nor powers, nor height, nor depth, nor anything else in all creation, will be able to separate us from the love of God in Christ Jesus our Lord.*[5]

Nothing can separate us from Christ, our Teacher – neither adversities in one's personal life (big and little failures, suffering, sickness ...) nor difficulties in the apostolate (resistance by some to receiving Christ's teachings,

---

4. J. Escrivá, *The Forge*, 675
5. Rom 8:35,37-39

hostility from an environment that flees from the Cross and all sacrifice ...). In Christ we will always find our strength.

46.2 This miracle is a figure of the Holy Eucharist, in which the Lord gives himself as food.

In the miracle of the multiplication of the loaves and the fishes, Christ uses the same words and behaviour as He later employs for the institution of the Eucharist.[6] This miracle is not only a demonstration of divine mercy; it is also a prefiguring of the Holy Eucharist,[7] which the Lord explains in the synagogue of Capharnaum.[8] This is the interpretation given by many Fathers of the Church. The liturgy of the Mass recalls the gesture of the Lord when He lifted his eyes up to heaven. The words of the Roman Canon are as follows: *Et elevatis oculis in caelum, ad Te Deum Patrem suum omnipotentem*, and looking up to heaven, to you, his almighty Father ... We remember that miracle as we prepare for an even greater miracle, that being the changing of bread into his Body, which is to be offered as spiritual food for all mankind.

The miracle by the lakeside showed to men the power and love of Jesus. That power and love are what allow us to find the Body of Christ under the sacramental species. Down through the centuries it is the Eucharist that can feed the multitude of the faithful. As Saint Thomas put it in the sequence which he composed for the Mass of 'Corpus Christi', *Sumit unus, sumunt mille ... Whether one receives or a thousand do, each receives the same as the other, He cannot be exhausted ... This is how the miracle acquires its significance, without losing any of its*

---

6. cf Matt 26:26; Mark 14:22; Luke 22:19; 1 Cor 11:25
7. cf *The Navarre Bible*, notes to John 6:11 and Mark 6:41
8. cf John 6:26-59

reality. It is wondrous in itself, but it ends up being even more wonderful than expected. It evokes the image of the Good Shepherd who feeds his sheep. It can be seen as a foreshadowing of the new order. Enormous multitudes will come to join in the eucharistic feast, where they will be fed in a miraculous way with an incredibly superior food.[9]

The crowds that seek out our Lord are evidence of the strong impression his Person makes on people. Many go so far as to follow Jesus into the desert itself, quite a way from the main roads and towns. They travel without provisions. They don't want to lose any time in their haste to get a glimpse of the Lord. This is a good example for us whenever we face some difficulty in receiving Communion or visiting the Blessed Sacrament. To have an encounter with the Master is worth any sacrifice.

Saint John reports that the multitude grew very excited as a result of the miracle.[10] *If all those people became so enthusiastic and were ready to acclaim you over a piece of bread, even granting that the multiplication of loaves was a very great miracle, shouldn't we be doing much more for all the many gifts you have granted us, and especially for giving us your very self unreservedly in the Eucharist?*[11]

In Holy Communion we receive Jesus, the Son of Mary, the One who performed that great miracle many years ago. *In the Host we possess the Christ of all the mysteries of Redemption – the Christ of Mary Magdalene, of the Prodigal Son, of the Samaritan woman, the Christ resurrected from the dead, seated at the right hand of the Father ... The marvellous presence of Christ in our midst should completely transform our life ... He is here with us*

9. M. J. Indart, *Jesus in his World*, Barcelona, 1963
10. John 6:14
11. J. Escrivá, *op cit*, 304

– in every city, in every town … [12] He waits for us. He misses us when we are tardy in coming.

46.3 We should look for our Lord in Communion. We should prepare for each Communion as if it were the only one of our life.

The eyes of all look to thee, and thou givest them their food in due season. Thou openest thy hand, thou satisfiest the desire of every living thing. This is today's Responsorial Psalm. [13]

Jesus, really present in the Holy Eucharist, gives this sacrament an infinite supernatural efficacy. Whenever we want to express our love for someone, we give presents, we do favours, we make ourselves available to the person in question … But we always come up against one limitation, namely, that we cannot give away our very self. Jesus Christ can do that. He gives us his very self. And we can unite ourselves to him. We can identify ourselves with him. And we can find him every day in Holy Communion. He waits for us. He is there waiting for each one of us. He does not wait for us to ask for things. He cures us of our weaknesses. He protects us against danger, against temptations that would separate us from him. He lifts up our spirits. Each Communion is a fountain of graces, new light and a new impulse that strengthens us in handling daily life with human elegance and supernatural outlook.

How much we partake of these benefits depends in good measure upon the quality of our interior dispositions. The sacraments *produce a greater effect in proportion to the good dispositions of the recipient.* [14] We improve our disposition, our desires for greater holiness, by going to

---

12. M. M. Philipon, *The Sacraments in Christian Life*
13. Ps 144:15-16
14. St Pius X, Decree, *Sacra Tridentina Synodus*, 20 December 1905

Confession frequently. It is our love which will lead us to a greater eucharistic piety. As Pope John Paul II said during his first papal journey to Spain, *This love will bring you ever closer to the Lord. I ask you to make good use of the sacrament of Confession, which leads us to the Eucharist, just as the Eucharist leads us to Confession.*[15] Both these sacraments help the soul to love in a more delicate, refined and pure manner.

When the moment of receiving Communion draws near, our desires of reparation, of faith and of love should grow more fervent. *Have you ever thought how you would prepare yourself to receive Our Lord if you could go to Communion only once in your life? We must be thankful to God that he makes it so easy for us to come to him; but we should show our gratitude by preparing ourselves to receive him very well.*[16] One day it will be our last time. Soon afterwards we will be meeting Jesus face to face, the Lord with whom we have been united sacramentally. How pleased Jesus must be by our acts of faith and love!

---

15. John Paul II, *Address*, 31 October 1982
16. J. Escrivá, *op cit*, 828

EIGHTEENTH SUNDAY: YEAR B

47. THE BREAD OF LIFE

47.1 Manna is the symbol and figure of the Holy Eucharist, which is the true spiritual food.

Jesus said to them, 'I am the bread of life; he who comes to me shall not hunger, and he who believes in me shall never thirst'.[1]

Following the miracle of the multiplication of the loaves and the fishes, the enthusiastic multitude went again in search of Jesus. When they discovered that He and his disciples had already departed, they got into their boats and sailed for Capharnaum. According to Saint John in today's Gospel it was there that the revelation of the Holy Eucharist took place.[2]

With the miracle of the previous day, Jesus had awakened the crowd's deepest hopes and longings. Thousands of people had left the comfort of their homes to come and hear him. They wanted to make him their king. But the Lord departed from them. Upon meeting them again, Jesus says to the people, *Truly, truly, I say to you, you seek me, not because you saw signs, but because you ate your fill of the loaves*. Saint Augustine comments: *You seek me for worldly motives, not for spiritual ones. How many people there are who seek Jesus solely for worldly ends!... Rarely does someone look for Jesus for the sake of Jesus*.[3] We want to be among those few.

---

1. *Communion Antiphon*, John 6:35
2. John 6:24-35
3. St Augustine, *Commentary on St John's Gospel*, 25, 10

This attachment to earthly goods is not what Jesus is looking for in men. With great courage and an infinite love, He presents to the people the ineffable treasure of the Holy Eucharist, in which He becomes food for us. It does not matter to him that many of his loyal followers will abandon him as a result of this revelation. Jesus begins the discourse by hinting at the great mystery: *Do not labour for the food which perishes, but for the food which endures to eternal life, which the Son of man will give to you ... Then they said to him, 'What must we do, to be doing the works of God?' Jesus answered them, 'This is the work of God, that you believe in him whom he has sent'.*

Despite the fact that many of those present had only the previous day witnessed a great miracle, they said, *Then what sign do you do, that we may see, and believe in you? What work do you perform? Our fathers ate the manna in the wilderness; as it is written, 'He gave them bread from heaven to eat'.*

In today's First Reading we are shown how Yahweh manifested his Providence to the Israelites in the desert.[4] He sent down manna from heaven to feed them. This bread is a symbol and figure of the Holy Eucharist which Christ first announced in this small city on the shores of the Sea of Galilee. Jesus Christ is the true food which transforms us and gives us the strength to live our Christian vocation. Pope John Paul II has pointed out in this regard: *It is only by means of the Eucharist that we are able to live the heroic virtues of Christianity, such as charity to pardon one's enemies, the love which enables us to suffer, the capacity to give one's life for another; chastity at all times of life and in all situations; patience in the face of suffering and the apparent silence of God in human history*

---

4. Ex 16:2-4; 12-15

or our very own existence. Therefore, strive to always be eucharistic souls so as to be authentic Christians.[5]

With the words of the poet Dante, we petition the Lord, *Give us this day the daily manna, without which he goes backward through this harsh wilderness who most labours to advance.*[6] Truly, life without Christ is a harsh wilderness. It is a way of life where it is especially difficult to reach the journey's end.

47.2 The *bread of life.*

When the Jews tell Jesus that Moses had given them the bread of heaven, Jesus replies that it was not Moses, but his Father who had given them *the true bread from heaven. For the bread of God is that which comes down from heaven, and gives life to the world.*

The Lord presents himself as superior to Moses. Not even Moses had had the audacity to claim that he himself gave the food which never perishes, which lasts unto eternal life. Jesus promises much more than Moses. Moses promised a kingdom, a land of milk and honey, earthly peace, numerous sons, physical health and all the other earthly goods … Thus you would fill your bodies here on earth with perishable goods. In contrast, Christ promised a food which would never perish but would last forever.[7]

Those present at the synagogue of Capharnaum knew that the manna was a symbol of the messianic goods. It was for that reason that they asked Jesus to work a similar sign. Yet they had no idea that the manna was indeed a figure of that great messianic good, the Holy Eucharist.[8]

Jesus tells the Jews that the manna in the desert was

5. John Paul II, *Homily*, 19 August 1979
6. Dante Alighieri, *The Divine Comedy: Purgatory*, XI, 13-15
7. St Augustine, *Commentary on St John's Gospel*, 25, 12
8. cf *The Navarre Bible*, *in loc*

not the true bread from heaven since those who ate of it did die. He says that his Father will give them the true bread from heaven. They respond, *'Lord, give us this bread always.'* Jesus said to them, *'I am the bread of life; he who comes to me shall not hunger, and he who believes in me shall never thirst'*. Our Lord leaves no room for doubt that this bread is a reality. He repeats the verb *to eat* eight times. Christ will become food so that we might gain a new life, the life which He has brought to us: *The bread which I shall give for the life of the world is my flesh.* This is not a bread from the earth. It is a bread *which came down from heaven, not such as the fathers ate and died; he who eats this bread will live forever.* In the Holy Eucharist we become *flesh of his flesh and blood of his blood.*[9] The Eucharist is the supreme realisation of those words of Holy Scripture that have God *rejoicing in his inhabited world and delighting in the sons of men.*[10] The Blessed Sacrament is *Emmanuel*, 'God with us', the food of eternal life.

He was the greatest madman of all times. What greater madness could there be than to give oneself as he did, and for such people? It would have been mad enough to have chosen to become a helpless Child. But even then, many wicked men might have been softened, and would not have dared to harm him. So this was not enough for him. He wanted to make himself even less, to give himself more lavishly. He made himself food; he became Bread. Divine Madman! How do men treat you? How do I treat you?[11] How do I prepare to receive you, Lord? How is my faith, my joy, my desire? We should make some resolutions in preparation for our next Communion, perhaps within the

---

9. St Cyril of Jerusalem, *Catechesis*, 22, 1
10. Prov 8:31
11. J. Escrivá, *The Forge*, 824

next few minutes or hours. It cannot be like so many of the previous times. We have to receive with greater love.

47.3 We receive the same Christ in every Communion. His presence in the soul.

When we receive Communion, we receive Christ himself with his Body, his Blood, his Soul and his Divinity. He gives himself to us in an intimate union which binds us to him in a real way. Our life is transformed into his life. In Holy Communion Christ is not only God *with* us, but God *in* us.

After we receive Communion, Christ is truly, really, substantially present in our soul. We can apply here those words of the Lord to Saint Augustine: *I am the food of grown men. Grow, and you shall feed upon me. You will not change me into yourself, as you change food into your flesh, but you will be changed into me.*[12] Christ gives us his life! He divinizes us! He transforms us into himself! The infinite merits of the Passion are poured out into our soul. He sends us strength and consolation. He leads us to his Most Sacred Heart, to transform our sentiments into his sentiments. The Eucharist holds all the graces and fruits of eternal life for humanity and for each individual soul. This is because the sacrament *contains all the spiritual good of the Church.*[13] If we frequently consider the effects which this sacrament can have on the soul we will come to treasure Holy Communion and spiritual communions. We will see the value of receiving our Lord as often as we can, on a daily basis if possible. We will prepare ourselves well for each Communion. Each and every day we will say to Jesus, *Lord, give us this bread always*.

---

12. St Augustine, *Confessions*, 7, 10, 16; 7, 18, 24
13. Second Vatican Council, Decree, *Presbyterorum ordinis*, 5

The soul will be raised to a supernatural plane. Christ's virtues will vivify it. Then we will be able to say with confidence, *It is no longer I who live, but Christ who lives in me.*[14]

Those words of the Lord during the Last Supper are also fulfilled with every Communion: *If a man loves me, he will keep my word, and my Father will love him, and we will come to him and make our home with him.*[15] The soul becomes the temple and tabernacle of the Holy Trinity. The life of the three Divine Persons will transform it, nurturing in it the divine seed that was implanted in Baptism.

When we draw near to receive him we should say, *Lord, I hope in you. I adore you, I love you, increase my faith. Be the support of my weakness. You, who have remained defenceless in the Eucharist so as to be the remedy for the weakness of your creatures.*[16] We go to Holy Mary. For thirty-three years she was in his physical presence. She treated him with the greatest respect and love imaginable. We unite ourselves to her sentiments of adoration and love.

14. Gal 2:20
15. John 14:23
16. J. Escrivá, *op cit*, 832

EIGHTEENTH SUNDAY: YEAR C

48. TO BE RICH BEFORE GOD

48.1 Only God can fill our heart.

If then you have been raised with Christ, seek the things that are above, where Christ is, seated at the right hand of God. Set your minds on the things that are above, not on things that are on earth, exhorts Saint Paul in the Second Reading of the Mass.[1] Things of the world last a relatively short period of time and they cannot fulfil the longings of the human heart.

The life of man on earth is brief.[2] The greater part of it is spent in pain and suffering. Every life passes like the wind; barely a trace is left behind.[3] In the best of cases, one might amass a great fortune only for it soon to be left to others. What does all this pain and effort add up to? Is it all for nothing? As we are reminded in the first reading: *Vanity of vanities! All is vanity.*[4]

In the face of this emptiness and inconsistency, all this pointlessness, God is *the rock of our salvation. Let us come into his presence with thanksgiving; let us make a joyful noise to him with songs of praise!*[5]

Nevertheless, the human heart has a tremendous capacity to seek the things of the world without paying any attention to the transcendent meaning of life. The human

---

1. *Second Reading*: Col 3:1-5; 9-11
2. Wis 2:1
3. Ps 89:10
4. Eccles 1:2
5. *Responsorial Psalm*, Ps 94

heart tends to become attached to worldly goods as the one and only goal in life, forgetting what is really important. In today's Gospel, the Lord takes advantage of a question about inheritances to teach us about the true worth of things in the light of eternity.[6] He brings up the subject of death, of our own death, to make his point: *The land of a rich man brought forth plentifully; and he thought to himself, 'What shall I do, for I have nowhere to store my crops?' And he said, 'I will do this: I will pull down my barns, and build larger ones ... And I will say to my soul, Soul, you have ample goods laid up for many years; take your ease, eat, drink, be merry'.*

The Lord teaches us that putting our hearts into the pursuit of wealth and worldly well-being is foolishness. Neither happiness nor authentic human life itself are founded on worldly goods. *A man's life does not consist in the abundance of his possessions.*[7] The rich man discloses his 'value system' in his mental dialogue. He sees himself in a very secure position because he has great resources. He bases his stability and his happiness on this wealth. For him, as for many people, living is a matter of enjoying as much pleasure as possible. It is to do as little as need be, to eat, to drink, 'to have a good time', to lay up ample goods *for many years*. This is his ideal. In his life there is no reference to God, much less to other people. He sees no need to share his goods with others less fortunate than himself.

And how does he plan to maintain this thoroughly materialistic lifestyle? *I will store ...* Yet in the end, all of his calculations are for nothing. The things of this world give a fragile and insufficient security since our lives will

---

6. Luke 12:13-21
7. Luke 12:15

never be fulfilled without God.

We can ask ourselves today during this time of prayer, 'Where is my heart?' Because we know that our destination is Heaven, we have to make positive and concrete acts of detachment with regard to what we own and what we use. How much do we share our goods with the needy? How much time and wealth do we contribute to apostolic works?

48.2 Our earthly life is short and fleeting. Taking advantage of the noble things of the earth so as to win Heaven.

Despite the fact that He has been overlooked, God interrupts the rich man in his ruminations to pass judgment on his chosen way of life: *Fool! This night your soul is required of you; and the things you have prepared, whose will they be?' So is he who lays up treasure for himself, and is not rich toward God.*

Our passage upon the earth is a time of testing. The Lord himself has given it to us. As Saint Paul teaches, *For here we have no lasting city, but we seek the city which is to come.*[8] On a certain day the Lord will come to settle accounts with us, to determine how well or ill we have administered his gifts. His gifts include intelligence, health, material goods, a capacity for friendship, the power to give joy to those around us ... The Lord will come only once, perhaps when we least expect him, like a thief in the night,[9] like lightning flashing across the sky.[10] He ought to find us well prepared. Tying ourselves down to the world, forgetting that our end is in Heaven, will lead us to live a disoriented life of complete idiocy. *Fool* is precisely what God calls the man who lives only for the world. We

---

8. Heb 13:14
9. Matt 24:43
10. Matt 24:27

certainly have to walk with our feet on the ground, taking care to safeguard our future and the future of those who depend upon us. But we cannot forget that we are pilgrims, no more than *actors in a show. No one is permanently made king or wealthy, since at the end of the performance we will all find ourselves as paupers*.[11] Worldly goods are but the means for us to attain the goal which the Lord has pointed out. These goods can never become the 'be-all and the end-all' of our existence.

Our life on earth is short and limited: *This night your soul is required of you*. Perhaps we think of death in terms of something remote, as if we will live forever. Yet the Lord speaks of *this night*. Our days are numbered. We are in the hands of God. Within a few years, maybe not that many, we will find ourselves face to face with him.

Meditating on our final end should motivate us to sanctify our work – 'redeeming the time' – as we strive to make up for lost time.[12] It should help us to take advantage of our circumstances in order to make reparation for sins and to become detached from earthly goods. One day like any other day will be our last day on earth. Today, thousands of people have died or will die in the most diverse of circumstances. Those people were probably unaware that their time was up, that they would have no more time to improve. Some have died with their hearts immersed in things of little or no importance in terms of eternal life. Others have died who have been involved in exactly the same activities but have kept their sights on God. It is these latter people who have come into possession of that marvellous treasure which *neither rust nor moth consumes* ...[13]

11. St John Chrysostom, *Homily on Lazarus*, 2, 3
12. Eph 5:16
13. Matt 6:20

48.3 Good use of time with respect to God. Detachment.

At the moment of death the state of the soul is fixed forever. Afterwards, it is impossible to change. The destiny which awaits us is the consequence of our behaviour on earth: *If a tree falls to the south or to the north, in the place where the tree falls, there it will lie.*[14] This is the reason for the Lord's frequent warnings to be on watch.[15] Death is not the end of existence, but the beginning of a new life. Christians cannot 'write off' or minimise the importance of our temporal existence since it is the very means by which we prepare for our definitive life with God in Heaven. To yield a rich harvest before God we have to sanctify this same ordinary life and the use of material goods. Every other 'lifestyle' is built upon sand: *Surely every man stands as a mere breath! Surely man goes about as a shadow! ... man heaps up, and knows not who will gather!*[16]

Inasmuch as the goods of this world are intended for the glory of God, we should use them with a sense of detachment, not complaining either when these goods may be lacking. The absence of some good, if it is God's will, should not take away our peace. We should know how to be happy in times of prosperity and in adversity. Whether we are rich or poor, we should share what we have with others – by creating new jobs, if that be in our power, by promoting works of culture and formation, by giving generously to the good works of the Church.

By considering our death we can also learn how to make good use of the days that remain to us. *My children, the world is slipping through our fingers. We cannot lose any time, for the time is short ... I understand Saint Paul very*

---

14. Eccles 11:3
15. cf Matt 24:42-44; Mark 13:32-37
16. Ps 39:7

*well when he writes to the Corinthians: 'Tempus breve est!'
How brief is our sojourn upon the earth! For a coherent
Christian, these words ought to ring true in the depths of the
soul. They are a reproach for our lack of generosity and a
constant invitation to loyalty. Truly, we have so little time to
love, to give, to do penance.*[17] Are we going to allow our
hearts to be tied to the things of this world?

Meditation on the eternal truths is a good antidote
against sin and a real help towards giving a Christian
meaning to life. These thoughts can inspire us to pay
proper attention to our daily work, to our relations with
others and to our duties in charity towards those most in
need. That will be our way into Heaven.

---

17. J. Escrivá, quoted in *Newsletter* No. 1

EIGHTEENTH WEEK: MONDAY

49. CHRISTIAN OPTIMISM

49.1 To be realistic in a supernatural way is to rely always on the grace of God.

A great multitude follow Jesus into the desert.[1] They follow him without giving a thought to distance, heat or cold, because their needs are great. They sense that they are welcome. They listen attentively to those words which give meaning to their lives, so attentively that they neglect life's necessities. They have brought no food to eat and there is no place to buy any food out there. This problem does not seem to have bothered them, nor does it seem to bother Jesus. When the disciples become aware of the situation at dusk, however, they go to the Master and say, *This is a lonely place, and the day is now over; send the crowds away to go into the villages and buy food for themselves*. This is a statement of fact which is evident to all. But Jesus knows of a higher reality, of possibilities which even his most intimate disciples cannot discern. And so he answers them, *They need not go away; you give them something to eat*. The disciples, being keenly aware of their lack of provisions, reply, *We have only five loaves here and two fishes*.

The disciples see *objective* reality. They know that this small amount of food will not suffice to feed the multitude. This is what may happen to us when we take stock of our own strengths and possibilities. The

---

1. cf Matt 14:13-21

difficulties before us may appear larger than life and beyond our power to influence. Mere human objectivity can lead us to discouragement and pessimism. It can cause us to forget the radical optimism which is part and parcel of the Christian vocation. As popular wisdom would have it: *He who fails to include God in his reckonings does not know how to add.* He does not know how to add because he leaves out the most important factor. The Apostles made a very precise count of their resources. They counted up the exact number of loaves and fishes available. But they forgot to consider that Jesus was at their side. And this fact radically alters the situation. The *real* reality is something different from *objective* reality. *In apostolic undertakings it's very good – it's a duty – to consider what means the world has to offer you ($2 + 2 = 4$). But don't forget – ever –that your calculations must fortunately include another term: God $+ 2 + 2 ...$* [2] To neglect this reality is to misread the true situation. To be supernaturally realistic, we need to count upon the grace of God which is an ineluctable *fact*.

Christian optimism is rooted in God, who says to us: *I am with you always, to the close of the age.*[3] With him we can do anything. We are victorious even when we are defeated. This is the optimism so characteristic of the saints. Saint Teresa of Avila would often repeat, with her good humour and supernatural spirit: *Teresa can do nothing alone. Teresa and a maravedí (a penny, say), less than nothing. But Teresa, a maravedí and God can do anything.*[4] It is the same with us. *Cast away that despair produced by the realization of your weakness. It's true: financially you are a zero, and socially another zero, and another in virtues,*

2. J. Escrivá, *The Way*, 471
3. cf Matt 28:28
4. A. Ruiz, *Teresian Anecdotes*, Burgos, 1982

and another in talents ... But to the left of these zeros is Christ. And what an immeasurable figure it turns out to be.[5] How this realization changes our entire outlook at the hour of beginning an apostolic work, at the moment of personal conversion, in the realities of ordinary life!

49.2 A Christian's optimism is the result of faith.

Christian optimism is a result of faith, not of circumstances. The Christian knows that the Lord has his best interests in mind. The Lord knows how to draw fruit even from apparent failure. At the same time, He asks us to use all of the human means at our disposal, leaving no stone unturned. We should count on the five loaves and the two fishes. By themselves they won't make much of a meal for so many hungry people at the end of a long day, but they nevertheless play an indispensable part in the working of the miracle. The Lord sees to it that failures in the apostolate (someone does not respond, someone turns his back on us, etc ...) serve to sanctify us and sanctify others. Nothing is lost. On the other hand, what will never give any fruit are omissions and excuses, behaviour like throwing up our hands before a hostile environment. The Lord wants us to put our loaves and fishes to good use, while placing our trust in him with rectitude of intention. Some fruits will come at once. Other fruits will come at the time and in the way the Lord wants. One thing is beyond doubt – fruits will always be forthcoming. We have to convince ourselves that we are nothing, and that we can do nothing without Jesus at our side. *He, to whose power and knowledge all things are given, protects us by means of his inspirations against all foolishness, ignorance, wild tantrums or hardness of heart.*[6]

---

5. J. Escrivá, *op cit*, 473
6. St Thomas, *Summa Theologiae*, 1-2, q 68, a 2, ad 3

A Christian's optimism gets strong reinforcement from prayer. *Christian optimism is not a sugary optimism; nor is it a mere human coincidence that everything will turn out all right. It is an optimism that sinks its roots in an awareness of our freedom, and in the sure knowledge of the power of grace. It is an optimism which leads us to make demands on ourselves, to struggle to respond at every moment to God's calls.*[7] It is not the optimism of the egoist who seeks only his personal tranquillity, who closes his eyes to reality, saying 'Everything will work out in the end'. He uses that as an excuse so that he will not be bothered. He goes so far as to deny the evil in others in order to avoid worries and responsibility. The radical optimism of one who follows Christ closely does not delude him as to the nature of reality. Quite the contrary; the Christian is able to confront the whole truth without being demoralized by it. The Christian knows that his Father God will never leave him. He believes that abundant fruit will be harvested from that field – those circumstances, those friends – in which it seemed that only weeds could grow. The Christian is confident that *the work of the good is never destroyed, but that in order to bring forth fruit, the ear of corn begins by dying in the earth. The Christian knows that the sacrifice of goods is never in vain.*[8]

49.3 Our optimism is rooted in the Communion of Saints.

Monsignor Knox points out that Jesus worked this miracle not just for anybody, but rather for people who had been following him for days, people who had earnestly been searching for him. According to Knox, the multitude is a prefiguring of the Church. Those five thousand seated

---

7. J. Escrivá, *The Forge*, 659
8. G. Chevrot, *The Well of Life*, 185

on the hillside were united as followers of Christ. They fed upon the same bread, that foreshadowing of the Holy Eucharist, which came from the hands of Christ. *How naturally a common meal serves for a symbol of fraternity; how easily a scratch party of guests get on together if you take them out for a picnic in the open air! Just imagine what it must have meant, later on, if one of those five thousand met, by accident, one of the others; what fellowship must have been imposed on them by their common store of reminiscences! 'Yes, don't you remember, I was sitting about seven or eight off you, and Peter – or John, or James, or Judas – came round with the crust which looked as if it could never satisfy more than two; we both seemed to be in starvation corner, didn't we? And then when he got to the end of the row the crust was still there'.*[9]

We can take part at the same table, at the same Banquet. We can receive the same Bread, wherein Christ comes to us, which is multiplied without ceasing. Those who follow Christ are united by a very strong bond. *Recognise in yourself a limb, a branch of Christ, (the body, the vine) living, grafted-on and ingrowing, nourished by his strength and grace.*[10] The *Communion of Saints* teaches us that we all form one Body in Christ. Through this communion we can help one another in a most efficacious way. Somewhere, at this very moment someone is praying for us, someone is helping us with sanctified work, with prayer, with suffering offered up. We are never alone.

The *Communion of Saints* serves as the constant fuel of our optimism because we can always count on the mysterious but very real help of those who partake of the same Bread.

---

9. *ibid*
10. B. Baur, *In Silence with God*, 206

And they all ate and were satisfied. And they took up twelve baskets full of the broken pieces left over. And those who ate were about five thousand men, besides women and children.

We are moved by Christ's generosity to appeal to him with confidence. We too have spent many days with him. *Ask him without any fear, and insist. Remember that scene of the multiplication of loaves we read about in the Gospel. Notice how magnanimously he says to the Apostles, How many loaves do you have? Five? ... How many are you asking for? And he gives six, a hundred, thousands ... Why? Because Christ sees all our needs with divine wisdom, and with his almighty power he can and does go far beyond our desires. Our Lord sees much farther than our poor minds can discern and he is infinitely generous.*[11] He will once again perform miracles as soon as we place the little we have at his disposal. He thinks in terms which greatly exceed our poor human calculations. What a shame if we were ever to hang on to the five loaves and two fishes with which the Lord would readily work miracles!

---

11. J. Escrivá, *The Forge*, 341

EIGHTEENTH WEEK: TUESDAY

50. MEN OF FAITH

50.1 Faith in Christ. With him, we can do everything; without him we are incapable of taking a single step.

Immediately after the multiplication of the loaves and fishes, our Lord himself took leave of the crowds and ordered the disciples to set out in their boats.[1] It must have been late in the evening. After a long day of work, attending to those who sought him out, Jesus felt compelled to pray. He walked up a nearby hill and, after nightfall, remained there alone, in conversation with His Father in Heaven.

From that hilltop Jesus saw the Apostles far offshore; and their boat – buffeted by the waves, the wind against them – was in danger. The Pasch was near and there was a full moon, so Jesus could make out the little craft in the middle of the lake. But in the fourth watch of the night, around three in the morning, well before sunrise, He came to them walking upon the sea. Seeing a vague figure coming over the surface of the sea toward the place where they were struggling, they were filled with fear. *It is a ghost!*, they said. And they began shouting out in terror. But then our Lord revealed himself. *Take courage; it is I, do not be afraid.* Christ always presents himself in this manner in the life of a Christian, giving encouragement and serenity. Peter takes courage; led on by his love, moved by his desire to be close to the Master, he makes

---

1. Matt 14:22-36

an unexpected request: *Lord, if it is thyself, bid me come to thee over the water.* Love's daring has no limits, and our Lord yields easily to the request. And He said, *Come.* Peter got out of the boat and began to walk on the water toward Jesus. Those were stirring moments for all: Peter gave up the safety of the boat at Jesus' word. He did not remain clinging to the side of the vessel, but went towards Jesus, who was now only a few yards away from his disciples. Awestruck, they contemplate the Apostle moving forward on the swirling waves. Peter walks on the water. Faith and confidence in his Master are all that sustain him – only that.

The difficulties that surround us don't matter if we walk with faith and confidence toward Jesus, who is waiting for us. It doesn't matter if the waves are high and the wind strong, or that it's not natural for man to walk on water. If we look to Jesus, we can do anything; and looking at him is the virtue of piety. If through prayer and the sacraments we remain close to Jesus, we will remain on the right path. If our gaze wanders away from Jesus, we will sink; we will be incapable of even a single step, even on firm ground.

50.2 When faith diminishes, difficulties seem greater.

Peter's faith, great at first, was soon to diminish. He realized the force of the waves and the wind (Saint John states that the wind was strong), that it was impossible for a man to walk on water. He worries about the difficulties and forgets the only thing that was keeping him afloat: the word of the Lord. He paid attention to the obstacles and his faith diminished: the miracle was linked to complete trust in Christ.

At times, God asks for things which seem apparently impossible, but which become a reality when we act with faith, with our sight fixed on the Lord. On a certain occasion, the Founder of Opus Dei, Blessed Josemaría Escrivá, told a daughter of his who was going to another country where there would be difficulties inseparable from the beginning of the apostolic work: *When I ask something of you, my daughter, don't tell me that it's impossible, because I know that already. Since I began the Work, our Lord has asked me to do many impossible things ... and they've become a reality!*[2] And they have kept on happening!: so it was with their apostolic work in many countries ... and vocations came, and with them people who were willing to help out in that work with great generosity and detachment. In many ways he told them: *Men of faith are needed and the great works of scripture will be repeated.* Those great works are done each day on earth .. This is the way it has always been in the history of the Church.

It is God who keeps us afloat and makes us effective in the midst of those apparent *impossibilities*, of an environment which often goes against the Christian ideal. It is He who makes us walk on water – on one condition: we should keep our eyes set on Christ and not allow obstacles and temptations to distract us.

In his gospel commentary Saint John Chrysostom points out that Jesus taught Peter, through personal experience, that all his fortitude came from Him. Left to his own devices, Peter could only expect weakness and misery.[3] *When our cooperation is lacking,* he added, *God also ceases to help us.* That is why as soon as Peter began to fear and doubt he also began to sink.

When faith diminishes, difficulties seem greater: *Living faith depends on my ability to respond to God, who calls*

---

2. P. Berglar, *Opus Dei – Life and work of the Founder*
3. St John Chrysostom, *Homilies on the St Matthew's Gospel*, 50

me and wants to treat me as a friend, as One who is the great witness of my life. So if I respond to him and love him, and if He is someone familiar in my life, if I live close to Him, I am safeguarding my faith, because my faith is founded on God ... On the other hand, if I keep my distance from God, if I forget him, if I keep him outside my life and am submerged in merely human and material things, if I let myself be carried away by what is immediately in front of me and God fades from my soul, then how will I have a living faith? If I don't speak with Christ, what is there left of my faith? That is why, in the final analysis, all obstacles to a life of faith may be reduced – in their root – to a withdrawal, a separation from God: we cease to deal with him face to face.[4] Then it is that temptations and obstacles gain strength. Peter would have remained firm on the waters and would have reached the Lord if he had not separated his confident gaze from the Lord. All the tempests put together, those within the soul and those arising from outside, cannot shake us as long as we have firm recourse to prayer. To abandon prayer, to pray with little intimacy or sincerity, exposes us to sink into discouragement, pessimism and temptation.

Our faith should never falter even when the difficulties are enormous, even though they seem to crush us under their weight. *What does it matter if the whole world with all its power is against you? You ... go forward!*

Repeat the words of the psalm: 'The Lord is my light and my salvation. Whom shall I fear? ... Si consistant adversum me castra, non timebit cor meum.' Though my enemies surround me, my heart shall not waver.[5]

4. P. Rodriguez, *Faith and Life of faith*, Pamplona, 1974
5. J. Escrivá, *The Way*, 480

50.3 Jesus always comes to our aid.

Then Peter got out of the boat and walked on the water to come to Jesus. But seeing the wind was strong, he was afraid; and as he began to sink, he cried out, saying *Lord, save me!* And Jesus at once stretched forth his hand and took hold of him saying, *O thou of little faith, why didst thou doubt?* And when they got into the boat the wind fell.

Amidst dangers, obstacles and doubts we should look to Christ: let us run with patience to the fight set before us; looking toward the author and perfecter of faith, Jesus,[6] we read in the Epistle to the Hebrews. Christ should be a clear, sharply-defined figure for us. We have contemplated him so many times that we cannot confuse him with a ghost, as the disciples did that night. His features, his voice, his gaze are unmistakable. He has looked at us so many times! He is the beginning and the culmination of Christian life. *If you want to be saved*, writes Saint Thomas Aquinas, *look upon the face of your Christ.*[7] Dealing with him habitually, in prayer and through the sacraments, is the only guarantee of staying on our feet, as children of God, in the middle of the rough seas in which we live.

What's more, together with Christ the conflicts and labours we confront almost daily strengthen our faith and hope, and unite us more closely to Him. The same occurs to *the trees that grow in shady, sheltered places: while externally they appear to thrive, they are feeble and easily hurt. However, the trees that grow on the pinnacles of the tallest mountains, buffeted by many winds, constantly exposed to harsh conditions, beaten by fierce storms and covered by snow, these grow as strong as iron.*[8]

---

6. Heb 12:1-2

7. St Thomas, *Commentary on the Epistle to the Hebrews*, 12:1-2

8. St John Chrysostom, *Homily on the glory of tribulation*

Peter stopped looking at Christ and he sank. But he knew enough to return immediately to Him to whom all is submitted. *Lord, save me!*, he cried with all his strength when he felt all was lost. And Jesus, with infinite affection, stretched out his hand and pulled him up. If we see that we are sinking, that temptations and difficulties are overwhelming us, let us go to Jesus. He always stretches out his hand to us, for us to hold tight. He will never let us sink, if we do the little required of us. God has also placed our Guardian Angel next to us to help us in all adversity and to serve as a powerful aid on our road to Heaven. Let us deal with this friend confidently; let us ask his help in small things and great things, and we will find the fortitude we need for victory.

EIGHTEENTH WEEK: WEDNESDAY

51. THE VIRTUE OF HUMILITY

51.1 The humility of the Syrophoenician woman.

In the Gospel of today's Mass,[1] Saint Matthew records that Jesus retired with his disciples to the lands of the gentiles, in the region of Sidon and Tyre. There, a woman came to them shouting loudly: *Lord, Son of David, have mercy on me! My daughter is cruelly tormented by the devil.* Jesus heard her but did not respond. Saint Augustine comments that He did not answer her precisely because He knew what she was to receive. He did not remain silent in order to refuse her, but so that she – through her humble perseverance – would merit the favour.[2]

The woman probably insisted for a long time, so that the disciples – tired of her efforts – told the Master: *Send her away, for she is crying after us.* Our Lord explained to her that He had come to preach first to the Jews. But the woman – despite the negative response – prostrated herself before him saying: *Lord, help me!*

The Canaanean woman's persistence led our Lord to repeat his answer using an image which she understood at once: *It is not right to take the children's bread and cast it to the dogs.* Again He tells her that He has been sent to the sons of Israel and should not show preference for pagans. Our Lord's loving and welcoming gesture would remove any hint of harshness from the expression He uses. His

---

1. Matt 15:21-28
2. St Augustine, *Sermon 154 A*, 4

words filled the woman with confidence. With great humility, she replied: *It is true Lord, but even the dogs can eat of the crumbs which fall from their masters' table.* She recognized her true place; *she confessed as her lords those whom He called children.*[3] Saint Augustine himself says that the woman *was transformed by humility*, and deserved to sit at the table with the children.[4] She conquered the heart of God, receiving the favour she requested as well as a great compliment from our Lord: *O woman! Great is your faith! Let it be done as you wish. And at that instant, her daughter was healed.* Later, she would surely be one of the first gentile women to embrace the Faith, and she would preserve from that moment a lasting gratitude and love for our Lord.

We, who are far from the faith and humility of this woman, fervently ask the Master, *Dear Jesus, if I have to be an apostle you will need to make me very humble.*

Everything the sun touches is bathed in light. Lord, fill me with your clarity, bathe me in your divinity so that I may identify my will with your adorable Will and become the instrument you wish me to be. Give me the madness to undergo the humiliation you underwent, which led you to be born poor, to work in obscurity, to endure the shame of dying sewn by nails to a piece of wood, to your self-effacement in the Blessed Sacrament.

May I know myself: may I know myself and know you. I will then never lose sight of my nothingness.[5] Only thus will I be able to follow you as you wish, and as I wish: with a deep faith, a great love and without placing any obstacles in the way.

---

3. *ibid, Sermon 60* A, 2-4
4. *ibid*
5. J. Escrivá, *Furrow*, 273

51.2 The active nature of humility.

In the account of the life of Saint Anthony, Abbot, it is said that God showed him the world beset with the snares the devil had prepared to entrap men. Following the vision, the saint was filled with fear, and asked, *Lord, who can escape so many snares?* And he heard a voice that answered, *Anthony, he who is humble can escape, for God gives his grace to the humble, but the proud fall into all the traps the devil sets. Yet the devil does not dare to attack the humble man.*

If we want to serve the Lord, we must desire and ask for the virtue of humility with insistence. To truly desire this virtue, we should keep in mind that the opposite of humility – the capital sin of pride – is the greatest obstacle to the vocation we have received from the Lord. It is what harms family life and friendship, what opposes our true happiness most of all. It is the devil's foremost ally in our soul, with which he tries to undo the work that the Holy Spirit is constantly carrying out.

Living the virtue of humility is not only a matter rejecting the motions of pride, selfishness and vanity. In fact, Jesus and Mary, who possessed the virtue of humility to the full, never experienced any inclination toward pride. The word 'humility' derives from the Latin word *humus* (soil or earth). Etymologically, 'humble' signifies inclined towards the earth; the virtue of humility consists in bowing down before God and everything that is of God in creatures.[6] In practical terms, it leads us to recognize our inferiority, our littleness and indigence before God. The saints experience great joy in becoming nothing before God, recognizing that only He is great and that all human

---

6. R. Garrigou-Lagrange, *The Three Ages of the Interior Life*, vol II, p. 670

greatness is, by comparison, empty and a lie.

Humility is based on truth,[7] and above all on the great truth that the distance between the creature and the Creator is infinite. That is why we should frequently take time to remind and persuade ourselves that everything good in us is from God, that all the good that we have done has been suggested and brought to fruition by him, with the help of his grace. We do not say a single aspiration without the impulse and grace of the Holy Spirit.[8] Ours are the defects, sins and selfishness. *These miseries are less than nothing, because they are a disorder and reduce our soul to a truly deplorable state.*[9] Grace, on the other hand, makes our soul shine so that even the angels are awed by the brightness of the divine gift.

The Canaanean woman did not feel humiliated by Jesus' comparison emphasizing the difference between Jews and pagans. She was humble and knew her place with respect to the chosen people. Because she was humble she was not ashamed to persevere, prostrating herself before Jesus in spite of the apparent rejection. Because of her humility, daring and perseverance, she obtained a great favour. Humility has nothing to do with timidity, with fickleness or with a mediocre life lacking in ambition. Humility discovers that everything good in us, both in the order of nature and in the order of grace, belongs to God for from his fullness we have all received.[10] And such profusion of gifts moves us to be grateful.

---

7. St Teresa, *The Interior Castle*, VI, 10
8. 1 Cor 12:3
9. R. Garrigou-Lagrange, *op cit*, vol II, p.674
10. 1 Cor 1:4

51.3 The road to humility.

To the question, 'How shall I become humble?' corresponds the immediate answer, 'Through the grace of God'. … Only the grace of God can give us a clear vision of our true condition and the awareness of the dignity that comes from humility.[11] That is why we should desire this virtue and ask for it incessantly, convinced that with it, we shall love God and be capable of great enterprises despite our weakness …

Together with this petition we should accept the humiliations – usually small – that may arise each day in different ways: during our work and in our dealings with others, when we are conscious of our weakness or make mistakes, great or small. One day, it is said, Saint Thomas Aquinas was pulled up for a supposed grammatical error while reading. He corrected it as indicated. Later, his companions asked him why he had made the correction since he himself must have known that the original text was faultless. *Before God*, the saint replied, *better a fault of grammar than a fault of obedience and of humility*. We walk the way of humility when we accept humiliations, great or small, and when we accept our defects and struggle to overcome them.

He who is humble can do without praise or flattery in his work because his hope is in the Lord, who is truly the source of all his riches and happiness and gives meaning to all he does. *One of the reasons why men are so prone to praise one another, to overestimate their own value and abilities, to resent anything that tends to lower them in their own eyes or in the eyes of others, is that they see no hope for happiness outside themselves. That is why they are often so hyper-sensitive, so resentful when they are criticized, so upset*

---

11. E. Boylan, *This Tremendous Lover*, p. 81

by anyone who contradicts them, so insistent on getting their own way, so desirous of being well known, so anxious to be praised, so determined to control their surroundings. They secure themselves to themselves like a shipwrecked man holding on to a straw. And life goes on, and they move further and further away from happiness ... [12]

He who struggles to be humble does not seek out praise, and if praises come, he tries to refer them instead to the glory of God, the author of all good things. Humility does not consist so much in despising oneself as in forgetting oneself, joyfully recognizing that we possess nothing that we have not received. It leads us to become God's little children, who find all their strength in the strong hand of their Father.

We learn to be humble by meditating on the Passion of our Lord, by considering his greatness in the face of so many humiliations, allowing himself as He did to be led like a sheep to its shearers, as had been prophesied;[13] by considering his humility in the Holy Eucharist where He waits for us to visit him and speak with him, to be received by anyone who wants to attend the sacred Banquet He prepares for us daily; by considering his patience in the light of so many offences. We will learn to walk the path of humility if we pay attention to Mary, *the handmaid of the Lord*, who had no other desire than to do the Will of God. We can also approach Saint Joseph, who spent his life serving Jesus and Mary, fulfilling the task that God had entrusted to him.

---

12. *ibid*, p. 82
13. Is 53:7

EIGHTEENTH WEEK: THURSDAY

52. YOU ARE THE CHRIST

52.1 *You are the Christ, the son of the Living God:*
confess in this way the divinity of Jesus Christ.

Jesus was in Caesarea Philippi, in the northern
confines of Jewish territory where the population was
predominantly pagan. There He asked his disciples with
complete confidence, *Who do men say the Son of Man is?*[1]
The Apostles, familiar with the opinions the people had of
him, replied, *Some say John the Baptist; and others Elias;
and others Jeremias or one of the prophets.* Many of those
who listened to him thought highly of Him, but did not
know who He really was. The Master turned to them and
affectionately asked, *But who do you say that I am?* From
his own – those who follow him closely – He seemed to
demand a clear, uncompromising confession of faith. They
should not conform to a superficial popular opinion, so
subject to change. They should know him well and make
him known, for they have left everything to live a new life
with him.

Peter answered firmly: *You are the Christ, the Son of
the Living God.* It is a clear affirmation of his divinity, as
confirmed by Jesus' reply: *Blessed are you Simon, son of
John, for flesh and blood has not revealed this to you, but
my Father in Heaven.* Peter must have been profoundly
moved by the Master's words.

Even today there are varying and divergent opinions
concerning Jesus: there is a great deal of ignorance

---

1. Matt 16:13-23

regarding his person and mission. Despite the preaching and apostolate of the Church over twenty centuries, many souls have still not discovered Jesus' true identity. He still lives among us and asks, *And you, who do you say that I am?* With the help of God's grace, which is never lacking, we too should proclaim with firmness – with the supernatural firmness of faith – 'You, Lord, are my God and my King: perfect God and perfect Man, *centre of the universe and of history*,[2] centre of my life and the motive and cause of all my actions.'

During his Passion, when He is about to complete his mission on earth, the Chief Priest asks Jesus, *Are you the Messiah, the Son of the Blessed One?* Jesus replies, *I am, and you will see the Son of Man seated at the right hand of the Father, and coming with the clouds of heaven.*[3] With this response He not only affirms that He is the Messiah whom they await, but also declares the divine transcendence of his messianism, attributing to Himself Daniel's prophecy of the Son of Man.[4] The Lord uses the strongest possible words found in the Bible to declare his divinity. It is then and on this account that they condemn Him for blasphemy.

Only the clarity of supernatural faith allows us to know that Jesus is infinitely superior to all creatures: He is *the only Son of God, born of the Father before all things were made: God from God, Light from Light, true God from true God, begotten not made, one in Being with the Father, by whom all things were made; who for us men and for our salvation came down from heaven, and by the power of the Holy Spirit was born of the Virgin Mary and became man* ...[5] He was begotten of the Father,[6] but remains in full

---

2. John Paul II, Encyclical, *Redemptor hominis*, 1
3. Mark 14:61-62
4. cf Dan 7:13-14
5. *Roman Missal*, Nicene creed
6. cf John 8:42

communion with him, because He has the same divine nature. In union with the Father, He will send the Holy Spirit,[7] who will keep what He keeps, for He keeps as his own all that is of the Father.[8]

He comes as supreme Law-giver: *Before, it was said to the ancients ... But I say to you now ...* [9] In the old law, it was stated, *Thus speaks Yahweh,* but Jesus does not teach in another's name: *I tell you ...* In his own name He imparts the divine teaching, and sets forth precepts that affect the essence of man. He exercises the power to forgive sins, any sin.[10] As all Jews knew, this power pertains only to God. Not only does He personally forgive sins, but He gives the power of the keys, the power to rule and forgive, to Peter and the Twelve Apostles and their successors.[11] He promises, at the end of the world, to sit as the only judge of the living and the dead.[12] No one before or since has ever dared attribute to himself those awesome powers.

Jesus demanded – demands – of his disciples an unwavering faith in his person, to the point of bearing the Cross on their shoulders: *he who does not pick up his cross and follow me is not worthy of me.*[13] What He asks for his heavenly Father, He also asks for himself: a solid faith, an unlimited love.[14]

We who wish to follow him very closely, when we are before the Tabernacle say to him with Saint Peter: *Lord, you are the Christ, the Son of the Living God.* Truly, *he who*

---

7. cf John 15:26
8. cf John 16:11-15
9. Matt 5:21-48
10. cf Matt 11:28
11. cf Matt 18:18
12. cf Mark 14:62
13. Matt 10:38
14. cf K. Adam, *Jesus Christ*, p.171

finds Jesus finds a good treasure; truly, a good above all other good. He who loses Jesus loses a great deal, much more than the entire world. Very poor is he who lives without him, and very rich he who is with Jesus.[15] Let us not ever leave him. Let us make our love firm with many acts of faith, with the courage to make our faith and our love for the living Christ known in any environment.

52.2 Christ: perfect God and perfect Man.

Even after so many years Jesus remains for many, who lack the supernatural gift of faith or who live immersed in lukewarmness, a hazy and indistinct figure. Just as the apostles answered him that day, we too can tell him: some say you were a man of high ideals, while others ... The words of the Baptist ring true even today: *In the midst of you there has stood one whom you do not know.*[16]

Only the divine gift of faith allows us to proclaim, in union with the Magisterium of the Church: *We believe in our Lord Jesus Christ, who is the Son of God. He is the eternal Word, born of the Father before all things were made, and consubstantial with the Father* ...[17] We believe that in Jesus Christ there are two natures – one divine and the other human, distinct yet inseparable. He is one Person, the Second Person of the Blessed Trinity, uncreated and eternal, who became man by the power of the Holy Spirit in the most pure womb of Mary. Born in the direst poverty, He was acclaimed by the angels in Heaven. He suffered hunger and thirst. He felt fatigue and at times needed to rest, on a rock or at the edge of a well. So tired was He that He fell asleep at sea on the fishermen's boat. He wept at the tomb of his friend, Lazarus. He was

15. Thomas à Kempis, *Imitation of Christ*, II, 8:2
16. John 1:26
17. Paul VI, *Creed of the People of God*, 30 June 1968

overwhelmed with grief and feared death before suffering the humiliations of his crucifixion.

Jesus is also perfect Man. This most Holy Humanity of Jesus, equal to ours in everything but sin, has become our way to the Father. He lives today. Why do you seek the one who lives among the dead?[18] He is the same today as then. *'Iesus Christus heri, et hodie, ipse et in saecula'* (*Heb 13:8*). *How I love to recall these words! Jesus Christ, the very Jesus who was alive yesterday for his apostles and the people who sought him out; this same Jesus lives today for us, and will live forever. Yet at times we poor men fail to recognize his ever-present features because our eyes are tired and our vision clouded.*[19] Our vision is clouded because we lack love.

52.3 Christ: *the Way, the Truth and the Life.*

Christian life consists in loving, imitating and serving Christ. The heart has an important rôle in this life to such an extent that if, through lukewarmness or a hidden pride, our life of piety suffers it becomes almost impossible to move ahead. To follow Christ closely means to be his friends. That friendly, intimate union leads us to follow even the smallest of his precepts: love is expressed in deeds. After many attempts – all in vain – to find Christ, Saint Augustine shares with us his experience: *I looked all around for the strength I needed to delight in You and could not find it, until I at last embraced the Mediator between God and man: the Man, Jesus Christ, who is above all things and blessed for all time. It is He who calls and tells us, 'I am the Way, the Truth and the Life'* (*John 14:6*).[20] We are to love a man – Jesus Christ!

---

18. cf Luke 24:5
19. J. Escrivá, *Friends of God*, 127
20. St Augustine, *Confessions*, 7,18

Jesus Christ is the only *Way*. No one can go to the Father except through him.[21] Only through him, with him and in him can we reach our supernatural destiny. The Church brings this to our attention each day in Holy Mass: *Through Him, with Him, in Him, in the unity of the Holy Spirit, all glory and honour is yours ...* Only through Christ, his Most Beloved Son, will the Father accept our love and homage.

Christ is also the *Truth*. He is the absolute and total truth, uncreated Wisdom, who reveals himself to us in his most Holy Humanity. Without Christ, our life would be a vast lie.

The Old Testament narrates that, at God's command, Moses lifted up his hand and struck the rock two times, and water came forth so abundantly that all his thirsty people drank their fill.[22] That water symbolized the Life that pours forth from Christ and springs up unto life everlasting.[23] He is our Life because He merited grace for us, supernatural life for our soul; because that life flows from him – in a special way – in the sacraments; because He communicates his life to us. All the grace we possess, that of all humanity – fallen and redeemed – is God's grace given to us through Christ. We receive grace in many ways, but the spring from which it flows is one: Christ himself, his most Holy Humanity united to the Person of the Word, the Second Person of the Blessed Trinity.

When in the intimacy of our hearts our Lord asks, *And you, who do you say that I am?*, we should respond with the faith of Peter: *You are the Christ, the Son of the Living God, the Way, the Truth and the Life ...* Without him my life would be completely empty and I would be lost.

---

21. cf John 14:6
22. cf *First Reading*, Year I: Num 20:1-13
23. cf John 4:14, 7:38

EIGHTEENTH WEEK: FRIDAY

53. LOVE AND THE CROSS

53.1 The greatest manifestation of love.

Jesus called his disciples, and leaving everything behind, they followed him. They accompanied the Master on the roads of Palestine, to villages and towns. They shared joys and fatigue and hunger. At times they risked their reputations and indeed their very lives for Jesus. At first they accompanied him externally, but little by little an interior disposition to follow him took root: their souls were transformed. This deeper disposition requires more than mere detachment, and even more than abandoning house and home, family and material possessions. In the Gospel[1] of today's Mass our Lord says, *He who wishes to come after me, let him deny himself, take up his cross and follow me.*

Denying oneself means refusing to be the centre of one's own attention. The true disciple must be centred on Christ, to whom must be directed all thoughts and cares, so that our entire day truly becomes an offering to God.

To carry the cross means that one is willing to die. Whoever picks up the cross and carries it squarely accepts his destiny and knows that his life will end on that cross. Carrying the cross means that a firm resolution has been made; it indicates that we are willing to follow him – if necessary unto death – that we wish to imitate him in everything without placing obstacles between us. To follow

---

1. Matt 16:24-25

Christ we should identify our will with his; He took up his cross without hesitation. He carried it to Calvary, where He offered himself to God the Father in an offering of infinite merit and love.

We should consider frequently that his Passion and Death on the Cross are the greatest expression of his love for the Father and for us. Certainly, the smallest act of love He performed, his most insignificant work – even as a child – had infinite merit, sufficient to obtain for all men over all of time the grace of salvation; to obtain for them eternal life and all the grace they would need to obtain it. In spite of this He was still willing to suffer the horrors of his Passion and Death on the Cross to show us how much He loves the Father, and how much He loves each of us. Sometimes He expressed to his disciples the urgency that filled his soul: *I have a baptism to be baptised with, and how distressed I am until it is accomplished ...* [2] The Holy Spirit has written through Saint John: *God so loved the world that He gave his only begotten Son.* [3] Jesus freely gave up his life for us because He loved us, for *greater love than this no one has, that one lay down his life for his friends.* [4]

Jesus Christ cannot restrain his desire to give his life for our love. If we want to follow him, not just externally but deeply, identifying ourselves with him, how can we reject the Cross, the sacrifice so intimately related with love and self-giving? Being close to Christ will lead us to complete self-surrender, to true love, to the greatest joy. Forgetting ourselves, identifying ourselves with his holy will in all things, cleans, purifies, makes transparent and divinizes our soul. *To have the Cross is to have joy: it is to have you Lord!* [5]

---

2. Luke 12:50
3. John 3:16
4. John 15:13
5. J. Escrivá, *The Forge*, 766

53.2 The meaning and fruits of suffering.

A holy soul once experienced difficult trials. One calamity after another befell her, and each succeeding disaster seemed worse than the one before. Finally, that soul turned affectionately to our Lord and asked, *But Lord, what have I done to you?* And in the depths of her heart came the reply, *You have loved me.* She thought of Calvary and understood a little better how our Lord wanted to purify her and draw her close to the salvation of many who were lost, far from God. She was then filled with peace and joy.[6]

In our lives we will encounter sorrows, as all men do. *If you have difficulties, be assured that they are a proof of the fatherly love the Lord has for you.*[7] These are good moments to look with love upon Christ on the Cross, to understand that from the Cross He is telling us *I love you more, from you I expect more.* Perhaps it is a painful illness that disrupts the plans we have made, or a misfortune affecting those whom we love most, or some kind of professional failure. *Lord, what have I done to you?*, we will ask. And He will respond in silence that He loves us; that He wants an unlimited acceptance of his divine will; that his *logic* is different from human reasoning. Then, when we accept and abandon ourselves, we come to understand – though perhaps later – what a great good are those difficulties. How thankful will we then be to our Lord![8]

Often, though, we will find the Cross in the ordinary and even trivial things that we encounter in the course of run-of-the-mill days: fatigue; lacking the time we would like to do things; having to renounce a pleasant plan that we had made; bearing with love the defects of persons

---

6. R. Garrigou-Lagrange, *The Saviour*, p. 311
7. J. Escrivá, *op cit*, 815
8. J. Tissot, *The Interior Life*, p. 318

with whom we live and work or, in connection with them, some small, unexpected humiliation; aridity in prayer ... Our Lord awaits us there as well. He asks that we accept those contradictions – great or small – without sterile complaints, without bitterness or rebellion. He asks for our love, taking up that which goes against us and offering it as a valuable jewel. Our small contradictions united with those of Christ on the Cross acquire an infinite value to make reparation for the many sins committed daily the world over, and for our sins as well.

Sorrows borne with and for love bear many other rich fruits: they serve as satisfaction for our sins; they purify our soul; *they deepen and strengthen our character and personality. They are the only way to acquire a certain special understanding and sympathy for our neighbour. In fact, they open us to Christ's own interior life, and thus unite us more closely to him. Often, deep suffering sets its mark on a decisive moment in our lives and leads us to a renewed fervour and hope,*[9] to a new way – fuller and deeper – of understanding our own existence. But pain and suffering should not mean sadness. When we carry our Cross together with Christ, our soul is filled with peace and a deep joy amidst all its trials. The life of the saints is full of joy, a joy the world does not understand because its roots are sunk in God.

53.3 Seeking out mortifications.

If anyone will come after me ... We want nothing in the world but to follow Christ closely. No other thing – not even our own lives – do we love more than this: identifying ourselves with him; making the desires and sentiments that He had on earth our own. We are close to him

---

9. E. Boylan, *This Tremendous Lover*, p. 119

not only when things are going well, but also when we accept adversities with patience, happy to be able to accompany him on the way of the Cross, uniting our sufferings with his.[10]

If, however, we were only to await the trials and contradictions, the pain we cannot avoid, our love would lack generosity. We would be content with just getting by. *We would have a reluctant disposition, that might be described in these words: Mortification? Life has enough sorrows! I have enough worries already!*

However, interior life depends too much on mortification not to seek it out actively. Those mortifications which arise spontaneously are important and valuable, but should not serve as excuses to flee from generous voluntary sacrifices, the sign of a true spirit of penance. 'I will freely offer you sacrifice; I will sing your name, O Yahweh, your name, because it is good' (Ps 53:8).[11]

The Church proposes that we consider the penitential aspect of our lives one day each week – on Fridays – by reflecting on the Passion of Christ. On this day, many Christians consider with greater care the sorrowful mysteries of Christ's life, or they accompany him on the Way of the Cross, or they read or meditate on his Passion. It is a good day to examine more carefully how we habitually bear contradictions and the generosity – fruit of love – with which we seek out voluntary mortifications in little things; or how we struggle against our selfishness, laziness or the desire to be well thought of, to be the centre of attention. Other points for examination might include the small mortifications that make the lives of others more

---

10. Paul VI, Apostolic Constitution, *Paenitemini*, 17 February 1966, 1
11. R. M. Balbin, *Sacrifice and Joy*, Madrid, 1975.

enjoyable; being cordial in our dealings with others; not giving in to bad moods that perhaps will lead to brusque manners; smiling when we tend to be more serious; being punctual in our work or studies; eating a little less of what we like most or a little more of what we like least; not eating between meals; keeping our desk, wardrobe or room neat and orderly; not giving in to curiosity; guarding our senses with refinement; not complaining about excessive heat or cold or heavy traffic ...

As we finish today's meditation on the words of Jesus, *if anyone wishes to come after me, let him deny himself, take up his cross and follow me*, we request of him in the intimacy of our prayer, *Grant me, Jesus, the Cross with no Simon of Cyrene to help me. No, that's not right; I need your grace, I need your help here as in everything. You must be my Simon of Cyrene. With you, my God, no trial can daunt me ... But what if my cross should consist of boredom or sadness? In that case I would say to you, Lord, with You I will gladly be sad.*[12] *As long as I don't lose You, no sorrow will be a sorrow at all.*[13]

---

12. J. Escrivá, *op cit*, 252
13. *ibid*, 253

EIGHTEENTH WEEK: SATURDAY

54. THE POWER OF THE FAITH

54.1 Faith is able to move mountains. The greatest miracles occur daily in the Church.

From the great crowds awaiting Jesus' arrival, a man came forward and threw himself on his knees before him saying, *Lord, have pity on my son ...* [1] The attitude and words of this father show that his prayer is humble. He appeals not to the power of Jesus, but to His compassion. He does not advance his own merits nor does he offer anything of value. He looks to Jesus' mercy.

To seek out the merciful heart of Christ is to be heard always: the man's son would be healed even though the apostles were unable to heal him earlier. Later, privately, the disciples asked our Lord why they couldn't cure the possessed boy. He said to them, *Because of your little faith, for amen I say to you, if you have faith like a mustard seed, you will say to this mountain, remove from here, and it will remove. And nothing will be impossible to you.*

When we truly live by faith, we participate in God's omnipotence. Thus our Lord would say at another time, *He who believes in me, the works that I do he also shall do, and greater than these he shall do, because I am going to the Father. And whatever you ask in my name, that I will do in order that the Father be glorified in the Son. If you ask me anything in name, I will do it.* [2] And Saint Augustine

---

1. Matt 17:14-20
2. John 14:12-14

comments, *He who believes in me is not greater than I; but I will then do greater things than those I do now. I will do more through him who believes in me, than what I now do on my own.*[3]

Our Lord told the apostles in this passage of the Gospel from today's Mass that they would be able to *move mountains* from one place to another, an expression that has become proverbial. These words of our Lord – and more – are fulfilled each day in the Church. Some Fathers of the Church point out that 'mountains are moved' whenever a person – with the assistance of grace – attains what human strength alone cannot attain. Such is the case with the work of our personal sanctification that the Holy Spirit carries out in our soul and in the apostolate. Although it may pass unnoticed, this work is much more sublime than the moving of mountains, and is carried out daily in the lives of many holy souls.

The Apostles and other saints through the centuries have also performed wonderful miracles in the physical order; but the greatest and most important miracles have been, are and will be those of souls that have been submerged in the death of sin, in ignorance or spiritual mediocrity, and are reborn and grow up in the new life of the sons of God.[4] *'Si habueritis fidem, sicut granum sinapis ... If you have faith like the grain of a mustard seed ... '*

What promises are contained in this exclamation of the Master!,[5] promises for our interior life, for the apostolate, for everything we need ...

---

3. St Augustine, *Commentary on St John's Gospel*, 72,1
4. *The Navarre Bible*, in loc
5. J. Escrivá, *The Way*, 585

54.2 The greater the obstacles, the greater the grace.

Lord, why could we not cure the boy? Why could we not do good in your name? Saint Mark[6] and many manuscripts which record this text, add these words of our Lord: *This kind* (of devil) *can be cast out only by prayer and fasting.*

The Apostles were unable to free this possessed boy because they lacked the faith required, a faith that should have been manifested in prayer and mortification. We too may encounter some who need these means to arouse them from the prostration of sin or religious ignorance ... Something similar occurs with different metals: they melt at different temperatures. The hard interior of some souls – perhaps more ingrained in bad habits – requires more energetic supernatural means. Let us not leave these souls sunk in their lethargy for want *of prayer and fasting.*

Our Lord teaches us that faith as tiny as a mustard seed is capable of moving mountains. Let us ask frequently throughout this day and during this time of prayer for that faith that prompts us to use the supernatural and human means generously. *This is the victory that overcomes the world: our faith.[7] With this faith, the mountains – the most formidable obstacles we may encounter along our way – will crumble before us, because our God does not lose battles. Walk then, 'in nomine Domini', with joy and security in our Lord's name. Without pessimism! If difficulties arise, God's grace will abound. If more difficulties appear, from heaven we will have poured down on us even more of God's grace. If there are many difficulties, we can count on all the greater access of grace. Divine assistance is proportional to the obstacles that the world and the devil erect against the*

---

6. Mark 9:29
7. 1 John 5:4

apostolic work. That is why I dare to affirm that difficulties are good, because where they exist we will have more of God's assistance: where the offence has abounded, grace has abounded yet more (Rom 5:20).[8]

The greatest obstacles to the miracles that even today our Lord wishes – with our help – to work in souls arise above all from within us. With a human outlook, we can narrow the horizons that our Lord continually opens in the lives of our friends and acquaintances, relatives and colleagues. We should never think that anyone is *a hopeless case* in the apostolate. As the saints have demonstrated, the word 'impossible' does not exist in the vocabulary of one who truly lives by faith. *God is always the same. It is men of faith that are needed: when He has them there will be a renewal of the wonders we have read of in the Holy Scriptures.*

'Ecce non est abbreviata manus Domini: The hand of God the Lord', his power, 'has not grown weaker!'[9] Even today He works the same marvels as He did then.

54.3 Faith with deeds.

Christ lays down one condition: we must live by faith; then we will be able to move mountains. And so many things need moving ... in the world, but first in our own hearts. So many obstacles placed in the way of grace! We have to have faith therefore: faith and good works, faith and sacrifice, faith and humility. For faith makes us all-powerful: 'If you only will believe, every gift you ask for in your prayer will be granted' (Matt 21:22).[10]

Faith should be put into practice daily. *'Estote factores verbi et non auditores tantum'* – Be doers of the word and

---

8. A. del Portillo, *Letter*, 31 May 1987, 22

9. J. Escrivá, *op cit*, 586

10. *idem*, *Friends of God*, 203

not hearers only.[11] Carry out in your life the word of God; do not limit yourselves to merely listening to it or acknowledging it, exhorts the Apostle James. This is not enough. It is necessary to live those truths, to fulfil them. Faith should generate a life of faith, which is a manifestation of friendship with Jesus Christ. We should approach God with our lives, our works, our sorrows and joys ...with everything![12]

All too often difficulties arise from or are exaggerated by our lack of faith. We may pay too much attention to attendant circumstances or we may become excessively prudent, an attitude that may result from a lack of rectitude of intention. *There is nothing – however simple – that our lukewarmness won't present to us as difficult and costly. Conversely, there is nothing – however difficult and costly – that our fervour and determination won't present to us as pleasant and agreeable.*[13]

A life of faith leads to a healthy *superiority complex*, born of a deep personal humility because – as Saint Augustine recalls – *faith belongs to the humble, not to the proud.*[14] Faith results from the deep conviction that one's efficacy comes entirely from God, not from oneself. This confidence leads the Christian to confront the obstacles he may encounter in his soul or in his apostolate with a *will to win*, even though the fruits of his efforts may be late in coming. With prayer and mortification, with friendship and joy, we will be able to perform those great miracles in souls. We will be able to *move mountains*, to bring down barriers which appeared insurmountable, to bring our friends to Confession, to help others regain the road that

---

11. Jas 1:22
12. P. Rodriguez, *Faith and Life of faith*
13. St John Chrysostom, *De compunctione*, 1:5
14. St Augustine, *Catena aurea*, vol VI, p.297

leads to our Lord. The faith that will enable us to move mountains is nurtured in an intimate relation with Jesus, in prayer and in the sacraments.

Our Mother Mary will show us how to be filled with faith and love and daring in that course our Lord has marked for us in the middle of the world. She is that *good instrument, completely identified with the mission received. Once she learns of God's plan, she makes it her own. Her plans are not something added on. In the just fulfilment of these plans, she completely disposes her intelligence and will and all her energies. She is never an inert puppet: not when she sets out joyfully through the mountains of Judaea to visit her cousin Elizabeth; not when, truly exercizing her duty as mother, she seeks and finds the Child Jesus in the temple of Jerusalem; not when she causes our Lord's first miracle; not when she appears – without being called – at the foot of the Cross on which her Son died ... By saying 'Be it done' she freely disposes her entire person to the fulfilment of her calling. This calling does not seem foreign to her: God's interests are her own interests. She does not run the risk that Her plans might pose an obstacle to the plans of God; her plans are perfectly identified with his.*[15]

---

15. J. M. Pero-Sanz, *The Sixth Hour*, Madrid, 1978

NINETEENTH SUNDAY: YEAR A

55. GOD ALWAYS HELPS

55.1 He never failed his friends.

The First Reading of today's Mass[1] presents the prophet Elias who, fatigued and disheartened by many trials, seeks refuge in a cave on Mount Horeb, the holy mountain where God showed himself to Moses. There, Elias was told: *Go out and wait for the Lord.* A powerful hurricane passed shattering mountains and destroying boulders. A mighty earthquake and fires followed, but God was not to be found in the hurricane or in the earthquake or in the fire. Then a soft breeze passed – like a whisper – and God was there. In this way, God expressed his mysterious spirituality and his gentle benevolence towards the weakness of man. Elias now felt strengthened for the new mission that our Lord wanted him to fulfil.

The Gospel[2] tells of one of the tempests the Apostles experienced when our Lord was not with them in the boat. It occurred after the multiplication of the loaves and fishes. The Lord instructed them to set out for the opposite shore while He sent the people off, for it was already quite late. From the top of a hill where he was recollected in prayer, He did not forget his disciples. He could see that a strong wind was blowing against them. Our Lord saw them struggling with the waves and gale-force wind trying to reach the place He had suggested.

---

1. 1 Kings 19:11-13
2. Matt 14:22-33

Finishing his prayer, he sets out to help them.

During the fourth quarter of the night Jesus nears the boat; it was being buffeted by the waves and in danger of capsizing. The Gospel tells us that the disciples were filled with fear as they saw Jesus approaching, walking on the turbulent waters. They thought He was a ghost. Saint Mark, who recorded this unforgetable moment as recounted to him by Saint Peter, writes that Jesus walked past them as if to continue on his way. They all began to shout. Jesus then came closer and said: *Have confidence; it is I, do not fear.* These were consoling words that we too have often heard – many times and in different ways – in the intimacy of our heart when faced with a disconcerting situation, or in difficulties or trying times.

If our life is the fulfilment of what God wants for us – like Elias who goes to Mount Horeb at God's command, or the Apostles who do as Jesus said even though the wind *was against them* – then divine help will never be lacking. In moments of weakness, of fatigue, in the most difficult situations, Jesus shows himself and tells us: *it is I, do not fear.* He never fails his friends.[3] If we have no other goal in life but to seek his friendship and serve him, how could He ever abandon us when the winds of temptation, of fatigue, of difficulties in the apostolate go against us? He will not pass us by and go on his way. *If you have confidence in him and a cheerful disposition – His Majesty is quite partial to this – do not be afraid of lacking anything.*[4] What could we possibly lack if we are his friends in the middle of the world, if we want to follow him day after day among all those others who abandon him?

---

3. cf St Teresa, *Life*, 11:4
4. *idem*, *Foundations*, 27:12

55.2 Christ is the firm anchor on whom we should rely.

When the Apostles heard Jesus, they were filled with peace. Then Peter shouted out a daring and courageous request: *Lord, if it is You, then command that I go out to You on the water.* The Master, who was still a few yards from the boat, answered: *Come.* Peter had much faith, and gave up the security of the boat out of confidence in Jesus' words. *Leaving the boat, he began to walk on the water towards Jesus.* They were impressive moments. Moments of firmness and love.

Then Peter stopped looking at Jesus and began to notice the difficulties around him. Seeing that the wind was so strong, he became fearful. He forgot for a moment that the strength holding him up on the water did not depend on the circumstances, but on the Will of the Lord, who rules over heaven and earth, life and death, all nature, the winds and the sea ... Peter began to sink, not because of the waves but because his confidence in him who can do all things wavered. He cried out to Jesus: *Lord save me!* Jesus immediately extended his hand, held him up and said: *Man of little faith, why have you doubted?* In moments of weakness or tiredness, when we see ourselves sinking, we should look to Jesus' firm hand to steady ourselves. In our prayer we can cry out to him: *Lord, save me!*

Sometimes the Christian may stop looking at Christ and pay more attention to things that separate him from God. These things may endanger his faith and lead him to sink down if he does not react promptly. From the moment one begins to lose the clarity of his faith or the vocation received from God, *he should make a sincere examination of conscience. He will not fail to see that – perhaps for some time – his life of piety has been a bit lax, his prayer less frequent or more distracted, he has been less demanding on himself. Is not a sin all the more detrimental*

when its seriousness is deliberately hidden from the sinner?
Surely, he does not struggle against his passions as before,
and may even complacently consent to some. A feeling of
resentment towards another that is allowed to fester, a lack
of honesty in certain questions that interest us, a friendship
that is too absorbing or simply the awakening of baser
instincts that are not rejected with vigour: little else is needed
to raise up clouds between ourselves and God. Thus, the
light of faith becomes darkened.[5]

To stay afloat Peter needed only to hold on to the
strong hand of the Lord, his Friend and his God. However
little, the disciple had to contribute his share; and his
share was the good will that God always asks of us. *When*
God our Lord gives us his grace, when He calls us by a
specific vocation, it is as if He were stretching out his hand
to us in a fatherly way. A strong hand, full of love, because
He seeks us out individually, as his own sons and daughters,
knowing our weakness. The Lord expects us to make the
effort to take his hand, his helping hand. He asks us to
make an effort and show we are free.[6]

The degree of effort our Lord asks to keep his disciples afloat in the face of a difficult situation may vary from
time to time, but the remedies are the same for all
throughout history: intensify prayer; be more sincere and
docile in spiritual direction; flee from dangerous occasions; obey promptly and with docility of heart; together
with prayer, use the human means – however small – we
have available … With Christ, in all battles, we will
emerge victorious, but we need to have complete
confidence in him. *Pray resolutely, using the words of the*
Psalmist: 'Thou Lord, art my refuge and my strength. I trust

---

5. G. Chevrot, *Simon Peter*
6. J. Escrivá, *Christ is passing by*, 17

in thee.'

I promise you that He will preserve you from the ambushes of the 'noontide devil' when you are tempted and even when you fall, and when your age and virtues ought to have proved a solid safeguard and you should have known in your heart that He alone is your stronghold.[7]

55.3 Confidence in God. He never arrives late to rescue us, if we go to him with faith and use the means available to us.

Peter stayed on his feet – even when facing the greatest difficulties – as long as he acted with supernatural outlook, with faith, with confidence in the Lord. Later, in order to stay afloat, to receive God's help, he had to cooperate, because *when our cooperation is lacking divine help also ceases.*[8] It was our Lord who helped him to go on.

Peter recovered his faith and confidence in Jesus. He climbed aboard the boat with him, and at that moment the wind ceased and calm was restored to the seas and to the hearts of the disciples. They recognized Jesus as their Lord and God. Those who were in the boat worshipped him, saying, *Truly, you are the Son of God*.

The experience of our personal weakness will serve for us to find Jesus who puts out his hand and enters our heart, giving us great peace in the midst of any trial. We should learn never to be afraid of God, who presents himself in ordinary things, as well as in the physical or moral sufferings we may experience in our lives. *Have confidence; it is I, do not fear.* God never delays coming to our rescue, and never fails to remedy every need. He

---

7. *idem*, *The Forge*, 307
8. St John Chrysostom, *Homilies on St Matthew's Gospel*, 50, 2

arrives – at times in a hidden and mysterious way – at the opportune time. And when, for whatever reason, we find ourselves in a difficult situation – with the wind against us – He comes close to us. He may pass as if to continue on so that we will call out to him, but He will not delay in coming to our side when we do.

If at times we realize that we are out of our depth, that we are sinking, we should repeat with Peter, *Lord, save me!* We should neither doubt his Love nor his merciful hand. We should not forget that *God does not demand the impossible. Instead, when He makes a request, He asks that we do what we can do, that we ask for what we cannot do and for his help to carry it out.*[9]

What certainty our Lord gives us! *He has guaranteed his protection. I do not depend on my own strength. I have in my hands his written word. This is my strength, my certainty, my tranquil haven. Even if the entire world is shaken, I read the written word I carry with me, for it is my fortress, my defence. And what does this word tell me? 'I will be with you until the end of the world,' it says.*

Christ is with me. What shall I fear? Let the waves of the sea and the fury of the powerful come upon me. That will not weigh me down any more than a spider's web.[10] Let us not let go of his hand. He does not let go of ours.

We end our prayer asking Our Lady to intercede for us. She will help us to cry out confidently the liturgical prayer, *Renew O Lord, the marvels of your love.*[11] May we live firmly anchored in your love.

---

9. St Augustine, *On nature and grace*, 43
10. St John Chrysostom, *Homily before departing for the desert*
11. *Divine Office*, Sunday of the Third Week, Vespers

NINETEENTH SUNDAY: YEAR B

56. THE LIVING BREAD

56.1 Communion restores and renews our strength, so that we may reach heaven. The Viaticum.

In the First Reading of today's Mass[1] we read that Elias the prophet, fleeing from Jezabel, went to Horeb, the holy mountain. During the long and difficult journey, he felt so tired he wished to die. *Enough, Yahweh,* he said. *Take up my soul, for I am no better than my fathers.* And lying down there, he fell asleep. But an angel of the Lord woke him and offered him bread saying, *Rise up and eat, for you still have a long journey ahead.* Elias *arose, ate and drank, and strengthened by the meal walked forty days and forty nights to the mountain of God.* What he could not do of his own strength, he could do with the meal that the Lord gave him when he was most distraught.

The holy mountain which was the prophet's destination is an image of heaven. The forty days of travel represents our journey through life, during which we too encounter temptations, difficulties and fatigue. At times we too may find ourselves distraught and without hope. As the Angel does, so does the Church invite us to nourish ourselves with the bread – in all ways unique – that is Christ himself, present in the Holy Eucharist. In him we will find the strength to reach heaven, in spite of our weakness.

Holy Communion was called the *Viaticum* during the

---

1. 1 Kings 19:4-8

early years of Christianity, drawing an analogy between this sacrament and the viaticum, or provisions of food and money, that Romans took with them on long journeys. Later, this term was reserved for the spiritual assistance – in particular, the Holy Eucharist – that the Church gives to her children during the final and definitive stage of their journey to eternal life.[2] The first Christians had the custom of taking Communion to those imprisoned, especially when their martyrdom drew near.[3] Saint Thomas teaches that this sacrament is called the Viaticum because it prefigures the joy of possessing God in our true homeland, and because it makes it possible for us to reach that goal.[4] It is our great help during our life, and especially near the end of the road when the attacks of the enemy may be all the more intense. This is the reason why the Church has always recommended that no Christian should die without it. From the very beginning, the need – and the obligation – to receive this sacrament was evident, even though one might already have received Communion on that day.[5]

We may also recall today the obligation – at times grave – that we have to do everything possible so that no relative, friend or colleague of ours dies without the spiritual assistance that our Mother the Church provides for the final moments of our journey.

This is the best and most effective and perhaps the last possible manifestation of charity and affection towards those persons here on earth. The Lord rewards us with a deep joy when we fulfil this most agreeable though at

---

2. cf A. Bride, *Viatique*, in DTC, XC, 2842-2858
3. cf St Cyprian, *De lapsis*, 13; *Vita Basilii* 4: PG 29, 315; *Acts of the Martyrs*, etc.
4. cf St Thomas, *Summa Theologiae*, 3, q.74, a.4
5. *Code of Canon Law*, canon 921,2

times difficult duty.

Throughout our life, deeds should express our gratitude to our Lord for many things, but especially for having given us Holy Communion. Our gratitude will be shown in preparing to receive him better each day, and in receiving him fully aware that He gives us more than he gave Elias – all the strength we need to travel resolutely down the road of sanctity.

56.2 The Bread of life. Effects of Holy Communion in the soul.

I am the bread of life ... Jesus tells us in the Gospel of the Mass.[6] *If anyone eats of this bread, he shall live forever; and the bread that I will give is my flesh for the life of the world.*

Today our Lord forcefully reminds us that we need to receive him in Holy Communion in order to participate in the divine life, to overcome temptations, to foster and nourish the life of grace born in us through Baptism. Whoever receives Communion in a state of grace participates in the fruits of the Holy Mass and obtains benefits that are proper and specific to the reception of the Sacrament. He receives Christ himself, the source of all grace, really and spiritually. Thus, the Holy Eucharist is the greatest sacrament, the centre and summit of all the rest. The true presence of Christ in this sacrament gives it an infinite supernatural effectiveness.

There is no greater joy in this life than to receive our Lord. When we wish to give ourselves to others we often give them something that belongs to us, or something we know to symbolize a deeper attitude of affection, of love. But we always encounter some limitation to our self-

---

6. John 6: 48-51

giving. In Holy Communion, divine power surpasses all human limitations: under the Eucharistic species, Christ gives himself to us completely. Love achieves her ideal in this sacrament – complete identification with the person loved and longed for. *When two pieces of wax are put into the fire, they melt and become as a single thing. Something similar occurs when we participate in the Body of Christ and in his Precious Blood.*[7] Truly there is no greater joy or greater good than to receive Christ himself in Holy Communion with dignity.

The soul cannot but be grateful when, fighting off all routine, we frequently consider the richness of this sacrament. The Holy Eucharist is for the spiritual life what food is for the life of the body. Just as food strengthens us and prevents weakness and death, so the Holy Eucharist frees us from venial sins which weaken and debilitate the soul, and preserves us from mortal sins which cause its death. Food restores our strength and our health. *Through frequent or daily Communion spiritual life becomes fuller and the soul is enriched with virtues. The person receiving Communion receives a sure sign of eternal life.*[8] Just as food is needed for the growth of the body, the Holy Eucharist increases our sanctity and consolidates our union with God, *because participating in the Body and Blood of Christ transforms us into that which we receive.*[9]

Communion helps us to give of ourselves in family life; it moves us to work with joy and with perfection; it strengthens us to bear with human and supernatural elegance the difficulties and errors of ordinary life.

The Master is here and He calls you,[10] we are told

---

7. St Cyril of Alexandria, *Commentary on St John's Gospel*, 10:2
8. Paul VI, Instruction, *Eucharisticum Mysterium*, 15 August 1967, 37
9. *ibid*, 7
10. John 11:28

every day. Let us not ignore the invitation. Let us go with joy and well prepared to meet him. We have everything to gain from the encounter.

56.3 Frequent or daily reception of this sacrament. The Visit to the Blessed Sacrament; spiritual communions throughout the day.

Because we have many weaknesses we should frequently seek the Master in Holy Communion. *The banquet is prepared*[11] and many are invited, although few attend. How can we excuse ourselves? Love destroys all excuses.

The desire to receive this sacrament can be renewed often during the day by means of the spiritual communion that *consists in an ardent desire to receive Jesus in the Blessed Sacrament and in a loving conversation as if we had already received him*.[12] We will receive many graces and be given help to work better and serve others. It will be easier for us to place the Mass at the centre of our day.

The *Visit to the Blessed Sacrament* is also a very beneficial practice, *a manifestation of our gratitude, a sign of the love and adoration we owe our Lord*.[13] There is no better place than before the Tabernacle for those intimate, personal conversations that are required for permanent union with Christ. That is the most appropriate place for our dialogue with our Lord – as is clear from the lives of the saints – and for giving impulse to continuous prayer during work, in the street ... everywhere. Sacramentally present, the Lord sees us and hears us with greater intimacy. His heart still beats out of love for us and is *the source of all life and holiness*.[14] He invites us daily to

---

11. Luke 14:16
12. St Alphonsus Liguori, *Visits to the Blessed Sacrament*, Introduction, III
13. Paul VI, Encyclical, *Mysterium Fidei*, 3 September 1965, 67
14. *Litany to the Sacred Heart*; cf Pius XII, Encyclical, *Haurietis aquas*, 15 May 1956, 20, 34

return the visit that He made to us, coming sacramentally into our soul. He tells us, 'You too come away to a desert place to rest awhile.'

Near him we will find peace if we have lost it, strength to finish well the work at hand, and joy in the service of others. *What shall we do, you ask, in the presence of the Blessed Sacrament? Love him, adore him, thank him and ask him. What does a poor man do in the presence of a rich man? A sick man in the presence of a doctor? One who is thirsty at the sight of a crystal-clear fountain?*[15]

Jesus has what we lack and need. He is our strength along the road of life. Let us ask Our Lady to show us how to receive him *with the purity, humility and devotion* with which she received him, *with the spirit and fervour of the saints*.

---

15. St Alphonsus Liguori, *op cit*

NINETEENTH SUNDAY: YEAR C

57. WAITING FOR THE LORD

57.1 Foundations of theological hope.

The Liturgy of the Word this Sunday reminds us that life on earth is a short wait for our Lord's return. The faith which guides our footsteps is precisely *the certainty in things hoped for*,[1] as we see in the Second Reading. By means of this theological virtue the Christian acquires a firm certainty in regard to our Lord's promises, and a possession – in advance – of the divine gifts. Through faith, we know with certainty two fundamental truths of human existence: that we are made for heaven and therefore all else should be ordered and subordinated to this supreme end; and that our Lord wants to help us reach this end with an abundance of supernatural means.[2] Nothing should dishearten us on the road to sanctity because we lean on *three basic truths: God is all powerful; God has a great love for me; God is faithful to his promises. It is He, the God of mercies, who fills me with confidence. With him, I do not feel alone, or useless, or abandoned, but involved in a plan of salvation that one day will lead to Paradise*.[3] The Goodness, Wisdom and Omnipotence of God are the firm basis of human hope.

God is all-powerful. To him everything is subject – the wind, the seas, health and sickness, the heavens and the earth ... He uses and disposes everything for the

---

1. Heb 1:1
2. cf St Thomas, *Summa Theologiae*, 2-2, q. 17, a. 5 & 7
3. John Paul I, *Address*, 20 September 1978

salvation of my soul and of all men. He does not fail to look after the good of each of his children, even those who seem most alone and abandoned. God places his strength at the service of the salvation and sanctification of men. Only the misuse of freedom can render God's help sterile. But forgiveness is always possible. It is always possible to open the doors to let hope enter in. God is all-powerful. He can do everything; He is our Father and He is Love.[4]

God has a great love for me, as if I were his only Son. He never abandons me in my pilgrimage on earth. He looks for me when through my own fault I have lost him. He loves me with deeds, disposing everything for the good of my soul. The love of our earthly mother and father, with all its warmth, is only a pale reflection of God's love.

God is faithful to his promises in spite of our failings and lack of loyalty, our lack of correspondence to what Our Lord asks. He never fails us. He does not tire: He has patience – infinite patience – with men. While we walk on this earth, He does not abandon anyone; no one is a hopeless case, a lost cause. God is always the Father of the prodigal son, the Father who daily looks out impatiently, waiting for his son's return. He has a feast prepared for his arrival.

Our Lord awaits our sincere conversion and more generous correspondence. He wants us to be always vigilant and not fall into lukewarmness. Hope is intimately related with vigilance and depends to a great extent on love.[5]

---

4. G. Redondo, *Reasons for Hope*, Pamplona, 1977
5. cf J. Pieper, *Hope*

57.2 A vigilant waiting; the examination of conscience.

Jesus encourages us to be vigilant because the enemy never rests, he is always on the prowl;[6] and because love never sleeps.[7] In today's Gospel[8] our Lord warns us: *Let your loins be girt about you and your lamps burning. You yourselves be like men waiting for their master's return from the wedding, so that when he comes and knocks you may straightaway open to him.*

In those days, the Jews wore loose-fitting garments, and a belt was used in order to walk and perform certain chores comfortably. To *gird one's loins* was a graphic example of the need to prepare for a journey, to dispose oneself for the struggle.[9] Similarly, to *keep the lamps burning* is the attitude of one who keeps watch for or awaits the arrival of another.[10] When at the end of our lives our Lord arrives, He should find us prepared, awake and vigilant, like someone who lives for that day, serving out of love and determined to direct earthly realities – without losing his supernatural outlook – towards their true end. He should find us giving due value to earthly affairs – professional work, business, rest ... – without forgetting that none of this has an absolute value, but should instead help us love God more, win heaven and serve others better making the world a more just, human and Christian place.

A little time separates us from the definitive encounter with Christ. Each day that passes brings us a little closer to eternity. It may be this year or the following one ... Whenever it may be, it will always seem that life has passed too quickly. The Lord will come on the second

---

6. 1 Pet 5:8
7. cf Cant 5:2
8. Luke 12:32-48
9. cf Jer 1:17; Eph 6:14; 1 Pet 1:13
10. *The Navarre Bible*, notes to Luke 12:33-39 & 35

or third watch … *Since we do not know the day nor the hour, our Lord warns us to remain constantly vigilant, so that once we have completed our only time on earth (Heb 9:27) we may go into the wedding feast and be counted as one of the chosen.*[11] For those who have preferred to live with their backs to God, He will arrive completely unexpectedly, as a thief in the night.[12] *Know this: if the owner of the house knows at what time the thief were to arrive, he would not allow him to steal his belongings. You therefore, be prepared* … And Saint John Chrysostom comments that *with this, those who place greater care in guarding their riches than their souls from the thief are confused.*[13]

An *attitude of vigilance is opposed to negligence or carelessness which denote a certain weakness of the will.*[14] We are vigilant when we deepen our daily examination of conscience. *Take a good look at the way you behave. You will see that you are full of faults that harm you and perhaps also those around you.*

Remember, my child, that microbes may be no less a menace than wild beasts. Just as bacteria are cultivated in a laboratory, so you are cultivating those faults and those errors, with your lack of humility, with your lack of prayer, with your failure to fulfil your duty, with your lack of self-knowledge. Those tiny germs then spread everywhere.

You need to make a good examination of conscience every day. It will lead you to make definite resolutions to improve, because it will have made you really sorry for your shortcomings, omissions and sins.[15] The Lord should find us prepared at whatever hour He chooses to call upon us.

---

11. Second Vatican Council, Constitution, *Lumen gentium*, 48
12. 1 Thess 6:2
13. St John Chrysostom, in *Catena aurea*, vol 3, p. 204
14. St Thomas, *op cit*, 2-2, q.54, a.3
15. J. Escrivá, *The Forge*, 481

57.3 The struggle in little things.

We will be vigilant in love and far from lukewarm if we remain faithful in the little things of each day. If we consider these little details in the examination of conscience, we will easily find the signals that show us the way and those which may lead us astray. Little things are the prelude to greater things, and loving vigilance feeds upon them. He who pays no attention to things that appear to lack importance falls into the greatest temptations.

Saint Francis de Sales emphasizes the importance of conquering in small temptations, for there are many occasions to do so during the day, and many victories in small things are more important than a single great victory. Moreover, even though *wolves and bears are undoubtedly more dangerous than flies, they never cause as much discomfort or try our patience as much. It's easy*, the saint points out, *to avoid homicide, but how difficult to avoid anger over little things. It is easy to avoid stealing our neighbours belongings, but how difficult it is at times to not desire them. It is easy not to spread false rumours about our neighbour, but difficult to avoid lying in our conversations. We easily avoid drunkenness, but how difficult it is at times to live sobriety.*[16]

Small daily victories strengthen the interior life and make the soul more sensitive to divine things. They are common situations: living *the heroic minute* on waking or starting our work; overcoming our curiosity by putting down that frivolous magazine that, at best, is a waste of time; offering a mortification at meals; living sobriety during a social engagement; offering pleasant conversation to others ... We are certain that *for all the battles we win against those small enemies there will be a precious stone*

---

16. cf St Francis de Sales, *Introduction to the Devout Life*, IV, 8

placed in the crown of glory that God prepares for us in his holy kingdom.[17]

If we make an act of love with each temptation, with all those things in ourselves or others that may separate us from God, we will be filled with peace, and that which could have been an offence against God we will turn into a victory. Furthermore, writes the saint, *when the devil sees that his temptations move us to love God, he will cease to tempt us.*[18]

If we are faithful in little things we will be girded, vigilant, on the alert when our Lord arrives. Our life will have been a joyful wait, while we joyfully carry out the task our Lord has entrusted to us in the world. Then we will fully understand the words of Jesus: *Happy the servant whom his master finds thus on his return. Truly I say to you that he shall be placed at the head of all his possessions.* His arrival is near at hand; we should always remain vigilant.

---

17. *ibid*
18. *ibid*, IV, 9

NINETEENTH WEEK: MONDAY

58. THE TRIBUTE FOR THE TEMPLE

58.1 To be good Christians, we should be exemplary citizens.

They had just arrived in Capharnaum, we read in the Gospel of the Mass,[1] and the tithe collectors of the temple approached Peter asking, *Will your master not pay the didrachma?* Every Jew over the age of twenty was required to pay an annual sum of two dracmas to support the worship of God in the temple of Jerusalem. This was an obligation for all, even the Jews not living in Palestine. Peter's affirmative answer – given without consulting Jesus – suggests that our Lord usually paid this tax. The conversation probably took place outside the house. Our Lord was not close by at the time, so when Peter entered the house, Jesus, already inside, asked, *What do you think Simon? From whom do the kings of the earth receive tribute or custom, from their own sons or from others?*

Under the ancient monarchies the tribute was considered a special payment for the benefit of the royal family. Hence Jesus' question to Peter: *From whom do the kings of the earth receive tribute?* The answer was easy: 'from their subjects, from the others.' *The sons are exempt.* With respect to the payment of the tribute, Jesus is in the same position as the sons of the king. By declaring himself exempt, He teaches us that He is God's own Son, and lives in the Father's house.[2] He is not obliged to pay the tribute.

---

1. Matt 17:21-26
2. cf John 16:15

But the Lord wished to fulfil his duties as a citizen, as other men did. However, He made his divinity patent to all in the way He obtained the money for the payment. This Gospel account, recorded only by Saint Matthew, also shows us our Lord's poverty, for He lacked even two drachmas, a small sum in those days. Significant also is that our Lord paid Peter's share along with his own. *But that we may not give offence to them,* said Jesus to Peter, *'Go down to the sea and cast a hook, and take the first fish that comes up. And opening its mouth, you will find a stater. Take that and give it to them for me and for you'. The stater equalled the sum of four drachmas.*[3]

Saint Ambrose comments that this is a great lesson *that teaches Christians submission to the temporal authority, so that no one should disobey the edicts of a king of the earth. If the Son of God paid the tribute, are you perhaps great enough to refuse payment? Even He, who possessed nothing, paid the tribute. You, who seek the riches of the earth: why do you not recognize the duties which go along with these goods? Why do you consider yourself above the world?*[4]

From these and other passages we learn that in order to imitate the Master we should be good citizens who fulfil their duties at work, in the family and in society. Paying fair taxes, voting according to our conscience and participating in public services are part of these duties. *Love and respect the ways of behaving by which you may live in amity with other people. Have no doubt either that your loyal submission to duty can be the means for others to discover Christian integrity, which is the fruit of divine love, and to find God.*[5]

3. cf F. Spadafora, *Biblical Dictionary*, Barcelona, 1968
4. St Ambrose, *Commentary on St Luke's Gospel*, IV, 73
5. J. Escrivá, *Furrow*, 322

58.2 The first Christians: examples for our life in the middle of the world.

After the descent of the Holy Spirit at Pentecost, the Apostles were clearly aware that they had been sent out by the Lord to make him present in the midst of society. They – like the Master – were not of the world.[6] The world would often reject them. Seldom would they enjoy the benevolent smile men reserve for something that is their own. Without being of the world, without being worldly, the first Christians rejected customs and behaviour that were incompatible with the faith they had received, although they never felt out of place in the society to which they rightfully belonged. In their preaching they would lay special emphasis on their special place in the very heart of society. There, they would exercise their influence fully: *salt* is for seasoning and preserving from corruption the lives of all men; *yeast* is united completely with the flour and thus acts to ferment and raise the entire mass; their *light* should shine before men so that others – convinced through the deeds they have seen – may glorify the Father in heaven.

The first Christians did not seek isolation, nor did they put up barriers to hide behind and defend themselves in times of fierce persecution. Their attitude during these trials was neither pugnacious nor faint-hearted. They were serene and, like yeast, unapparent within the mass of society. The Christian presence in the world was a radical affirmation, and all the fury of the persecutors was incapable of shaking the serene and positive attitude of the Christians. They were exemplary citizens. The violence of the persecutions did not make them into maladjusted or anti-social people, nor did it change their basic attitude of

---

6. John 17:16

solidarity with other men, their peers. *We are accused of separating ourselves from the popular masses of the State*, writes Tertullian, *which is false, because the Christian knows that he is in the same boat as his fellow citizens, shipmates in a common earthly destiny. If the Empire is shaken by violence, this evil affects all her subjects, ourselves included.*[7] At times slandered and misunderstood, the Christian remained faithful to his divine vocation and to his human vocation. He occupied his proper position in the world, exercised his rights and carefully fulfilled his duties.[8]

The first Christians were not just good Christians, they were exemplary citizens too because their duties as citizens were the obligations of a well-formed conscience. Fulfilling them, they sanctified themselves. They obeyed just civil laws, *not only out of fear of punishment, but also as a matter of conscience,*[9] writes Saint Paul to the first Christians of Rome. He adds: *for this reason – in conscience – you pay them the tribute.*[10] *As we learned from him* (from Christ), writes Saint Justin Martyr in the middle of the second century, *we pay the tribute and contributions, fully and promptly ... Thus, though we adore only God, we gladly obey you in all the rest, fully acknowledging that you are the kings and governors of men, and praying that along with the Imperial power you also possess a skill in governing that is full of wisdom.*[11]

We might ask ourselves today in our prayer whether we are known to be good citizens who punctually fulfil their duties, whether we are good neighbours, good colleagues to our fellow workers ...

7. Tertullian, *Apologetics*, 28
8. cf D. Ramos, *The Witness of the Early Christians*, Madrid, 1969
9. Rom 13:5
10. Rom 13:6
11. St Justin, *Apologia*, I, 17

58.3 Be present wherever the good of society is decided.

The Church has always encouraged Christians, *citizens of the temporal city and of the eternal city, to faithfully fulfil their temporal duties, guided always by the spirit of the Gospel.*[12] The others should see in us the light of Christ reflected in honest work, in which we carefully fulfil our due obligations to our employer and fellow employees, and to society through the payment of just taxes. Similarly, students should strive to form their conscience properly in their new profession, and professors should prepare their classes daily, improving their lessons year after year, without falling into routine or mediocrity. Mothers should take care of the home, their children, their husbands, if necessary paying a fair sum to whoever may assist them with the household chores ...

Good Christians cannot be bad citizens. Mistaken are they who affirm that *we have no home here and look only to the future* (cf Heb 13:14), and therefore are careless as regards their temporal affairs. They do not realize that their faith obliges them to fulfil these duties with perfection, according to their personal calling.[13]

The Christian cannot be satisfied with fulfilling only his family and religious duties. He should be present, if possible, where the affairs of the neighbourhood, town or city are decided. His life has a social and political dimension that springs from faith and affects the exercise of the virtues, the essence of Christian life. *From this perspective, the social and political dimension of charity acquires its full nobility and dignity. It is an effective love for other persons that is realized in the pursuit of the common good of society.*[14] As Christians who are called to be saints in the

---

12. Second Vatican Council, Constitution, *Gaudium et spes*, 42
13. *ibid*
14. Spanish Episcopal Conference, *Catholics in Public Life*, 22 April 1986, 60 and 63

middle of the world, we should always keep present *the nobility and moral dignity of social and political commitments, and the great opportunities they offer to grow in faith, in hope, in love and in fortitude, in detachment and generosity. When these social and political commitments are lived with a Christian spirit, they become a strenuous school of perfection and a demanding means of living the virtues.*[15]

If we are citizens who fulfil our duties in an exemplary way we can thus show the way to Christ to many. In our days, *a new and unformed mass has arisen in lands of old Christian heritage, while the world – in all its breadth – is a field of apostolic action that should reach all men, a task to which all Christians are committed. Today, the church and all of her children are enrolled in a mission, and the leaven should now exercize her renewing function.*[16] This is possible when we realize that we are full-fledged citizens, with rights to exercise and duties to fulfil, and with a desire to face up to the difficulties that life in the midst of the world entails.

---

15. *ibid*
16. J. Orlandis, *The Christian vocation of the man of today*, Madrid, 1973,

NINETEENTH WEEK: TUESDAY

59. THE LOST SHEEP

59.1 God loves us always, even when we stray.

In the Gospel of the Mass[1] we read one of the parables of divine mercy which most moves the heart. A man with a hundred sheep – a large flock – loses one, probably because the sheep strayed, lagging behind the others as they looked for new pastures. And Jesus asks, *Will not the shepherd leave the other ninety nine in the fields and go to look for the lost sheep?* Saint Luke records our Lord's words: *And when he finds it, he places it on his shoulders with joy*[2] to return it to the flock.

How often has Jesus sought us out, in spite of our lack of generosity and correspondence! Even though we do not deserve his care and stray through our own fault, He seeks us out again and again.

None of the sheep received so much attention as the one that had strayed. The care that divine mercy pours out on sinners – on us – is overwhelming. How can we refuse the shoulders of the Good Shepherd if at times we lose the way? How can we not love frequent Confession, where we find Christ? We should take for granted that we are weak and will stumble. It is this very weakness, when we acknowledge it, that will attract the divine mercy, which comes to us with greater help and greater love. *Jesus, our Good Shepherd, hurries to find the hundredth sheep that had lost the way ... A marvellous condescendence of God*

---

1. Matt 18:12-14
2. Luke 15:6

*for him to seek man out; what great dignity must man have
to be sought out by God in this way!*[3]

We can always count on Christ's love. Even during
the worst moments of our life He does not stop loving us.
We can always count on his help to return to the right path
if we have lost it, to begin and begin again. He keeps us
fighting, and *a leader on the battlefield values more the soldier who, having fallen back in flight at first, returns to the
fray and attacks the enemy with valour, than he does the soldier who never ran but never showed outstanding courage.*[4]
He who never sins is not sanctified, but he is who always
repents, trusting in the love God has for him, getting up
and getting on with the fight. To have defects is not in
itself bad. The only evil lies in making a truce with them,
not struggling against them, thinking that they are part and
parcel of our character or our nature. Making such a truce
would lead to spiritual mediocrity. Our Lord does not
want this to happen to those who follow him.

59.2 God loves each one personally.

Jesus loves each one as he is, with his defects. His
love does not lead him to idealize men. He sees them with
their paradoxes and weaknesses, with their great potential
for good and with their misery that is so often evident.
Christ knows what is in man. Only He knows![5] He loves us
the way we are.

How well Jesus understands the human heart, and
what a positive conception He has of our abilities! *Jesus'
eye knows how to look beyond the veil of human passions
and penetrate the inmost self of man, where man is most
alone, poor and naked.*[6] He understands us always, and

---

3. St Bernard, *Sermon for the First Week in Advent,* 7
4. St John Chrysostom, *Homilies on the First Epistle to the Corinthians*
5. John Paul II, *Homily,* 22 October 1978
6. K. Adam, *Jesus Christ,* p. 112

always encourages us to continue struggling. If only we could realize Christ's personal love for each person, his care and solicitude for each one!

God loves us. This is the greatest reality of our lives, the one capable of raising our spirits always, the one that makes us happy in spite of sorrows and contradictions. Jesus loves us always despite the deep-rooted wretchedness that lies in the human heart. *His love, 'in spite of everything', is so incomparable, so unique, so maternally tender and generous, that it will be inscribed forever in the memory of humanity ... His love for humanity is very different from the abstract benevolence preached by thinkers and philosophers. It is not simply doctrine, but life. Moreover, it is to suffer and to die with man. The Lord does not settle for merely examining human misery and prescribing a remedy to ease it. He makes actual contact with that misery. He cannot bear to know of it without taking it upon himself. The love of Jesus surpasses the bounds of his own heart in order to attract others to himself, or better, in order to go out of himself, identifying himself with others so as to live and suffer with them.*[7]

He calls men brother and friend, and so sympathetically binds his fortune to theirs that He looks upon anything done for another as being done for him.[8] Constant are the Evangelists' statements that He felt compassion for the people.[9] He had compassion on them because *they were like sheep without a shepherd.*[10] He is moved by misfortune and pain. He cannot reject a suffering soul, not even the Syrophoenician woman, a pagan.[11] He is quick to

---

7. *ibid*, p.113-114
8. Matt 25:40
9. Mark 8:2
10. Mark 6:34
11. Mark 7:26

attend those who came to him, even when doing so led others to claim that He was breaking the Sabbath.[12] He mingles with publicans and sinners, even though those who feel that they themselves fulfil the Law well are scandalized. Not even when in agony does He fail to tell the good thief, *Today you will be with me in Paradise*.[13]

His love does not tolerate class distinctions. He welcomes the rich – like Nicodemus, Zacchaeus and Joseph of Arimathea – and poor folk – like Bartimaeus, a beggar, who once cured followed him along the way. On his journeys, women at times accompanied him to assist him.[14] He attends more promptly those with troubled bodies and above all, those with troubled souls. His concern for those most in need is not exclusive; it is not limited to those without fortune or friends. There are evils common to all social classes – loneliness, lack of affection ...

Our life is the story of Christ's love for us. He has looked at us with a love of predilection and has time and again sought us out when we had lost our way. We ought to ask ourselves today how we are corresponding to our Lord's constant solicitude for us. What efforts do we make to receive the sacraments frequently and devoutly? Do we strive to recognize Christ in spiritual direction and when we receive fraternal correction? Do we look with gratitude upon those to whom the Church has entrusted, as our Pastors, the care of our souls? Do we know how to exclaim in those situations, *It is the Lord!*?

---

12. Mark 1:21
13. Luke 23:43
14. Luke 8:3

59.3 Our life is the story of Christ's love; He has often looked upon us with predilection.

Jesus loved me and gave himself up for me.[15] This is the great truth that consoles us. Jesus shows his love by giving his life. He loves each of us as if each one were the sole object of his affections. We should meditate often on this truth: God loves me. This surpasses the most improbable expectations of the human heart. No one – without divine Revelation – would dare to guess at or acknowledge this sublime vocation to which each and every person is called: to be God's son or daughter, called to live a close relationship as a friend, to participate in the very Life of the three divine Persons. Considered with earthbound eyes, it seems a dream, or scarcely credible, but it is the truth, the great truth that should move us to correspond.

Jesus never stops loving us, helping us, protecting us, talking to us, not even in our moments of sheer ingratitude, or after we have committed the greatest disloyalty. Perhaps it was during such sad circumstances that our Lord has been most attentive to us, as today's parable suggests. Among the hundred sheep in the flock, only the one that was lost had the honour of resting on the good shepherd's shoulders. *I will be with you always,*[16] in each situation, at every moment, our Lord tells us. And especially when we begin that final journey towards him.

Certain that our Lord is close to us, we should be moved to begin and begin again in the interior struggle, without being disheartened by the negative experience of our defects and sins. Every moment we live is unique, and therefore provides a good opportunity to begin again,

---

15. Gal 2:20
16. Matt 28:20

because – as we read in the book of Deuteronomy – *the Lord will go before you. He will be with you: He will not leave you or abandon you. Do not fear or be cowardly.*[17]

For many centuries the Church had placed on the lips of priests and faithful, at the beginning of the Mass, the words of the Psalm: *I will go to the altar of God, of God who gives joy to my youth.*[18] These words were repeated when the priests and people were young, and when they had long since passed the years of their maturity. They are the cry of the soul going straight to Christ, who knows he is loved and desires love.

God loves me. And John the apostle writes, 'Let us love God, then, since God loved us first'. As if this were not enough, Jesus comes to each one of us, in spite of our patent wretchedness, to ask us, as He asked Peter, 'Simon, son of John, do you love me more than these others?'

This is the moment to reply: 'Lord, you know all things. You know that I love you!' adding, with humility, 'Help me to love you more. Increase my love!'[19] These are aspirations that can serve us today. They will bring us closer to Christ. He awaits our correspondence with him.

---

17. *First Reading, Year I: Deut 31:8
18. Ps 42:4
19. J. Escrivá, *The Forge*, 497

NINETEENTH WEEK: WEDNESDAY

60. THE POWER TO FORGIVE SINS

60.1 The promise of the sacrament of Penance and its institution. Giving thanks for this sacrament.

Jesus is well aware of our weaknesses and failings. That is why He instituted the sacrament of Penance. He wanted us to be able to straighten out our ways whenever necessary. Christ had the power to forgive sins and He exercised it on a number of occasions – with the woman taken in adultery,[1] with the good thief hanging from the cross,[2] with the paralytic of Capharnaum ...[3] He came *to seek and to save the lost*,[4] just as he does now in our own day.

The Prophets had prepared the way and foretold this restoration of all things in Christ and the reconciliation of man with God. It is reflected in the words of Isaiah: *Come now, let us reason together, says the Lord: though your sins are like scarlet, they shall be as white as snow; though they are red like crimson, they shall become like wool.*[5] This was also the mission of the Baptist, who came to preach *a baptism of repentance for the forgiveness of sins.*[6] How is it then that people wince when the Church preaches the need for Confession?

Jesus shows his mercy above all in his approach to

---

1. John 8:11
2. Luke 23:43
3. Mark 2:1-12
4. Luke 19:10
5. Is 1:18
6. Mark 1:4

sinners. *'I know the plans I have for you, plans for peace and not affliction'* (Jer 29:11). *This was God's promise through Jeremiah. The liturgy applies these words to Jesus, for it is through him that God reveals his infinite love for us. He did not come to condemn us, to remind us of our pettiness and lack of virtue. He came to save us, to pardon us, to excuse us, to bring us peace and joy.*[7] He sought to pardon those men and women he met on the roads and in the villages of Palestine. He wants to pardon everyone who lives on the earth for the rest of time. This is why He gave the Apostles and their successors the power to forgive sins down through the centuries. After Peter recognised Jesus as the Messiah, the Lord solemnly promised to give him the power to forgive sins.[8] Shortly thereafter, we read in today's Gospel, He extended this power to the rest of the Apostles: *Truly, I say to you, whatever you bind on earth shall be bound in heaven, and whatever you loose on earth shall be loosed in heaven.*[9] This promise was fulfilled on the day of the Resurrection: *Receive the Holy Spirit,* said the risen Lord; *If you forgive the sins of any, they are forgiven; if you retain the sins of any, they are retained.*[10] This was Christ's first gift to his Church.

The sacrament of Penance is a marvellous sign of the love and mercy with which God looks upon men. *For though God has been offended, yet He is still our Father; and even though He has been provoked to anger, He remains fond of his children. One thing only does He seek, which is not vengeance for our offences, but rather true repentance and the conversion of our hearts.*[11] In today's

---

7. J. Escrivá, *Christ is passing by*, 165
8. Matt 16:17-19
9. Matt 18:18
10. John 20:23
11. St John Chrysostom, *Homilies on St Matthew's Gospel*, 22, 5

prayer we give thanks to the Lord for this great gift of for-giveness. Now that we are in prayer before him, each one should ask the question: Are my confessions well-prepared and thorough?

60.2 Reasons for our gratitude.

There are many reasons why this sacrament is such an incredible gift. These reasons should move us to be thankful to Our Lord, to love this sacrament more every time we receive it. Prayerful consideration of these rea-sons should help us to be faithful to a plan for frequent confession.

First of all, we should realize that Confession is not merely a spiritual remedy by which the priest can heal a sick soul or revive a soul dead to the life of grace. This is a lot, but to our Father God it seems very little. Remember how in the parable of the Prodigal Son the father did not forgive his son by means of an emissary. He ran right up to him so as to forgive him in person. So it is with Our Lord. He seeks out the sinner. He makes himself present in the person of the confessor. It is Jesus who absolves us, since every sacrament is the action of Christ.

In Confession we encounter Jesus,[12] in the same way that the good thief met him, as did the woman caught in adultery, the Samaritan woman and so many others. We meet Jesus as Peter did after his denials. Inasmuch as the remission of sins is an action of Christ, it is at the same time an action of his Mystical Body, the Church.

We should also give thanks for the universality of this power granted to the Church in the person of the Apostles and their successors. The Lord is ready to forgive every-thing in everyone, always, as long as he finds the proper

---

12. cf Second Vatican Council, *Sacrosanctum Concilium*, 7

dispositions. *God's omnipotence is particularly shown in sparing and having mercy, because in this is it made manifest that God has supreme power, that He freely forgives sins.*[13]

Jesus says to us: *I came that they may have life, and have it abundantly.*[14] In Confession he gives us the opportunity to empty all worldliness from the soul, to have a thorough cleaning out. *Imagine that God wants you to be overflowing with honey, but you are full of vinegar. Where can God put the honey?* asks Saint Augustine. *First you have to empty and clean out the container ... You have to clean it out even if it takes a lot of effort scrubbing the thing. That's what has to be done to receive this mysterious reality.*[15] The Holy Spirit will increase the sensitivity of our soul if we make the little effort required to confess our sins frequently, to examine our consciences diligently and make good resolutions. We will acquire an interior refinement of soul characterised by a horror of mortal sin. We will flee from the occasions of mortal sin while we grow in our hatred of venial sin. In this manner Confession fills us with confidence in the struggle. Those who practise it have found it to be 'the sacrament of joy'.[16] How can we fail to thank Our Lord for this proof of his mercy? Shouldn't we appreciate this sacrament more each time we receive it? Shouldn't we get others to know its immense value?

The Holy Spirit teaches us *the meaning of sin* through his unceasing action in the sacrament of Penance. The Holy Spirit teaches us to suffer more over sin, to understand the gravity of offending God. We will then be filled

---

13. St Thomas Aquinas, *Summa Theologiae*, I, q 25, a 3 ad 3
14. John 10:10
15. St Augustine, *Commentary on the First Epistle of St John*, 4
16. cf Paul VI, *General Audience*, 23 March 1977

with a filial desire to make reparation for our faults. Our spirit of penance will be shown in that our confessions will be punctual, contrite and well-prepared. We thank the Holy Spirit for having inspired the Fathers of the Church to encourage frequent Confession.[17] With this aid we make progress in humility. We combat with energy un-Christian customs. We confront lukewarmness head on. We strengthen our will and increase sacramental grace in ourselves by virtue of the sacrament of Penance.[18] How many benefits we receive from the Lord through this wonderful sacrament!

60.3 Only a priest can forgive sins. Confession, a judgment of mercy.

The power to forgive sins was given to the Apostles and their successors.[19] The only people who have the faculty to forgive sins are those who have received Holy Orders. Saint Basil compared Confession to caring for the sick. He commented that just as many do not understand the sicknesses of the body, many do not know the sicknesses of the soul. They cannot be healed by just anybody.[20] The priest gets his power directly and freely from God, unlike the physician, whose power derives from his knowledge, his professional prestige or his reputation in the community.

By divine decision, the confessor acts in the place of Christ in judging the dispositions of the sinner, his judgment being based on the penitent's sorrow and desire for personal amendment. This judgment precedes the absolution that leads into a fuller communion with the Church.

---

17. cf Pius XII, Encyclical, *Mystici Corporis*, 29 June 1943, 39
18. *ibid*
19. cf *Ordo Poenitentiae*, 9
20. St Basil, *Brief Rule*, 288

As a consequence, the sacrament of Penance is a real judgment to which the sinner willingly submits.[21] But it is a judgment so ordered that the guilty are to be forgiven. *Consider what depths of mercy lie in the justice of God! For, according to human justice, he who pleads guilty is punished, but in the divine court, he is pardoned. Blessed be the holy sacrament of Penance.*[22]

The priest cannot absolve someone who has not repented of his sin. Nor can he absolve someone who will not make restitution for something that has been stolen. He cannot absolve someone who will not forgo the proximate occasions of sin, much less anyone who will not seriously commit himself to avoiding sin and improving his life. Such individuals exclude themselves from the fount of mercy.

The judgment in the sacrament of Penance is a foreshadowing of and a preparation for the definitive judgment which will take place at the end of our lives. We should try to understand the profound nature of the grace and mercy that are present when our sins are forgiven. Our gratitude if we do so will have no limits. It will be shown in our effort to glorify God eternally for his wonderful compassion. Yet Our Lord wants this gratitude to be evident in this life also. We thank God and ask that his Church be never short of holy priests who are willing to impart this sacrament with love and dedication.

---

21. cf Council of Trent, Dz 899
22. J. Escrivá, *The Way*, 309

NINETEENTH WEEK: THURSDAY

61. OUR DEBT WITH GOD

61.1 The innumerable benefits from the Lord.

We read in today's Gospel, *Therefore the kingdom of heaven may be compared to a king who wished to settle accounts with his servants.*[1] When this king began his reckoning, one was brought to him who owed him *ten thousand talents,* an immense sum that could not possibly be paid back. This first debtor symbolizes our own situation; we owe God so much that we can never hope to pay the debt. We owe him the gift of our creation. He preferred to create us as we are rather than in another way. He created our bodies with the help of our parents, but He created our immortal souls as well as our bodies in a direct, unrepeatable act. He made our bodies and souls to be eternally happy in Heaven. We find ourselves in the world by his express desire. We owe God our conservation in existence, since without him everything would return to nothing. He has given us the energies and qualities of our body and spirit, our health, our life and all the goods we possess. Over and above this natural order, we are in his debt for his supernatural benefits such as the Incarnation of his Son, the Redemption, our divine filiation, our being called to participate in the divine life here on earth and later in Heaven with the glorification of body and soul.

We are indebted to God for the immense gift of being sons and daughters of the Church, in which we have the

---

1. Matt 18:23-35

blessing of receiving the sacraments, especially the Holy Eucharist. In the Church we share through the Communion of Saints in the good works of the other members of the faithful. At any moment we are receiving graces through those other members, those who are at prayer or who are offering up their work or their sufferings ... We are also continually receiving benefits from the saints in Heaven, from the holy souls in Purgatory and from the angels. All of these graces reach us through the intercession of Mary, our Mother. Their source lies in the infinite merits of Christ, our Head,[2] our Redeemer and Mediator. These helps are bestowed on us daily, keeping us from sin, lighting up our souls, moving us to fulfil our duties, to do the good that is possible in every moment, to be silent when others complain, to go to the defence or the assistance of the most needy ...

We owe God for the grace that is always necessary for any good works, to be true to our resolutions, to deepen our desires to follow Jesus Christ and to make progress in the acquisition of the virtues. In a very special way we are indebted to God for the wonderful grace of our vocation, from which we have drawn so many other graces and helps ...

Truly, we are insolvent debtors who have not the wherewithal to pay our debt. We can only adopt the attitude of the bankrupt servant in the parable: *So the servant fell on his knees, imploring him, 'Lord, have patience with me, and I will pay you everything'.* Since we are his sons, we can petition him with an unlimited confidence. Fathers do not remember the loans they have made out of love to their little children. *Draw strength from your divine filiation. God is a Father – your Father! – full of warmth and*

---

2. cf St Thomas Aquinas, *Summa Theologiae*, 3, q 8

infinite love. Call him Father frequently and tell him, when you are alone, that you love him, that you love him very much, and that you feel proud and strong because you are his son.[3] Our older brother, Jesus Christ, will more than pay in full for all of us.

61.2 The Mass is the most perfect act of thanksgiving we can offer to God.

'Have patience with me, and I will pay you everything.'

In the Holy Mass we offer with the priest *this holy and perfect sacrifice*, an act of thanksgiving of infinite value. We unite to this sacrifice the poverty of our own thanksgiving: *Look with favour on these offerings*, we pray each day, *and accept them as once you accepted the gifts of your servant Abel, the sacrifice of Abraham, our father in faith, and the bread and wine offered by your priest Melchisedech.*[4] *Through him, with him, in him, in the unity of the Holy Spirit, all glory and honour is yours, almighty Father, for ever and ever.* With Christ, united to him, we are enabled to say: *'I will pay you everything'*.

The Mass is the most perfect act of thanksgiving we can offer to God. The whole life of Christ was one continuous act of thanksgiving to the Father, an interior attitude which became apparent on different occasions in words and gestures, as we know from the Gospels. *Father, I thank thee that thou hast heard me*, exclaims Jesus after the resurrection of Lazarus.[5] Similarly, at the multiplication of the loaves and fishes Christ gives thanks before the food is distributed to the people.[6] At the Last Supper *He took bread, and when he had given thanks he broke it ...*,

---

3. J. Escrivá, *The Forge*, 331
4. *Roman Missal, Eucharistic Prayer I*
5. John 11:41
6. cf Matt 15:36

and He took a cup, and when He had given thanks He gave it to them . . . [7]

It is through the miracle of the curing of the ten lepers that we get an insight into Our Lord's desire for gratitude. *Was no one found to return and give praise to God except this foreigner?*[8] asks Jesus in disbelief. Christ frequently warns his disciples about the sin of ingratitude. They should be wary of the fate of those who are blessed with many gifts but give no thanks for any of them. Since they are accustomed to receive things they have come to think of the gifts as their rightful due. But everything is a gift from God. To be in harmony with God presupposes that we receive his favours with the grateful spirit of one who knows the value of what he is getting. *If you knew the gift of God, and who it is that is saying to you, 'Give me a drink', you would have asked him and He would have given you living water;*[9] so said Our Lord to the Samaritan woman who was on the verge of shutting herself off from grace.[10]

Our thanksgiving to God for so many, many gifts which we cannot repay is what we must unite to Christ's thanksgiving in the Holy Mass. He who is grateful can see the good things of this world with clear eyes. This is why we should participate every day in the Holy Sacrifice of the Mass, telling our Father God, in union with Jesus Christ: How good you are, Father! Thank you for everything! I give you thanks for those goods which I can see all around me, and for those others, so many others, which you have given me yet are hidden from my sight.

What shall I render to the Lord for all his bounty to me?[11] we might ask ourselves each day with the Psalmist.

---

7. Luke 22:19; Matt 26:27
8. Luke 17:18
9. John 4:10
10. cf J. M. Pero-Sanz, *The Sixth Hour*, 267
11. Ps 115:2

We will not find a better way to give due thanks than by participating in the Holy Mass each day with greater and greater devotion, offering to the Father the sacrifice of the Son, to which we add our humble personal oblation. *Bless and approve our offering, making it acceptable to you, an offering in spirit and in truth.*[12] Christ's presence in the Tabernacle is another motive for giving thanks with a heart full of joy.

61.3 Gratitude towards all people; always forgiving every offence.

Although the entire Mass is an act of thanksgiving, this aspect is especially pronounced in the Preface. With joyful spirit we confess and proclaim that *it is our duty and our salvation, always and everywhere, to give you thanks through your beloved Son, Jesus Christ.*

Always and everywhere, to give you thanks ... This is what our attitude should be towards God. We should be grateful at every moment, in whatever circumstances. This includes those times when we have trouble understanding some event. *God is very pleased with those who recognise his goodness by reciting the 'Te Deum' in thanksgiving whenever something out of the ordinary happens, without caring whether it may have been good or bad, as the world reckons these things. For everything comes from the hands of our Father: so though the blow of the chisel may hurt our flesh, it is a sign of Love, as he smooths off our rough edges and brings us closer to perfection.*[13] Everything that happens is a continuous call *ut in gratiarum actione semper maneamus*, that we remain always in an ongoing act of thanksgiving.[14]

Ut in gratiarum actione semper maneamus ... We

---

12. *Roman Missal, op cit*

13. J. Escrivá, *op cit*, 609

14. *Roman Missal, Prayer after Communion*, Feast of St Justin

have to bring this attitude to the fore in our daily life. We need to take advantage of the little happenings of each day to show our gratitude in family life, at work, with our friends ... We show our gratitude to the man who sells us a newspaper, to the clerk who attends to us, to the driver who allows us to enter into traffic, to the friendly pharmacist at the corner shop.

In this passage from the Gospel the Lord shows us another way to settle our accounts with him. This includes all the debts we have contracted through our sins and omissions. The Lord wants us to forgive those offences which are done to us. In the worst kind of situation we can imagine, the sum of those offences we receive will not exceed *one hundred denarii,* a somewhat ridiculous amount compared with the ten thousand talents (some sixty million denarii). If we know how to forgive the offences done to us by others (perhaps even to the extent of a really grievous injury), then Our Lord will not hold against us the enormous debt we owe to him. This is the condition Jesus imposes at the conclusion of the parable. And this is what we say to God each day when we pray the Our Father: *Forgive us our trespasses as we forgive those who trespass against us.* When we forgive and forget, we imitate Our Lord, since *nothing makes us more like unto God than to be always willing to forgive.*[15]

We finish our meditation with a prayer that has been traditionally popular with the faithful: *I thank you, my God, for having created me, redeemed me, made me a Christian and given me life. I offer you my thoughts, words and actions of this day. Do not allow me to offend you and give me strength to flee from occasions of sin. Increase my love for you and for everyone.*

---

15. St John Chrysostom, *Homilies on St Matthew's Gospel,* 19:7

NINETEENTH WEEK: FRIDAY

62. MATRIMONY AND VIRGINITY

62.1 Matrimony, a Christian vocation. Its dignity, unity and indissolubility.

Today's Gospel[1] presents us with the scene where the Pharisees seek to entrap Jesus with a tricky question: *Is it lawful to divorce one's wife for any cause?* There were different schools of thought on how to interpret the Scriptures on this issue. Divorce was commonly allowed. The question had to do merely with the casuistry behind the motives, yet our Lord takes advantage of this idle question to delve into the very heart of the matter, which is the fact of indissolubility. As supreme author of all legislation, Christ restores matrimony to its original essence and dignity, to the way intended by God: *Have you not read that He who made them from the beginning made them male and female, and said, 'For this reason a man shall leave his father and mother and be joined to his wife, and the two shall become one'? So they are no longer two but one. What therefore God has joined together, let no man put asunder.*

Our Lord proclaimed the unity and indissolubility of matrimony for all time over and above any human consideration. There are many reasons which support the indissolubility of the marriage bond – the nature of conjugal love, the good of the children, the good of society ... But the fundamental reason for the indissolubility of

---

1. Matt 19:3-12

marriage is that it is the Will of the Creator. This is how He wanted marriage to be – one and indissoluble. The marital bond is so strong that it can be broken only by death. Saint Francis de Sales uses this image to explain the doctrine: *If the adhesive is good, two pieces of fir wood glued together will stick so fast to one another that it is easier to break them in any place other than the one where they have been joined together.*[2] So it is with matrimony.

Husband and wife need to see marriage in terms of a vocation which is a gift from God.[3] When marriage is viewed in this way, everything about family life and conjugal duties, the education of the children, the struggle for economic security – all of these demands – take on a supernatural meaning.[4] They become opportunities to draw close to God. Husband and wife then look with eyes of faith upon the many challenges that face them, confident in the knowledge that God will provide. Such is the way of sanctity for the married person.

Because of our Faith and the teachings of the Church we Christians are blessed with a more perfect understanding of the nature of matrimony, of the importance that the family has for each person, for the Church and for society. As a consequence, we have a responsibility to defend this human and divine institution in these times when it is under attack from many quarters by means of magazine articles, the special publicity given to sensational scandals, television series that little by little deform the consciences of millions of viewers ... When we give others sound doctrine, that of the natural law enlightened by faith, we are doing a great good to the whole of society.

We should consider now in our prayer whether we

---

2. St Francis de Sales, *Introduction to the Devout Life*, 3, 38
3. cf Second Vatican Council, *Lumen gentium*, 11
4. cf J. Escrivá, *Christ is passing by*, 23

are defending the family – especially its weakest members, who suffer the most harm – from these attacks. Are we trying our best to live those virtues which are of such help to everyone – mutual respect, a spirit of service, friendship, understanding, optimism, a joy that is independent of feelings, a concern for everyone, but especially the most needy …

62.2 The many fruits of virginity and apostolic celibacy.

Our Lord's doctrine concerning the indissolubility and dignity of marriage proved such a shock to those present that even his disciples had occasion to comment, saying, *If such is the case of a man with his wife, it is not expedient to marry*. Then Jesus went on to affirm the value of celibacy and virginity for the love of the Kingdom of Heaven. The complete surrender to God, *indiviso corde*,[5] without the mediation of conjugal love, is one of the most precious possessions of the Church.

Those who have received the call to serve God in matrimony must do so precisely in the faithful fulfilment of their marital duties. For them, this is a sure road to heaven. Those who have received the vocation to apostolic celibacy will find in their total commitment to God the grace necessary to live happy lives and attain sanctity in the midst of ordinary life if this be their call from God. They are everyday citizens with a well-defined professional calling, fully given to God and to the apostolate without limits and without conditions. The call to complete dedication is a special sign of affection from God. He gives specific graces to help his children on this path. The Church grows in sanctity because of the fidelity of Christians, each one responding to the personal call he has

---

5. 1 Cor 7:33

received from the Lord. *This is a precious gift of divine grace given by the Father to certain souls (Matt 19:11; 1 Cor 7:7), whereby they may devote themselves to God alone the more easily, due to an undivided heart.*[6] This complete self-giving to God *has always been held in particular honour in the Church. The reason for this was and is that perfect continency for the love of God is an incentive to charity, and is certainly a particular source of spiritual fecundity in the world.*[7]

Both matrimony and virginity are necessary for the growth of the Church. Both presuppose a specific vocation from the Lord. Virginity and celibacy do not contradict the dignity of matrimony. Quite the contrary; they act to reaffirm it. *Marriage and virginity or celibacy are two ways of expressing and living the one mystery of the covenant of God with his people.*[8] If one does not esteem virginity, one has not understood the dignity of matrimony in all its fullness. Indeed, *when human sexuality is not regarded as a gift of great value given by the Creator, the renunciation of it for the sake of the Kingdom of Heaven loses its meaning.*[9] As Saint John Chrysostom has written, *Whoever denigrates marriage also diminishes the glory of virginity. Whoever praises it makes virginity more admirable and resplendent.*[10]

The witness of love manifested in virginity or apostolic celibacy is a source of joy to the sons and daughters of God. This witness becomes a new way to see Our Lord in this world, to contemplate his face by means of his creatures. This is a shining example of the purity of the

---

6. Second Vatican Council, *op cit*, 42
7. *ibid*
8. John Paul II, Apostolic Exhortation, *Familiaris Consortio*, 22 November 1981, 16
9. *ibid*
10. St John Chrysostom, *Treatise on virginity*, 10

Church for both Christians and non-believers. It brings with it a special youthful spirit and a joyful apostolic efficacy. *In spite of having renounced physical fecundity, the celibate person becomes spiritually fruitful, the father and mother of many, cooperating in the realization of the family according to God's plan. Christian couples therefore have the right to expect from celibate persons a good example and a witness of fidelity to their vocation until death. Just as fidelity at times becomes difficult for married people and requires sacrifice, mortification and self-denial, the same can happen to celibate persons, and their fidelity, even in the trials that may occur, should strengthen the fidelity of married couples.*[11]

God so loved this virtue, comments Saint Ambrose, *that He did not want to come to earth without it, being born of the Virgin Mother.*[12] We frequently ask our Blessed Lady that there will always be people in the world to answer this call of the Lord, people who know how to give God an undivided heart. It is this kind of sacrifice which will permit an unlimited generosity to others.

62.3 Holy purity, guardian of both human and divine love.

To live out the fullness of one's vocation it is necessary to live holy purity in accord with one's state in life. God gives the graces necessary to those called to matrimony as well as to those called to give their whole hearts, so that they all may be faithful. Holy purity is not the most important virtue, but it is indispensable for anyone wishing to enjoy intimacy with God. It may happen that in some environments this virtue has gone out of fashion. It may seem that to live the virtue and all of its consequences will

---

11. John Paul II, *op cit*
12. St Ambrose, *Treatise on Virginity*, 1

appear to many people as incomprehensible or utopian. We should remember that the first Christians also had to confront a hostile and aggressive environment in this and in other areas of morality.

With the passage of time the pastors of the Church felt that they were under obligation to spell out the parameters of Christian conduct. The counsels of Saint John Chrysostom are a good example. They seem almost as if they were directed to many Christians of our own day: *What do you want us to do? Go up into the mountains and become monks? What you are saying makes me want to cry. You think that modesty and chastity are just for monks? No. Christ laid down common laws for all of us. And so, when He said: 'everyone who looks at a woman lustfully'* (Matt 5:28), *He was not speaking to a monk, but to the man in the street ... I do not forbid you to marry, nor do I forbid you to enjoy life. I only ask that you do this with temperance, not with impurity, not with countless sins. I do not lay it down as a law that you go into the mountains and out into the deserts. I want you to be good, modest and chaste even though you are in the middle of the world.*[13]

What wonderful things we can accomplish in the world by living holy purity with refinement! We will bring the *bonus odor Christi,*[14] the sweet fragrance of Christ, to all the places that we frequent.

This virtue is accompanied by others which do not attract much attention but which do add up to a general comportment which is always attractive. We can take as examples of these virtues details of modesty in dress, in neatness, in sports and recreation. We would also include the refusal to listen to or engage in conversations that are

---

13. St John Chrysostom, *Homilies on St Matthew's Gospel*, 7, 7
14. 2 Cor 2:15

beneath the dignity of a Christian and of any decent person, the planning of vacations so as to avoid sloth and moral harm ... and, above all, the cheerful example of our own life, optimism in the face of ups and downs, and a genuine love of life ...

The virtue of purity is so important to every apostolate in the middle of the world that we can think of it as the guardian of Love. It is precisely here that this holy virtue is nourished and acquires meaning. It protects and defends both human and divine love. If our love were to die out, it would be very difficult, even impossible, to live this virtue in all its youthful fullness.

NINETEENTH WEEK: SATURDAY

63. THE BLESSING OF THE CHILDREN

63.1 Christ's love for children and for those who become like children.

Jesus loved with predilection the sick, the needy and children. This is the repeated testimony of the Gospels. He had a special affection for these groups of people because they are always in need of help. In addition, they possess the qualities which He set down as indispensable for entering into his Kingdom.

There are two occasions in the Gospels when Jesus blesses children and presents them as a model to his disciples. One took place in Capharnaum in Galilee while the other happened in Judaea, probably near Jericho, on the way to Jerusalem. We read of this second event in today's Gospel:[1] *Then children were brought to him,* relates Saint Matthew. We can be sure that they were brought by women – by their mothers or their grandmothers or their sisters. They had entered into the house where Jesus was, probably nudging forward their little ones until they were right in front of Our Lord, *that he might lay his hands on them and pray* for them. It would seem as if it was Christ's accustomed way with children. Perhaps the commotion this would cause had somewhat distracted the adults listening to the Master. And so *the disciples rebuked the people*. But the Lord intervened: *Let the children come to me,* He tells them, *and do not hinder them; for to such*

---

1. Matt 19:13-15

*belongs the kingdom of heaven. And he laid his hands on
them and went away.*

By declaring that the Kingdom of Heaven belongs to
children Jesus teaches us, first of all, that children have a
definite place there. As a consequence, great care should
be taken in the preparation and guidance of children.
More than anything else, they should be baptized as soon
as possible, as Holy Mother Church has urged repeatedly
in every epoch.[2] *That this law extends not only to adults but
also to infants and children, and that the Church has
received this from Apostolic tradition, is confirmed by the
unanimous teaching and authority of the Fathers. Besides, it
is not to be supposed that Christ the Lord would have
withheld the Sacrament and grace of Baptism from children,
of whom He said: Suffer the little children, and forbid them
not to come to me ...*[3] *Parents are obliged to see to it that
infants are baptized within the first weeks after birth ...*[4]

Through Baptism children receive the life of Christ.
They become sons and daughters of God in a completely
new manner, becoming heirs to Heaven. Our Lord looks
with special favour on those mothers who have their children baptized promptly, and who make the effort to teach
them the truths of the Faith, regardless of the sacrifices
involved.

Our Lord also reveals to us in this Gospel passage
that his Kingdom belongs to those who become 'as children'. This means having a clean heart and soul, being sincere and uncomplicated, without pride or pretensions.
Before God we are indeed as little children, and should
act accordingly. *Being at the start of life, the child is open to*

---

2. cf Sacred Congregation for the Doctrine of the Faith, *Instruction on
Infant Baptism*, 20 October 1980
3. *Catechism of the Council of Trent*, II, 2, 32
4. Code of Canon Law, 867, 1

any adventure. So it should be with you. Don't put any obstacle in the way of your progressive union with Christ, a process which should continue throughout your whole life.[5]

63.2 Life of childhood and divine filiation.

In the Incarnation the Son of God could have presented himself to mankind as an angel, or as an all-powerful sovereign. Yet he chose to present himself in the weak and fragile condition of a new-born babe. He chose to be helpless as a child, as if He needed protection and love.

God has wanted us to imitate his Son in this choice, to become what in fact we are – helpless children constantly in need of God's assistance. *See what love the Father has given us, that we should be called children of God; and so we are.*[6] These few words capture the fundamental truths of our Faith. They show us how we should deal with our God. To become like children ... this requires a real change of heart that will transform all of our thoughts and actions. What must we do to become like children? First of all, we really have to want to be sons of God, ever docile to his Will, being of clean mind and body, humble and sincere. This desire is evident in the lives of the saints. As they have become more and more transformed by the action of the Holy Spirit they have increasingly seen themselves as sons of God. To become like children in the spiritual life is more than simply a beneficial and praiseworthy devotion. It is the expressed desire of the Lord. Although not every saint has manifested this attitude explicitly, this has been the work of the Holy Spirit in the heart of each and every one.[7]

---

5. C. Lubich, *Words of Life*, 47
6. 1 John 3:1
7. cf B. Perquin, *Abba, Father*, 142

A foolish child wails and stamps his feet when his loving mother puts a needle to his finger to get a splinter out. A sensible child, on the other hand, perhaps with his eyes full of tears – for the flesh is weak – looks gratefully at his good mother who is making him suffer a little in order to avoid much greater harm. Jesus, may I be a sensible child.[8] This is our request in this time of prayer – that we learn how to understand sickness, pain, apparent professional failure ... that we shall find in such setbacks the providential hand of a Father who never ceases to watch over his sons and daughters. We will accept with a smile whatever life has to offer us, in good times as in bad, and we will see it as something sent or else permitted by Someone who is infinitely wise, Someone who is infinitely in love with us.

A life of childhood has nothing to do with behaving childishly. *A foolish child wails and stamps his feet* ...: childishness has to do with personal immaturity, with a lack of self-discipline, with an overall absence of personal struggle. Such behaviour can accompany people throughout their entire life. There are those who enter into old age, and even go to their deaths, without knowing that they are children of God. True spiritual childhood entails real maturity – supernatural vision, consideration of events with the eyes of faith and with the help of the Holy Spirit. This maturity brings with it sincerity and simplicity: its possessor has become a *sensible child* ... In contrast, he who readily accedes to his whims, who gives in to his emotions and his every idea, who is constantly preoccupied with himself, this person will not make progress on the way of spiritual childhood. The man who is simple as a child is completely taken up with the glory of his Father God, just as his Master was in his earthly life.

---

8. J. Escrivá, *The Forge*, 329

The true child, the true son, the true daughter, has a steady relationship with *Abba*, his and her Father.[9]

63.3 Spiritual childhood and humility.

Our piety should be filial, full of love for our Father. How can we really serve God with love if we do not begin by recognizing him as a Father overflowing with love for his children? Many Christians live apart from God or have lost touch with God because they have not discovered the truth of their divine filiation. Spiritual childhood has been the first step in the interior life of many souls. Give us, Lord, this sense of divine filiation. Help us to meditate upon it frequently.

Truly, I say to you, whoever does not receive the kingdom of God like a child shall not enter it.[10] *Why is it that children are eligible for the Kingdom of Heaven?* asks Saint Ambrose *Perhaps it is because, ordinarily, there is no malice in them. They don't know how to lie. They don't lie to themselves. They have no desire for luxury. They aren't drawn to riches. They are uninterested in ambition. But the virtue here resides not in what they lack interest in or know nothing about, but in what they don't want to do. The virtue lies not in their inability to sin, but in their unwillingness to sin. Therefore, the Lord is not referring to childhood as it is, but to the innocence that all children share.*[11]

In the Christian life we arrive at maturity precisely at the moment when we become children before God, children who abandon themselves completely into God's loving embrace. Then we see the events of the world as they really are, with their true meaning. Our only preoccupation will be to give thanks to our Father and Lord.

---

9. cf B. Perquin, *op cit*, 143
10. Luke 18:17
11. St Ambrose, *Commentary on St Luke's Gospel*, 18, 17

The life of childhood requires in us the supernatural virtue of fortitude so that we may overcome our tendency to pride and self-sufficiency. Filial piety builds up our hope; it reinforces our confidence that we will attain our end. It gives us peace and joy in this life, for we are no longer facing life's difficulties alone. No matter how great our problems may be, the Lord will never abandon us. This certainty will keep us going, no matter what obstacles lie in our path. Without it, no advance is possible.

We ask the Blessed Virgin, our Mother, to take us by the hand since we are her little children. We ask her to have even greater care whenever our age or our experience of life require her guidance.

TWENTIETH SUNDAY: YEAR A

64. THE IMPORTANCE OF PRAYER

64.1 How to ask. The Lord pays special attention to the prayers of his children.

In the Gospel of today's Mass[1] Saint Matthew tells us that Jesus and his disciples withdrew to the district of Tyre and Sidon. He went from the shores of the Sea of Galilee to the coast of the Mediterranean. There a Gentile woman approached him. She was a Canaanite, a descendant of the original peoples of Palestine, the land which God had promised to the Jews. She cried out with a loud voice: *Have mercy on me, O Lord, Son of David; my daughter is severely possessed by a demon*.

Despite the woman's cries, the Evangelist relates of the Lord that *he did not answer her a word*. According to Saint Mark, this first encounter took place in a house, and it was here that the woman *fell down at his feet*.[2] It seemed as if Our Lord did not pay any attention to her.

Later on, when Jesus and his companions were getting ready to leave the house, Saint Matthew writes that the disciples complained to Jesus: *Send her away*, they said, *for she is crying after us*. The woman perseveres in her clamour, but the response of Jesus seems curiously cold: *I was sent only to the lost sheep of the house of Israel* The woman refuses to give up: *But she came and knelt before him, saying, 'Lord, help me'*. What faith! What humility! What steadfastness there is in her petition!

---

1. Matt 15:21-28
2. Mark 7:24-25

Jesus uses the image of the Kingdom to explain how He must first preach the Gospel to his Jewish brethren, the chosen people: *It is not fair to take the children's bread and throw it to the dogs*, He says. But the woman, armed with an unshakable faith, will not take 'No' for an answer: *Yes, Lord, yet even the dogs eat the crumbs that fall from their master's table*. She enters into the parable and conquers the heart of Christ, provoking one of the greatest compliments uttered by Our Lord as well as procuring the miracle she requested: *O woman, great is your faith! Be it done for you as you desire. And her daughter was healed instantly*. This was the reward for her perseverance.

The noble mothers who appear in the Gospels are always seeking the best for their children. They know how to appeal to Jesus for assistance and favours. On one occasion it was the mother of James and John who approached the Lord to seek advancement for them. Another time it was the widow of Naim who was weeping for the young man who had been her only child. Perhaps it was only an anguished and pleading look into the eyes of Christ that led him to bring the body back to life ... The woman in today's Gospel is a perfect model of constancy in prayer, a model intended for all those who tire easily of praying to God.

Saint Augustine relates in his *Confessions* how his mother, Saint Monica, never ceased to implore God for the conversion of her son. Nor did she weary of asking good and wise people to speak to her son to dissuade him from his erroneous ways. One day a holy bishop said to her these words by way of consolation: *Go your way; as sure as you live, it is impossible that the son of these tears should perish.*[3] Much later, Saint Augustine himself was to write: *If I did not perish in error, it was due to the daily tears*

---

3. St Augustine, *Confessions*, 3, 12, 21

of my mother, who was so full of faith.[4]

God listens in a special way to the prayer of those who know how to love, even though at times it may appear that He is deaf to the entreaty. He wants our faith to become more strong, our hope to become more profound, our love to become more trusting. He wants everyone to have the desire and the humility that a good mother has.

64.2 Characteristics of prayer: perseverance, faith and humility. Seeking the help of others to join in our prayers.

The prayer of petition plays an important role in the life of men and women. Although the Lord provides countless blessings without our ever asking for them, He has set aside many graces the granting of which will depend upon our personal prayer, or upon the prayers of others who are close to him. Saint Thomas teaches that our petitions do not change the Divine Will, but instead win for us what has already been set aside for us if we should ask.[5] As a result, we should petition the Lord without ceasing. Who knows how many blessings are waiting for us if only we ask for them? We should ask others to pray for the fervent intentions we have in our hearts, to pray for all the blessings we need and can receive from the Lord. Saint Thomas says that this is one of the reasons why Jesus did not reply immediately to the Canaanite woman. He wanted the disciples to intercede for her. In this way He shows us the importance of the intercession of the saints.[6] The Gentile woman wanted an extraordinary miracle. That required an extraordinary kind of prayer, accompanied by enormous faith and deep humility.

---

4. *idem*, *Treatise on the gift of perseverance*, 20, 53
5. St Thomas, *Summa Theologiae*, 2-2, q 83, a 2
6. *idem*, *Catena Aurea*, vol II, p 338

Perseverance is a prerequisite to all petition – *They ought always to pray and not lose heart;*[7] this was Christ's teaching. *Persevere in prayer. Persevere, even when your efforts seem sterile. Prayer is always fruitful.*[8] The prayer of the Canaanite woman was successful from the very first moment. Jesus was only waiting for her to prepare her heart to receive the great blessing she asked for.

We have to petition with faith. Faith *nurtures prayer, and prayer, as it grows, leads to firmness in faith.*[9] Both are intimately united. This woman had a great faith: *She shows her belief in the divinity of Christ when she calls him Lord. She shows her belief in the humanity of Christ when she calls him Son of David. The woman asks for nothing based on her merits. She only invokes the mercy of God by saying: 'Have mercy on me'. And she doesn't ask for mercy for her daughter, but mercy for herself, because her daughter's pain is truly her pain. In order to win Christ's compassion she gives a full description of the suffering when she states: 'my daughter is severely possessed by a demon'. From these words the divine Doctor learns about her ailment, its gravity and its origin – the gravity when she says 'severely possessed'; the origin at the words 'by a demon'.*[10]

Perseverance in prayer comes from a life of faith, of confidence that Jesus is always listening to us. This faith leads us to a complete abandonment into the hands of God. *Tell him: Lord, I want nothing other than what you want. Even those things I am asking you for at present, if they take me an inch away from your Will, don't give them to me.*[11] I want only what you want, because it is what you want.

---

7. Luke 18:1
8. J. Escrivá, *The Way*, 101
9. St Augustine, *Homily 115*
10. St Thomas, *Catena Aurea*, vol. II, pp 336-337
11. J. Escrivá, *The Forge*, 512

64.3 Above any other petition, asking for the needs of our souls. Asking for material needs insofar as they bring us closer to God.

The Canaanite woman teaches us another characteristic of true prayer besides perseverance. She teaches us the importance of humility. Prayer can rise up only from a humble and repentant heart: *A humble and contrite heart, O God, thou will not despise.*[12] God resists the proud and gives his grace to the humble,[13] to the person who sees himself as *servus pauper et humilis*.[14]

The Lord wants us to ask him for many things. First of all, we should ask for what refers to our souls since *the sicknesses they can contract are severe. It is our souls Our Lord mainly wants to cure of these ailments. If He works to cure the body, He has done so for the sake of the soul.*[15] It can happen that *as soon as we contract a physical malady, we will leave no stone unturned until we are free of its effects. On the other hand, when the sickness affects the soul we respond with vacillation and delay ... We make the primary secondary and the secondary primary. We treat the symptoms and not the disease.*[16] What our souls can really use are the grace to fight against our defects, more rectitude of intention in our work, perseverance in our vocation, light to receive more fruit from Holy Communion, a more refined sense of charity, docility in spiritual direction and more apostolic zeal ... Our Lord also wants us to ask for other things we need, such as help to recover after a small defeat; employment, if we need a job; good health ... And all of these we seek insofar as they will lead us to

---

12. Ps 50:19
13. cf 1 Pet 5:5; Jas 4:6
14. cf *Divine Office*, Hymn for the Solemnity of Corpus Christi
15. St John Chrysostom, *Homilies on St Matthew's Gospel*, 14, 3
16. *ibid*

love God more. We don't want anything that will take us away from what is really important – to be always united to Christ.

Jesus is most pleased when we pray for others. Saint John Chrysostom teaches: *Necessity obliges us to pray for ourselves. Fraternal charity obliges us to pray for others. God finds the prayer motivated by charity to be more meritorious than the prayer motivated by necessity.*[17]

We should pray for all those in our families and for everyone the Lord has put by our side. Parents have a special obligation to pray for their children, especially if they have fallen away from the Faith. Parents should also pray for those children who have been called to a life in his service. We should accompany our prayers with works so that God will hear our pleas more promptly – by offering, for example, hours of work or study for a particular intention in question, by accepting God's will in suffering or in the face of contradictions and by practising charity and mercy at every opportunity.

Christians in all times have felt moved to present their petitions through holy intercessors, through each person's Guardian Angel, and through the special mediation of Our Blessed Mother, Holy Mary. Saint Bernard says that *our Advocate rose to Heaven, where she could act on behalf of our salvation as Mother of the Judge and Mother of Mercy.*[18] We should never fail to go to Our Lady each day, since so much depends on her.

---

17. *idem, Catena Aurea*, vol. I, p. 354
18. St Bernard, *Sermon on the Assumption of the Blessed Virgin Mary*, 1, 1

TWENTIETH SUNDAY: YEAR B

65. THE PLEDGE OF ETERNAL LIFE

65.1 Holy Communion is a foretaste of Heaven and a guarantee of reaching it.

The First Reading of today's Mass[1] includes the Lord's timeless invitation to all men and women: *Come, eat of my bread and drink of the wine I have mixed*. The banquet is an image which is frequently to be found in Sacred Scripture. It is used to announce the coming of the Messiah, full of good things and blessings. In a special way the banquet is a prefiguring of the Holy Eucharist, wherein Christ gives himself to us as food. Saint John speaks to us of this meal, recalling those final words of Jesus in the synagogue of Capharnaum: *I am the living bread which came down from heaven, that a man may eat of it and not die*. And then he adds: *He who eats my flesh and drinks my blood has eternal life, and I will raise him up on the last day. For my flesh is food indeed, and my blood is drink indeed ... This is the bread which came down from heaven, not such as the fathers ate and died; he who eats this bread will live forever*.[2]

As food for the soul, Holy Communion increases the supernatural life of the recipient. At the same time and as a consequence, Holy Communion builds up our defences against what is not from God, whatever is in opposition to Christ. It helps us combat our inclination to evil while strengthening us against sin. It enkindles our charity and

---

1. Prov 9:1-6
2. John 6:51-58

inspires contrition for our falls. It also erases the effects of venial sins we have confessed, and preserves us from mortal sin.

In addition, the Holy Eucharist is a pledge of eternal life and a foretaste of Heaven. A pledge is what is given as a guarantee for the fulfilment of a promise.[3] In Holy Communion we have an 'advance' on the life to come and an enormous help towards achieving it – that is, if we remain faithful to the Lord.

In an ancient Antiphon used in Eucharistic devotion, we pray: *O most holy banquet at which we receive Christ ... the soul is filled with grace and we are given a pledge of future glory*. The image of the banquet is often used in Sacred Scripture to describe the great joy and happiness to be found in union with God. The Lord himself announces that He will no longer drink of the fruit of the vine, *until that day when I drink it new with you in my Father's kingdom*.[4] He makes reference to a new wine,[5] because now there shall be no need for ordinary food and drink. Now we are to have Christ for all time in a vibrant union, without limit. We have in Holy Communion the foretaste and guarantee of this definitive union, and *it becomes manifest to all the members of the Mystical Body of Christ, beyond the limits of distance or temporal life itself, because space and time cannot contain the Glorious Christ here present*.[6]

What happiness to be able to be with Christ and enter in some way into Heaven while still here on earth! *Build up a gigantic faith in the Holy Eucharist. Be filled*

---

3. cf W. Morris, ed., *The American Heritage Dictionary of the English Language*, Boston, 1969, p. 1006
4. Matt 26:29
5. cf Is 25:6
6. C. Lubich, *The Eucharist*

with wonder before this ineffable reality. We have God with us; we can receive him every day and, if we want to, we can speak intimately with him, just as we talk with a friend, as we talk with a brother, as we talk with a father, as we talk with Love itself.[7]

65.2 The Holy Eucharist is also a pledge of the future glorification of the body.

The Second Vatican Council teaches that Holy Communion is *a sacrament of love, a sign of unity, a bond of charity, a paschal banquet in which Christ is eaten, the mind is filled with grace, and a pledge of future glory is given to us*.[8] This eternal glory is not only for the soul, but for the body, for the whole person.[9] The Lord made reference to the whole person when He promised that whoever should eat His flesh, would live in Him and would never die, but would rise with Him on the last day.[10] The Eucharist proclaims the death of the Lord until He comes again at the end of time,[11] when our earthly bodies will be resurrected and united with our souls. Therefore those who enter into the joy of God forever will do so in both body and soul.

Jesus is *the Life,* not just of eternal life, but also of the supernatural life of grace that works in the souls of people still on earth. When Jesus arrives in Bethany to raise Lazarus from the dead, he says to Martha: *I am the resurrection and the life; he who believes in me, though he die, yet shall he live, and whoever lives and believes in me shall never die.*[12] The Lord repeats in Bethany the teaching

---

7. J. Escrivá, *The Forge*, 268
8. Second Vatican Council, *Sacrosanctum Concilium*, 47
9. cf M. Schmaus, *Dogmatic Theology*, vol. VI
10. cf John 6:54
11. 1 Cor 11:26
12. John 11:25

He had given earlier in Capharnaum, the teaching we find in today's Gospel: he who receives him will not die.

The Fathers of the Church call Communion *the medicine of immortality, the antidote for death, the means to live always in Jesus Christ*.[13] Saint Irenaeus teaches that just as the branches of the vine on the ground bear fruit in due season, the grain of wheat has to fall into the earth and die before it will multiply, so that *through the wisdom of God this bread and wine may become the Eucharist, which is the Body and Blood of Christ. The same cycle takes place with our bodies, which are fed on the Eucharist and eventually laid in the earth to become corrupted, to rise again in due time* ...[14] The Eucharist acts as the seed of future glorification for the body, making it incorruptible for eternity. The Eucharist sows within the human person the germ of immortality, since the life of grace is more perdurable than death.

Saint Gregory of Nyssa explains that man took in the food of death (with original sin), and therefore should take the medicine which will work as an antidote. This medicine is none other than the Body of Christ, *who has overcome death and is the fount of Life*.[15]

If at any time we should become depressed at the thought of death, we should fill ourselves with hope in the knowledge that death is a step on the road to everlasting life. Our soul will live on, to be later reunited with our glorified body. It is like someone who, abandoning his home during a catastrophe, is consoled by the thought that he is on the way to a better dwelling, one that he will never again have to quit. The Holy Eucharist is not only an anticipation, it is a *sign that acts as a guarantee* of the promise

---

13. St Ignatius of Antioch, *Letter to the Ephesians*, 20, 20
14. St Irenaeus, *Against heresies*, 5, 2, 3
15. cf St Gregory of Nyssa, *Catechetical discourses*, 37

the Lord has made to us: *he who eats my flesh and drinks my blood has eternal life, and I will raise him up at the last day*.

65.3 While we journey to the house of the Lord, the knowledge of our weaknesses should lead us to seek strength in Communion.

Look carefully then how you walk, not as unwise men but as wise, making the most of the time, because the days are evil, warns Saint Paul in the Second Reading of today's Mass.[16] Now, as then, *the days are evil*, and the time is short. There is a very little space of time separating us from our definitive life with God, but there are in this interval many chances that we may not achieve that final union with him.

The Apostle encourages us to use our time well. Even more, we should make up for the time we may have lost. According to Saint Augustine, to redeem time is *to sacrifice present interests for the sake of eternal interests. In this way we purchase eternity with the coin of time*.[17] We should take advantage of all the circumstances and events of our lives to give glory to God, to reaffirm our love for him above all that goes on in this transient world.

Through Holy Communion Christ teaches us to look upon the present with the eyes of eternity. He throws light on what is truly important in every situation, in every event. He illumines the future and gives transcendent meaning to our work when it is well done. His light grows stronger every day, leading us on to a new and eternal existence, whose reality is such that the world becomes like a shadow.[18] We find in the Holy Eucharist the

---

16. Eph 5:15-20
17. St Augustine, *Homily 16*, 2
18. cf 1 Cor 7:31

strength we need to undertake what remains of the journey to the Father's house. *The Holy Eucharist is an eternal pledge to us. It assures us of Heaven. This is the dowry sent to us by Heaven as a promise that one day it will be our resting place. What is more, Jesus Christ will cause our bodies to rise again with greater glory, insofar as we have frequently and reverently received him in Communion.*[19]

The knowledge of our weaknesses should lead us to seek strength in Communion. In this sacrament *it is Christ himself who gives shelter to the traveller worn out by the roughness of the road. Christ comforts man with the warmth of his understanding and love. In the Eucharist there is the fulfilment of those sweet words: 'Come to me, all who labour and are heavy laden, and I will give you rest'* (*Matt 11:28*). *This personal and profound assistance is to be found in the divine Bread which Christ offers to us at the eucharistic table. This is our final end as we travel the ways of this world.*[20] If we are faithful, one day we will enter with him into Heaven. Then what had been the guarantee of a promise will become a reality – our life joined to the Life for all eternity.

Ecce Panis angelorum, factus cibus viatorum, vere panis filiorum: behold the bread of Angels, made into the food of travellers, truly the bread of the sons.[21] Give us, Lord, the strength to travel with human and supernatural dignity along our way upon this earth, our eyes fixed firmly on our goal.

---

19. St Jean Vianney, (The Curé d'Ars), *Homily on Holy Communion*
20. John Paul II, *Homily*, 9 July 1980
21. *Roman Missal, Solemnity of the Most Holy Body and Blood of Christ*, Sequence *Lauda Sion*

TWENTIETH SUNDAY: YEAR C

66. THE FIRE OF DIVINE LOVE

66.1 Faith in the love God has for us and always has had.

Fire is used frequently in Sacred Scripture as a symbol of the Love of God, a love which works to cleanse men of their impurities. Love is like *the fire which never says, 'Enough'*.[1] Love is ignited by contact with God: *My heart became hot within me. As I mused, the fire burned*, exclaims the Psalmist.[2] On the day of Pentecost the Holy Spirit came down upon the Apostles in the form of tongues of fire, to purify their hearts and prepare them for the mission of extending the Kingdom of Christ throughout the world.[3]

Jesus says to us in today's Gospel: *I came to cast fire upon the earth; and would that it were already kindled!*[4] Love finds its ultimate expression in Christ himself: *For God so loved the world that he gave his only Son*.[5] Jesus surrendered his life freely for us. *Greater love has no man than this, that a man lay down his life for his friends*.[6] This is why He tells us of his holy impatience to fulfil his Baptism by dying on the Cross and redeeming mankind: *I have a baptism to be baptized with; and how I am constrained until it is accomplished!*[7]

---

1. Prov 30:16
2. Ps 38:3
3. Acts 2:2-4
4. Luke 12:49
5. John 3:16
6. John 15:13
7. Luke 12:50

The Lord wants the fire of his love to set alight our hearts, to light them up completely. He loves each one of us with a personal love, as if each one of us were the only object of his love. He has never ceased to love us, to help us, to protect us, to communicate with us ... even when we are ungrateful, when we sin or even when we sin gravely. The Lord always shows forth his benevolence. God does not love us with a conditional love. He loves us totally, without any conditions, with all of his being, which is infinite. This mystery of love is particularly apparent in the case of his Mother, the Blessed Virgin.

Mary, Our Mother, is a mirror in which we should see ourselves. She lived a normal life in such a way that none of her relatives or neighbours knew what was in her heart. Not even Joseph would have known, had not God revealed it to him. Our Blessed Lady, God's most favoured creature, remained always in a state of absolute normality. At the time of the Annunciation, when God's special love for her was especially evident, she accepted God's eternal plan for her. How great was her faith! To think that she carried within her the salvation of Israel, the fulfilment of all the prophecies! She not only believed in God's absolute love, but believed without the slightest reservation.

Mary teaches us to love God without limits. She helps us now to examine our conscience concerning the quality of our love for God. *It doesn't make sense to have a half-hearted love for a God who loves us with such ardour.*[8] Is our heart on fire like that of the Blessed Virgin? Or has our heart gone cold, becoming a heap of ashes?

God loves me. This is the fundamental fact of my existence. Everything else pales in importance.

---

8. St Alphonsus Liguori, *Visits to the Blessed Sacrament*, 4

66.2 Love calls for love. This response is best shown in deeds.

Love calls for love. This response is best shown in deeds, in the daily effort to relate to God, to identify our will with his Will. In today's Second Reading we are given encouragement for this daily struggle.[9] Secure in the knowledge that *we are surrounded by so great a cloud of witnesses*, the saints, we should take advantage of their example and their assistance. *Let us also lay aside every weight, and sin which clings so closely, and let us run with perseverance the race that is set before us, looking to Jesus the pioneer and perfecter of our faith* ... We have our sights set on him, like the runner who will not let anything keep him from his goal. We will avoid any and all occasions of sin with decision and vigour, though *you have not yet resisted to the point of shedding your blood*. We have to be ready to go thus far, if necessary, in our struggle to avoid sin, even venial sin. It is better to die than to offend God, if only in a minor matter.

We need to say 'Yes' to Love many times a day. We need to respond to Jesus in the thousand ordinary events of daily life: by denying ourselves and serving those others with whom we live and work; by living temperance and sobriety through small mortifications of the senses; by being punctual in the fulfilment of our duties; by being orderly at home and at work; by making the effort required to pray well; by happily accepting the Will of God whenever it does not fit in with our own plans or desires ... This is how we say 'Yes' to God in the little victories of each day. There are many times when we have to say 'No' to ourselves if we are to honour our 'Yes' to Love: by guarding our eyes; by giving up many comforts and

---

9. Heb 12:1-4

conveniences; by refusing to leave off work early ... The Holy Spirit can give us many indications as to how best to respond to Christ's infinite love for us.

Love is shown in sorrow for sins, in contrition. There are so many times when we say 'No' to Love, perhaps without paying much attention. It is then we have to make a deeper act of love in response to our having offended God. We should seek out the divine mercy to be found in the sacrament of Confession. *He who does not truly repent, does not truly love; obviously, when we love another person we suffer at having offended him. This is one of the effects of real love.*[10]

Then flew one of the seraphim to me, having in his hand a burning coal which he had taken with tongs from the altar. And he touched my mouth, and said: 'Behold, this has touched your lips; your guilt is taken away, and your sin is forgiven'.[11] We ask the Lord to purify our souls with the fire of his love. *O Jesus, strengthen our souls, open out the way for us, and above all, intoxicate us with your Love. Make us into blazing fires to enkindle the earth with the heavenly fire you brought us.*[12]

66.3 Inspiring others with the love of Christ

We Christians should be a flame that enkindles, just as Jesus enkindled his disciples. No one who has known us should be left indifferent. Our love should be something alive, a burning fire that sets off other fires of love and apostolate. The Holy Spirit will work through us, blowing upon embers that appear to have gone out, but which can still be revived and return to the fullness of Christian life. It does not matter that we see ourselves as useless

---

10. St Thomas, *On the precept of Charity*, 205
11. Is 6:6-7
12. J. Escrivá, *The Forge*, 31

nonentities, as obstacles rather than as fitting instruments. Our Lord wants only that we give our all. He will do the rest. We should not forget that it takes only a tiny spark to ignite a forest fire. How pleased the Lord is to hear us offer him the little that we are! *You wrote: My King, I hear you proclaiming in a loud voice that still resounds: 'Ignem veni mittere in terram, et quid volo nisi ut accendatur?'* – *I have come to cast fire upon the earth, and what will I but that it be kindled! Then you added: Lord, I answer, with all my heart, with all my senses and faculties: 'Ecce ego quia vocasti me!'* – *here I am because you have called me. May this answer of yours be a daily reality.*[13]

True love for God is shown in the apostolate, in our desire that others may know and love Jesus Christ. *With the amazing naturalness of the things of God, the contemplative soul is filled with apostolic zeal: 'My heart was warmed within me, a fire blazed forth from my thoughts'. What could this fire be if not the fire that Christ talks about: 'I have come to cast fire upon the earth, and what will I but that it be kindled?' An apostolic fire that acquires its strength in prayer,*[14] in close union with Christ.

This is the furnace at which we fuel our apostolic zeal. In front of the Tabernacle we will receive light and strength. We will speak to Jesus about the children, about our parents, about our brothers and sisters, about our friends, about that person we recently met, about those people we encounter at work and in our family life. No one should go away from us empty-handed. To everyone, in one way or another, with a word, with our example, with our prayer, we should announce that Christ is passing by, that Christ is waiting for us, that Christ wants us to serve

---

13. *ibid*, 52
14. *idem, Christ is passing by*, 120

him. *Through the world still echoes that divine cry: 'I have come to cast fire upon the earth, and what will I but that it be kindled?' And you see: it has nearly all died out ... Don't you want to spread the blaze?*[15]

We tell Jesus that He can count on us, upon our paltry strength and our meagre talents: *Ecce ego quia vocasti me*. Here I am, Lord, because you have called me. And we ask Our Blessed Lady, *Regina Apostolorum*, to teach us to be courageous in leading others to her Son.

---

15. *idem, The Way*, 801

TWENTIETH WEEK: MONDAY

67. JOY AND GENEROSITY

67.1 The rich young man. The joy of giving.

After the blessing of the children, Jesus left that place and was setting out again on the road when a young man came and knelt before him, saying: *Good Teacher, what must I do to inherit eternal life?*[1] Jesus looked upon that young man with great hope. The disciples stopped to observe this roadside encounter. The scene depicted in today's Gospel is one of special beauty.[2] Perhaps the rich young man had listened to Jesus on another occasion. Maybe this was the first time he had the nerve to speak directly to him. He carried in his heart a longing to give himself, to love more ... perhaps he was unhappy about his life. So, when the Lord tells him to keep the Commandments, the young man says that he has obeyed them, then asks: *Quid adhuc mihi deest? What do I still lack?* This is the question that so many men and women have asked themselves on recognizing that something is missing in their lives.

Jesus, who is so attentive to the slightest movement of souls, is moved at the sight of this clean and restless heart. It was at this moment that He looked upon the young man and loved him, according to Saint Mark.[3] The steady gaze of Jesus, that penetrating and unforgettable look, is in itself no less than an invitation. Christ is inviting the young

---

1. Mark 10:17
2. Matt 19:16-22
3. Mark 10:21

man to follow him by leaving behind all of his possessions. In other words, the invitation is to empty out his heart so as to fill it with the things of God, to exchange a love of material goods for the love of Christ, to become materially poor but spiritually rich.[4]

But the young man was not generous. He chose to keep his riches, which he could go on enjoying for a period of years, but he lost his opportunity to have Jesus, whom he would have had forever. The rich young man did not expect this answer from the Master. God's plans do not usually match with our plans, which are largely fabricated by our imagination. God's plans have been prepared from all eternity. They are the best plans we could possibly imagine, though at times they can upset us.

Upon hearing these words from Jesus the young man *went away sorrowful; for he had great possessions.* Everyone present saw how he walked away from the most loving invitation of the Lord. It is certainly possible that some time later the young man would find excuses for his lack of generosity. This would perhaps give him back some degree of tranquillity, though never the peace of soul which is the fruit of self-sacrifice. Maybe he thought he was too young, or that he needed more time to consider the matter ... What a disaster! What a missed opportunity! When it comes to such a meeting with Jesus, one ends up by either following him or getting lost. Each encounter is crucial. Jesus never leaves anyone indifferent. The choice is one way or the other.

Once someone has received the loving glance of the Lord, it is never forgotten. It becomes impossible to live as before. Joy is the fruit of generosity, of responding fully to the calls which Christ makes to each one of us in our state

---

4. cf M. J. Indart, *Jesus in his World*

of life. Life becomes full of joy and peace as the result of our complete abandonment to the Will of God, to be tested on a daily basis.

67.2 Christ passes by and beckons.

The young man refused to take the hint, and the Gospel goes on to say: 'abiit tristis' (Matt 19:22), he went away forlorn ... *He lost his happiness because he refused to hand over his freedom to God.*[5] If he would not use his freedom to follow Christ, our true destiny, of what use was his freedom to him anyway?

Sadness takes root in the heart like a noxious weed when we distance ourselves from Christ, when we deny his call, when we lack generosity. This spiritual sickness *is a vice caused by a disordered love for oneself.*[6] We can also grow sad because of poor health, exhaustion or pain. But this sadness of the heart has its origin in pride, in egoism: behind that aversion from enduring such privations may lurk a streak of vanity; behind that physical pain might be hiding a refusal to accept the Will of God; in that discouragement upon seeing one personal fault after another there could be more sorrow for self than sorrow for having offended Christ ... *If God has pardoned me, if his most merciful love encompasses me, how can I remain sad? If anyone feeds his sorrow with anxiety about his guilt for sins committed, that man should know that he is only fooling himself.*[7] Our faults and sins should be a motive for true repentance and a renewal of joyful love.

Our Lord frequently meets us on the pathways of our lives. Sometimes He asks a lot from us so as to give us more. At other times He looks for little things like the

---

5. J. Escrivá, *Friends of God*, 24

6. St Thomas, *Summa Theologiae*, 2-2, q 28, a 4, ad 1

7. C. Lopez Pardo, *On Life and Death*, Madrid

fulfilment of a duty, fidelity to our plan of life,
mortification of the imagination, details of refined charity
... It can happen that the Lord will cross our path so as to
invite us to follow him more closely, without leaving our
place in the world but with an unconditional surrender of
our heart. *We have to learn how to give ourselves, to burn
before God like the light placed on a lampstand to give light
to those who walk in darkness; like the votive lamps that
burn by the altar, giving off light till their last drop of oil is
consumed.*[8] This is what He asks of everyone, of each one
in the place and state to which he is called, in the particular and specific vocation he or she has received from God.
Vocation is the most important aspect of our life. Once it
is known, our vocation is the business that should occupy
all our energies, with the help of divine grace, until the end
of our days.

67.3 Sadness causes much harm to the soul. Looking for joy in the act of giving.

He went away sorrowful. We know nothing more
about that young man. His story ends in disappointment.
Who knows? He could have been one of the Twelve. But
he did not want to give his assent, and Jesus respected his
freedom. The freedom he had was one that the young man
did not know how to use. Saint Basil criticizes him with
these words: *The vendor does not become sad that he has
to barter the goods he has at fairs to acquire the merchandise he wants; but you become sad at exchanging the chance
of eternal life for a handful of dust.*[9] He preferred to keep
his dust, his wealth, instead of choosing the imperishable
gift offered by Christ.

---

8. J. Escrivá, *The Forge*, 44
9. St Basil, in *Catena Aurea*, vol VI, 313

Sadness does a good deal of harm to the soul. *Like a moth in clothing, or a maggot in wood, sorrow gnaws at the human heart,*[10] and predisposes one to evil. We have to react right away if at any time sadness should come over our soul: *Delight your soul and comfort your heart, and remove sorrow far from you, for sorrow has destroyed many, and there is no profit in it.*[11] From this state nothing can be expected but unfortunate consequences.

Because our lives are oriented towards following Christ, it is logical that we should always be filled with joy. This is the only true joy in the world, a joy without limit, a joy without end. It is compatible with suffering, with illness, with failure ... *Christian joy excludes and combats sadness in a definitive way. Envy, discouragement, depression all are incompatible with it. One of the fruits of Christian joy is the suppression of these pains, which are so perilous to the spiritual life.*[12]

A sorrowful soul is at the mercy of many temptations. How many sins have had their origin in sadness? How many noble ideals have been undone because of it! If at any time we should feel the pull of sadness, we should examine the cause with sincerity in our prayer. We will frequently find that we are lacking in generosity with God or with others. *Laetetur cor quaerentium Dominum* – 'Let the hearts of them rejoice who seek the Lord'.

There you have light to help you discover the reasons for your sadness.[13] We can always increase our joy if we are seriously following the footsteps of Our Lord in our prayer, in our effort to maintain presence of God. We should also examine our generosity with others – by

---

10. Prov 25:20
11. Sir 30:23
12. J. M. Perrin, *The Gospel of Joy*, Madrid, 1962
13. J. Escrivá, *The Way*, 666

having an interest in their health and in their aspirations, by making those small but constant sacrifices on their behalf ...

If we should ever feel sad at heart, we should ask ourselves: In what area am I not being generous with God? How can I be more generous with other people? Do I worry too much about myself and my own affairs, my health, my future? ... We should find both the cause and the remedy forthwith. In the meantime, we should seek to improve our friendship with the Lord and to increase our generosity towards others, if only in small details of service. We have to open our hearts to our spiritual director, who truly understands and appreciates our holy ambitions.

Filled with the joy Christ gives us, we can do a great deal of good in the world around us. One of the best forms of charity is to transmit this joy to others. Many can find God in the practical expressions of this attractive and profound sentiment. *Holy Mary, Cause of our Joy*, pray for us. Win for us the grace to follow Christ ever more closely. Obtain for us the grace that we may never turn our backs on him, not even in the little things of our every day life.

TWENTIETH WEEK: TUESDAY

68. THE CHRISTIAN MEANING OF THE GOODS OF THE EARTH

68.1 The goods of the earth have been ordered by God for the supernatural end of the person.

The Apostles looked on with sorrow as the young man declined to follow Christ by giving up his material wealth. They saw him take his leave with that sadness peculiar to those who will not correspond with divine love. Everyone there was disappointed at the thought that the rich young man could have been one of Christ's disciples.

Our Lord chose to say to the Apostles at that very moment: *Truly, I say to you, it will be hard for a rich man to enter the kingdom of heaven.* He then repeated himself to give emphasis: *Again I tell you, it is easier for a camel to go through the eye of a needle than for a rich man to enter the kingdom of God.* The disciples *were greatly astonished.*[1]

Whoever fills his heart with the things of this world is simply incapable of having a meaningful encounter with the Lord. Man was made to tend towards and have his end in God. He can reach God through material things or he can make material things his god. The human heart can follow either path. It is a clear choice of going one way or the other. As Our Lord taught on another occasion: *You cannot serve God and Mammon.*[2]

'Mammon' is the Aramaic term used by Our Lord to

---

1. Matt 19:23-25
2. Matt 6:24

signify material wealth. The word *refers to an idol. Why did Christ allude to an idol? For two reasons: first, because an idol is a substitute for God, and second, because of the nature of wealth. Besides serving as a means of exchange, 'mammon' also serves as an instrument of power, a means of controlling people and events, a source of contention between persons. The idol offers man a dominion over Creation which is in direct contradiction to man's role as revealed by the Creator.*[3]

Anyone who places his hopes on the things of this world is practising a form of idolatry,[4] thereby corrupting his soul with something impure.[5] How often do those people end up joining forces with *the kings of the earth who wage war against the Lord and against his anointed.*[6]

A disordered love for material goods, whether few or many in number, is a serious obstacle to the following of Christ. This is the lesson we learn from the incident involving the rich young man in yesterday's meditation. Christians have to examine frequently their sense of detachment from things, as will be shown in details of the way they live sobriety and temperance. Am I really detached from the things of this world? Do I value the needs of my soul more than the needs of my body? Do I use material goods in a way that brings me closer to God? Do I avoid unnecessary expenditures? Do I refuse to satisfy my whims? Do I fight against the tendency to create false needs? Do I take good care of the things I own and of the things I am responsible for? ... What a shame if we were to stop following Christ for the sake of something really unimportant!

---

3. J. M. Lustiger, *Secularity and Theology of the Cross*, Madrid, 1987
4. Col 3:5
5. cf Eph 4:19; 5:3
6. cf Ps 2:2

68.2 Wealth and personal talents need to be ordered to the service of the common good. Living poverty in the middle of the world. The sanctification of temporal realities.

A Christian who lives in the midst of the world should never forget that the goods of this earth are in fact *goods* that should serve to benefit one's family and society as a whole. We Christians must sanctify ourselves by the way in which we put these goods to use. There is nothing further from the spirit of true poverty than to view the world and its riches with suspicion or contempt. God looks with favour on authentic progress and material development. We all have to struggle against poverty, misery and every kind of situation that degrades human dignity.

The poverty of a normal Christian is not a matter of exterior appearance. Christian poverty has to do with something deeper, with the orientation of the human heart. It has to do with being humble before God, recognising one's total dependence on him. This kind of poverty is shown in a faith proved by works. If someone has this virtue and is blessed with material wealth, then that person's Christian response will be one of detachment and charity. The person who lacks material wealth is not justified in the sight of God for that reason alone. The poor person has to struggle to acquire the virtues necessary to live poverty in a Christian way. A poor person can certainly act with generosity. The poor person, too, has to be detached – from what little he possesses.

Jesus was always very close to the poor, the sick and whoever was in need. Yet among those drawn to his Person there seems to have been a number of wealthy people. For example, the women who took care of the material needs of the Master and his Apostles must have been fairly well-to-do. A few of the Apostles, like Matthew and

the sons of Zebedee, were men of some means. Joseph of
Arimathea was a man of substance who was specifically
identified as one of Christ's disciples.[7] It was he and
Nicodemus who had the privilege of taking down the body
of Our Lord from the Cross.[8] Joseph gave Christ his tomb,
and Nicodemus contributed, we are told, a mixture of
myrrh and aloes *weighing about one hundred pounds*. The
family of Martha, Mary and Lazarus was probably of considerable social standing, since we know that 'many Jews'
went to mourn the death of Lazarus. Christ asked the rich
tax-collector Zacchaeus if He could stay in his home, and
later accepted him as a disciple.[9] The very cloak that Jesus
wore was valuable, as shown by the fact that it was woven
from top to bottom without seam ...

*Earthly goods are not bad, but they are debased when
man sets them up as idols, when he adores them. They are
ennobled when they are converted into instruments for good,
for just and charitable Christian undertakings. We cannot
seek after material goods as if they were a treasure. Our
treasure is Christ and all our love and desire must be centred
on him* ...[10] He is the truth that defines our life, and
above which there is no other. We need to imitate him,
according to our personal circumstances. We can never
assume that we are thoroughly detached, since it is the
nature of every man and every woman to create personal
idols, to have unnecessary 'needs', to spend more than is
really necessary, to give in to one's whims. As the Second
Vatican Council teaches us, ... *man should regard the
external things that he legitimately possesses not only as his
own but also as common in the sense that they should be*

7. Matt 27:57
8. John 19:38
9. Luke 19:5
10. J. Escrivá, *Christ is passing by*, 35

able to benefit not only him but also others.[11]

We should examine how detached we are from material things and ask ourselves whether we have our hearts utterly set upon the Lord. This involves both things of the moment and things of lesser consequence, since *one clear sign of detachment is genuinely not to consider anything as one's own*.[12]

68.3 Developing one's God-given talents for the sake of others.

We should develop all the talents the Lord has given us, without false modesty or hesitation. We should employ all of our energies to foster true social progress, a progress that is ever more worthy of man. Since we are all children of God, every person should be allowed conditions of life that are in accord with human dignity. We have to give what we can to institutions and foundations which elevate man from ignorance and sub-human conditions. We should work for solutions to those inequalities and social barriers that cry to Heaven for remedy: on the one hand there are many who have to struggle every day to survive, while on the other hand there are squanderers who offend mankind as well as their Creator with their selfish profligacy.

We will come across many difficulties in this effort, both internal and external. Egoism is deeply rooted in our hearts, and our present environment seems totally given over to a culture of consumerism. Such an environment brings with it a strong wave of sensuality, which *entails a proliferation of moral deviations of every kind: eroticism, the exaltation of pleasure, the abuse of alcohol and drugs, etc. It*

---

11. Second Vatican Council, *Gaudium et spes*, 69
12. J. Escrivá, *The Forge*, 524

is obvious that these excesses have appeared as a conse-
quence of the profound dissatisfaction of men and women
who have become alienated from God ... The results are all
around us: men and women without ideals, without criteria
and good judgment,[13] who have risen up against the Lord
and against his Christ.[14]

For the great majority of Christians, following Christ
means sanctifying oneself in the middle of the world. It
means developing one's talents and possessions for the
good of others, beginning with one's own family. The aim
and object of Christian life cannot be the mere accumula-
tion of riches. Such conduct can only result in a massive
impoverishment of the human person. Temperance in the
possession and use of material goods frees the Christian to
follow Christ. The Blessed Virgin knew more than anyone
else how to live this virtue. She will help us to form in this
respect a good, concrete resolution.

---

13. A. Fuentes, *The Christian meaning of Riches*, Madrid, 1988
14. cf Ps 2:2

TWENTIETH WEEK: WEDNESDAY

69. AT ALL HOURS OF THE DAY

69.1 The Lord calls everyone to work in his vineyard. He calls us to be co-redeemers with him in the world.

In today's Gospel the Lord speaks about a father of a family who goes out to hire labourers to work in his vineyard – at daybreak, at nine o'clock in the morning, at twelve noon, at three in the afternoon ... [1] He promises to pay the first group one denarius for a day's work. The remaining groups are in turn also hired as it transpires for the same just wage. At day's end, at five o'clock in the afternoon, the father goes out again, only to find still more labourers without work. He asks them: *Why do you stand here idle all day?* And they reply: *Because no one has hired us.* So the owner sends them also into the vineyard.

Our Lord wants to teach us a fundamental lesson: God calls each and every person to his service. Some people receive Christ's invitation at 'daybreak', in their youth. They have been blessed with a special kind of divine predilection. Others receive Christ's call 'later in the day'. Everyone hears the call in different circumstances. The denarius we receive at the end of the day is eternal glory, a participation in the life of God.[2] In addition, we are given an incomparable happiness while here on earth, knowing that we are working for the Master, spending our lives for Christ.

To work in the Lord's vineyard, no matter how old we

---

1. Matt 20:1-16
2. cf F. M. Moschner, *Parables of the Kingdom of Heaven*, 215

are, is to collaborate with Christ in the Redemption of the world: spreading good doctrine, in season and out of season; encouraging others to go to the sacrament of Confession; inviting others to follow Christ more closely with our life of prayer; teaching catechism; helping to raise funds for new apostolic instruments; leading someone away from a situation that could result in an offence against God; suggesting to others the possibility of a vocation ...

Whoever feels called to work in the Lord's vineyard should indeed *take part in the divine plan of redemption. He should make progress personally towards salvation himself and help others reach this end as well. By helping the others, he acts to save himself.*[3]

It will not be possible to follow Christ if at the same time we failed to transmit the joy of our calling to everyone. *He who is totally absorbed in his own interests has not yet entered into the Lord's vineyard.*[4] The people who work for Christ are those who are *ever vigilant to win new souls. They are in a hurry to bring others to the vineyard.*[5] There is an urgency about it because our time in life is short.

69.2 We do apostolate in whatever time or place we find ourselves. The example of the first Christians.

The Lord goes out to hire labourers for his vineyard at different hours and in different places. Every hour, every minute is a good time for apostolate, to bring others to the vineyard so that they too can be of service. God calls each single one of us in accordance with his personal circumstances, with his virtues and his defects alike. Countless numbers of people have died without the knowledge of Christ because no one brought them the

---

3. John Paul II, *On prudence*, 25 October 1978
4. St Gregory the Great, *Homilies on the Gospels*, 19, 2
5. *ibid*

news. Are we too going to be paralysed, unable to talk about God? *You might tell me, 'Why should I make an effort?' It is not I who answer you, but Saint Paul: 'Christ's love is urging us'* (2 Cor 5:14). *A whole lifetime would be little, if it was spent expanding the frontiers of your charity.*[6]

The first Christians understood very well that the apostolate knew no boundaries of persons, places or situations. Apostolate usually began with their own families – *They persuaded their servants and children, if they had any, to become Christians because of their mutual love. Once they became Christians they called each other 'brothers' without distinction.*[7] Many were the families that received the Faith from their slaves, from the youngest of the servants and children to the oldest. Perhaps they were followed by their neighbours, their clients, their customers, their social acquaintances ... The spread of the Gospel throughout the army was speeded by the virtues and the martyrdom of the first Christians. The army itself 'provided' martyrs in Italy, in Africa, in Egypt and along the shores of the Danube. The final persecution began with a purge of the legions.[8]

All situations are favourable for bringing souls to Christ, even those situations that may appear to be the least opportune. Before a Roman tribunal in Caesarea, Saint Paul speaks as a prisoner brought before the procurator Festus and King Agrippa. He reveals the mysteries of the Faith with such conviction that *as he thus made his defence, Festus said with a loud voice, 'Paul, you are mad; your great learning is turning you mad'.* The Venerable Bede comments: *They considered it madness that a man in*

---

6. J. Escrivá, *Friends of God*, 43
7. Aristides, quoted by D. Ramos, *The Testimony of the early Christians*
8. A. G. Hamman, *Daily Life of the early Christians*, Madrid, 1986

chains would choose to speak of his inner beliefs rather than of the calumnies of his enemies.[9]

Later on, Agrippa says to Paul: *In a short time you think to make me a Christian!* And Paul responds: *Whether short or long, I would to God that not only you but also all who hear me this day might become as I am – except for these chains.*[10]

And how is it that we cannot patiently bring our relatives, neighbours and friends to the Lord? Our love for Christ is clearly shown by our apostolic spirit. We will not miss a single opportunity. Every hour is a good hour to bring workers to the Lord's vineyard. All ages are good ages for us to serve as co-redeemers.

69.3 Every person who comes into contact with us should be moved to live closer to Christ.

It is surprising that the father in the parable went out at the very end of the day, when there was little left to do. It is also surprising to learn the explanation given by those who even at that late hour are unemployed: *Because no one has hired us.* No one has given us the good news that the owner of the field is looking for labourers to work his vineyard. Is this not the same answer given by many baptized Christians today? Their faith is languishing because no one has made use of them. *You have spoken to one person and another, and yet another, because you are consumed by zeal for souls ... You must persevere, and no one afterwards will be able to excuse himself by saying 'Quia nemo nos conduxit' – nobody has called us.*[11] Not one of our relatives, our friends, our neighbours ..., not even someone with whom we spent an afternoon, or shared a

---

9. St Bede, *Commentary on the Acts of the Apostles, in loc*
10. Acts 26:24-32
11. J. Escrivá, *Furrow*, 205

journey, or worked in the same office, or studied at the same school ... not one should be unaffected by our love for Christ. When love is great it shows itself at the slightest opportunity.

Many will be moved by the words we speak with vigour and with the joy of the Master. Others will be helped by our good example of work well done, of serenity in the face of suffering, of manifest charity towards others ... All will feel urged by our prayer and by our profound joy, which are the fruits of following Christ. No one who has known us should be able to say at the end of his life that he was never called.

Some of the labourers complained about the wages they were given. No matter, since the Lord gave to each one the agreed amount – one denarius. Those malcontents did not understand that to serve the Lord is an honour and not a duty. To work for Christ is to reign. To be called by God from the public square is reason for giving thanks. While serving as apostles in the middle of the world we find more than enough compensation. We are trying to love Christ and to serve him ever more faithfully as we seek new labourers to work for him. The Lord will never forget that service. We should keep in mind that the denarius itself is stamped with *the image of the King*.[12] God gives up his own life for us. And at the end of time, he will give us glory without end: *each shall receive his wages according to his labour*.[13]

Come with me to Mary, the Mother of Christ. You, who are our Mother and have seen Jesus grow up and make good use of the time He spent among men, teach me how to spend my days serving the Church and all mankind. My

---

12. St Jerome, *Commentary on the Gospel of St Mark*, 4, 3
13. 1 Cor 3:8

good Mother, teach me, whenever necessary, to hear in the depths of my heart, as a gentle reproach, that my time is not my own, because it belongs to Our Father who is in Heaven.[14] We ask Saint Joseph also, to teach us how to spend our lives in Christ's service while we go about our ordinary activities in the midst of the world.

TWENTIETH WEEK: THURSDAY

70. THE WEDDING FEAST

70.1 It is Christ himself who invites us.

In many of Our Lord's parables we find an insistent invitation to us all, to each one according to his or her own circumstances. Today we read about a king who prepares a wedding feast for his son and sends out his servants to call those who have been invited.[1]

The image of the banquet was quite familiar to the Jewish people: the Prophets had foretold that with the coming of the Messiah Yahweh would prepare a wondrous feast for all nations: He would get ready *a feast of fat things, a feast of wine on the lees, of fat things full of marrow, of wine on the lees well refined.*[2] The banquet signifies the plenitude of goodness that flows from the Incarnation and the Redemption, and the priceless gift of the Blessed Eucharist.

In this parable Jesus illustrates how we often respond coldly and indifferently to God's generosity: He sent his servants to call the guests, but they didn't want to come. In Our Lord's telling of this parable there is a note of sadness, foreseeing as He does the many excuses that will be made to him over the centuries. The carefully prepared food stays on the table and the room remains empty, because Jesus does not compel anyone to come.

The king sends his servants out once more: *Tell those who are invited, Behold, I have made ready my dinner, my*

1. Matt 22:1-14
2. Is 25:6

oxen and my fat calves are killed, and everything is ready; come to the marriage feast. However, the guests pay not the slightest heed: one goes off to his farm, another to whatever else is his business. Others not only reject the invitation but revolt against the king: *The rest seized his servants, treated them shamefully, and killed them.* They react violently to the invitation of Love.

Jesus calls us to come closer to him, to a greater level of commitment and confidence. Every day He invites us to the table He has prepared. He both invites us and gives himself as food – the great banquet is, of course, a symbol of Holy Communion.

Jesus himself is the food we need for our sustenance; He is *the remedy for our daily needs,*[3] without which our souls would weaken and die. Jesus awaits us every day, hidden under the appearances of bread, so that we can go and receive him full of love and gratitude. *The wedding is ready,* He tells us; but many are absent, because they don't appreciate the most wonderful marvel of the Blessed Eucharist. They respond to Our Lord's invitation with a variety of silly excuses because they don't appreciate what love there is in every Communion.

Saint John Chrysostom exhorts us: *Consider the great honour done to you, and the table of which you partake. He whom the angels tremble to behold, unable to look upon him face to face because of the brightness He radiates, is the one with whom we feed ourselves, mingling with Him and becoming one body and flesh with Christ.*[4]

Many will absent themselves, and so he expects us to be present. He desires, with an intensity we can scarcely imagine, that we receive him with great love and joy. He

---

3. St Ambrose, *On the sacred mysteries of the altar*, 4, 44
4. St John Chrysostom, *Homilies on St Matthew's Gospel*, 82, 4

sends us out to call others: *Go therefore to the thoroughfares, and invite to the marriage feast as many as you find.* He expects many, and sends us out to do a loving, patient, and effective apostolate, and to teach our many friends and acquaintances what an uncontainable joy it is to find Christ. Perhaps this is what happened to us: *Remember where you were called: at a crossroads. And what were you like then? Limp and lame of soul, which is much worse than any physical deformity.*[5] However, our merciful Lord wanted to have us close to him.

70.2 Preparing well for Holy Communion. Avoiding routine.

We shouldn't come into Our Lord's presence thoughtlessly and carelessly. *But when the king came to look at the guests, he saw there a man who had no wedding garment; and he said to him, 'Friend, how did you get in here without a wedding garment?'*[6]

Each day we are invited to approach the Eucharistic banquet, which has been prepared for us with such great care. We are aware in ourselves of habits, attitudes, errors and aspects of our character which perhaps don't correspond with the great honour being done to us by Jesus Christ.

We should examine ourselves so that we don't appear before Our Lord in what amounts to rags, since we have a tendency to disguise our defects and justify our behaviour. *On this earth, when we receive an important person, we bring out the best – lights, music, formal dress. How should we prepare to receive Christ into our soul? Have we ever*

---

5. *ibid*, 69, 2
6. Matt 22:11-12

thought how we would behave if we could only receive him once in a lifetime?[7] We wouldn't sleep the night before, we would have thought out well what we would say, what we would ask and how we would ask it; everything we could do wouldn't be enough ... That is how we should receive Jesus every day.

One man invited to the wedding certainly heard the invitation and went to the wedding cheerfully enough, but he was inappropriately dressed and didn't give due consideration to what was required of him. We can't just receive Our Lord any old way, distracted, inattentive, not fully realizing what we are about. To receive Holy Communion worthily we should above all be in the state of grace. Our Mother the Church teaches us and warns us that *no one who has a mortal sin on his conscience shall dare receive the Holy Eucharist without making a sacramental confession, regardless of how contrite he may think he is.*[8]

As well as that, such a great gift requires us to get ourselves ready in body and soul as best we can – by frequent Confession, even though we may not have any mortal sins; by intensifying our desire for purification and increasing our acts of faith, love and humility at the moment of receiving Our Lord. *Love is repaid with love ... In the first place it will be love for Christ himself. A Eucharistic encounter is, in fact, a loving encounter.*[9] Frequent communion should never mean lukewarm communion. Fighting lukewarmness means preparing and doing what we can to ensure that Our Lord does not find us distracted when he comes into our hearts. It would betoken a great lack of refinement to approach Communion with our

---

7. J. Escrivá, *Christ is passing by*, 91
8. Council of Trent, Dz 1646
9. John Paul II, *Address*, Madrid, 31 October 1982

mind on other matters. Lukewarmness is nothing but a lack of love, and is typified by not receiving Communion in the right frame of mind. We know we can never manage to receive Jesus as worthily as he deserves: our grasp of what is involved is so limited. However, Our Lord expects us to make what effort we can. *If any important or high-ranking person, or even one who is just wealthy or powerful, were to tell us he was to come to our house, how we would have everything gleaming, hiding away anything the visitor or our friend would find unsightly! He who has perpetrated evil acts, let him firstly cleanse the dirt and stains if he wants to prepare his soul as a fit dwelling.*[10]

70.3 Love for Jesus in the Blessed Sacrament.

You have prepared a banquet for me ... [11] What joy it gives to think that Our Lord makes it so easy for us to receive him! What a joy to know that He wants us to receive him!

Frequent Confession is the best way to prepare for frequent Communion. Besides, we can always have a still deeper desire for purification, and have greater faith and refinement in our dealing with Jesus present in this holy Sacrament. Our effort to live in God's presence during the day, and the very fact of trying to perform our daily duties as best we can, helps us to receive him in Communion with greater love. It also makes us feel an ever-greater need to make atonement to Our Lord for our mistakes, and to fill the day with acts of thanksgiving and spiritual communions so that our heart is more and more firmly centred on Our Lord during our work, our family life and in everything we do.

---

10. St Gregory the Great, *Homily 30 on the Gospels*
11. *Responsorial Psalm*, Ps 22

On finishing our prayer we can make our own the plea Pope John Paul II addressed to Jesus in the Sacred Host: *Lord Jesus! We come to you knowing you are calling us and love us just as we are. 'You have the words of eternal life; and we have believed, and have come to know, that you are the Holy One of God' (John 6:69). Your Eucharistic presence began with the sacrifice of the Last Supper and continues as a communion and a gift of your entire self. Increase our faith ... You are our hope, our peace, our Mediator, our brother and friend. Our heart is filled with joy and hope in knowing that you 'always live to make intercession for us' (Heb 7:25). Our hope turns into confidence and Paschal joy, hastening us on our way to the Father in your company.*

We want to share your sentiments and to value the things you value, because you are the centre, the beginning and end of everything. Sustained by this hope we desire to implant this scale of Gospel values in the world where God and his gifts for salvation will hold pride of place in the hearts of men and in their attitudes of practical living.

We want to love like you, who gives life and all you are. We would like to say with Saint Paul: 'For me, to live is Christ' (Phil 1:21). Our life is meaningless without you. We want to learn 'to be with him whom we know loves us', because 'with such a good friend at your side any suffering can be borne'...

You have given us your Mother to be our own, to teach us how to meditate and adore in our hearts. She, in receiving the Word and putting it into practice, became the most perfect Mother.[12]

---

12. John Paul II, *loc cit*

TWENTIETH WEEK: FRIDAY

71. WITH ALL OUR HEART

71.1 The first Commandment of the Law: to love God with our whole being.

Loving God is not just something very important for man. It is the one absolutely important thing, the one for which man was created, and so it is his fundamental task on earth and will be his sole occupation forever in heaven. It is the means whereby he attains happiness and complete fulfilment. Its absence makes man's life empty. A soul who loved Our Lord very much, and who led a life of much physical suffering, left behind some very pertinent words: *What frustrates a life is not pain but lack of love*. The one great failure in life is to have lived without loving: it may be that many other things have been achieved, but what is really important, namely, loving God, is left undone.

In the Gospel of today's Mass[1] we read how a Pharisee came to Jesus and asked him a question *to test him*, to twist his words: *Teacher, which is the great commandment in the law?* Perhaps he was waiting to hear Jesus say something that would enable him to accuse him of contradicting Scripture. But Jesus replied: *You shall love the Lord your God with all your heart, and with all your soul and with all your mind. This is the great and first commandment*. God is not asking for a bit of room in our heart, in our soul or in our mind, for just a share in our

---

1. Matt 22:34-40

love: he wants it all – not just a little love, some part of our life, but all we have got. *God is All, the Only One, the Absolute, and must be loved 'ex toto corde', absolutely,*[2] without limit or measure.

Christ, God made man, who comes to save us, loves us with a very personal love; He is *a jealous lover*, asking for all our love. He expects us to give him what we have, to follow that vocation to which he called us one day, and He continues to seek us out in the middle of the chores and circumstances – pleasant or otherwise – of our daily lives. *God has a right to ask us: Are you thinking about me? Are you aware of me? Do you look to me as your support? Do you seek me as the Light of your life, as your shield ..., as your all?*

Renew, then, this resolution: In times the world calls good I will cry out: 'Lord!' In times it calls bad, again I will cry: 'Lord!'[3] Every circumstance should be an opportunity for loving him with our whole heart, with our whole soul, with our whole mind, with our whole strength and life, not only when we pay him a visit in a church or when we receive Holy Communion, but also in our work, in our sufferings and failures, at times of receiving unexpected good news. We have to say to him often in the depths of our heart: *Jesus, I love you*, I accept this difficulty serenely for you, I will finish this task well because I know that it will please you, knowing that it is not all the same to you if I do it well or badly. Now in our prayer we can say to him: Jesus I love you ..., but teach me to love you more; may I learn to love you with my heart and my with deeds.

---

2. F. Ocáriz, *Love for God, Love for men*, Madrid
3. J. Escrivá, *The Forge*, 506

71.2 We must also love God with our affections.

My son, give me your heart, and let your eyes observe my ways.[4]

Saint Thomas Aquinas, commenting on the command to love God with all our heart, teaches us that the origin of love is two-fold: involved alike are our affections or emotions, and our reason. Love is emotional when the person concerned is unable to live without the object of his love. And it is governed by the dictate of reason when the person loves what he grasps with his mind. We should love God in both these ways, with our will and with a heart that is human too, with the affection with which we love other human beings,[5] with the only heart we possess. Our heart and our emotions are integral parts of our personality. Saint John Chrysostom, writing against the Manichean notion that human feelings are essentially evil, comments: *As human beings it is impossible for us to be completely deprived of our emotions; we can control them, but we cannot live without them. Besides, emotion can be advantageous if we are able to use it when needed.*[6] When we read the Gospel we see Christ's love as at once human and supernatural, full of warmth, vibrancy and tenderness in addressing his heavenly Father as well as in the company of men. He is moved at the sight of a widowed mother who has lost her only son; He weeps for a dead friend; He is pained by the lack of gratitude of the lepers cured of their sickness; He is always cordial and open to all, even during the terrifying and sublime moments of his Passion. We who desire to follow Jesus very closely, to be truly his disciples, should remember that the Christian life consists not so much *in thinking a lot as in loving a lot.*[7]

---

4. Prov 23:26
5. cf St Thomas, *Commentary on St Matthew's Gospel*, 22, 4
6. St John Chrysostom, *Homilies on St Matthew's Gospel*, 16, 7
7. cf John Paul II, *Homily*, Avila, 1 October 1982; St Teresa, *The Interior Castle*, IV, 1, 7

From the emotional and sentimental points of view we realize how much we ourselves need help, protection, affection and happiness. At times these very deep feelings can and should be a channel for seeking God, for telling him we love him, that He must help us stay close to him. If our actions were the result only of cold and rational choices, or if we tried to ignore the affective side of our being, we wouldn't be living our human life to the full as God wished, and in the long term we could stop loving him altogether. God made us body and soul, and Jesus the Master tells us to love him fully with all our faculties of heart and mind and all our strength.

At times we may perhaps feel cold and listless, with our hearts unresponsive, our feelings fluctuating unpredictably. We shouldn't then make do with following Our Lord unwillingly, like one who is fulfilling a heavy duty or swallowing an unpalatable medicine. We have to take steps to get out of such a state as this – unless it happens to be a case of passive purification allowed by Our Lord – it would only be lukewarmness, a lack of true love. We must love God with an unshakable will, and always, when possible, with those other worthy feelings of our hearts. Most times it will be possible, with God's help, to awaken our affections and inflame our hearts anew, even although at the time there is no interior satisfaction to be had.

At other times God treats us as an affectionate mother would, rewarding her child unexpectedly with a sweet, or simply giving it to him as a special sign of affection. And the child, who loves his mother always, is ecstatic with delight, and in his desire to show his grateful appreciation, even offers voluntarily to do whatever his mother wants. The child would never dream of thinking that his mother doesn't love him when she doesn't give him sweets, and if he has any common sense he will be able to see his mother's love also behind a correction or a visit to the doctor. It is the same with our Father God, who loves us far more than this. At times like these we should make good use of those affectionate consolations to get closer to God, to respond more generously in our daily struggle, even though we know that the ultimate essence of love is not to be found in our feelings.

71.3 Expressions of piety.

Scripture tells us: *My heart is like wax; it is melted within my breast.*[8]

Love of God, like all true love, has to be cultivated, protected and nourished. Without affection, we need to show some signs of affective piety, like the heartfelt kissing of a crucifix or a glance at a picture of Our Lady, not trying to reach God only by 'willpower', which eventually wears thin and impoverishes our relationship with Christ. *Your mind is sluggish and won't work: you try to collect your thoughts in God's presence, but it's useless: there's a complete blank.*

Don't try to force yourself, and don't worry. Look: such moments are for your heart.[9] Perhaps it's the moment to say a few words with the simplicity of our early childhood, consciously saying a number of aspirations with great piety and affection. People who are drawn to the love of God fully realize how important it is to do and say the same things every day – certain words, actions and gestures, which when performed with Love give rise to the promise of many others to come.[10]

Recourse to Our Lord's most holy Humanity enables

---

8. Ps 21:14
9. J. Escrivá, *The Way*, 102
10. cf J. Escartín, *Meditation on the Rosary*, Madrid

us to love God with all our heart. It may lead us perhaps to read from time to time a Life of Christ, contemplating him as perfect God and perfect man, seeing how He relates to those who come to him, with merciful compassion and love for all. We should particularly meditate on his Passion and death on the Cross, on his limitless generosity the more He suffers. At other times we can even address God in the words of human romance, making use, for example, for genuine and elevated prayer, of the old songs that sing of a pure and noble love.

Love of God, like every true love, is not merely sentimental. It is not emotionalism or empty sentimentality, because it should give rise to a multitude of practical expressions; even more, it should govern every single aspect of our life. *'Love means deeds, and not sweet words.' Deeds, deeds! And a resolution: I will continue to tell you often, Lord, that I love you. How often have I repeated this today! But, with your grace, it will be my conduct above all that shows it. It will be the little things of each day which, with silent eloquence, will cry out before you, showing you my Love.*[11]

---

11. J. Escrivá, *The Forge*, 498

TWENTIETH WEEK: SATURDAY

72. DOING AND TEACHING

72.1 Our deeds should show that Christ is alive.

In the Gospel of today's Mass[1] we read of Our Lord's warning his disciples against the Scribes and Pharisees who had set themselves up in Moses' chair and taught the Scriptures to the people, but whose lives were far removed from what they taught: *Practise and observe whatever they tell you, but not what they do; for they preach but do not practise.* Saint John Chrysostom comments: *Is there anything more lamentable than a teacher whose only way of saving his pupils is to tell them not to heed the life of the one speaking to them?*[2]

Our Lord asks everyone to give good example in their daily lives and in a fruitful apostolate. There are many admirable examples around us, but we have to pray that, among Christians, those who lead and govern, people of influence, parents, teachers, priests and everyone who is in any way *a good shepherd* for others will grow daily in holiness. The world is in need of *living examples*.

Christ is the fullness of unity of life; his words and deeds are profoundly consistent. What He says is perfectly consistent with what He does, which is always something marvellous and complete. *We have seen strange things today,*[3] as people said when He had forgiven the sins of the paralytic man and then cured him. Even the Pharisees

---

1. Matt 23:1-12
2. St John Chrysostom, *Homilies on St Matthew's Gospel*, 72, 1
3. Luke 5:26

exclaimed, disconcerted: *What are we to do? For this man performs many signs*.[4] However, they rejected the witness of the deeds and so became blameworthy: *If I had not done among them the works which no one else did, they would not have sin*.[5] On other occasions He invited them to believe through what was obvious to all: *Believe me for the sake of the works themselves*.[6] Our Lord considered his deeds a means of making his teaching known: *These very works which I am doing bear me witness*.[7] Christ proclaimed the marvellous truth of revelation in word and deed, both in his hidden life and in his public ministry.

We have to show everyone that Christ is still alive by living heroically the events of our daily lives. The apostolic vocation which we all received at Baptism means giving witness in word and deed to the life and teaching of Christ. People said of the early Christians *See how they love one another*. The pagans were really edified by this behaviour and those who conducted themselves in this way had *favour with all the people*,[8] as the Acts of the Apostles tell us. As a result, *the Lord added to their number day by day those who were being saved*.[9] Those who were converted to the faith made good use of every opportunity to explain the reason for their hope,[10] and in order to spread their joy to others: *Those who were scattered went about preaching the word*.[11]

Many gave the supreme witness of martyrdom to the faith they professed. We too are ready to go to that extreme

---

4. John 11:47
5. John 15:24
6. John 14:11
7. John 5:36
8. Acts 2:47
9. *ibid*
10. cf 1 Pet 3:15
11. Acts 8:4

if Our Lord asks for it. In his apparent madness the martyr becomes a powerful attractive force that leads people to Christ: many conversions are the result of having beheld a martyr's example. Hence the name *martyr*, meaning witness, signifies having given testimony for Christ.

Normally Our Lord asks us to give a Christian witness through our ordinary lives, engaged in the same ways of earning a living, tackling the same concerns as other folk. *We have to act in such a way that others will be able to say, when they meet us: This man is a Christian because he does not hate, because he is ready to understand, because he is not a fanatic, because he is willing to make sacrifices, because he shows that he is a man of peace, because he knows how to love.*[12]

72.2 Jesus began to do and to teach ... The witness of deeds well done and of charity for all men.

Love is expressed in deeds: *coepit facere et docere*,[13] Jesus began to do and to teach; He *proclaimed the Kingdom with the witness of his life and the power of his Word.*[14] He wasn't content just to preach, or with being a Teacher who enlightened with a wonderful doctrine; on the contrary, *'coepit facere et docere' – Jesus began to do and then to teach. You and I have to bear witness with our example, because we cannot live a double life. We cannot preach what we do not practise. In other words, we have to teach what we are at least struggling to put into practice.*[15]

In his long years as a tradesman in Nazareth, Our Lord teaches us the redemptive value of work and calls us to attain the greatest possible prestige in our profession or

---

12. J. Escrivá, *Christ is passing by*, 122
13. Acts 1:1
14. Second Vatican Council, *Lumen gentium*, 35
15. J. Escrivá, *The Forge*, 694

area of study. He asks us to work without slovenliness, with intensity and methodically, while at the same time being courteous and considerate with those around us – our colleagues, our clients, our superiors or those in our charge. We must also show Christ's teaching in the supernatural way we try to put up with illness or unexpected reverses, in the way we spend our leisure time, in our manner of coping with financial difficulties, or with the way we handle professional success if Our Lord allows it, in the way we enjoy ourselves and in our habitual cheerfulness even when it is very hard to smile. For a Christian, Christ is the greatest reason for him to be happy always. That joy – springing from our peace of soul – will be a convincing sign to others, causing them to feel moved to seek him.

The good example that stems from a living faith always has the power to attract others. It is not a matter of giving witness to ourselves, but to Our Lord. We should act in such a way that *men should be able to recognise the Master in his disciples*,[16] being able to say with Saint Paul: *I urge you, then, to be imitators of me, as I am of Christ*.[17] He is the one and only Model with whom we should compare ourselves. Above all, we should imitate him in the way he relates to everyone. Charity was the distinguishing characteristic Jesus left us, and through it we have to be recognizable known as Our Lord's disciples: *By this all men will know that you are my disciples, if you have love for one another*.[18] It is, along with cheerfulness and professional prestige, the indispensable means of carrying out apostolate with those close to us. *Before wanting to make saints out of all of those people we love, we have to make*

---

16. *idem, Christ is passing by*, 105
17. 1 Cor 11:1
18. John 13:35

*them happy and joyful, for nothing better prepares the soul
for grace than joy.*

*You already know ... that when you have in your
hands the hearts of people you wish to improve, if you are
able to attract them through the meekness of Christ you have
already gone half-way on your apostolic road. When they
love you and trust you, when they are at ease with you, the
field is ready for sowing. For their hearts are open like fertile
ground, ready to receive the white grain of your word as an
apostle or educator ...*

*Let us never lose sight of the fact that Our Lord has
promised his effectiveness to friendly faces, to cordiality, to
good manners, and to clear, persuasive words that direct
and form without wounding. 'Blessed are the meek, for they
shall inherit the earth.' We should never forget that we are
men and women relating to other men and women, even
when what we want is to do good to souls. We are not
angels: therefore our appearance, our smile, our manners,
are factors conditioning the effectiveness of our apostolate.*[19]

72.3 Example is not enough: we have to give doctrine, making use of all opportunities, and even creating them.

To do and to teach: example and doctrine ... *It is not
enough to do in order to teach,* writes Saint John Chrysostom, *and it is not I who say so, but Christ himself: 'He who
does them (i.e. the commandments of the Law) and
teaches them shall be called great' (Matt 5:19). If the mere
act of doing were sufficient to teach men, the second part of
Our Lord's saying would be superfluous, for it would have
been sufficient for him to have said 'he who does'. When He
distinguishes the two things, he gives us to understand that
in perfecting souls both deeds and words have their role and*

---

19. S. Canals, *Jesus as Friend*

are mutually necessary.[20] We are not talking about contradictories, about things that are largely opposed to each other or separate: to speak is a sign, an announcement about Christ; and to do something is also a sign, a way of teaching which confirms the truth of what is spoken. *This witness of life, however, is not the sole element in the apostolate; the true apostle is on the lookout for occasions of announcing Christ by word, either to unbelievers to draw them towards the faith, or to the faithful to instruct them, strengthen them or incite them to a more fervent life.*[21] What meaning could our good example as Christians have for unbelievers if we did not also speak about the *treasure*, Christ, which we have found? We don't bear witness to ourselves, but to Christ. We are his witnesses in the world, and a witness doesn't testify to himself: he gives testimony to some truth or to some deeds that he ought to teach. What Jesus asks us is both to live out our faith and to proclaim his doctrine.

We make Our Lord known through the example of our life, looking for occasions to speak out, not missing a single opportunity. Our task consists to a large extent in making the way to Christ cheerful and attractive. If we behave like that, many will be encouraged to follow it and to bring the joy and peace of the Lord to other men and women.

When that village woman, moved by Jesus' doctrine, paid a compliment to Our Lord's mother, Jesus replied: *Blessed rather are those who hear the word of God and keep it.*[22] Nobody has fulfilled that advice as Mary did. To her, who for us is a beautiful example of all the virtues, we entrust ourselves in order to carry out our resolutions to give good example in our daily behaviour.

---

20. St John Chrysostom, *On Priesthood*, 4, 8
21. Second Vatican Council, *Apostolicam actuositatem*, 6
22. Luke 11:28

TWENTY-FIRST SUNDAY: YEAR A

73. THE POPE, PERMANENT FOUNDATION OF UNITY

73.1 Jesus promises that Peter will be the rock upon which he will build the Church.

The Gospel of the Mass[1] shows us Jesus and his disciples in the neighbourhood of Caesarea Philippi. They had arrived there after leaving Bethsaida and taking the northern road along the edge of the lake.[2] As they walk along, Jesus asks the Apostles, *Who do men say that the Son of man is?* Then, after they have relayed the various opinions people have, Jesus asks them directly, *'But who do you say that I am?'* We all know this moment – says John Paul II – *in which it is no longer sufficient to speak about Jesus by repeating what others have said. You must say what you think, and not quote an opinion. You must bear witness, feel committed by the witness you have borne and carry this commitment to its extreme consequences. The best friends, followers and apostles of Christ have always been those who heard within them one day the definitive, inescapable question, before which all others become secondary and derivative: 'For you, who am I?'[3]* A person's life, his whole future, *depends on the clear, sincere and unequivocal answer, without rhetoric or subterfuge, that he gives to this question.[4]*

---

1. Matt 16:13-20
2. cf Mark 8:27; Luke 9:18
3. John Paul II, *Homily at Belo Horizonte*, 1 July 1980
4. ibid

This question that Jesus puts to all his followers finds a special resonance in the heart of Peter, who, moved by a special grace, replies: *You are the Christ, the Son of the living God*. Jesus calls Peter *blessed* for this truth-filled reply in which he openly confesses the divinity of him in whose company he has already spent some months. This is the moment chosen by Christ to tell Peter that upon him will fall the Primacy of the whole Church. *And I tell you, you are Peter, and on this rock I will build my church, and the powers of death shall not prevail against it. I will give you the keys of the kingdom of heaven, and whatever you bind on earth will be bound in heaven, and whatever you loose on earth will be loosed in heaven*. He will be the *rock*, the firm foundation upon which Christ will build his Church, in such a way that no power will be able to overthrow it. And Our Lord himself has wanted Peter to feel supported and protected each day by the veneration, the love and the prayer of all the faithful. How do we pray every day for the Pope and his intentions? He has an awesome responsibility and we cannot leave him on his own. If we want to be really united to Christ, we have to be united in the first place to the person who takes his place here on earth. *May the daily consideration of the heavy burden that weighs upon the Pope and the bishops move you to venerate and love them with real affection, and to help them with your prayers*.[5]

73.2 Love for the Pope.

I will give you the keys of the kingdom of heaven, and whatever you bind on earth will be bound in heaven.

The keys signify power: *I will place on his shoulder the key of the house of David*, we read in today's First

---

5. J. Escrivá, *The Forge*, 136

Reading,[6] the reference being to Eliakim, the steward of the royal palace. The power promised to Peter, which will be conferred on him after the resurrection,[7] is immensely superior to this. He is not given the keys of an earthly kingdom, but of the Kingdom of Heaven, that kingdom which is not of this world but which is nurtured here and which will last forever. Peter has the power to *bind and loose*, that is, to absolve or to condemn, to gather or to exclude. This power is so great that whatever he decides on earth will be ratified in heaven. To exercise it, he counts on a special help from the Holy Spirit.

From the first day he met Jesus he will be forever known as *Cephas, Petrus*, the Rock. *And I tell you, you are Peter, and on this rock I will build my church.*[8] By changing his name Our Lord wished to underline the new mission his Apostle Simon has been given: that of being the firm foundation of the new edifice of the Church. *It is as if Our Lord had said to him* – writes Saint Leo the Great – *I am the unbreakable stone, I am the cornerstone ... the foundation apart from which no one can build. But you are also the 'rock', because through my power you have acquired such firmness that you, by participation, share with me the power which I have by right.*[9]

From the very beginnings of Christianity the faithful have venerated the Pope. The Prince of the Apostles is everywhere mentioned before the others,[10] and makes frequent use of his special primacy and authority over the rest: he proposes the election of a new Apostle to replace Judas;[11] he is the one who speaks to the crowd on

---

6. Is 22:19-23
7. cf John 21:15-18
8. John 1:42
9. St Leo the Great, *Homily 4*
10. Matt 10:2ff; Acts 1:13
11. Acts 1:15-22

Pentecost and makes the first converts;[12] he replies to the Sanhedrin on behalf of all;[13] he punishes Ananias and Sapphira with full authority;[14] he admits Cornelius, the first Gentile, into the Church;[15] and he presides at the Council of Jerusalem and rejects the attempts of the Jewish Christians to impose circumcision on the Gentile converts, laying it down that salvation is to be had only through faith in Christ.[16]

These great spiritual powers are given to Peter for the good of the Church, and since the Church has to last until the end of time, these powers are handed down throughout history to those who take Peter's place. The Church's Magisterium has always stressed this point. In the Second Vatican Council's dogmatic Constitution on the Church we read: *This sacred synod, following in the steps of the First Vatican Council, teaches and declares with it that Jesus Christ, the eternal pastor ... put Peter at the head of the other apostles, and in him He set up a lasting and visible source and foundation of the unity both of faith and of communion. This teaching concerning the institution, the permanence, the nature and the import of the sacred primacy of the Roman Pontiff and his infallible teaching office the sacred synod proposes anew to be firmly believed by all the faithful.*[17] The Roman Pontiff is the successor of Peter; united to him we are united to Christ. He is his Vicar here on earth, the one who takes his place.

Our love for the Pope is not just a natural affection, based on his holiness, his likeableness etc. When we

---

12. Acts 2:14-36
13. Acts 4:8ff
14. Acts 5:1ff
15. Acts 10:1ff
16. Acts 15:7-10
17. Second Vatican Council, *Lumen gentium*, 18

journey to see the Pope, to listen to what he has to say, we do it in order to see, to touch and to hear Peter, the Vicar of Christ. He is, whoever he happens to be, *the sweet Christ on earth*, in the phrase of Saint Catherine of Siena. *Your deepest love, your greatest esteem, your most heartfelt veneration, your most complete obedience and your warmest affection have also to be shown towards the Vicar of Christ on earth, towards the Pope.*

We Catholics should consider that after God and the most Holy Virgin, our Mother, the Holy Father comes next in the hierarchy of love and authority.[18]

73.3 Where Peter is, there is the Church, there is God. Listen to the Pope's teaching and make it known.

An ancient formula sums up in a few words all the teaching about the Roman Pontiff: *Ubi Petrus, ibi Ecclesia, ibi Deus.*[19] Where Peter is, there is the Church, there too is God. *The Roman Pontiff* – says the Second Vatican Council – *as the successor of Peter, is the perpetual and visible source and foundation of the unity both of the bishops and of the whole company of the faithful.*[20] *And what would become of this unity if there were not one head over all the Church, to bless it and care for it, and to unite all its members in the profession of one faith and join them together in the bond of charity and of union?*[21] Unity would be smashed into a thousand pieces and we would wander like scattered sheep, without a sure faith in which to believe, without a clear path to follow.

We want to be with Peter, because with him we have the Church, with him we have Christ; and without him we

---

18. J. Escrivá, *The Forge*, 135
19. St Ambrose, *Commentary on Psalm 12*, 40, 30
20. Second Vatican Council, *Lumen gentium*, 23
21. Gregory XVI, *Commissum divinitus*, 15 June 1835

will not find God. And because we love Christ we love the Pope – with the same charity. And since we are attentive to Jesus, to his desires, to his actions, to his entire life, in the same way we are united to the Roman Pontiff in even the smallest details: we love him above all for the One he represents and of whom he is the instrument. *You must love, venerate, pray and mortify yourself for the Pope, and do so with greater affection each day. For he is the foundation-stone of the Church and, throughout the centuries, right to the end of time, he carries out among men that task of sanctifying and governing which Jesus entrusted to Peter.*[22]

In the *Acts of the Apostles* we see clear evidence of the love and devotion the first Christians had for Peter: *they even carried out the sick into the streets, and laid them on beds and pallets, that as Peter came by at least his shadow might fall on some of them.*[23] They were happy to make do with *the shadow of Peter*. They knew well that very close to him there was Christ! His word confers on us a noonday clarity in the midst of the confused welter of opinions which, today just as in former times, are proclaimed by so many false prophets and false teachers. Let us have a hunger to know the teachings of the Pope and to make them known in our environment. That is the light which illuminates men's consciences. Let us make the resolution to receive his word with internal docility and obedience, with love.[24]

---

22. J. Escrivá, *The Forge*, 134
23. Acts 5:15
24. cf Second Vatican Council, *Lumen gentium*, 25

TWENTY-FIRST SUNDAY: YEAR B

74. FOLLOWING CHRIST

74.1 Like the Apostles, we follow Christ forever, like a goal towards which we direct our steps.

The First Reading of today's Mass[1] tells us about the moment when the Chosen People, having crossed the Jordan, are about to enter the Promised Land. Joshua gathered all the tribes of Israel together at Sichem and said to them: *If you be unwilling to serve the Lord, choose this day whom you will serve, whether the gods your fathers served in the region beyond the River, or the gods of the Amorites in whose land you dwell; but as for me and my house, we will serve the Lord.* And all the people answered him: *Far be it from us that we should forsake the Lord ... We also will serve the Lord, for he is our God.*

In the Gospel of the Mass[2] we also find Jesus posing the same question to his disciples. After the announcement of the Eucharist in the synagogue at Capharnaum many of his disciples abandoned their Master because they found his teaching about the mystery of the Eucharist difficult to accept. Jesus is left with only his closest followers, and He wants them to reaffirm their loyalty and their unconditional confidence in him. So Our Lord turns to those men who have followed him thus far and asks them: *Will you also go away?* And Peter answers in the name of all: *Lord, to whom shall we go? You have the words of eternal life; and we have believed, and have*

---

1. Jos 24:1-2, 15-17, 18
2. John 6:61-70

come to know, that you are the Holy One of God. The Apostles say *Yes* once more to Christ. What would become of them without Jesus? Where would they go? Who would satisfy the longings of their hearts? Life without Christ, then as now, is life without meaning.

We too have said *Yes* to Jesus, for always. We have embraced Truth, Life, Love. We have directed that freedom which God has given us towards its only valid objective. The day on which Our Lord looked upon us in a special way we told him that He would be the goal towards which we would direct our steps; and we have since told him on many other occasions: *Lord, to whom shall we go?* Without you nothing has any meaning.

Today is a good opportunity to examine the sincerity of our self-surrender to Our Lord, to see if we joyfully put aside anything that prevents us from following Jesus. *Ask yourself now – I too am examining my conscience – whether you are holding firmly and unshakeably to your choice of Life? When you hear the most lovable voice of God urging you on to holiness, do you freely answer 'Yes'?*[3] To say *yes* to Our Lord in all circumstances means also saying *no* to other paths, to other possibilities. He is our Friend; only He has the words of eternal life.

74.2 The signposts on the road. Our freedom in following them.

Like those disciples who reaffirmed their full adherence to Christ at Capharnaum, at all times and in all places there are many men and women who, having walked perhaps for a long time in darkness, eventually find Jesus and see the path that leads to heaven open and marked out before them. So it has happened in our lives

---

3. J. Escrivá, *Friends of God*, 24

too. At last we discover that our freedom was given us not just to go from one place to another without a fixed reference point, but rather to make for a goal: Christ! Then we began to understand the surprisingly joyful character of the freedom that chooses Jesus and draws us closer to him, and rejects what separates us, because *by itself freedom is insufficient: it needs a guide, a pole-star.*[4] The North Pole of our freedom, which points out at every moment the direction we should take, is Our Lord, because *to whom shall we go* if not to him? What would we do with these few short days of life that God has given us? What is there that is worth a straw without Him?

For many people, unfortunately, freedom means following one's impulses or instincts, allowing oneself to be carried along by one's passions or by whatever one feels like doing at the time. Many people think like this, and they forget that *freedom is certainly an inalienable and basic human right, but for all that it is not characterized by the possibility of being able to choose evil, but for 'the possibility of being able to choose the good in a responsible fashion', recognizing it and desiring it as such.*[5] A person who has a mistaken and impoverished notion of freedom will reject the idea that there is a valid and obligatory goal for all mankind to follow, because it will appear to him as something opposed to freedom.[6]

If we have chosen Christ, if He is truly the object of our striving and of all our actions, over and above any other, then everything that teaches us how to journey towards him, or that highlights the obstacles that separate us from him, we will see as an enormous benefit, as a sure guide for which we are deeply grateful. A traveller in an

---

4. *ibid*, 26
5. John Paul II, *Address*, 6 June 1988
6. cf C. Burke, *Conscience and Freedom*

unknown land takes care to read a map, asks people who know the way and follows the signposts, and does so willingly because he wants to get to his destination. In no way does he consider that his freedom is being restricted, nor does he consider it a humiliation to have to depend on maps, signposts or guides to get where he is going. If he is unsure, or begins to feel lost, the signposts he meets are for him an occasion of reassurance and relief.

In fact, very often we rely more on maps or signposts than on our own sense of direction, of whose untrustworthiness we have plenty of experience. When we follow the signposts we don't have any sense of being imposed upon; rather do we welcome them as a great help, a fresh piece of information which we immediately proceed to make our own. This happens with the Commandments of God, with the laws and the teaching of the Church, and with the advice we receive in spiritual direction or which we look for in difficult situations. They are like signposts which in various ways guarantee our freedom, the free choice which we made to follow Christ and not explore other paths which lead to places where we don't want to go. *The Church's authority, in its teaching on faith or morals, is a 'service'. It is like the signposts on the road leading to heaven. It ought to be trusted because it enjoys a divine authority. It is not imposed on anyone. It is simply offered to mankind. And each one can, if he or she wishes, make it his own.*[7]

We shouldn't be surprised if sometimes these divine signposts invite us to abandon paths or roadways that appear more attractive, and lead us instead along others that are steeper and narrower and harder. Although we may be asked to give up a comfortable existence, we will

---

7. *ibid*

always have joy, even when we feel that the going is heavy, that our life has the achievement of a difficult goal ahead of it, which we opted for perhaps a goodly number of years ago, or maybe only a few days back. Let us head for the summit, where Christ is waiting for us.

74.3 True freedom. Renewing our self-surrender to Our Lord.

The signposts Our Lord gives us have to be trusted. They are not restrictions imposed on mankind, they are not onerous burdens. They are radiant sources of light which illuminate the road, enabling us to see and to travel more easily. The person who tries to respond sincerely to the grace of God will discover true freedom by following Jesus. On hearing his voice one sees, at last, one's way: *the commandments then are not seen as an imposition from outside, but as a requirement that is born within, and to which, therefore, the Christian submits willingly, 'freely', because he knows that in this way he fulfils himself more fully.*[8] And we take the free decision through which we seek after good in our work, in honest recreation, in family life, in friendship, in all noble things – a decision that is often renewed, through which we adhere to Christ and thus achieve that fullness of being to which we have been called.

John Paul II tells us that *man cannot be genuinely free or foster true freedom unless he recognizes and lives the transcendence of his being over the world and his relationship with God; for freedom is always the freedom of man made in the image of his Creator ... Christ, the Redeemer of man, makes us free. The Apostle John records the words: 'If the Son makes you free, you will be free indeed' (John*

---

8. John Paul II, *Address*, 6 June 1988

8:36). And the Apostle Paul adds: 'Where the Spirit of the Lord is, there is freedom' (2 Cor 3:17). To be set free from injustice, fear, constraint and suffering would be useless if we were to remain slaves in the depths of our hearts, slaves of sin. To be truly free, man must be liberated from this slavery and transformed into a new creature. The radical freedom of man thus lies at the deepest level, the level of openness to God by conversion of heart, for it is in man's heart that the roots of every form of subjection, every violation of freedom, are found.[9]

Each day we follow Christ we experience more strongly the joy of our choice and the broadening out of our freedom, at the same time as we see around us the slavery of those who at some stage turned their back on God or who didn't want to know him. *Slavery or divine sonship, this is the 'dilemma' we face. We can choose to be children of God or slaves to pride, to sensuality, to the fretful selfishness which seems to afflict so many souls.*

Love of God marks out the way of truth, justice and goodness. When we make up our minds to tell Our Lord, 'I put my freedom in your hands,' we find ourselves loosed from the many chains that were binding us to insignificant things, ridiculous cares or petty ambitions.[10] When we choose Christ as the purpose of our life we have gained everything.

Lord, to whom shall we go? You have the words of eternal life. Let us reaffirm today our following of Christ, with a lot of love, trusting in his merciful help; and with complete freedom we can tell him: *I put my freedom in your hands.* Let us also imitate her who said: *Behold, I am the handmaid of the Lord; let it be in me according to your word.*

9. John Paul II, *Message for World Peace Day*, 8 December 1980, 11
10. J. Escrivá, *Friends of God*, 38

TWENTY-FIRST SUNDAY: YEAR C

75. CATHOLIC AND UNIVERSAL

75.1 God wants all men to be saved. The Redemption is universal.

Apart from its other disastrous consequences, original sin produced the bitter fruit of propagating divisions among men. Pride and selfishness are rooted in the first sin and are the fundamental causes of hatred, isolation and division. The Redemption, on the other hand, brings about the union of mankind through the charity of Christ whereby we become children of God and brothers and sisters of one another. Our Lord, through his redemptive love, becomes the focal point of mankind. This is what was foretold by the prophet Isaiah, as we read in the first reading at this morning's Mass:[1] *I am coming to gather all nations and tongues; and they shall come and shall see my glory, and I will set a sign among them. And from them I shall send survivors to the nations, to ... those that have not heard of my fame or seen my glory; and they shall declare my glory among the nations. And they shall bring all your brethren from all the nations as an offering to the Lord, upon horses, and in chariots, and in litters, and upon mules, and upon dromedaries, to my holy mountain Jerusalem, says the Lord, just as the Israelites bring their cereal offering in clean vessels to the house of the Lord*. It is a great calling of all peoples to faith and salvation, without distinction of language, race or degree of social

---

1. Is 66:18-21

advancement. The prophecy comes to pass with the coming of the Messiah, Our Lord Jesus Christ.

In the Gospel,[2] Saint Luke records Jesus' reply to one who asked him a question as they journeyed towards Jerusalem: *Lord, He was asked, will those who are saved be few?* Jesus didn't choose to answer the question directly. The Master goes further than that and stresses the essential facts. They ask him about numbers, and he speaks about the manner: *Strive to enter by the narrow door.* And he goes on to teach them that in order to enter the Kingdom – which is the only thing that really counts – it is not enough to belong to the Chosen People, or to have a false confidence in him. *Then you will begin to say, 'We ate and drank in your presence, and you taught in our streets.' But the Lord will say, 'I tell you, I do not know where you come from; depart from me, all you workers of iniquity.'* All those divine privileges are not enough. What is needed is a faith with works, the kind of faith to which we have all been called.

All of mankind have a vocation to go to heaven, Christ's definitive Kingdom. This is what we have been born for, because God *desires all men to be saved*.[3] When Christ died on the Cross, the Temple veil was torn in two[4] as a sign that the separation between Jews and Gentiles was ended.[5] From then on, all men are called to form part of the Church, the new People of God, which, *whilst remaining one and only one, is to be spread throughout the whole world and to all ages in order that the design of God's Will may be fulfilled: he made human nature one in the beginning, and has decreed that all his children who are*

---

2. Luke 13:22-30
3. 1 Tim 2:4
4. Luke 23:45
5. cf Eph 2:14-16

scattered shall be finally gathered together as one.[6]

The Second Reading[7] points out what our mission is in this universal task of salvation: *Therefore lift your drooping hands and strengthen your trembling knees, and make straight paths for your feet, so that what is lame may not be put completely out of joint but rather be healed.* It is a call to be exemplary in order to encourage, with our conduct and with our charity, those who are wavering and have less strength. Many will lean upon us; others will understand that the narrow path that leads to heaven becomes a broad way for those who love Christ.

75.2 We are Christ's apostles. We belong in the world.

I am coming to gather all nations and tongues ... and I will send survivors to the nations, to Tarshish, Put, and Lud, who draw the bow, to Tubal and Javan, to the coastlands afar off.[8] *And men will come from east and west, and from north and south, and sit at table in the kingdom of God.*[9] This prophecy has already been fulfilled, and there are still very many people who do not know Christ, perhaps even in our own family, among our friends and the people we meet every day. It is possible that many have heard often about him but in reality don't know him. We too can repeat to those with whom we come in contact with the words of John the Baptist: *Among you stands one whom you do not know.*[10]

Our Lord wants us to play a part in his mission to save mankind, and has provided apostolic zeal as an integral component of the Christian vocation. The person

---

6. Second Vatican Council, *Lumen gentium*, 13
7. Heb 12:5-7, 11-13
8. Is 66:18
9. Luke 13:29
10. John 1:26

who decides to follow Jesus, as we have done, becomes an apostle with very definite responsibilities for helping others find the *narrow door* that leads to heaven: *Inserted as they are in the Mystical Body of Christ by Baptism and strengthened by the power of the Holy Spirit in Confirmation, it is by the Lord himself that they are assigned to the apostolate.*[11] All Catholics, whatever their age or background, in all circumstances of their lives, are called to *bear witness to Christ all the world over.*[12]

Apostolic zeal, the desire to draw many people to Our Lord, does not require us to do anything odd or peculiar, and much less to neglect our family, social or professional duties. It is precisely in those situations – in our family, at work, with our friends, in everyday human relationships – that we find scope for an apostolic activity which may often be silent, but which is always efficacious.

In the middle of the world, where God has placed us, we have to bring Christ to others: with our example, putting our faith into practice; by being always cheerful; by our refusal to be perturbed by the difficulties which are the normal lot of mankind; by, with our word, always being ready to encourage and thereby letting people see the greatness and the wonder of finding and following Jesus; in some cases it can be by helping people to go to the Sacrament of forgiveness, and in others, by putting new heart into people who perhaps have been on the point of abandoning the Master.

Let us ask ourselves today in our prayer if the people who know us can readily recognize us as disciples of Christ. Are we not only Christians, but seen to be Christians? Let us consider how many we have helped to take a

---

11. Second Vatican Council, *Apostolicam actuositatem*, 3
12. *ibid*

decisive step on the path to heaven. How many have we spoken to about God, or invited to a recollection, or recommended that they should read a good book which would help their soul to improve? Whom have we helped to go to Confession, or to whom explained the Church's teaching on family or marriage? To whom have we shown the grandeur of being generous in almsgiving, in the number of children people have, or in following Christ in an unconditional self-giving? It was said of the first Christians that *what the soul is to the body, Christians are to the world*.[13] Could the same be said of us in family life, among our colleagues at work or our fellow-students, or in the cultural or sporting associations to which we belong? Are we the soul that infuses the life of Christ into society wherever we happen to be?

75.3 Our Lord sends us forth. Begin with those near at hand.

Go into all the world and preach the gospel to the whole creation,[14] we read in the responsorial psalm at Mass. These words of Christ are very clear: He doesn't excuse anybody of any generation, of any people or nation, from the task his disciples have to carry out. Nobody we meet is excluded; as somehow unsuited to follow Our Lord, all are called by him – the elderly and the very young, from the child just learning to stammer his first words to the youth or the adult in full maturity, from our neighbours, to those who direct our affairs and those we employ. We see the Apostles dealing with people from all sorts of backgrounds: some were very well educated, others had never even heard of the existence of Palestine;

---

13. *Letter to Diognetus*, 6
14. Mark 16:15

some held very important positions, others did manual work of unexceptional notice in their surroundings. But none were excluded from the Apostolic preaching. And people who at first lacked courage or were too timid or too comfortable to associate themselves with the apostolate became fully identified with the universal mission they were given.

Every generation of Christians needs to redeem, to sanctify its own time. In order to do this, those of any era must understand and share the desires of other men – their contemporaries and equals – in order to make known to them, with a 'gift of tongues', how they are to correspond to the action of the Holy Spirit, to that permanent outflow of rich treasures that comes from Our Lord's heart. We Christians are called upon to announce, in our own time, to this world to which we belong and in which we live, the message – old and at the same time new – of the Gospel.[15] In this task of evangelization we have to reckon with *a completely new and disconcerting phenomenon, namely, the existence of a militant atheism which has already invaded entire peoples;*[16] an atheism which exhorts men to turn their backs on God, or at least to forget about him. We are faced with ideologies which use powerful means of diffusion, like television, newspapers, the cinema, the theatre, in the face of which many Christians feel themselves defenceless and lacking in the necessary formation to be able to cope with them.

To all these men and women, wherever they may be, in their more exalted moments or in their crises and defeats, we have to bring the solemn and unequivocal message of Saint Peter in the days that followed Pentecost: Jesus is the

---

15. J. Escrivá, *Christ is passing by*, 132
16. John XXIII, Apostolic Constitution, *Humanae salutis*, 25 December 1961

*cornerstone, the redeemer, the hope of our lives. 'For there is
no other name under heaven given among men by which we
must be saved' (Acts 4:12).*[17]

Our Lord makes use of us to light up the way for
many others. Let us consider today all the people we have
closest to us: sons and daughters, brothers and sisters,
relations, friends, colleagues, neighbours and clients. Let
us begin our apostolate with them, without worrying about
the fact that at times we seem to be no good at it, that we
are terribly few for all that has to be done. Our Lord will
multiply our strength, and our Mother Mary, *Regina Apostolorum*, will greatly assist our constant, patient and adven-
turous toil.

---

17. J. Escrivá, *Christ is passing by*, 132

76. DOCILITY IN SPIRITUAL DIRECTION

76.1 We need someone to guide our soul on its journey towards God.

Grace to you and peace from God the Father and the Lord Jesus Christ, writes Saint Paul to the Christians of Thessalonica. *We are bound to give thanks to God always for you, brethren, as is fitting, because your faith is growing abundantly, and the love of every one of you for one another is increasing.*[1] Thanks to the Holy Spirit's help, the first Christians benefited from the self-sacrificed vigilance of their pastors. The Pharisees, by contrast, were unable to guide the Chosen People effectively because, through their own fault, they remained in darkness, and laid upon the children of Israel a hard and heavy burden, one which moreover didn't lead them to God. In the Gospel of today's Mass[2] Our Lord calls them *blind guides,* incapable of showing others the right path to follow.

One of the greatest graces we can get is to have someone to guide us along the pathways of the interior life; and if we haven't yet found someone to teach us and advise us, in God's name, in the construction of our spiritual edifice, then let us ask God for it now: *every one who asks, receives, and he who seeks finds, and to him who knocks it will be opened.*[3] He will not fail to give us this great gift.

In spiritual direction God provides us with a person

---

1. 2 Thess 1:1-3
2. Matt 23:23-26
3. Matt 7:8

who knows the way well, to whom we open our heart and who acts as a teacher, a doctor, a friend, a good shepherd in the things that relate to God. That person points out to us the possible obstacles, and invites us to strive higher in our interior life and to fight on specific points more effectively. Thanks to the director's help we are continually encouraged to keep going, we discover new horizons and our soul is roused to a hunger and thirst for God which lukewarmness, always lurking nearby, would like to quench. From earliest times the Church always recommended the practice of spiritual direction as a very effective means of making progress in the interior life.

It is very difficult for one to be his or her own guide in the interior life. It can happen very often that the impulses of our nature, the lack of objectivity with which we see ourselves, our self-love, the tendency to be drawn to what we like most or what we find easiest to do, can all tend to obscure the path to God – even though at the beginning it was perhaps very clear – and when that happens we begin to get bogged down, to get discouraged and lukewarm. *A soul without a director is like a kindled coal, which, left by itself, cools instead of burning.*

He who insists on being left to himself, without a director to guide him, is like an unowned tree by the wayside; however fruitful it may be, the travellers pick its fruit, and none of it ripens.[4]

It is a very special grace from God to have a person who can help us effectively in our sanctification and in whom we can confide in a very human and at the same time a supernatural way. What a joy it is to be able to communicate our deepest feelings, so as to direct them to

---

4. St John of the Cross, *Spiritual Maxims*, 177-178, in *The Living Flame of Love*

God, to someone who understands us, who encourages us, who opens new horizons for us, who prays for us and has a special grace to help us!

In spiritual direction we encounter Christ himself, who listens to us attentively, who understand us, and who gives us new energies and insights to help us keep going.

76.2 Supernatural outlook in spiritual direction.

In spiritual direction one needs a lot of common sense and a great supernatural outlook. For this reason *one does not confide in just anyone, but in someone who deserves trust either because of what he is or because of the position in which God has placed him in relation to us*.[5] For Saint Paul the person chosen by God was Ananias, who strengthened him during his conversion; for Tobias it was the Archangel Raphael, in human form, who was entrusted by God to guide him and counsel him in his long journey.

Spiritual direction needs to have a supernatural environment if it is to be effective: it is God's voice that we are listening for. In order to get advice on something minor or to share the everyday concerns of life, it is enough for us to go to someone discreet and prudent who is able to understand us. But in matters that have to do with the soul we have to identify in prayer the person who for us can be the *good shepherd*, because *if we consider the matter from merely human motives we run the risk of not being understood; and then our joy becomes bitterness, and the bitterness becomes misunderstanding. Then we feel uneasy; we feel uncomfortable because we have talked too much to the wrong person about the wrong matter.*[6] We shouldn't choose *blind guides* who, rather than helping us,

---

5. F. Suárez, *Mary of Nazareth*, p.74
6. *ibid*, pp. 75

cause us to stumble and fall.

We need to have a supernatural attitude in spiritual direction if we are to avoid looking around for the sort of advice that fits in with our own whims, advice that would drown out with its apparent authority the voice of our soul. Especially to be avoided is the tendency to keep changing advisers until we find the most *benevolent* one.[7] This is a temptation that can occur especially in more sensitive areas: whenever sacrifice is called for, in things that perhaps we are not prepared to change, in the attempt to adapt God's Will to our own will: for example, on discovering a vocation that calls for a greater degree of self-giving; or having to abandon an undesirable friendship; or, in the case of married people, being ready to have many children.

Let us ask God to make us persons of upright conscience, who seek his Will and who are not carried along by human considerations: men and women who really want to please Him, and not seekers after a false 'tranquillity' or who want to be well thought of. In the same way, it would be a lack of supernatural outlook to be excessively attached to what people think, or what they might think, of us. Supernatural outlook leads to sincerity and to simplicity.

The interior life requires time in order to mature, and things cannot be improvised overnight. We will surely have defeats, which will help us to be more humble, as well as victories, which display the power of grace at work in us. We need to begin and begin again, many times, not giving way to discouragement and not looking for immediate results, although at times they may come: it may be that Our Lord doesn't want to give them to us now, in order to give us something better later.

---

7. cf J. Escrivá, *Conversations*, 93

76.3 Constancy, sincerity, docility.

Behind a cheerful ascetical struggle there has to be spiritual direction. It cannot be sporadic or erratic, because it is meant to follow step by step the ups and downs of our effort. There also has to be *constancy* when the going gets more difficult: because we are short of time, or because of pressure at work, or exams: God rewards that effort with new insights and graces. On other occasions the difficulties are internal: laziness, pride, discouragement because things are going badly, because we haven't managed to get anything done of what we had planned. This is when we have more need of the fraternal chat, or of Confession, from which we always come away more hopeful and cheerful, and with a new determination to keep fighting. Just as a picture is painted stroke by stroke, and a stout hawser is woven from many strands, so too in the continuity of spiritual direction, week after week, the soul is forged; and little by little, with defeats and victories, the Holy Spirit constructs the edifice of our holiness.

As well as constancy, *sincerity* is absolutely necessary: we always begin by speaking about the most important thing, which perhaps also happens to be the thing we find most difficult to say. This approach is essential, not only at the beginning but also later on. At times fruits can be slow in coming because of not having given from the beginning a clear picture of what we are really like, or becoming distracted by incidental background and not getting to the root. Sincerity has to be just that: no dissimulation, exaggerations or half-truths; spelling things out, in detail, though with refinement, and when necessary calling things by their name. We need to reveal our errors and mistakes, our character defects, without trying to disguise them with false justifications or arguments more or less in vogue at the moment. Why? How? When? These are the circumstances which make more personal, more revealing, the state of our soul.

Another condition for spiritual direction to be fruitful is *docility*. Those lepers whom Jesus ordered to show themselves to the priests as if they were already cured were docile.[8] So too are the Apostles when Our Lord has them tell the people to sit down and give them to eat, in spite of the fact that they themselves have already done their calculations and are aware of the scarcity of their provisions.[9] Peter was docile when he let down the net, even though he was well aware that there were no fish in that part of the lake, nor was it the right time of day.[10] Saint Paul allows himself to be guided; his strong personality, evident in so many ways on many occasions, now enables him to be docile. First of all his companions lead him to Damascus, then Ananias returns him his sight, and he then becomes ready to do battle for his Lord.[11]

That person cannot be docile who is determined to be stubborn, obstinate, incapable of assimilating an idea different from the one he already has or which contradicts his own experience. The proud person is incapable of being docile, because in order to learn and to allow oneself to be guided, it is necessary to be convinced of one's own insignificance and neediness in all the affairs of the soul.

Let us have recourse to the Blessed Virgin Mary in order to be constant in the work of our soul's direction, and to be sincere, opening our heart completely, and docile, like *clay in the potter's hand*.[12]

8. Luke 17:11-19
9. Luke 9:10-17
10. cf Luke 5:1ff
11. Acts 9:17-19
12. Jer 18:1-7

TWENTY-FIRST WEEK: TUESDAY

77. THE OBLIGATIONS OF JUSTICE

77.1 Justice and the dignity of man.

The Law of Moses prescribed the paying of tithes:[1] it meant the tenth part of the fruits of the earth; produce like corn, wine and oil had to be paid towards the maintenance of the Temple. Over and above this the Pharisees also paid tithes on mint and dill and cummin, aromatic plants that were grown in kitchen gardens for flavouring food. This was a misleading display of generosity with God, because at the same time as they were punctilious in these matters they neglected other more important obligations towards their neighbour. It is for this hypocrisy that Our Lord castigates them: *Woe to you, scribes and Pharisees, hypocrites! For you tithe mint and dill and cummin, and have neglected the weightier matters of the law, justice and mercy and faith; these you ought to have done, without neglecting the others*.[2]

Our Lord does not despise the paying of tithes on mint and dill and cummin: it could indeed have been a genuine expression of love for God, just as in the case of a person who offers flowers to someone he loves, or to Our Lord in the Tabernacle. What Jesus rejects is the hypocrisy lurking behind this display of false zeal, whereby they justified the non-fulfilment of essential duties of justice, mercy and faith. Christians cannot ever allow themselves to fall into a similar state of hypocrisy: our

---

1. Lev 27:30-33; Deut 14:22ff
2. Matt 23:23

voluntary offerings are pleasing to God when we fulfil the obligatory and necessary ones determined by the virtue of justice, which requires us to render to every one his own, and which is enriched and perfected by charity. *These you ought to have done, without neglecting the others* ...

Justice is founded on the inviolable dignity of the human person, created in God's image and likeness and destined to enjoy eternal happiness forever in heaven. If we consider the respect that all men are due *from the standpoint of divine revelation, inevitably our estimate of it is incomparably increased. Men have been ransomed by the blood of Jesus Christ. Grace has made them children and friends of God, and heirs to eternal glory.*[3]

Proper regard for the rights of individuals begins with the just ordering of civil law, to the upholding of which we Christians have to contribute with all our strength as exemplary citizens, beginning with the laws that defend the right to life, that first of all rights, from the very moment of conception. But this contribution, which we always have to make to the best of our abilities, however limited they may be, isn't enough. Every day we encounter many opportunities to be honest in our relations with our fellow men – for example, when making judgements about others, how easily and how readily we sometimes fall into rash judgement in the most elementary of ways! In speech we have to avoid not only calumny and false accusations, but also detraction, gossip that needlessly reveals our neighbour's genuine defects and diminishes his standing among his colleagues or acquaintances and in society at large. Justice in our actions, finally, requires us to give to each person what is his due, or his own ...

How can our works be pleasing to God if we don't act

---

3. John XXIII, *Pacem in terris*, 11 April 1963, 10

considerately in thought, word and deed towards our
brothers and sisters for whom Jesus gave his life?

77.2 Social justice goes beyond what is strictly owed.

Acting justly towards our neighbour is not simply a
question of avoiding doing him or her any harm. Nor is it
simply a matter of denouncing unjust situations as they
crop up. Complaining about the state of the world is pointless unless it gives rise to more prayer and action to
remedy the situations we grumble about.. Every Christian
has to ask himself how he puts the virtue of justice into
practice in the normal circumstances of life – within the
family, at work, in social relations and so on. Being just
towards those with whom we have daily contact means,
among other duties, respecting their right to their good
name, to privacy, to a sufficient financial remuneration.
*These requirements cannot be limited to the economic
sphere alone, as regards, for example, justice in in the payment of wages and salaries. The demands of Christian living
and ethics range wider than that, and include considerations
such as the respect for life, fidelity and truth, the cultivation
of reliability, competence, industriousness and honesty, the
rejection of all forms of cheating, a sense of social responsibility and indeed of generosity, which ought always to inspire
Christians in the performance of their work and in the exercise of their professional activities.*[4]

Calumny, backbiting and gossip can be real and
flagrant manifestations of injustice, because *among temporal goods the integrity of one's reputation appears to be
the most important, and through its loss man is deprived of
doing much good.*[5] The Apostle Saint James says that *the*

---

4. Spanish Episcopal Conference, *Catholics in public life*, 22 April
   1986, 113-114
5. St Thomas, *Summa Theologiae*, II-II, q.73, a.2

tongue is an unrighteous world among our members:[6] it can serve to praise God, to converse with him, to communicate with one another, or it can do incalculable harm unless there is a determined effort on our part never to speak badly of anyone.

It is not infrequent to encounter offences against justice by word. For this reason God asks us Christians to defend it, and not to let ourselves be led, either by word-of-mouth rumours or by what we pick up from the media, into making hasty judgements about people. We should never give vent to a negative judgement about persons or institutions, nor should we set ourselves up as inquisitors and executioners of the lives of others. This requires us to take steps to be well informed; and if we ever have the duty to judge, we have to listen to both sides, making due allowance for circumstances and always respecting the fundamental good intentions of the persons concerned, which only God himself really knows. People who work in the communications media, or who have access to them, have a special responsibility in this regard because of the great good or considerable damage they can do.

We have to fulfil the duties of justice towards those whom God has entrusted to us, dedicating time to them, helping with their formation, or taking special care of anyone who, through sickness, age or any special conditions, is particularly in need of attention. We know well that fathers or mothers, for example, would not do well if they could find time for their own relaxation and entertainment while not dedicating the necessary time to their children's education or to those whom God might have entrusted to their care. The same could be said of those who put their own interests and preferences, from which with a little

---

6. Jas 3:6

good will and little difficulty they could manage to abstain, before the needs of others.

We act justly when we render to every one what is his own. Employers, for example, are required to pay their employees a wage that is in accordance with the requirements both of law and of a right conscience. At times it is not uncommon to have to pay more than the minimum legal wage, because circumstances can arise in which one would err against justice if one were to pay only what the law requires. There can be cases where it is legal, but unjust, to lay workers off, or to pay salaries that are in line with wage levels but which offend human dignity: *justice does not consist exclusively in an exact respect for rights and duties, as in the case of arithmetical problems that are solved simply by addition and subtraction.*[7] The Christian employer gives importance above all to being just in the sight of God, which leads him to go beyond what the law strictly requires, bearing in mind the personal and family circumstances of the persons working for him.

77.3 The overall purpose of economics.

Economics has its own laws and mechanisms, but these laws are neither immutably self-sufficient nor supreme, nor are their mechanisms sacrosanct and untouchable. The Church's Magisterium reminds us that the world of economics ought not to be thought of as independent and autonomous, but as subject to the over-riding principles of social justice which correct the defects and shortcomings of the economic order by making allowance for the dignity of the human person.[8]

Social justice requires also that workers' living

---

7. J. Escrivá, *Friends of God*, 168
8. cf Pius XI, *Quadragesimo anno*, 15 June 1931, 37

conditions are not left to the mercy of market forces, as if their labour were merely merchandise to be bought and sold;[9] and one of the principal occupations of the State and of employers *must be this: to give work to everyone*,[10] as unemployment is one of the greatest evils that can afflict a country and is the cause of many other harmful consequences for individuals, for families, and for society itself.

A person employed in a workshop, in a university or in a commercial business would not be acting in accordance with justice if he were not to carry out his job conscientiously, in a professionally competent way, while taking good care of the tools, equipment and other property of the company (or library, hospital, workshop etc.) he works for, or of the house in the case of domestic employees. Students would be lacking in justice towards society and towards their families, at times seriously, if they didn't make good use of the time during which they are supposed to be studying. In general, examination marks can be a good source of material for examination of conscience. Very often poor application to one's studies can be the cause of afterwards not being professionally competent and of not giving value for money to one's employers through lack of adequate preparation. These are points on which we ought to examine ourselves often, if we are to carry out conscientiously, before God and men, our duties to our neighbour, thereby fulfilling the requirements of *justice, mercy and faith* in agreements, contracts and promises.

Let us ask Our Lady for this rectitude of conscience, so that we can contribute to making the society in which we live a worthy place for the sons and daughters of God to live together in harmony.

---

9. cf John Paul II, *Sollicitudo rei socialis*, 30 December 1987, 34
10. John Paul II, *Address in Morumbi Stadium*, 3 July 1980

TWENTY-FIRST WEEK: WEDNESDAY

78. LOVING OUR DAILY WORK

78.1 The example of Saint Paul.

Work is a gift from God and a great benefit for man, *even though it bears the mark of a 'bonum arduum', in the terminology of Saint Thomas ... It is not only good in the sense that it is useful or something to be enjoyed; it is also good as being something worthy, that is to say, something that corresponds to man's dignity, that expresses this dignity and increases it.*[1] A life without work is deformative, and through work man *becomes more a human being,*[2] more dignified and more noble, if he carries it out as God intends he should.

Work is a consequence of the divine command to mankind to subdue the world.[3] This task, which became arduous through original sin,[4] *is the hinge of our holiness, and the supernatural and human means whereby we bring Christ with us and do good to all.*[5] It is, as it were, the backbone of the human race, that which sustains all aspects of life, and through which we work out our own sanctification and that of others. An incorrect attitude to our daily work, a wrong emphasis in the meaning we give to our professional occupation, can have an effect on our entire life, including in our relationship with God. That is why we readily appreciate the evils that accrue from

---

1. John Paul II, *Laborem exercens*, 14 September 1981, 9
2. *ibid*
3. cf Gen 1:28
4. cf Gen 3:17
5. J. Escrivá, *Letter*, 14 February 1950

laziness, from things badly done or only half-finished. *The tool that lies unused, its edge dulled by rust, becomes blunt and worthless; but put to use it is much more valuable and pleasing, and becomes as bright as silver. So too, land which is allowed indefinitely and carelessly to lie fallow produces nothing good, only coarse grasses, weeds, thistles and worthless trees; but land that is cultivated or properly tended is rich with pleasant fruits. In a word, all beings are ruined by neglect and are improved by being put to use according to their natures;*[6] in man's case, this means through work.

Saint Paul, in the First Reading today at Mass,[7] reminds the Christians of Thessalonica how he behaved while he was preaching among them: *You remember our labour and toil, brethren; we worked night and day, that we might not burden any of you.*[8] And later on, in his Second Letter, he says: *You yourselves know how you ought to imitate us; we were not idle when we were with you; we did not eat anyone's bread without paying, but with toil and labour we worked night and day, that we might not burden any of you.*[9] With this example the Holy Spirit has given us a clearly-defined rule of behaviour: *If any one will not work, let him not eat.*

Today, in the peace and repose of our prayer, we have to bear in mind that God expects from us the same spirit of industriousness and hard work which we observe among those early Christians. One of the very early Patristic writings has left us this admirable testimony: *Let every one who comes to you in the name of the Lord be received; but, after testing him, you will know him, for you know right and wrong. If the one who comes to you is a traveller, help*

6. St John Chrysostom, *Homily on Priscilla and Aquila*
7. *First reading.* Year 1: 1 Thess 2:9-13; Year 2: 2 Thess 3:6-10, 16-18
8. 1 Thess 2:9
9. 2 Thess 3:7-8

*him as much as you can; but he shall not remain with you
more than two or three days unless there is need. If he
wishes to settle among you and is a craftsman, let him work
and eat. If he has no trade, provide according to your conscience, so that no Christian shall live among you idle. If he
does not agree to do this, he is trading on the name of
Christ; beware of such men.*[10]

78.2 The value of work well done.

In his years in Nazareth Our Lord has given us a
wonderful example of the importance of work and of the
human and supernatural perfection with which we have to
carry out our professional tasks. *The fact that Jesus grew
up and lived just like us shows us that human existence and
all the ordinary activity of men have a divine meaning. No
matter how much we may have reflected on all this, we
should always be surprised when we think of the thirty years
of obscurity which made up the greater part of Jesus' life
among men. He lived in obscurity, but, for us, that period is
full of light.*[11] His very way of speaking, the parables and
images that he used afterwards in his preaching, reveal to
us a man who has experienced work at first hand: he
speaks always for the person who *is struggling, for ordinary
folk whose lives are governed by the law of normality, the
predictable pattern of events for people everywhere. This is
the background to Christ's preaching, and in this climate his
teachings have always remained graphically anchored. He
was not the 'philosopher' or the 'visionary' but the craftsman, a man who worked, like ordinary people.*[12]

In Saint Joseph, our Father and Lord, we also have
the example of a life of work, an ordinary one like our

---

10. *Didache*, 12
11. J. Escrivá, *Christ is passing by*, 14
12. R. Gómez Pérez, *Faith and Life*, Madrid

own; and we can entrust to him today our dedication to our professional tasks. It was he who initiated Jesus into his craft and who taught him the skills of an accomplished master in the use of the tools of his trade, of saw, chisel, plane and file.

During his public life the Master called to his service people who were accustomed to work: Saint Peter, a fisherman by occupation, returns again to his fishing as soon as he gets the opportunity;[13] Saint Matthew receives the call to follow Our Lord while he is sitting at his desk in the tax office; and so too all the others.

When Saint Paul left Athens and came to Corinth, he found there a Jew named Aquila, originally from Pontus, and his wife Priscilla. He joined up with them, and since they were of the same trade – they were both tent-makers – he stayed in their house and worked along with them.[14] During the eighteen months he spent in Corinth Saint Paul wrote those demanding instructions to the Christian community of Thessalonica, since he saw that many of the evils which befell them were due to the fact that some of them were more given to idle chatter and to wandering about from house to house than in spending their time attending to their duties.

We, for our part, ought to consider frequently the technical perfection of our work – whether we begin it and end it according to a fixed timetable, even though many of our colleagues, or even all of them, for whatever reason, do otherwise; whether we carry it out in an orderly fashion, not leaving the hardest and least attractive part to the last; whether we work intensely, making the best use of time, trying to avoid the interruptions of unnecessary or

---

13. cf John 21:3
14. cf Acts 18:1-3

less urgent conversations or telephone calls; whether we
are keen to improve the quality of our work through
further training or study, trying to be up to date in the
latest advances being made in ours as in every profession;
whether we strive for excellence, as occurs when we are
genuinely interested in something, but with reasonable
balance and rectitude, without detriment to the time we
owe to our family, to our brothers or sisters, to the apostolate, and to our own formation. Let us consider, too,
whether we duly look after the implements we use, if
either they are our own or belong to our employers. Let us
contemplate Jesus in the workshop at Nazareth; let us ask
Our Lord to allow us to enter there with the eyes of faith,
and there we will see if our work really has the quality and
the high degree of competence which He expects of those
who follow him.

78.3 Love for our profession.

We have to love our work and do it well, because it is
a command we have received from our Father God.
Everyday work is the ordinary means to develop one's personality, to support one's family and oneself, and to contribute to enterprises of apostolate and formation. We have
to love it, and it has to be at the same time material for
our prayer, because work is also one of the highest human
values, a means whereby each individual contributes to the
progress of society, and above all because it is a way to
holiness. Every day we can place before Our Lord all the
things we have tried to do well: students, for example, can
offer well-filled hours of intense study; housewives can
offer their loving attention to the needs of their children
and husbands, to the care of the thousand and one details
that go to make their house a real home; doctors can add
to their professional skill and expertise the friendly and

warm way they deal with their patients, and nurses can offer long hours of constant service, as if each of their patients were Christ himself. When doing our work we have many opportunities of turning our souls to God: with cries for help, with acts of thanksgiving, and with repeated intentions giving him all the glory in the completion of whatever enterprise we have on hand.

As ordinary lay faithful we do not sanctify ourselves 'in spite of' our work, but *through* our work; we encounter Our Lord in the various incidents that go to make up its daily routine, some of them pleasant and others less so; it is in this arena that the human and supernatural virtues are perfected.

In many cases, love for our profession will cause us to spend perhaps our entire life in the same occupation. That doesn't go against the legitimate ambition we might have for promotion or to get a better position or job. But this desire of advancement, which forms part of a good professional outlook, shouldn't give rise to unease or dissatisfaction, as if professional success and an increased salary were the the only or predominant motives we should have. As Christians we cannot measure careers solely in terms of money, as if this were the only thing that mattered in the long run. Our profession is the milieu in which our personality is developed and perfected; it is a way of serving others, the means of contributing to social progress, and the place of our encounter with God.[15] All this has to be taken into account when evaluating one's professional work.

Saint Paul, like most other men, dedicated a certain amount of time to daily work in order to earn his living. But while he was working he still continued to be the

---

15. cf Second Vatican Council, *Gaudium et spes*, 34

Apostle of the Gentiles, God's chosen vessel, and he made use of his trade to bring others to Christ. That is what we have to do too, whatever our job and our niche in society happens to be. And if it should be our lot to be sick or incapacitated, then in those very circumstances we have to be a light to others, perhaps even more than would otherwise be the case, to enable them see the way that leads to God and feel moved to embark upon it themselves.

TWENTY-FIRST WEEK: THURSDAY

79. VIGILANCE AND CHARITY

79.1 The spiritual life requires constant vigilance.

The whole Gospel is a call to us to remain awake, watchful and on guard against the enemy who never sleeps, as we await the Lord's arrival. That decisive moment, when we have to present ourselves before God with our hands filled with the fruits of a Christian life will arrive when we least expect it. *Watch, therefore, for you do not know on what day your Lord is coming*, we read in the Gospel at Mass this morning.[1] *But know this, that if the householder had known in what part of the night the thief was coming, he would have watched and would not have let his house be broken into*.

For the Christian who remains awake, the last day will not come *like a thief in the night*;[2] there will be no panic or confusion, because each day will have been an encounter with God in the simple and everyday business of living. Saint Paul compares this watchfulness to the *statio* or guard-duty of a well-armed sentry who doesn't allow himself to be taken by surprise.[3] He frequently speaks about the Christian life as one of being on guard, like a soldier on active service.[4] The Christian, too, lives frugally and is not easily surprised by the enemy because he is

1. Matt 24:42-51
2. 1 Thess 5:2
3. cf 1 Thess 5:4-11
4. cf J. Precedo, *The Christian in the military terminology of Saint Paul*, Rome

awake through prayer and mortification.

Our Lord warns us in many ways, in different parables, against negligence, carelessness and half-hearted love. A loving heart is a vigilant heart, both over itself and over others, because God also expects us to be watchful and on guard over those who are especially united to us by the bonds of faith, of blood and of friendship.

When Our Lord speaks about the coming of the *thief in the night*, which we read about today in the Gospel at Mass, He is teaching us not to allow ourselves to be distracted from the great enterprise of our salvation. He doesn't want us to think of vigilance merely as something negative – to watch doesn't mean just to stay awake for fear of what might happen if we fell asleep. To watch *means being alert, on the qui vive; it means craning your neck out of the window in the hope that you will be the first to cry out, 'Look! He's coming!'*[5] To watch means to be looking forward with eager expectation to Our Lord's coming. It means striving with all our strength to bring to Jesus all the people entrusted to our care, and many others besides. Thanks to the Communion of Saints we are like the sentry who raises the alarm when he spots the enemy, or the lookout who waits expectantly for his Master's arrival in order to announce the good news to all. Our model is that prudent servant who has been placed in charge of his Master's estate and who, while awaiting his return, spends his time *doing a hundred little jobs against time; always a room to be dusted here, a floor to be polished there, a fire to be made up in this room or that, so that the house shall look a hundred per cent welcoming when he steps inside. Each of us has got a job to do; each of us should be inspired to do it better, especially if it looks as if*

_____

5. R. A. Knox, *A Retreat for Lay People*

we hadn't got much time to do it in.[6]

To watch, to be alert, we must overcome sleepiness and lukewarmness. We do this by struggling to put into practice the things we hear in spiritual direction, by having a clearly-defined *particular examination*, and by being diligent in our daily *general examination*.

79.2 The day on guard.

The early Christians fulfilled Our Lord's *new commandment*[7] so well that the pagans were able to recognize them by the love they had for one another, and by their universally courteous behaviour. Their charity was expressed in their concern for one another's needs and, in times of difficulty, by helping all their brothers and sisters to remain steadfast in the faith. There existed among them the custom which Tertullian called the *statio*, a military term meaning 'being on guard',[8] of fasting and doing penance twice a week with the aim of preparing to receive the Blessed Eucharist with greater purity of soul and of praying for those who were in even greater danger or need. We know, for example, that Saint Fructuosus was fasting on the day he suffered martyrdom because it was his *statio*, his 'day on guard'.[9] Other early Christian documents give us more information about these matters.

Our Lord expects us to practise charity in a special way with those to whom we are united by the bonds of our common faith: *'See how they love one another and are ready to die for one another',* say the pagans ... *As regards the term 'brethren' whereby we address one another, they form a mistaken idea ... By the law of nature, our common*

---

6. *ibid*, pp.45-46
7. cf John 13:34
8. cf A. G. Hamman, *The daily life of the early Christians*, p.200
9. cf *Martyrdom of St Fructuosus*, in *Acts of the Martyrs*, Madrid

mother, they too are our brethren, but with what greater rea-
son do we call brethren those who acknowledge God as our
common Father, who imbibe the same Spirit of holiness,
those who, having emerged from the same womb of
ignorance, gaze in wonderment at the same light of truth![10]

If we suffer because of mankind's neediness, how are
we not going to have a vigilant charity towards those who
share our own ideals! It can also be of help to us, as it was
to the first Christians, to have a fixed day of the week on
which to be even more attentive to the needs of our brothers and sisters in the faith, helping them with even more
fervent prayer, with an even greater spirit of penance, with
more signs of esteem than ever, and with a kindlier fraternal correction. It means being especially vigilant in our
charity towards the people for whom we have a greater
obligation in duty, like the sentry who guards the camp,
like the alert lookout watching for the enemy's approach.

'Custos, quid de nocte? – Watchman, how goes the
night?'

May you acquire the habit of having a day on guard
once a week, during which to increase your self-giving and
loving vigilance over details, and to pray and mortify your-
self a little more.

Realise that the Holy Church is like a great army in
battle array. You, within that army, are defending one 'front'
on which there are attacks, engagements with the enemy and
counter-attacks. Do you see what I mean?

This readiness to grow closer to God will lead you to
turn your days, one after the other, into days on guard.[11]

---

10. Tertullian, *Apologeticus*, 39
11. J. Escrivá, *Furrow*, 960

79.3 What to do on the day on guard.

Go, set a watchman, let him announce what he sees, says the prophet Isaiah. *When he sees riders, horsemen in pairs ... riders on camels, let him listen diligently, very diligently. Then he who saw cried: Upon a watchtower I stand, O Lord, continually by day, and at my post I am stationed whole nights*.[12] The sentry is constantly watching, night and day, for the Babylonian invaders who would sweep away everything and impose their own idols. The watchman is vigilant in order to save his people. That is how we too have to be.

As an aid to vigilance and greater fraternity, like the early Christians, we too can have a day every week when we are particularly mindful of the needs of others. On that day we should say with special intensity: *cor meum vigilat, my heart is awake*.[13] We all need one another, we can all help one another. In fact, we are continually benefiting from the spiritual goods of the Church, from all the prayer, all the sacrifices, all that work well done and offered to God, all the suffering of sick people everywhere. At this very moment, someone, somewhere, is praying for us, and our soul is revitalized by the generosity of people whom perhaps we do not know, or of someone unsuspected, very close beside us. Some day, when we enter God's presence in the moment of the particular judgement, we will finally see the sum total of all the effort that on many perilous occasions kept us afloat, and which on others helped us to draw a little closer to Our Lord. If we are faithful, we will also contemplate then, with unbounded joy, the efficacy of all our own sacrifices, toils and prayers in the lives of our brothers and sisters in the

---

12. Is 21:6-8
13. Cant 5:2

faith, including those things we did for them which at the time may have appeared inconsequential and of little value. Perhaps we will see too the souls that were saved thanks to our prayers and mortifications and to our action in their lives.

Everything we do has repercussions and makes an unguessed-at impact on the lives of others. This consideration ought to move us to fulfil our duties faithfully, offering our work to God, the motive praying with devotion, knowing that our work, our sickness and our prayers, closely united to the prayer and the Sacrifice of Christ renewed daily on the altar, constitute a powerful support for all. On occasions, the help we can offer will be one of the fundamental motives of our fidelity to God, to begin again and again, to be generous in mortification. Then we can make our own Our Lord's prayer: *pro eis sanctifico ego meipsum*, for their sake I sanctify myself.[14] This, then, is the motive for us to begin once more, to finish this task, to do that mortification. Jesus will look upon us then with particular affection and will not let us go from his side. There are few things more pleasing to him than those which directly refer to his brethren, who are our brothers too.

This vigilant charity, this *day on guard*, supports everybody. *'Frater qui adiuvatur a fratre quasi civitas firma.'* A brother helped by brother is like a walled city.

Think for a moment and make up your mind to live the fraternal spirit I have always asked of you.[15]

The day on guard ... A day to be more vibrant in charity, with our example, with many simple services to all, with small mortifications that make life more pleasant for others; a day in which to ask ourselves whether we help

---

14. cf John 17:19
15. J. Escrivá, *The Way*, 460

those who need it with fraternal correction, a day in which to have more frequent recourse to Mary, *harbour of the shipwrecked, consolation of the world, ransom of captives, joy of the sick*,[16] saying the Rosary, or perhaps the *Memorare*, praying to her for the person we know needs some special help at that moment.

---

16. St Alphonsus Liguori, *Visits to the Blessed Sacrament*, 2

TWENTY-FIRST WEEK: FRIDAY

80. THE OIL OF CHARITY

80.1 Intimacy with Jesus is the oil which keeps the light of charity alight.

In the Gospel of today's Mass[1] we read about a Jewish custom which Our Lord makes use of to let us see how vigilant we have to be personally and with regard to our duties towards our neighbour. Jesus tells us: *the kingdom of heaven shall be compared to ten maidens who took their lamps and went to meet the bridegroom.* It was the custom for the bridesmaids to wait in the bride's house for the bridegroom to arrive. Our Lord is trying to teach us what sort of attitude we should have towards his coming. It is He who comes to us, and we for our part have to wait for him with a spirit of watchfulness, our love awake, because, as Saint Gregory the Great says commenting on this parable, *to sleep is to die.*[2]

The parable tells us that five of the maidens were *foolish*: they didn't bring enough oil with them in case the bridegroom was late in coming. The other five were foresighted – *wise* – and *took flasks of oil with their lamps.* Because of the long delay, all of them fell asleep. At midnight they were awoken by the cry *Behold, the bridegroom!*, but the only bridesmaids who were ready and who were admitted to the wedding, were the ones who had remembered to bring oil with them. The others, in spite of their efforts, had to remain outside.

---

1. Matt 25:1-13
2. St Gregory the Great, *Homilies on the Gospels*, 12, 2

The Holy Spirit is teaching us that it is not enough just to have started out on the path that leads to Christ; we have to remain on it, continually alert, because the natural tendency of every man and woman is to lower the level of self-giving that the Christian vocation requires. Little by little, almost without realizing it, the soul gives in to the tendency to make Christ's call compatible with a comfortable existence. We have to be eternally on our guard against the pressure of an environment whose guiding principle is the insatiable search for comfort and the easy way. If not, we will end up like those maidens: at first they are full of good will, but they quickly get tired and cannot go out to meet the *Bridegroom*, for whom they have been preparing all day. If we are not alert, Our Lord will find us without the lustre of good works, asleep, with our lamp extinguished. What a pity if a Christian, after years and years of struggle, were to find at the end of his days that his acts were bereft of supernatural value because they lacked the oil of love and charity! Let us not forget that the light of charity ought to permeate all our family and social relations, our dealings with our friends, our clients, and even the people we meet only from time to time.

The theological virtue of charity has to illuminate all our acts, everywhere and in every moment: when we are feeling well and when we are sick, when we are tired, in moments of failure; when we are with people we get on well with and also with those we find more abrasive or difficult; at work and at home; in a word, always. *The well-disposed soul has always got a lively, firm and resolute determination to forgive, to endure, to help, and an attitude that always moves it to perform acts of charity. If this desire of loving, and of loving disinterestedly, has taken root in the soul, it will have the most convincing proof that its communions, confessions, meditations and its whole life of prayer are in good order and sincere and fruitful.*[3]

The oil that keeps charity alight is prayer that is attentive and full of love: intimacy with Jesus. It is not hard to see that charity is often not practised even by many people who call themselves Christians. *But if we then consider things from a supernatural point of view, we can also see what is the root cause of this sterility: the absence of a continuous and intense, person-to-person relationship with Our Lord Jesus Christ, and an ignorance of the work of the Holy Spirit in the soul, whose very first fruit is precisely charity.*[4]

80.2 The lustre of good works.

The decision to follow Christ is born of Love, and in Love it finds its nourishment. A readiness to give in easily is a sign that the noble ideal of following the Master has lost its appeal. We have to be very sincere with God and with ourselves if we are to be always open to his requests and ready to combat selfishness. The soul that is attached to an easy-going form of existence and who avoids self-denial and sacrifice, or who is motivated only by personal satisfaction, will not find the strength necessary to give itself to God and to its neighbour with all its heart.

There are others too who afflict their bodies with abstinence, but through this very abstinence of theirs they look for material recompense. They teach others, they give many things to the needy, but in reality they are 'foolish virgins', because they seek only the reward of fleeting praise.[5] These are those who lack rectitude of intention; their works remain empty.

Our Lord asks us for perseverance in love. Love has

3. B. Baur, *In Silence with God*, p. 247
4. J. Escrivá, *Friends of God*, 236
5. St Gregory the Great, *Homilies on the Gospels*, 12, 1

to grow continually, experiencing in each moment and situation the joy of following Christ. *Be strong, and let your heart take courage, all you who wait for the Lord!*,[6] the Holy Spirit tells us; without getting discouraged, persevering in our daily effort, so that Love will find us waiting when it comes. *Are not the prudent virgins* – says Saint Augustine – *the ones who persevere until the end? For no other cause, for no other reason, would they have been allowed to enter but for having persevered until the end ... And because their lamps are burning right up to the last moment, the doors are opened wide for them and they are told to enter:*[7] they have discovered what their lives are about.

When the soul loses this attitude of vigilance, when it gives in to venial sin and allows its friendship with Our Lord to grow cold, it remains in darkness, without light for itself or for those who had the right to the influence of its good example. When the spirit of mortification is abandoned and prayer is neglected, the light dims and eventually goes out, *and after so many labours, after so many toils, after all that courageous effort and the hard-won victories over the evil inclinations of nature, the foolish virgins had to retire shamefacedly, their lamps extinguished and their heads lowered.*[8] The love of God does not consist in having begun – not even with a lot of effort – but in persevering, in beginning again and again.

As regards the foolish virgins, *it's not that they hadn't done anything. They had tried to do something ... But in the end they were to hear his stern reply: 'I do not recognise you.'* Either they didn't know how to get ready properly or they didn't want to and they forgot to take the sensible precaution of buying oil in due time. They were not generous

---

6. Ps 31:24
7. St Augustine, *Sermon 93*, 6
8. St John Chrysostom, *Homilies on the Gospels*, 78, 2

*enough to carry out properly the little that had been
entrusted to them. They had been told with many hours to
spare, but they had wasted their time.*

*Let us take a good honest look at our own lives. How
is it that sometimes we just can't find those few minutes it
would take to finish lovingly the work we have to do, which
is the very means of our sanctification? Why do we neglect
our family duties? Why that tendency to rush through our
prayers, or through the Holy Sacrifice of the Mass? How are
we so lacking in calm and serenity when it comes to
fulfilling the duties of our state, and yet so unhurried as we
indulge in our own whims? You might say that these are
trifling matters. You're right, they are, but these trifles are the
oil, the fuel we need to keep our flame alive and our light
shining.*[9]

The desire to love Christ always more and more, the
readiness to fight against our defects and weaknesses,
beginning again and again, is what keeps the flame alight.
This is the oil that doesn't allow the light of charity to go
out. Our Lord waits for us in our work, at home, in our
pastimes. We are all His, in whatever situation we find
ourselves. The light of charity ought to shine always.

80.3 Being light for others.

The people closest to us are the ones who ought to
benefit most from the attitude of vigilance Our Lord wants
us to have in our hearts. At times people can be influenced
a lot by a purely materialistic outlook on life or by the bad
example of people who should give a lead to others. We
sometimes experience very strongly the weight of our passions pulling us down, but it can always be overcome by
the power of an ardent charity. *Frater qui adiuvatur a fratre*

---

9. J. Escrivá, *Friends of God*, 41

quasi civitas firma,[10] a brother helped by a brother is like a walled city that no enemy can assault. Good is always stronger than evil. Our lives have a great importance, because we have to be like burning lamps that light the way for many people.

Our Lord wants us to provide the shelter and protection of our fraternal concern to the people we are close to through ties of blood or friendship, and indeed to all mankind: helping them daily with our prayer, alerting them opportunely and gently through fraternal correction whenever we see them falling into customs or habits that are not in keeping with their Christian state, giving them some helpful advice to improve their family life or their work, being quick with a word of encouragement when they are feeling down, being understanding with their shortcomings and defects and helping them to overcome them. We can even help people a lot by the way we greet them, because, as Saint Thomas says, *our greeting is a sort of prayer*:[11] in it we wish people peace of soul, that God would bless them, and so forth.

Frater qui adiuvatur a fratre quasi civitas firma, a brother helped by a brother is like a walled city. If we let ourselves be helped and we truly give ourselves to the people around us, we can expect that Christ will come and bring us into the wedding feast, to Love without measure and without end.

---

10. cf *Divine Office*, Fourth Sunday of Lent, Evening Prayer II, intercessions (Prov 18:19)
11. St Thomas, *Catena Aurea*, I, p. 334

TWENTY-FIRST WEEK: SATURDAY

81. SINS OF OMISSION

81.1 The parable of the talents. We have received many benefits and gifts from God. We are their stewards, not their masters.

After Our Lord has reminded us of the need to be vigilant, he proposes to us in the Gospel of today's Mass[1] a parable that is a new call to responsibility in the face of the gifts and graces received. He tells us how there once was a rich man who went into a far country, but before leaving, he left all his belongings to his servants for them to look after and trade with. To one he gave five talents, to another two, and to another just one, *to each according to his ability*. A talent was equivalent to about one hundred pounds of silver, and was the unit used to measure very large sums of money.[2] In the time of Our Lord a talent was worth about six thousand pence, and in the Gospel a penny is mentioned as a day's wage for a labourer. So even the servant who received the least (just one talent) still received an enormous sum of money. The first lesson of this parable is that we have received immeasurable benefits from God.

Among the gifts we have received from God, the first of all is the gift of life itself. After that we have our intellect, the capacity to understand natural truths and to ascend from them to their Creator. Next, our will, the ability to desire the good, to love; and our freedom,

---

1. Matt 25:14-30
2. cf 2 Sam 12:30; 2 Kings 18:14

whereby we direct our path as children to our parental home. Then comes the gift of time, the span of days allotted us to serve God and give him glory. We have also received many material goods in order to carry out good works on behalf of our family, of society, and of those in need. On another incomparably higher and more exalted level, we have received the life of grace – a participation in the very life of God himself – which makes us members of the Church and sharers in the Communion of Saints; and God's vocational call to a life of closer union with him. To this we must add the gift of the Sacraments, especially the priceless gift of the Blessed Eucharist; the Mother of God, who is our Mother too; the seven gifts and the fruits of the Holy Spirit which constantly move us to be better; and a Guardian Angel to protect us.

Our life and the gifts that go with it have been given us as an inheritance which we have to invest wisely and which we will be one day called to account for. We are stewards of these goods, some of which are ours only for the short space of time of our earthly life. Afterwards Our Lord will say to us: *turn in the account of your stewardship* ... we are not owners: we are merely caretakers of God's gifts.

Life can be looked at in two ways: seeing ourselves as stewards and making everything productive for God's sake; or acting as if we were owners, for our own comfort, selfishness and whims. In our prayer today let us reflect on what attitude we have to the goods of this world, or perhaps to the way we use our time. Married people can think about their obligation to be generous in having children and in caring for their human and supernatural education, which is in most cases the greatest duty God has given them.

81.2 We have to make good use of our talents.

Our Lord expects to see his estate well looked after, and he expects a return in accordance with what he has bestowed. The reward is enormous: the parable teaches that the *much* of here below, of our life on earth, is very little in comparison to the reward of heaven. That is what happened to the first two servants: they made use of the talents they received and they gained with them as much again. And so they heard from the Master's lips the words *well done, good and faithful servant; you have been faithful over a little, I will set you over much; enter into the joy of your master.* They made the best bargain: they gained eternal happiness. The goods of this life, though manifold, are always *little* in comparison to what God gives to his own.

The third of the servants, by contrast, buried his talent in the ground and didn't trade at all: he wasted his time and made no profit. His life was full of omissions, of wasted opportunities, of time and materials squandered. He appeared before his Lord with his hands empty. As regards what was really important, his was a useless existence: perhaps he was busy in other ways, but he didn't carry out what was really expected of him.

To bury the talent God has given is to have the capacity to love and not to love, to be able to make people happy (something we can all do) and instead to leave them sad and unhappy. To have goods and not to use them profitably. To be able to bring others to God and not to take advantage of the opportunities that come from sharing the same work or job. To be able to make use of weekends to cultivate friendships or to spend time with the family, and instead of being dominated by comfort and self-seeking in ill-conceived forms of relaxation. Above all, to allow to sink into mediocrity an interior life that was meant to grow. It would be a great pity if, looking back over our life, we were to behold a long avenue of wasted opportunities, and to contemplate sorrowfully the abilities God has given us remain unproductive through laziness, carelessness or selfishness. We want to serve God, or better, it is the only thing we want to do. Let us ask Our Lord to help us give fruits of holiness: of love and sacrifice. And let us be very clear that it is *not enough, it is not sufficient*, not to do any harm: we have to trade with our talents, to positively do good.

For a student, to make use of one's talents means studying hard, making use of time intensely and not being foolishly led astray by the idleness of others, gaining through constant application, day by day, a well-earned prestige that will serve to bring others to God. For a wage-earner, for a housewife, to make use of one's talents means to do one's work in an exemplary fashion, intensely, distinguished by punctuality and good use of time. God will especially ask us to account for those people who in various ways have been placed under our care. Saint Augustine says that the person who has been placed over his brothers and doesn't care for them is like a scarecrow, *foenus custos*, a straw guardian, who doesn't even manage to scare away the birds who come and devour the grapes.[3]

Let us examine today the quality of our study or work, whichever it is, and let us ask Our Lord for the readiness to react decisively, if it should be necessary, with the help of his grace, which will not be lacking.

---

3. cf St Augustine, *Miscellanea Augustianensis*, I, p. 568

81.3 Omissions. Christian behaviour in social and public life.

Making use of our talents includes all aspects of private and public life. The effort to live a fully Christian life causes us to develop all aspects of our personality, for example, things like human relationships and the capacity to make friends. We have to exercise these qualities with initiative and faith so as to overcome the inhibition of what people might think in order to provoke a conversation which gets our relatives, friends or companions to improve humanly, spiritually, professionally, or in the way they fulfil their family duties, for example. It may happen that one of these conversations could be the catalyst to get some friend or sick relative back to the Sacraments. Let us consider if we really see ourselves as stewards of the goods Our Lord has given us. Do we really put them to good use or, on the contrary, do we squander them on unnecessary or even harmful purchases? Are we really generous in helping the Church and all those charitable works which constantly require the help of many people in order to keep going? May Our Lord be able to say joyfully to us some day: *I was hungry and you gave me food, I was thirsty and you gave me drink, I was naked and you clothed me.*[4]

God also expects of us a strongly Christian conduct in public life. We have to exercise our right to vote; to participate, according to our capacity, in professional associations, in parent-teacher associations, in trade unions; and we have to fight for better legislation if it is imperfect or clearly unjust in fundamental matters like pro-life issues, education and family law, even if our limited resources or expertise mean that it is an uphill task.

---

4. cf Matt 25:35ff

The time we have at our disposal is never enough to do all God wants: we don't know how much more we have left of the talent of time. Every day we can squeeze a lot from the gifts God has placed in our hands: a myriad of ordinary events, mostly very small, which God and others appreciate and take into account.

Frequent Confession helps us to avoid the omissions that impoverish the Christian life. *The person who is practising frequent Confession must be specially watchful about neglected duties (even if, often, they are only little things), about neglected inspirations and graces, about opportunities to do good left unused, about time wasted, about failure to show charity to the neighbour. He must excite himself to a deep and sincere contrition for these omissions and to a firm resolve to strive earnestly against even the smallest sins of omission that are in any way deliberate. If we come to Confession with this determination, we shall receive, together with the absolution pronounced by the priest, the grace to know our sins of omission better and to struggle against them more zealously.*[5] With the grace of the sacrament and the help of spiritual direction it will be easier for us to avoid those faults or sins and fill our life with fruits for God.

---

5. B. Baur, *Frequent Confession*

Twenty-second Sunday: Year A

82. THE CROSS IN OUR LIVES

82.1 There is no love without sacrifice. The Cross and mortification are unavoidable.

The Gospel of the Mass[1] describes the events that take place immediately after Peter's confession of Christ's divinity at Caesarea Philippi. First we hear Our Lord's words of praise for his disciple: *Blessed are you, Simon Bar-Jonah! For flesh and blood has not revealed this to you, but my Father who is in heaven.*[2] Jesus goes on to say that Peter is to be the foundation of his Church, but then begins to explain to his followers that he has to go up to Jerusalem and there suffer many things at the hands of the Jews, and finally die in order to rise on the third day.

The Apostles didn't understand this sort of talk at all, because they still thought of the Kingdom of God in political terms only. *And Peter took him and began to rebuke him saying, 'God forbid, Lord! This shall never happen to you.'* Carried away by his great love for his Master, Simon tried to dissuade Jesus from the way of the Cross, not yet understanding the immense benefit it was to be for mankind and how it would be the supreme sign of God's love for us. *Peter reasoned in a human fashion,* says Saint John Chrysostom, *and concluded that all Christ's talk of his Passion and Death were demeaning and unbecoming for him.*[3]

---

1. Matt 16:21-27
2. Matt 16:17
3. St John Chrysostom, *Homilies on St Matthew's Gospel*, 54, 4

Peter views Christ's earthly mission far too humanly, and so fails to realize that it was manifestly the will of God that the Redemption would be wrought through the Cross, and that *there was no more suitable way to rescue us from our misery*.[4] Our Lord answers his disciple with great vehemence, just as he did the tempter in the desert: *Get behind me, Satan! You are a hindrance to me; for you are not on the side of God, but of men.*

In Caesarea Peter had spoken under the impulse of the Holy Spirit; he now speaks from a totally materialistic perspective. The notion that the Cross, mortification, sacrifice, are in some way good and a means of salvation, will always strike a discordant note with people who, like Saint Peter on this occasion, view things from a worldly point of view. Saint Paul had to warn the early Christians about people who *live as enemies of the cross of Christ. Their end is destruction, their god is the belly, and they glory in their shame, with minds set on earthly things*.[5]

If we reason only in materialistic terms it is difficult for us to appreciate that pain and suffering, or indeed anything that requires an effort, can be worth while. On the one hand, we know by experience that the difficulties we encounter on our way can serve to purify and strengthen us and make us better. And yet it is clear that our nature of itself abhors suffering: we all aspire to happiness.

The fear of pain, above all if it is severe or persistent, is a deeply rooted instinct is us, and our first reaction in the face of something hard or difficult is to run away. That is why we find the Christian practice of penance difficult: we never find it easy, and no matter how hard we work at it we never manage to get accustomed to it.[6]

---

4. St Augustine, *De Trinitate*, 12, 1-5
5. Phil 3:18-19
6. cf R. M. de Balbín, *Sacrifice and Joy*, Madrid

Faith enables us to see and realize that without sacrifice the soul encounters no true love, no genuine joy, no lasting purification and no possession of God. The path to holiness passes through the Cross, and all apostolate is based upon it. It is the *living book in which we learn definitively who we are and how we ought to behave. This book is always open before us.*[7] Every day we have to approach and read it. And in it we learn who Christ is, the greatness of his love for us, and how we are to follow him. Any one who looks for God without sacrifice, without the Cross, will never find him.

82.2 Modern paganism and the search for material well-being at all costs. The fear of suffering.

... for you are not on the side of God, but of men. Peter will later come to understand profoundly the meaning of pain and sacrifice; along with the other Apostles, he will consider himself fortunate *that they were counted worthy to suffer dishonour for the name.*[8]

As Christians we know that our salvation and the path to heaven is to be found in the loving acceptance of pain and sacrifice. Is there any such thing as a fruitful life that doesn't contain suffering? *Are married couples sure of their love until they have suffered together? Is friendship not strengthened by hardships shared, or simply by having borne together the heat of the day or the fatigue and danger of an ascent?*[9] If we want to rise with Christ we have to accompany him on his journey to the Cross: we do this by accepting life's trials and tribulations with calmness and serenity. Being generous in voluntary self-denial, which purifies us interiorly, helps us understand the transcendent

---

7. John Paul II, *Address*, 1 April 1980
8. cf Acts 5:41
9. J. Leclerq, *Thirty meditations on the Christian life*, pp.217-218

meaning of life and affirms the soul's mastery over the body. Just like in Apostolic times, we have to bear in mind that the Cross Jesus preaches is a scandal to some and utter foolishness to others.[10]

Nowadays too there are many people who *are not on the side of God, but of men*. They have their gaze fixed on things here below, on material well-being, and chase after it as if it were the only thing that really counted. Mankind is suffering from a wave of materialism that is permeating everything and trying to take our civilization over completely. *This contemporary paganism is characterised by the search for material well-being at any cost, and by the corresponding disregard (or, to put it more accurately, fear, genuine panic) of anything that could cause suffering. With this outlook, words such as God, sin, cross, mortification, eternal life ..., become incomprehensible to a great number of people, who are ignorant of their meaning and content.*[11]

The pleasure-seeking mentality which makes enjoyment the supreme purpose of existence, has greatly affected customs and habits in the more developed countries in particular, but, as Pope John Paul II reminds us, it is also *the life-style of increasing groups inside the poorer countries*.[12] This radical materialism is suffocating the religious sense of nations and individuals, and is directly opposed to the doctrine of Christ, whom we hear once more in the Mass inviting us to take up our Cross as a necessary condition of following him: *If any man would come after me*, he tells us, *let him deny himself and take up his cross and follow me*.

Our Lord makes use of pain, of voluntary sacrifice, of poverty, of unheralded sickness, all of which, far from

---

10. cf 1 Cor 1:23
11. A. del Portillo, *Pastoral Letter*, 25 December 1985, 4
12. John Paul II, *Homily in Yankee Stadium*, 2 October 1979, 6

separating us from God, can unite us more closely with him. If we go to Jesus in the Tabernacle and offer him everything we find hard and difficult, we discover that *it is through Christ, and in Christ, that light is thrown on the riddle of suffering and death.*[13] This is the only way to lose the fear of suffering which will accompany us all the days of our life. We will manage to accept it with joy if we discover in it God's lovable will: *The great Christian revolution has been to convert pain into fruitful suffering and so to turn a bad thing into something good. We have deprived the devil of this weapon; and with it we can conquer eternity.*[14]

82.3 What will it profit a man if he gains the whole world and forfeits his life?

In our apostolate we have to tell everybody, by word and example, not to fill their hearts with the things of this world, because everything in this life is impermanent, it grows old and lasts but a moment. *Omnes ut vestimentum veterascent,*[15] they will all grow old like a garment. Only the soul that fights to retain its sense of divine awareness will remain forever young until the moment of the definitive encounter with its Maker. Everything else passes away, and quickly too. What a great pity it is to see so many people risking their eternal salvation, and indeed even their earthly happiness, for a few worthless trifles! *'What will it profit a man if he gains the whole world and forfeits his life?' What use to man are all the things of the earth, all that our intelligence and will can aspire to? What is the point of all that, if it is all to come to an end and sink out of sight; if all the riches of this world are mere theatre props and scenery, and if after all this there is eternity for*

---

13. Second Vatican Council, *Gaudium et spes*, 22
14. J. Escrivá, *Furrow*, 887
15. Heb 1:11

ever, and ever, and ever?[16]

The world and its riches can never be man's ultimate end. Even man's temporal end, which we Christians have the obligation of working for, does not consist strictly speaking in material accomplishments (the achievements of technology, science and industry), but in man's human dimension, in the perfecting of his faculties, social relationships and cultural values through the medium of work and material goods, which should always be at the service of the dignity of the human person.

Only a truly disinterested love, purified and moderated by temperance, can give its proper meaning to the legitimate striving after earthly goods. If God is really the centre of our life, then it will have many practical consequences for everyday living: marriage will be capable of overcoming all obstacles to achieve its primary end, which is to beget children for God and educate them for him; and family life will be a mutual and generous self-giving between spouses. Only if God is present, will art and public entertainment be worthy of man and a genuine expression of the richness of the human spirit. Only in God can the objective foundation of morality be properly understood, and the laws of nations be a faithful reflection of the divine law. Only here can man overcome all fear; only in the inevitability of suffering will he find a source of purification and of co-redemption with Christ. In a word, only the love that is rooted in generosity and sacrifice will enable the human person to obtain his eternal destiny in heaven.

---

16. J. Escrivá, *Friends of God*, 200

TWENTY-SECOND SUNDAY: YEAR B

83. TRUE PURITY

83.1 Cleanness of soul.

Saint Mark, who wrote his Gospel primarily for converts from paganism, in various passages explains for his readers' benefit the meaning of certain Jewish customs, the value of coins and so forth, so that they would be better able to understand Our Lord's teachings. In the Gospel of today's Mass[1] he tells us that the Jews, and especially the Pharisees, *do not eat unless they wash their hands, observing the tradition of the elders; and when they come from the market place, they do not eat unless they purify themselves; and there are many other traditions which they observe, the washing of cups and pots and vessels of bronze.*

These purifications were not done simply for hygienic reasons or out of politeness; they had in fact a religious significance, symbolizing the moral purity needed in order to approach God. In Psalm 24, which was part of the liturgical rite of entry to the Jerusalem sanctuary, it says: *Who shall ascend the hill of the Lord? And who shall stand in his holy place? He who has clean hands and a pure heart.*[2] Purity of heart appears as a condition for approaching God, for taking part in his worship and being able to behold his face. But the Pharisees hadn't got beyond the purely external level and even added to the intricacy of the rites while neglecting their fundamental

1. Mark 7:1-8
2. cf Ps 24:3-4

aspect, namely, cleanness of heart, of which all the rest was merely a sign and a symbol.[3]

On this occasion the Scribes and Pharisees who had come to Jerusalem were surprised that some of Jesus' disciples *ate with hands defiled, that is, unwashed*, and they asked Our Lord: *Why do your disciples not live according to the tradition of the elders, but eat with hands defiled?* Our Lord reacted strongly to this empty and formalistic attitude. *You hypocrites*, he said, *you leave the commandments of God, and hold fast to the traditions of men*. True purity – the *clean hands* of Psalm 24 (*innocens manibus* in Latin) is more meaningful than *washed hands* – has to begin with the heart, because *from within, out of the heart of man, come evil thoughts, fornication, theft, murder, adultery, coveting, wickedness, deceit, licentiousness, envy, slander, pride, foolishness*. All man's acts originate in his heart; and if this is unclean, then the entire person is unclean.

Sensuality, that is, the capital sin of lust, leaves a profound scar on the soul. However, this is not the only manifestation of impurity: also included is the inordinate desire for material goods, the attitude that leads a person to exploit others, to scheming, envy, or animosity; and also the tendency to think only about oneself to the exclusion of others; and interior sloth, the origin of daydreams and fantasies which undermine presence of God and application at work. Our external behaviour is coloured by our internal dispositions. Many external faults against charity can be traced to feelings of touchiness or irritability that should have been firmly rejected as soon as they first appeared.

What Jesus rejects is the mentality behind all those

---

3. cf John Paul II, *General Audience*, 10 December 1980

prescriptions; by then they had completely lost their original purpose. Instead, he teaches us to love that purity of heart whereby we are enabled to see God in our daily lives. He has told us so very often that he wants to reign in our feelings, to be with us at all times, to give a new meaning to everything we do. Let us ask him to always keep our heart clean of these disordered tendencies.

83.2 Purity in everyday life.

The purity of soul that Our Lord asks of his followers is far from being simply a matter of appearances. We are not expected to 'wash' our hands and plates and leave our heart unclean. Purity of soul (chastity, in the area of sensuality, and rectitude in our other feelings and inclinations) has to be really appreciated and joyfully sought after, basing our effort always on the grace of God. This interior cleanness (a necessary element of all love) is the consequence of a life-long, cheerful and unremitting struggle. The soul, if it is not to consent to attitudes and thoughts which separate it from God and from others, needs the help of a daily examination of conscience; it also needs to have a great love for frequent and worthy reception of the Sacrament of Penance, whereby God purifies and fills it with his grace and the heart is 'washed' clean.

Interior purity brings with it a strengthening and growth of love, along with man's elevation to the dignity to which he has been called. His ever greater awareness of this dignity[4] is in contrast to the great frequency with which he often appears to abandon it. *The human heart continues feeling today those same impulses that Jesus denounced as the cause and root of impurity: selfishness in*

---

4. cf Second Vatican Council, *Dignitatis humanae*, 1

all its forms, malicious intentions, the base motives that so often inspire man's conduct. But it seems as if at this moment in history we are witnessing something (the degradation of human love and a universal wave of impurity and sensuality) which, because of its gravity and extension, has not been experienced hitherto. This debasement of man affects the central core of his being, the very essence of his personality and, given its world-wide dissemination, has to be considered an unprecedented historical phenomenon.[5]

With the help of grace, which we can always count on if we don't hinder God's action in our souls, it is our Christian duty to show, with the example of our lives and with our word, that chastity is essential for everybody, men and women, adults and adolescents, and that everyone has to live it according to the conditions of the state to which God has called them; *it is a requirement of love, a dimension of its interior truth in man's heart,*[6] and it would not be possible to love God or our fellow man without it.

A sense of loyalty to our commitment to Christ, the virtue of fortitude, simple common sense, should all lead us to act intelligently and to avoid occasions that are injurious to the health of the soul and the integrity of the spiritual life. We have to safeguard our senses at all times. If necessary, we should avoid tuning in to certain TV or radio programmes. If the occasion arises, we should refuse to take part in smutty conversations, or better still, try to raise the tone. In the way we dress, in personal hygiene, when playing games, we cannot be careless about decorum and modesty. We cannot be seen in a place that is unbecoming for a good Christian, even though it is the fashion or most of our friends go there. At times we may

---

5. J. Orlandis, *The Eight Beatitudes*, pp.114-115
6. John Paul II, *General Audience*, 3 December 1980

be called upon to object strongly to indecent behaviour, and not have any complexes about doing so. It is no harm recalling that the word 'obscene' comes from ancient Greek and Roman theatre, and referred to those things which, because of their very intimate nature, *ought not to be performed on stage*, out of respect for the spectators. Even that pagan civilization, which was otherwise very permissive in its moral standards, understood that there are some things which are not done in public.

Perhaps at times it will not be easy to live in surroundings that have lost their Christian outlook. But then, Our Lord never promised us an easy way, but rather, the graces necessary to overcome difficulties. To let oneself be dragged along by what people think, or by fear of appearing unnatural, and so conforming to a 'pagan naturalness', would be a sign of mediocrity and a lack of personality, and above all, would show little love for the Master.

83.3 Keeping our heart unsullied. The role of frequent Confession.

From the depths of the human heart the Holy Spirit wishes to draw the source of that new life which little by little transforms our entire personality. One of the necessary elements in this activity (and at the same time one of the fruits of the interior life) is the virtue of purity, and chastity in particular:[7] *purity*, in English and in other languages, has come to mean the same thing as *chastity*, although in itself it has a wider meaning.[8] This Christian purity, chastity, has always been one of the Church's glories and one of the clearest signs of her holiness. Today too, like in the time of the early Christians, there are many

---

7. cf S. Pinckaers, *In search of happiness*, pp.141-142
8. cf John Paul II, *General Audience*, 10 December 1980

men and women who live a life of celibacy or virginity *for the sake of the kingdom of heaven*[9] in the middle of the world, though without being worldly; and there is a great multitude of Christian married couples, fathers and mothers of families, who live chaste and holy lives in the married state. Both the one and the other are witnesses to the same Christian love which matches itself to each one's vocation, because, as the Church teaches, *marriage and virginity or celibacy are two ways of expressing and living the one mystery of the covenant of God with his people.*[10]

All of us, each in the state in which we have been called (single, married, widowed, priest), ask God today to grant us a heart that is noble and clean, full of kindness towards all mankind and able to draw them all to God; capable of a limitless goodness for those who come, perhaps bleeding on the inside, looking for and at times imploring our support to help them stay afloat. An aspiration that perhaps can help us now, and on many occasions, is the prayer the Liturgy makes to the Holy Spirit on Pentecost Sunday:

> *Heal our wounds, our strength renew;*
> *On our dryness pour your dew;*
> *Wash the stains of guilt away.*
> *Bend the stubborn heart and will;*
> *Melt the frozen, warm the chill;*
> *Guide the steps that go astray.*[11]

And together with the petition, an effective resolution to do whatever is necessary to ensure that our heart is never disfigured, not only by impure thoughts and desires, but also by not being able to forgive readily. Let us resolve not to harbour any resentment or grievances

9. Matt 19:12
10. John Paul II, *Familiaris consortio*, 16
11. cf *Roman Missal*, Pentecost Sunday, sequence

against anybody for any reason; let us try with all our strength to avoid jealousy and envy, and all those things that stain the soul and leave it sad and lonely. Let us love the Sacrament of Penance, wherein our heart is purified ever more and more and is enlarged for doing good.

Whenever we find the going difficult, we can count on the help of our Mother the Virgin Mary, who was full of grace from the first moment of her conception, to teach us how to be strong and keep our heart clean and full of love for her Son.

TWENTY-SECOND SUNDAY: YEAR C

84. THE FIRST PLACES

84.1 The inordinate desire for praise and fame.

The readings of today's Mass tell us about a virtue that is the basis of all the others, namely, humility. It is so necessary that Jesus takes advantage of every opportunity to explain it to his followers. On this particular occasion Our Lord is invited to a banquet in the house of one of the leading Pharisees. Jesus notices how the guests, as they arrive, take up the the most honourable positions at table. Perhaps it is when they are already seated and have begun to talk that Our Lord tells them a parable[1] which ends with these words: *when you are invited, go and sit in the lowest place, so that when your host comes he may say to you, 'Friend, go up higher'; then you will be honoured in the presence of all who sit at table with you. For every one who exalts himself will be humbled, and he who humbles himself will be exalted.*

This parable reminds us of the need to know our place, to avoid being blinded by ambition and letting life become a frantic pursuit of ever greater goals, for which in many cases we are unqualified and which sooner or later would cause us to be humiliated. Ambition, one of the forms of pride, is often the cause of deep dissatisfaction in the person who suffers from it. *Why do you look for the first places? Why do you want to be above others?* asks Saint John Chrysostom.[2] Everybody has a natural appetite

---

1. Luke 14:1, 7-11
2. St John Chrysostom, *Homilies on St Matthew's Gospel*, 65, 4

(which in its proper place can be good and noble) for honour and glory. Ambition is simply a disordered tendency to look for honour, to exercise authority, or to have a position that is in some way superior, or at least appears to be so.

True humility is not opposed to the legitimate desire for personal advancement in social life, to enjoying the necessary professional prestige, to receiving the honour which is due to every human being. All this is compatible with a deep humility. But the humble person doesn't like showing off. He knows that his purpose in life is not to shine and be highly regarded, but to carry out a mission for God and for others.

The virtue of humility has nothing to do with being shy, timid or mediocre. It causes us to be fully aware of the talents Our Lord has given us and, without losing a right intention, want to make them fruitful in our lives. Humility counteracts the tendency to boast about our achievements and of thinking we are wonderful. It leads us to a wise moderation and to direct to God the desires of glory which are hidden in every human heart: *Non nobis, Domine, non nobis, sed nomini tuo da gloriam*[3] – not to us, O Lord, but to You be all glory due. Humility makes us always acknowledge that our talents and our virtues, both the natural ones and those of grace, come from God: *from his fullness have we all received.*[4] Everything good is from God; all that comes from us is imperfection and sin. And so, *the lively consideration of graces received makes us humble, because a knowledge of them excites gratitude.*[5] To penetrate, with the help of grace, into what we are and the greatness of the divine goodness, helps to keep us in our

---

3. Ps 113:1
4. John 1:16
5. St Francis de Sales, *Introduction to the Devout Life*, III, 5

place; in the first place, in our own minds: *Alas! do mules cease to be disgusting beasts simply because they are laden with precious and perfumed goods of the prince?*[6] asks Saint Francis de Sales. The parallels he sees between man's life and that of beasts of burden is a very valid one, echoing the words of Scripture: *ut iumentum factus sum apud te, Domine:*[7] we are like a donkey whose master, when he wishes to, loads with treasures of great value.

84.2 How to be humble.

In order to grow in humility we need to be able to appreciate, on the one hand, our nothingness; and on the other, all the gifts God has given us, the talents from which he expects fruit. *In spite of all our defects we are bearers of divine treasures of inestimable value: we are God's instruments. And since we want to be good instruments, the smaller and more miserable we see ourselves, in true humility, the more Our Lord will supply everything we are lacking.*[8] We will go through life conscious of our marvellous dignity of being God's instruments through whom he acts in the world. Humility means acknowledging our littleness, our nothingness, and *at the same time* knowing that we are *bearers of divine treasures of inestimable value*. This vision, the most real of all visions, leads us to be continually grateful to God and to be full of the greatest spiritual daring because we base everything on God. At the same time, it causes us to look upon our fellow men with great respect, while rescuing us from going around cadging the crumbs of praise and admiration which are so worthless and last so little. Humility avoids us developing an inferiority complex (often a consequence of wounded

---

6. *ibid*
7. Ps 72:23
8. J. Escrivá, *Letter*, 24 March 1931

pride), it makes us cheerful and serviceable with others and desirous of loving God: *Our Lord will supply everything we are lacking*.

In order to walk on the path of humility we have to learn to accept the humiliating events of life, which are inevitable anyway. We ask Our Lord that they would serve to unite us to him and that he would teach us to regard them as a heaven-sent opportunity to make reparation, to purify and to fill ourselves more and more with his love, without getting disheartened, and going to the Tabernacle if at any time they hurt a little more.

A sure means of growing in this virtue is total sincerity: first with oneself, leading to a self-knowledge that is achievable only in examination of conscience done in the presence of God; then, sincerity with God, which causes us to ask for pardon many times, because our weaknesses are many; and sincerity with the person who has charge of our spiritual welfare.

A readiness to change our minds is also a sure sign of humility. *Only the stupid are obstinate; the very stupid are very obstinate*.[9] Earthly affairs do not admit of only one solution. *Other people may also be right: they see the same question as you, but from a different point of view, under another light, with other shades, with other contours*,[10] and this confrontation of opinions is always enriching. The proud person who is never ready to give way to others, who always believes that he is right in things which are matters of opinion, can never participate in an open and enriching dialogue. Moreover, to admit our mistake when we have been in the wrong is not only a matter of humility, but of elementary honesty.

---

9. J. Escrivá, *Furrow*, 274
10. *ibid*, 275

Every day we encounter many opportunities to exercise this virtue: being docile in spiritual direction; taking well the indications and corrections we get; fighting against the ever-present temptation to vanity; stifling the urge to always have the last word; trying not to be the centre of attention; accepting that we were wrong in things in which perhaps we thought we were absolutely right; trying always to see our neighbour in an optimistic and positive light; not thinking that we are irreplaceable.

84.3 The benefits of humility.

Saint Francis de Sales reminds us that there is a form of false humility which makes us say *that we are nothing, that we are misery itself and the refuse of the world, but we would be very sorry if anyone should take us at our word or tell others that we are really such miserable wretches as we say. On the contrary, we pretend to retire and hide ourselves, so that the world may run after us and seek us out. We feign to wish ourselves considered as the last in the company and to sit down at the lowest end of the table, but it is with a view that we may be desired to pass more easily to the upper end. True humility does not make a show of herself or use many humble words.*[11] And Saint Francis goes on to add: *Let us never cast down our eyes except when we humble our hearts. Let us not seem to desire to be the lowest, unless we desire it with all our heart.*[12] True humility is full of simplicity and springs from the deepest recesses of the heart, because it is above all an attitude towards God.

The number of benefits that flow from humility is immense. The first of them is the grace of faithfulness, because pride is the greatest obstacle that can come

---

11. St Francis de Sales, *Introduction to the Devout Life*, III, 5
12. *ibid*

between God and us. Humility attracts to itself the love of God and the appreciation of men, whereas pride repels them both. That is why the First Reading at Mass[13] recommends us: *My son, perform your tasks in meekness; then you will be loved by those whom God accepts*. And the same passage says: *The greater you are, the more you must humble yourself; so you will find favour in the sight of the Lord. Many are lofty and renowned, but to the meek he reveals his secrets*. The humble soul penetrates more easily into the divine will and knows what God wants at every moment. And so it is always well balanced, knows how to be in its place and is always helpful; it even has a greater insight into human affairs because of its natural simplicity. The proud soul, on the contrary, closes the door to God's will, in which human happiness lies, because it has eyes only for its own way, its own preferences, its own ambition, the achievement of its own aims; even in human affairs it is often mistaken, because everything it sees is deformed by its sickly gaze.

Humility gives consistency to all the virtues. In a special way, the humble person respects others, their opinions and their things, and possesses a special fortitude, because he or she relies constantly on the goodness and omnipotence of God: *when I am weak, then I am strong*,[14] says Saint Paul. Our Mother the Virgin Mary, she in whom God did great things because he looked upon her humility, will teach us to occupy the place which corresponds to us before God and before men. She it is who will help us to progress in this virtue and to love it as a precious gift.

---

13. Sir 3:19-21, 30-31
14. 2 Cor 12:10

85. THE WORKS OF MERCY

85.1 Jesus is merciful. We must imitate his example.

Jesus returned to Nazareth, *where he had been brought up; and He went to the synagogue, as his custom was, on the Sabbath day.*[1] There they gave him the book of the prophet Isaiah to read. He opened the book at a passage which has a clearly Messianic meaning: *The Spirit of the Lord is upon me, because He has anointed me to preach good news to the poor. He has sent me to proclaim release to the captives and recovering of sight to the blind, to set at liberty those who are oppressed, to proclaim the acceptable year of the Lord.*

Jesus rolled up the book, handed it back to the attendant, and sat down. There was a great air of expectation among his listeners, all of whom had known him from boyhood. *The eyes of all in the synagogue were fixed on him.* Very likely Our Lady too was present. Our Lord then said to them quite plainly: *Today this scripture has been fulfilled in your hearing.*

In this passage[2] the prophet Isaiah foretold the coming of the Messiah to free his people from their afflictions. These words of Our Lord are, as Pope John Paul II says, *his first Messianic declaration. They are followed by the actions and words known through the Gospel. By these actions and words Christ makes the Father present among men. It is very significant that the people in*

---

1. Gospel of the Mass (Luke 4:16-30)
2. cf Is 61:1-2

*question are especially the poor, those without means of
subsistence, those deprived of their freedom, the blind who
cannot see the beauty of creation, those living with broken
hearts, or suffering from social injustice, and finally sinners.
It is especially for these last that the Messiah becomes a particularly clear sign of God who is love.*[3]

Later on, when John the Baptist's envoys ask him if
he is the Christ or if they have to wait for another, Jesus
tells them to go and relate to John what they have seen
and heard: *the blind receive their sight, the lame walk, lepers
are cleansed, and the deaf hear, the dead are raised up, the
poor have the good news preached to them.*[4]

Christ's love for men is shown especially in his
encounter with suffering, with anything in which human
weakness, both physical and moral, is to be seen. It thus
reveals God the Father's untiring concern for mankind, a
concern which *is love*[5] and *rich in mercy*.[6]

God's mercy is the fundamental core of Christ's
preaching and the main driving force behind his miracles.
The Church too *encompasses with her love all those who
are afflicted by human misery and she recognizes in those
who are poor and who suffer, the image of her poor and
suffering founder. She does all in her power to relieve their
need, and in them she strives to serve Christ.*[7]

And what else can we in turn do if we want to imitate
the Master and be good sons and daughters of the
Church? Every day we have countless opportunities to put
into practice Christ's teaching about how we ought to
behave when faced with suffering and hardship. In the first

---

3. John Paul II, *Dives in misericordia*, 30 November 1980, 3
4. Luke 7:22ff
5. 1 John 4:16
6. Eph 2:4
7. Second Vatican Council, *Lumen gentium*, 8

place, we have to be compassionate and merciful with our nearest neighbours, with those whom God has placed under our care, and with those most in need. Let us ask ourselves now, in the presence of God, how we rate our behaviour towards all these people. Am I aware of their pain (physical or moral), of their tiredness or their neediness? Am I quick to give them the help they need? Do I try to lighten the load they have to bear, especially when it exceeds their strength?

85.2 Concern for our neighbour's spiritual welfare.

... *He has anointed me to preach the good news to the poor. He has sent me to proclaim release to the captive* ... There is no greater poverty than that which arises from lack of faith, nor any greater slavery or oppression than that which is exercised by the devil in the soul of the sinner, nor more complete blindness than in the soul deprived of grace. As Saint John Chrysostom says, *sin produces the greatest of all tyranny.*[8]

If the greatest misfortune, the worst tragedy, that can befall anyone is to be separated from God, then the greatest work of mercy we can perform is to bring our relatives and friends to the life-giving fountains of the Sacraments, and especially to Confession. If their sorrows, sicknesses and misfortunes cause us to suffer, how much more do we suffer if we see that they don't know Christ, that they don't care for him or have abandoned him? True compassion begins with concern for the state of their soul, which with the help of grace we have to try to remedy. What a great work of mercy apostolate is!

All moral suffering, of any sort, invites our compassionate response. And so from the earliest times the

---

8. St John Chrysostom, *Commentary on Psalm 126*

Church has always held in high esteem the work of *instructing the ignorant*. Nowadays, just as illiteracy is everywhere on the decrease, religious ignorance is growing to an incredible extent, even in nations of long Christian tradition. *For one reason or another, whether through anti-Catholic prejudice or a lamentable disorientation and neglect, great masses of young Catholics are reaching adolescence totally ignorant of the most basic notions of the faith and the elementary practices of piety. Nowadays, to instruct the ignorant means above all to "evangelize" them, that is, to speak to them about God and the Christian life. Catechesis has become nowadays a work of mercy of prime importance.*[9]

What great good it does when a mother teaches the catechism to her children, and perhaps to her children's little friends! What a wonderful reward awaits those who generously spend time giving catechetical instruction, and to those who provide suitable books to enlighten men's minds and move their hearts! It means opening for them the path that leads to God: there is nothing they need more.

85.3 Other works of mercy.

Imitating Jesus in his merciful compassion for those in need can often mean giving support and company to the lonely, to the sick, to people who suffer a shameful or barefaced poverty. We try to share their pain and help them sanctify it, as well as trying to remedy their situation as far as we can. Think of how consoling it can be for such a person to have a spell of company, made possible perhaps by sacrificing a bit of free time we may have been looking forward to enjoying. Our simple and friendly

---

9. J. Orlandis, *The Eight Beatitudes*, pp.104-105

conversation with some sick or old person, which should never lack a certain supernatural tone – some uplifting news about the apostolate, maybe – leaves them with a little more faith and confidence in God. Tactfully and helpfully, we can offer them some little service, making their bed perhaps, or reading them part of some agreeable or possibly even amusing spiritual book.[10]

Every day it is getting more and more necessary to ask God to give us a merciful heart towards all, because as society becomes more dehumanized men's hearts are becoming harder and more insensitive. Justice is a fundamental virtue, it is true, but justice of itself is not enough: charity is needed too. No matter how much social legislation and working conditions improve, men will always need the warmth of a human heart, fraternal and friendly, which is able to identify with those situations that justice alone cannot remedy, because *Christian charity cannot be limited to giving things or money to the needy. It seeks, above all, to respect and understand each person for what he is, in his intrinsic dignity as a man and a child of God.*[11]

Mercy should cause us to forgive promptly and from the heart, even though the other party isn't sorry for what has happened or rebuffs our attempts to make up. The Christian cannot harbour any resentment in his heart; he is not at loggerheads with anybody. We have to love also those who are unhappy through their own fault, or even through their own evil actions. The only question God asks us is if that person is unhappy, if he is suffering, because *that is enough to make him worth your interest. Try, of course, to protect him from his evil passions, but the moment he suffers, be merciful. 'You shall love your*

---

10. cf St Jean Vianney, (The Curé d'Ars), *Sermon on almsgiving*
11. J. Escrivá, *Christ is Passing By*, 72

neighbour', not when he deserves it, but because he is your neighbour.[12]

God asks us to be compassionate in all situations in life. When we are called upon to judge our neighbour we have to do so from the most favourable angle. *Even though you see something very bad about your neighbour,* says Saint Bernard, *don't jump immediately to conclusions, but rather make excuses for him interiorly. Excuse his intention, if you cannot excuse his action. Think that he may have acted out of ignorance, or by surprise, or accidentally. If the thing is so blatant that it cannot be denied, even so, believe it to be so, and say inwardly: the temptation must have been very strong.*[13]

We frequently have to remember that if we are merciful, we will obtain from God that mercy which we need so much ourselves, particularly for those weaknesses, errors and failings that He understands so well. That confidence in God's infinite compassion will cause us to remain always very close to him.

Our Lady, *Queen and Mother of Mercy*, will give us a heart capable of having genuine compassion on all who suffer at our side.

---

12. G. Chevrot, *The Eight Beatitudes*, p. 128
13. St Bernard, *Sermon on the Canticle of Canticles*, 40

TWENTY-SECOND WEEK: TUESDAY

86. HE TAUGHT WITH AUTHORITY

86.1 Jesus teaches with divine power and strength.

The Evangelists repeatedly mention the surprised reactions that Jesus' teaching and his miracles provoke in the people, and even in his own disciples,[1] who are often seen to be afraid to ask him questions.[2] Their reluctance is a sign of the reverential awe which seized and captivated them, an awareness of his majesty reflected in his words and in his deeds. Saint Luke tells us in the Gospel of the Mass[3] how after Jesus had cured a possessed man *they were all amazed and said to one another: 'What is this word? For with authority and power He commands the unclean spirits, and they come out.'* And Saint Mark points out on another occasion how the people were astonished at his teaching, *for He taught them as one who had authority, and not as the scribes.*[4] The Second Person of the Blessed Trinity spoke through the medium of his Holy Humanity, and the people, aware of his extraordinary power, hastened to identify him with the most exalted and famous figures of their history: was he John the Baptist, or Elijah, or Jeremiah or one of the prophets?[5] They all fell very far short of the truth.

The people who listened to Jesus perceived clearly

---

1. cf Mark 9:6; 6:51; etc
2. cf Mark 9:32
3. Luke 4:31-37
4. Mark 1:22
5. cf Matt 16:14

the radical difference there was between the way the
scribes and Pharisees taught and the certainty and vitality
with which Christ pronounced his doctrine. Jesus doesn't
expound just a mere opinion, nor does He show any sign
of uncertainty or of doubt.[6] He does not speak, like the
prophets, in God's name, because He is not just another
prophet: he speaks in his own name: *I say to you ...* He
teaches people the divine mysteries and the nature of
human relationships, and he backs up his teachings with
his miracles. He explains his doctrine simply and
vigorously because He speaks of what He has seen,[7] and
He doesn't give long-winded explanations. *He demonstrates nothing, He doesn't try to justify himself, He doesn't
argue. He teaches. His authority imposes itself because the
wisdom that emanates from him is irresistible. When you
come to value this wisdom, when your heart is pure enough
to appreciate it, you know that there cannot be any other.
You don't feel any need to compare, to study. You see.*

*You see that this is the absolute; that before him every-
thing is but dust; you see that He is Life. Just as when the
sun rises the stars disappear, the same happens with all the
wisdom and all the opinions of men. Lord, to whom shall
we go? You have the words of eternal life.*[8]

Jesus continues to speak to each of us, personally, in
the intimacy of our prayer, when we read the Gospel every
day. We have to learn to listen to him also in the thousand
and one events of the day, including those which men call
failure or sorrow. *When you open the Holy Gospel, think
that what is written there – the words and deeds of Christ –
is something that you should not only know, but live. Everything, every point that is told there, has been gathered, detail*

---

6. cf *The Navarre Bible*, note to Matt 7:28-29
7. cf John 3:11
8. J. Leclerq, *Thirty meditations on the Christian life*, pp.53-54

by detail, for you to make it come alive in the individual circumstances of your life.

God has called us Catholics to follow him closely. In that holy Writing you will find the Life of Jesus, but you should also find your own life there ... Take up the Gospel every day, then, and read it and live it as a definite rule. This is what the saints have done.[9]

86.2 The daily reading of the Gospel.

Jesus' teaching had such power and authority that some of those who listened to him exclaimed that never before had anything like it been heard in Israel.[10] The Venerable Bede tells us that the scribes also taught the people what was written in Moses and the Prophets, but Jesus preached to the people as God and Lord of Moses himself.[11]

Christ's words were full of life; they penetrated to the bottom of men's hearts. When John the Baptist pointed out Jesus as He passed by, two of his disciples followed him and spent the day in his company. Saint John the Evangelist, the one who gives us the great dialogues of Jesus, on this occasion is silent; he only tells us that they met him *about the tenth hour*, about four in the afternoon. When, many years later, he wrote his Gospel, he wanted to leave us forever *the precise unforgettable moment of his first encounter* with the Master. What did Our Lord say to them? We only know the result from the words of Andrew, the other disciple who followed Jesus: *We have found the Messiah!*[12] he said to his brother Simon. That afternoon God entered into the deepest recesses of their hearts.

---

9. J. Escrivá, *The Forge*, 754
10. cf Luke 19:48; John 7:46
11. St Bede, *Commentary on St Mark's Gospel*, 1, 21
12. John 1:41

When we in turn open our hearts, Jesus' words pierce and transform us too, as happened to the men who had been sent to arrest him and returned empty-handed.[13] *Why did you not bring him?* said the Pharisees accusingly, to which they replied simply: *No man ever spoke like this man!*

In Jesus' words we find an infinite wisdom; He can be understood by philosophers and by the uneducated, by adolescents and by children, by men and women, by everybody. He speaks about the most sublime things in the simplest of language. His doctrine has a depth unlike any other, and yet is within reach of everybody. His preaching is full of familiar ideas and images which give his preaching an incomparable beauty and attractiveness. The smallest details serve to express the most sublime features of a new doctrine of mysterious and unfathomable depth.

Our Lord's whole life was an uninterrupted teaching process: *his silences, his miracles, his gestures, his prayer, his love for people, his special affection for the lowly and the poor, his acceptance of the total sacrifice on the Cross for the redemption of the world, and his Resurrection, are all the actualization of his word and the fulfilment of revelation ... These considerations ... all strengthen our fervour with regard to Christ, the Teacher who reveals God to man and man to himself, the Teacher who saves, sanctifies and guides, who lives, who speaks, rouses, moves, redresses, judges, forgives, and goes with us day by day on the path of history, the Teacher who comes and will come in glory.*[14]

In our daily Gospel reading we meet this same Christ who speaks to us, teaches us and consoles us. In our reading – just a few minutes a day – we get to know him better and better, to imitate his life, to love him. If we ask

---

13. John 7:46ff
14. John Paul II, *Catechesi tradendae*, 16 October 1979, 9

the Holy Spirit, the principal author of Sacred Scripture, to come to our assistance, we will be helped to be one more protagonist in the scene we read, or perhaps to draw some small but definite conclusion for the day.

86.3 Meeting Jesus in our Gospel reading.

Your prayer, says Saint Augustine, *is like a conversation with God. When you read, God speaks to you; when you pray, you speak to him.*[15] God speaks to us in many ways when we read the Gospel: He offers us the example of his life so that we can imitate him in ours; He shows us how to behave towards our brothers and sisters; He reminds us that we are children of God and that nothing ought to take our peace away; He invites us to forgive the little offences we suffer; He gets us to prepare well for frequent Confession, where our Heavenly Father awaits to give us an embrace; He asks us to be merciful today with our neighbour's defects, just as He himself was to a supreme degree; He leads us to sanctify our work, doing it perfectly, because it is what He himself spent so many years doing in Nazareth. Each day we can get some idea, some thought or resolution, to remember while we work. And so it is a very good idea to do those few minutes' reading early in the day so as to put into practice the little resolutions which can help us so much to improve. Some people actually read the Gospel standing up, as a reminder of the early Christian custom, which has been preserved in the Mass, whereby we stand for the Gospel in an attitude of prayerful vigilance.

It does our soul a lot of good to use the Gospel frequently as the source of topics for our prayer. On occasions, perhaps, we can try to enter the scene as someone

---

15. St Augustine, *Commentary on the Psalms*, 85, 7

joining a little group gathered around Jesus, or stopping at a doorway to hear the Master teaching, or standing at the shore of the lake. Perhaps we manage to hear only a part of the parable, or a few snatches of conversation, but it is enough for something to start stirring in the depths of our soul. On other occasions maybe we will be bold enough to say something to him, just like those others who said or shouted to him in their great need: *Domine, ut videam!,*[16] Lord, let me see, give light to my soul, set me on fire; or, echoing the words of the publican who didn't consider himself worthy to stand before his God: *God, be merciful to me a sinner;*[17] or perhaps those words of Peter, *Domine, tu omnia nosti ... Lord, you know everything, you know that I love you,*[18] will take on a new meaning for us, and we will confide to Jesus the sentiments of love and purification that fill our heart. Often, perhaps, we will contemplate his Holy Humanity, and on seeing him *perfect Man* we will be moved to love him more, to want to be more faithful to him. We will contemplate him at work in Nazareth, helping Saint Joseph, and later on looking after his Mother, or tired out, maybe, from many hours of preaching or from the strain of a long journey.

Every day, as we read the Gospel, Jesus passes beside us. Let us never fail to see and hear him, like those disciples who met him on the road to Emmaus. *'Stay with us, it is towards evening ... ' The prayer of Cleophas and his companion was effective.*

How sad it would be if you and I were not able to 'detain' Jesus who is passing by. What a shame not to ask him to stay![19]

---

16. Matt 10:51
17. Luke 18:13
18. John 21:17
19. J. Escrivá, *Furrow*, 671

87. HE IMPOSED HIS HANDS ON THEM

87.1 Helping and caring for people as Christ himself would do.

The Gospel of the Mass[1] tells us how at sunset people began to bring many sick people to Christ for him to cure them. It is quite possible that it was a Sabbath day, because the Sabbath observance, so scrupulously enforced by the scribes and Pharisees, would have ended at sunset. There were very many sick people: Saint Mark says that *the whole city was gathered together about the door*.[2] Saint Luke leaves on record the striking detail that He cured them by laying his hands upon each one, *singulis manus imponens*. He looks carefully at them and gives each one his full attention, because for him each person is unique. Everybody is always well received by Jesus, and is treated by him with the incomparable dignity that the human person always deserves.

Commenting on this passage of the Gospel, Saint Ambrose says that *from the beginning of the Church Jesus already sought out the crowds. And why? Because ... to cure people there are no established times or places. The medicine has to be applied in all times and places*.[3] The Gospel shows us Christ's tireless activity. It teaches us how we in turn have to behave with those who are far from the faith, with all those souls who haven't yet come to

---

1. Luke 4:38-44
2. cf Mark 1:33
3. St Ambrose, *Treatise on Virginity*, 8, 10

Christ to be healed. *No son or daughter of Holy Church can lead a quiet life, without concern for the anonymous masses – a mob, a herd, a flock, as I once wrote. How many noble passions they have within their apparent listlessness! How much potential!*

We must serve all, laying our hands on each and every one, as Jesus did, 'singulis manus imponens', to bring them back to life, to enlighten their minds and strengthen their wills so that they can become useful![4]

To serve all means treating them as Christ would have done in our place, with the same esteem, with the same courtesy, each one individually, allowing for their particular circumstances, their manner of being, the state in which they find themselves, without applying the same formula to everyone. They are the people we meet in the course of our business, through local involvement, journeys or common interests. And others we will go to look for wherever they happen to be, in order to bring them to God, *as a doctor looks after a patient. Just one single soul saved through another's mediation can be the source of pardon for many sins.*[5]

Let us resolve now in our prayer to be as concerned for our neighbours' welfare as were those who crowded around the doorway bringing Jesus the sick people to be cured. Let us see now in his presence if we treat them with the same attention, *singulis manus imponens*, as he did.

87.2 Patience and constancy in apostolate.

To reach Christ we have to travel along a road, sometimes a long one, with patience and constancy. He is expecting us to bring our friends, our study companions,

---

4. J. Escrivá, *The Forge*, 901
5. St John Chrysostom, in *Catena Aurea*, vol. 5, p. 238

our workmates, our children, our brothers and sisters. We can help them all as Jesus did – one by one, making allowance for each individual's circumstances, age or state of health, always remembering that they have been ransomed at the infinite price of Christ's redemptive Blood. In accompanying them to Jesus we invariably encounter resistance, perhaps for a long time. This is simply a consequence of man's difficulty in following God's plans because of the effects of original sin, subsequently added to by one's own sins. On occasions this obstruction is attributable to ignorance, in which case it should give us cause to pray, to offer mortifications and hours of work or study, to strengthen our friendship perhaps, all in direct proportion to the opposition we meet. Thanks to our faith we are well able to understand those in such straits and excuse them with a big heart, but realizing very well that the objective is to get them to know and love Jesus Christ. This is the greatest good we can do them, the greatest of all favours and benefits they can receive.

In all apostolate it is necessary to have a *patient attitude*. Patience is not the same thing as resignation or carelessness, but an attribute of the cardinal virtue of fortitude. It presupposes a tenacious perseverance in looking for the desired results. It is often necessary to proceed little by little, along an inclined plane as it were, without ever getting discouraged by our friends' not seeming to be making any progress, or by their even appearing to be going backwards. God allows for these situations and gives us all the necessary graces; from the very moment in which we decide, before the Tabernacle, to lead them to him, he has already placed his hands on each of them. Right from the beginning, Christ blesses our apostolic desire to bring to him all those souls whom we encounter in our daily lives.

If people are slow to respond, we have to remember

the patience that God has had with us, how much He has pardoned us, and the innumerable times we have made him wait. What a lot of waiting our God has had to do! How long He has waited at the door of our soul! If Our Lord had deserted us when we didn't respond, when we didn't want to hear his call, just think how far away from him we would be now! Our effort is never sterile, because in the apostolate we are moved by the love of God. Some people reach him after only a few days' contact, others after many years; some do so at the first conversation, others after a long delay; some are able to run from the beginning, others are scarcely strong enough to take a short step. We have to take each person as he is, according to his own human and supernatural circumstances, without getting tired, without giving up. A doctor doesn't use the same prescription for everybody, nor a tailor the same measurements or the same fitting. *Be patient, therefore, brethren*, Saint James tells us, *until the coming of the Lord. Behold, the farmer waits for the precious fruit of the earth, being patient over it until it receives the early and the late rain. You also be patient. Establish your hearts, for the coming of the Lord is at hand.*[6]

We need to keep after our friends, relatives and colleagues with supernatural doggedness, not being over-cautious or 'prudent' in the wrong sense, and all with a great charity and understanding, because we seek only their good. If the enemies of God try so hard to separate men from him, why shouldn't we do as much, since we seek their good? You know, Lord, that we want only what is best for them! And that 'best' is you, who gives yourself to those who choose to accept you.

6. Jas 5:7-8

87.3 Spreading Christ's teaching everywhere.

That afternoon, many people were cured and received a word of encouragement, a gesture of understanding, from the Master: *Now when the sun was setting, all those who had any that were sick with various diseases brought them to him; and He laid his hands on every one of them and healed them.* How happy the sick people must have been; and how happy, too, the people who had brought them to Jesus! Apostolate calls for sacrifice, but it is at the same time an immensely joyful undertaking. What a wonderful thing it is to bring our friends to Jesus so that He can impose his hands on them and heal them!

Early the following morning Jesus withdrew to a secluded place, as He was wont to do. *And the people sought him and came to him, and would have kept him from leaving them; but He said to them, 'I must preach the good news of the kingdom of God to the other cities also; for I was sent for this purpose.' And he was preaching in the synagogues of Judaea.*

Today too we find many people who don't know Christ. God wishes to imbue us with a sense of urgency for overcoming all that ignorance and for spreading good doctrine everywhere, using all sorts of methods and initiatives. As Pope John Paul II reminds us: *This mission is not the exclusive preserve of the sacred ministers or religious, but ought to embrace the entire ambit of secular society, of the family and the school. Every Christian has to participate in the task of Christian formation, to feel the urgent need to evangelize – something, says Saint Paul, 'that gives me no ground for boasting. For necessity is laid upon me'.*[7] Only if we look to Christ, if we love him, will we overcome

---

7. John Paul II, *Homily in Granada*, 15 November 1982; cf *Christifideles laici*, 30 December 1988, 33

laziness and love of comfort, will we emerge from the ivory tower that each of us tends to build for himself, will we make many blind people see Christ, many deaf people hear him, and many cripples walk beside him. God needs our cooperation.

Let us look at Christ now in our prayer, and let us also contemplate the people around us. What have we done up to now to lead them to God? Let us look at our own family, our colleagues at work or our study companions, those who live beside us, the people with whom we share a common interest, and the people we meet when travelling. Isn't it true that we haven't made very good use of many of the opportunities we have had? Haven't we got tired? Could it not be said to us some day that we didn't speak to these neighbours of ours about Christ, when this was what they really needed?

A consideration that should help us to be unwavering in apostolate is the great multiplying effect of all the good or evil that happens in the world. The people who that evening felt Christ stop beside them and impose his divine hands upon them knew in their hearts that their life couldn't go on being the way it was before. They became new apostles and went around everywhere spreading the good news about *the Way, the Truth and the Life*, whom they themselves had met. They announced it in their families, in their villages – in short, wherever they went. That is what we too have to do.

TWENTY-SECOND WEEK: THURSDAY

88. THE POWER OF OBEDIENCE

88.1 Obedience strengthens, and is fruitful.

Jesus was standing by the lake of Gennesareth with a great crowd who wanted to hear the Word of God; nearby, Peter and his companions were washing their nets after a night's fruitless fishing. Jesus, looking for some way to gain an entry into Simon's soul, asks him for a loan of his boat and to pull back a few yards from the shore; and seated there, he taught the multitude from the boat.[1] Perhaps Peter continued getting the vessel ready for the next night's fishing while at the same time listening to what the Master had to say; they already knew each other from the time Peter's brother Andrew had introduced them,[2] but he was totally oblivious of Our Lord's ambitious plans for him.

When he had finished speaking Jesus said to Simon: *Put out into the deep and let down your nets for a catch.* Perhaps by then they had finished cleaning their nets of the weeds and slime of the lake. Peter's every instinct was to say no: they were tired, all the more so because of their failure to catch anything; their nets were clean and neatly stowed for the next night's work and the time of day was in any case totally unsuitable for fishing. But there was something about Jesus' glance, his imperious yet winning manner, the extraordinary fascination He always has for

---

1. Luke 5:1-11
2. cf John 1:41

noble souls, that caused Peter to put put out from shore once more. His only reason for launching the boats was Jesus' command: *Master*, he said, *we toiled all night and took nothing! But at your word I will let down the nets. In verbo autem tuo*, at your word. That is a wonderful reason.

Very often, when we are waylaid by the weariness that comes from not seeing any results in our interior life or in the apostolate, when we have the sensation of total failure and have lots of reasons for wanting to give up, we should hear the voice of Jesus saying to us: *Duc in altum, put out into the deep*, begin once more, start off all over again, in my Name.

The secret of all progress and of every victory is, in fact, to 'know how to begin again', to learn from a failure and to try once more.[3] Through these apparent failures Our Lord is perhaps trying to tell us that we ought to act for more supernatural reasons, out of obedience, for him and only for him. *The power of obedience! The lake of Gennesareth had denied its fishes to Peter's nets. A whole night in vain.*

Then, obedient, he lowered his net again to the water and they caught 'a huge number of fish.'

Believe me: the miracle is repeated each day.[4]

If ever we find ourselves tired out and unable to begin again, we should look to Jesus beside us in the boat, inviting us to put into practice – with interior docility – with real effort, the advice we receive in Confession or in spiritual direction, and we will find the strength to go on. In this context Saint Teresa says: *I often thought my constitution would never endure the work I had to do, (but) the Lord said to me: 'Daughter, obedience gives strength'.*[5]

---

3. G. Chevrot, *Simon Peter*, p.16
4. J. Escrivá, *The Way*, 629
5. St Teresa, *Foundations*, Prologue, 2

88.2 Obedience is essential in order to follow Christ closely.

Peter put out onto the lake with Jesus in his boat and quickly discovered that the nets were filling with fish, so many in fact that they were in danger of breaking. *They beckoned to their partners in the other boat to come and help them. And they came and filled both the boats, so that they began to sink.* There was fish for everybody; obedience is always rewarded bountifully by God.

This passage of the Gospel is full of lessons for us: *at night*, in Christ's absence, their work had been in vain. The same occurs to those people who try to promote apostolic works without counting on God. If they insist on being guided by their own experience and by mere human factors, they end up in the greatest darkness. *You insist on trying to walk on your own, doing your own will, guided solely by your own judgement. And you can see for yourself that the fruit of this is 'fruitlessness'.*

My child, if you don't give up your own judgement, if you are proud, if you devote yourself to 'your' apostolate, you will work all night – your whole life will be one long night – and at the end of it all the dawn will find you with your nets empty.[6]

Peter showed his humility by listening to someone who wasn't a fisherman and so could be supposed to know nothing about the work in which he, Simon, had acquired so much experience and so much knowledge. Yet he trusts Our Lord; he has more confidence in Jesus' word than in his own years of toil. In this we can also see that Our Lord had already won him over and that very little more was needed to get him to leave everything for Jesus' sake.

Peter's trusting response to Jesus' words were the

---

6. J. Escrivá, *The Forge*, 574

final touches in his initiation. By eliciting from him this act of obedience and total confidence Our Lord had prepared the ground for his vocation.

Above and beyond any considerations of convenience or efficiency, the principal reason why obedience is so essential for the disciple of Christ is that it forms part of the mystery of Redemption: Christ *revealed to us his mystery; by his obedience he brought about our redemption.*[7] And so, anyone who wishes to follow the Master's footsteps cannot place any limits to his obedience. Jesus taught us to obey in easy things and in heroic things, because *He obeyed in things which were very weighty and difficult: unto death on the Cross.*[8]

Obedience causes us to want to identify our will in everything with the Will of God. This Will is manifested through our parents, our superiors and the normal duties of family, social and professional life. In a special way, God's Will for our soul is revealed to us in spiritual direction.

God expects of us, therefore, an upright conduct, which is characterised at every moment by the refined and cheerful manner in which we are subject, for his sake, to all forms of lawful authority, and in the first place to the Roman Pontiff and the Church's Magisterium.

If we stay with Christ He always fills our nets. In his presence, even what appears to be fruitless and pointless becomes effective and fruitful. *Obedience makes our actions and sufferings meritorious in such a way that, no matter how pointless they may seem, they in fact can be extremely fruitful. One of the wonderful things Our Lord has done is to have made the most useless things, like pain,*

---

7. Second Vatican Council, *Lumen gentium*, 3
8. St Thomas, *Commentary on Hebrews*, 5, 8, 2

meaningful; by his obedience and his love He has made it glorious.[9]

88.3 We mustn't resist God's Will.

Peter is dumbfounded at the catch they have just landed. In this miracle Our Lord manifests himself in a special way to Peter in particular. Peter looked at Jesus and then threw himself at his feet saying: *Depart from me, for I am a sinful man*. He realized how insignificant he was in comparison with Christ's supreme majesty. Then Jesus said to Simon: *Do not be afraid; henceforth you will be catching men*. When Peter and his fishing-companions *had brought their boats to land, they left everything and followed him*.

Jesus began by asking Peter for a loan of his boat and ended up with his life. Peter was destined to have an indelible effect on all those souls that Christ himself was to place in his care. He began by obeying in small things and Our Lord showed him the wonderful plans which He had prepared from all eternity for him, the poor fisherman of Galilee. Peter never suspected the transcendence and the value of his life. Thousands and thousands of people have enkindled their faith in the faith of those men who that day followed Jesus, and especially in that of Peter, who was to be the *rock*, the immovable foundation of the Church.

Nor can we foresee all the consequences of our following Christ faithfully. He continually asks us for a greater response, for more docility and more obedience to the things He gradually shows us. If we are faithful, some day He will let us see the full importance of having followed him with deeds. *Among those around you – apostolic soul – you are the stone fallen into the lake. With your*

---

9. R. Garrigou-Lagrange, *The Three Ages of the Interior Life*, II, p.683

*word and your example you produce a first circle ... and it
another ... and another, and another ... Wider each time
...*

*Now do you understand the greatness of your mis-
sion?*[10]

Let us not try to restrict God, as Peter didn't. *If you
are one of those who launch out into the deep, set the course
straight and firm ... If you give yourself to God give yourself
the way the saints did. Let no one and nothing occupy your
attention and slow you down: you belong to God. If you give
yourself, give yourself for eternity. Let neither the roaring
waves nor the treacherous undercurrent shake the concrete
solidity of your foundations. God depends on you: He leans
on you. Put all your energy into it and row against the
current ... 'Duc in altum'. Launch out into the deep waters
with the daring of those others who loved Christ.*[11]

Our Mother the Virgin Mary, *Stella Maris, Star of the
Sea*, will teach us to be generous with God when he asks
us for a loan of a boat and when he wants us to give him
our entire life. We shouldn't ask for any special conditions
in order to follow him.

---

10. J. Escrivá, *The Way*, 831
11. J. Urteaga, *Man the Saint*, pp. 130-131

89. FRIENDS OF THE BRIDEGROOM

89.1 Our Lord regards us as his intimate friends.

After the banquet which Matthew offered Our Lord and his friends on the occasion of his calling, some of the Jews came to Jesus and asked him why his disciples did not fast as the Pharisees and John's disciples did. And Jesus answered them: *Can you make wedding guests fast while the bridegroom is with them?* In an explicit reference to the death He was to suffer, He tells them that *the days will come when the bridegroom is taken away from them, and then they will fast in those days.*[1]

Among the Jews the bridegroom would be accompanied by some young men of his own age, his friends, like a guard of honour. They were called *the friends of the bridegroom,*[2] and their mission was to honour the person getting married, to join in his rejoicing, to take part in a special way in the celebrations that were held to mark the wedding. The wedding imagery appears frequently in Sacred Scripture to express the relationship between God and his people.[3] The New Covenant of the Messiah with his new people, the Church, is also described using this same imagery: John the Baptist referred to Christ as the Bridegroom, and to himself as *the friend of the bridegroom.*[4]

Jesus describes his followers as his intimate friends,

---

1. Luke 5:33-39
2. cf 1 Mac 9:39
3. cf Ex 34:16; Is 54:5; Jer 2:2; Hos 2:18ff
4. John 3:29

the friends of the bridegroom. We have been invited to participate more intimately in the joy of the wedding banquet, which is a figure of the boundless happiness of the Kingdom of Heaven. On many occasions Our Lord honoured his followers by describing them as his *friends*. One day the Master, stretching out his hand over his disciples, pronounced these consoling words: *Behold my mother and my brethren.*[5] And he taught us that those who believe and follow him with deeds – *whoever does the will of my Father in heaven* – occupy in his heart a place of privilege and are united to him with bonds that are stronger than those of blood. In the discourse at the Last Supper he tells them, in tones of endearing simplicity and sincerity: *As the Father has loved me, so have I loved you ... I have called you friends, for all that I have heard from my Father I have made known to you.*[6]

Our Lord offers himself as an example of genuine and unreserved friendship, attracting everybody with great tenderness and affection. As Saint Bernard puts it so well, *at that moment He allowed all the tenderness of his heart to escape; He opened his soul completely and from it there arose a most fragrant perfume, the perfume of a beautiful soul, of a generous and noble heart.*[7] And he became a faithful and self-effacing friend to all. From him there came that power of attraction that Saint Jerome compared to that of a powerful magnet.[8]

Jesus calls us his friends. He teaches us to receive everybody, to constantly extend and develop our capacity to make friends. We learn to do this only if we confidently open our heart to him in prayerful intimacy. *For this world*

---

5. cf Matt 12:49-50
6. John 15:9, 15
7. St Bernard, *Sermon on the Canticle of Canticles*, 31, 7
8. cf St Jerome, *Commentary on St Matthew's Gospel*, 9, 9

*of ours to set its course in a Christian direction – which is
the only one worth while – we have to exercise a loyal
friendship with all men, based on a prior loyal friendship
with God.*[9]

89.2 We learn from Jesus to have many friends. As Christians we are always open to others.

Jesus had friends among people of all social backgrounds and all walks of life, of all ages and circumstances, from people of high social standing, like Nicodemus or Joseph of Arimathea, to beggars like Bartimaeus. In most of the towns and villages the Master met people who loved him and who felt their friendship reciprocated by him, friends whom the Gospel doesn't always mention by name but whose existence can be deduced. In Bethany we find the sisters of Lazarus, whose trusting and at the same time painful message to Jesus is evidence of the strong bond of friendship that they had with him: *Lord, he whom you love is ill.*[10] *Now Jesus loved Martha and her sister and Lazarus*. When the Master reached Bethany, Lazarus had already died. And, to everybody's surprise, *Jesus wept. So the Jews said, 'See how he loved him!'*[11] Jesus weeps for his friend! He is not impervious to the sorrow of his close friends, nor to the emotional upheaval of someone confronted with the death of a dearly beloved relative. Jesus weeps silently, shedding manly tears, and the bystanders are astounded.

We should never tire of considering how much Our Lord loves us: *Jesus is your friend. The Friend. With a human heart, like yours. With loving eyes that wept for Lazarus.*

---

9. J. Escrivá, *The Forge*, 943
10. John 11:3
11. John 11:35-36

And he loves you as much as he loved Lazarus.[12]

Jesus liked to talk with those people who came to see him or who met him along the way. He made use of those conversations, which often started with something trivial, in order to enter fully into their souls and fill them with love. Anything and everything would be sufficient for his purpose in order to make friends and reveal to them the divine message he had brought to earth. We too ought not to forget that *friendship and charity are one and the same thing. They are a divine light which spreads warmth.*[13]

We can learn from Christ to have many friends, taking advantage of every opportunity of simple proximity, of work, study, chance encounters, pre-planned meetings ... The Christian is always open to others. With a friend one shares the best things one has; in our case, we have nothing to compare with the love we have for Christ, strengthened over the years through so many hours of prayer – think of all the things we have said to him! – and so much time spent beside the Tabernacle. Apostolic zeal and the good social graces we try to cultivate should help us find points of contact and understanding with our companions, our clients, with all sorts of people, as well as enabling us to overlook and forget the things that divide. We learn to forgo gracefully our own point of view in unimportant differences of opinion that could otherwise make mutual trust and understanding difficult.

If we regard ourselves as intimate friends of Jesus, it's logical that we would want to know all about friendship and be able, like him, to enter deeply into men's souls. Do we manage to communicate to others the love of Christ which we carry in our hearts?

12. J. Escrivá, *The Way*, 422
13. J. Escrivá, *The Forge*, 565

89.3 Charity perfects and strengthens friendship.

A faithful friend is a sturdy shelter; he that has found one has found a treasure. There is nothing so precious as a faithful friend, and no scales can measure his excellence.[14] So speaks Sacred Scripture about the value of friendship, at the same time as it teaches us how we have to seek it out, to use the means to find it. And once found, we have to cultivate it beyond the barrier of time or of distance, of all that tends to separate, of different tastes, opinions or interests.

Friendship requires us to help our friends. *If you discover some defect in your friend, correct him privately ... Corrections do a lot of good and are more valuable than a dumb friendship,*[15] which stands silently by, watching the friend drown. Friendship has to be persevering: *We shouldn't change our friends the way children do, who allow themselves to be tossed about by the fickle motions of sentimentality.*[16] *I will not be ashamed to protect a friend.*[17] *Don't abandon him in his hour of need, don't forget him, don't deny him your affection, because friendship is the mainstay of life. Let us carry one another's burdens, as the Apostle tells us. If a man's prosperity benefits all his friends, why shouldn't he count on their help in moments of adversity? Let us help our friend with our counsels, let us unite our efforts to his, let us share his afflictions.*

And when the occasion arises, let us put up with great sacrifices out of loyalty to our friend. We may perhaps have to face antagonisms to defend the cause of an innocent friend, and be prepared to receive insults when we try to reply and rebut those who attack and accuse him ... In

---

14. Sir 6:14-17
15. St Ambrose, *On the duties of ministers*, III, 125
16. *ibid*
17. Sir 22:25

adversity true friendship is tested, because in prosperity everybody appears faithful.[18]

Supernatural charity strengthens and enriches friendship. The love of Christ makes us more humane; it gives us a greater capacity to understand and it makes us more open to everybody. In Christ, the best of all friends, we learn to strengthen a relationship that perhaps was beginning to weaken, to remove some obstacle, to overcome the tendency to slide into a state of cosy isolation. When we are close to Jesus we learn to be better, to bring the people around us to holiness, because we can offer them our faith in him. Just think how many people down the centuries have journeyed along the path of friendship in Our Lord's company!

Look upon Christ. You know well that He counts you among his close friends. We are *the friends of the bridegroom*, and he calls us to share his favour and his possessions. The words of the Book of Sirach about friendship – *there is nothing so precious as a faithful friend*[19] – acquire their full meaning when applied to Christ: He showed his faithfulness by giving his life for each of us. Let us learn from him to be friends to our friends, and let us not cease to give them the best thing we have – our love for Jesus.

---

18. St Ambrose, *On the duties of ministers*, III, 126-127
19. Sir 6:14

90. OUR LADY'S FAITH

90.1 Saturday is traditionally dedicated to honouring our Lady; a weekly opportunity to meditate on her virtues.

For hundreds of years Christians have given special attention to Mary on Saturdays. Throughout history, and in our own times as well, theologians and ecclesiastical writers have explained some of the reasons that make this devotion particularly appropriate. Thus, Saint Peter Damascene writes that Saturdays commemorate the completion of God's work of creation. God rested on the seventh day, and Mary is the one in whom, *through the mystery of the Incarnation, God made for himself a holy resting-place.*[1]

Saturday, the Sabbath of the Old Law, is also an anticipation of the Lord's Day, a symbol and sign of heaven. Christ, risen from the dead, is the gateway to eternal life in heaven; and the Blessed Virgin is our way to Jesus, just as she was his way for coming into the world.[2]

Saint Thomas, also, points out that Saturday is dedicated to Mary because *on that day she kept faith in the mystery of Christ after his death.*[3] In any case, we Christians need a special day to honour our Lady and show her our love in a special way.

And so, since ancient times, special Marian devotions

---

1. St Peter Damian, *Opusculum 33, De Bono Suffragorum*, PL 145, 566
2. cf G. Roschini, *The Mother of God*, Madrid
3. St Thomas Aquinas, *On the Commandments*

have been held on Saturdays in churches, chapels and shrines throughout the world. Many Christians make a special effort to honour the Blessed Virgin in some special manner on this day. Some choose one favourite aspiration to repeat often throughout the day. Others pay a visit to a sick person, or to a poor family, or to someone who is lonely or suffering, in honour of our Lady. Still others visit a church or shrine dedicated in her honour, or simply make a special effort to be attentive in reciting the Rosary, the Angelus, or the *Hail, Holy Queen*.

There are many good Marian devotions. There is no need to practise every single one of them. But *anyone who doesn't live some of them, who doesn't express his love for Mary in some way, does not possess the fullness of the faith.*

Those who think that devotions to our Lady are a thing of the past seem to have lost sight of the deep Christian meaning they contain. They seem to have forgotten the source from which they spring – faith in God the Father's saving will, love for God the Son, who really became man and was born of a woman, and trust in God the Holy Spirit, who sanctifies us with his grace.[4]

If you look for Mary, you will necessarily find Jesus; and you will learn, in greater and greater depth, what there is in the Heart of God.[5] Let us consider how our own lives reflect this ancient Christian practice of special devotion to our Lady on Saturdays.

90.2 The obedience of faith.

This Saturday perhaps we can consider our Lady's great faith, a virtue in which she excels every other creature. Even before the angel announced to her that

---

4. J. Escrivá, *Christ is passing by*, 142
5. J. Escrivá, *The Forge*, 661

she was to be the Mother of God, Mary would meditate on the Scriptures; she would discover their deepest meaning as no one had ever done before. Her understanding, free from the effects of sin, was enlightened by faith and by the fullness of God's grace. In this light, and with the help of the gifts of the Holy Spirit, our Lady was able to fathom the depths of the Messianic prophecies. She longed for the Saviour's coming, and her insistent prayer was an echo of the constant petition of all the Patriarchs and the people of Israel throughout its history. But her prayer was more pleasing to God than theirs, for it came from a heart free from sin and full of faith and hope. With her earnest petition Mary gave glory to God more fully than did all the rest of creation.

The Blessed Trinity looked upon Mary with a special fondness. When the fullness of time came, with the angels of heaven looking on, God's messenger salutes her: *Hail, full of grace, the Lord is with you.*[6] Saint Luke recounts that Mary, when she heard the angelic greeting, *was greatly troubled at the saying, and considered in her mind what sort of greeting this might be.*[7]

Mary did not resist or place any limitations on the fulfilment of God's Will. She left herself totally open to whatever God might want from her. God had prepared the Blessed Virgin for her special mission, filling her with his grace. Now, with the revelation of her special calling, the seed sown by God on such good ground began to bear fruit through Mary's acquiescence: *fiat mihi secundum verbum tuum.*

Indeed, at the Annunciation Mary entrusted herself to God completely, with 'full submission of intellect and will'

---

6. Luke 1:28
7. Luke 1:29

(Dei Verbum, 5) *manifesting 'the obedience of faith' to him who spoke to her through his messenger. She responded, therefore, with all her human and feminine 'I', and this response of faith included both perfect cooperation with 'the grace of God that precedes and assists', and perfect openness to the action of the Holy Spirit, who 'constantly brings faith to completion by his gifts.*[8] The Annunciation brought with it the fulfilment of all that had been in our Lady's heart. *But it is also the point of departure from which her whole 'journey towards God' begins, her whole pilgrimage of faith.*[9]

The most immediate consequence of our Lady's faith is her full obedience to God's plan. And this consideration can help us to examine ourselves, to see whether our faith leads us to imitate her obedience – whether we are truly willing to fulfil God's Will in everything, unconditionally … desiring whatever God wills, whenever He wills it, and in whatever way He wills it.

We can especially ask ourselves how we accept the ordinary difficulties of our day – sickness, which we should love if it comes; suffering and sorrow; an unforeseen change in our plans; the failure of some project; in a word, anything that interferes with our own desires. Let us consider whether both success and failure, enjoyment as well as suffering, lead us to grow in holiness, instead of putting a distance between ourselves and our Lord.

90.3 Mary's life of faith.

Our Lady's life was not easy. She had to contend with trials and difficulties; but her faith overcame all obstacles and gained in strength with each victory. *Mary teaches us*

---

8. John Paul II, Encyclical, *Redemptoris Mater*, 13
9. *ibid*, 14

as a mother does, and, being a mother, she does so quietly. We need to have a sensitivity of soul, a touch of refinement, in order to understand what she is showing us by what she does more than by what she promises.

She teaches us to have faith. 'Blessed art thou for thy believing,' were the words of greeting uttered by her cousin Elizabeth when our Lady went up into the hill-country to visit her. Mary's act of faith had been a wonderful one: 'Behold the handmaid of the Lord; be it done unto me according to thy word.' When her Son was born she contemplated the greatness of God on earth: a choir of angels was present, and not only the shepherds, but also important men of this world came to adore the Child. Afterwards, however, the Holy Family had to flee to Egypt in order to escape Herod's murderous intent. Then, silence: thirty long years of simple, ordinary life, just like that of any other home in a small village in Galilee.[10]

Mary's faith shines silently in the years of her life in Nazareth. The Son born to her is a child who grows and develops like any other human being. He learns to walk, to talk, to work. Yet she knows that this child is the Son of God, the long-awaited Messiah. She knows that the helpless one in her arms is the Almighty; that those first halting words are pronounced by him who is infinite Wisdom; and that his childish games, and later on, his work as a boy and a young man, are the actions of the Creator of heaven and earth.

The Blessed Virgin looked at her son with love as her child and with reverence as her God. Her faith shone in the everyday events of her life. Her life of prayer grew in intensity through intimacy with Jesus; and thus she was able to give a supernatural meaning to all the events of her

---

10. J. Escrivá, *Friends of God*, 284

life, and sanctify *the ordinary everyday things – what some people wrongly regard as unimportant or insignificant: everyday work, looking after those closest to you, visits to friends and relatives.*[11]

Mary's faith reached its crown *iuxta crucem Iesu* – at the foot of the Cross. There, silently, she fulfilled God's will with the fact of her presence, and manifested the brightness and splendour and steadfastness of the faith in her heart.[12]

All of our Lady's life was lived in the obedience of faith. When we contemplate her, we can understand how *to believe means 'to abandon oneself' to the truth of the word of the living God, knowing and humbly recognizing 'how unsearchable are his judgements and how inscrutable his ways.' Mary, who by the eternal Will of the Most High stands, one may say, at the very centre of those 'inscrutable ways' and 'unsearchable judgements' of God, conforming herself to them in the dim light of faith, accepting fully and with a ready heart everything that is decreed in the divine plan.*[13]

We lack faith. The day we practise this virtue, trusting in God and in his Mother, we will be daring and loyal. God, who is the same God as ever, will work miracles through our hands.

Grant me, dear Jesus, the faith I truly desire. My Mother, sweet Lady, Mary most holy, make me really believe,[14] make me look at all the events of my life with a serene, unshakable, and operative faith.

---

11. J. Escrivá, *Christ is passing by*, 148
12. cf Second Vatican Council, *Lumen gentium*, 58
13. John Paul II, Encyclical, *Redemptoris Mater*, 14
14. J. Escrivá, *The Forge*, 235

Twenty-third Sunday: Year A

91. FAMILY PRAYER

91.1 Family prayer is very pleasing to our Lord.

Jesus frequently teaches us that salvation and the consequent union with God is, ultimately, a personal thing: nobody can take our place in this personal dealing with God. But He also desires that we support each other and that we help each other on our way towards our final goal. This union so pleasing to the Lord should be shown especially amongst those who have spiritual bonds with one another or are of the same family. This union, one that demands our living so many virtues, is so much desired by the Lord that He has promised as a special gift, to give us more easily what we ask for with unity of intention. Thus we read in the Gospel of the Mass: *I say to you further, that if two of you shall agree on earth about anything at all for which they ask, it shall be done for them by my Father in heaven. For where two or three are gathered together for my sake, there am I in the midst of them.*[1]

Prayer in common[2] has been practised in the Church from time immemorial. It is not opposed to nor can it be substituted for by private prayer which unites the Christian in an intimate way to Christ. Family prayer is in a special way very pleasing to Our Lord; it is one of the treasures we have received from previous generations so that we can get abundant fruit from it and pass it on to generations to come. *They have excellent means in the few, short daily*

---

1. Matt 18:19-20
2. cf Acts 12:5

religious practices that have always been lived in Christian families, and which I think are marvellous: grace at meals, morning and night prayers, the family rosary ... Customs vary from place to place, but I think one should always encourage some acts of piety in which the family can join together in a simple and natural fashion.

This is the way to ensure that God is not regarded as a stranger whom we go to visit in church once a week on Sunday. He will be seen and treated as He really is, not only in church, but also at home, because Our Lord has told us that 'Where two or three are gathered together in my name, I am there in the midst of them' (Matt 18:20).[3]

This prayer – John Paul II teaches, commenting on this passage of the Gospel *– has for its own object family life itself ... : Joys and sorrows, hopes and disappointments, births and birthday celebrations, wedding anniversaries of parents, departures, separations and homecomings, important and far-reaching decisions, the death of those who are dear to us, etc. – all of these mark occasions for God's loving intervention in the family's history. They should be seen as suitable moments for thanksgiving, for petition, for trusting abandonment of the family into the hands of their common Father in heaven. The dignity and responsibility of the Christian family as the domestic Church can be achieved only with God's unceasing aid, which will surely be granted if it is humbly and trustingly petitioned for in prayer.*[4]

Family prayer communicates a special fortitude to the whole family. The first and principal help we give to parents, to children, to brothers and sisters, is to pray with them and for them. Prayer fosters the supernatural vision that makes it possible for us to understand what is

---

3. *Conversations with Monsignor Escrivá*, 103
4. John Paul II, Apostolic Exhortation, *Familiaris Consortio*, 22 November 1981, 59

happening around us and in the family, and teaches us to
see that nothing is foreign to the plans of God: He always
shows himself to us as a father, and tells us that the family
is more his than ours. Prayer also enlightens us in those
events that without our being close to him would be
incomprehensible: the death of a loved one, the birth of a
handicapped child, sickness, economic difficulties ... With
Our Lord, we love his holy Will, and families instead of
disintegrating are united more strongly amongst themselves and with God.

91.2 Acts of piety in the home.

*But if anyone does not take care of his own, and espe-
cially of his household, he has denied the faith and is worse
than an unbeliever.*[5] Saint Paul wrote to Timothy, reminding us of the obligation we all have concerning those the
Lord has placed under our care. One of the principal obligations that parents have with respect to their children –
as also, at times, do older brothers and sisters with
younger brothers and sisters – is that of teaching them
how to deal with God. This task is so important, that it can
be considered essential. As the years go by, these first
seeds sown continue to bear fruit, perhaps even until the
moment of death. For many, this has been the spiritual
help that has meant most to them.

*Experience shows in all Christian environments what
good effects come from this natural and supernatural introduction to the life of piety given in the loving atmosphere of
the home. Children learn to place God first and foremost in
their affections. They learn to see God as their Father and
Mary as their Mother, and learn to pray by following their
parents' example. In this way one can easily see what a*

---

5. 1 Tim 5:8

*wonderful apostolate parents are called to, and how it is
their duty to live a fully Christian life of prayer, so that they
can communicate their love of God to their children. This is
something more than merely teaching them.*[6]

The Christian family has always known how to pass
on from parents to children simple and brief prayers, easy
to understand, that make up the seeds of piety: aspirations to Jesus, to our Mother Mary, to Saint Joseph, to the
Guardian Angels ... perennial prayers, repeated
thousands of times in each generation. Children quickly
learn for themselves these teachings and prayers that are
so obviously a part of their parents' lives. When they are a
little older, they will have assimilated and incorporated
into their lives the meaning of saying grace before and
after meals, of offering to Our Lady something that is
somehow difficult ... greeting with a kiss or with a glance
the pictures of Our Mother, remembering one's Guardian
Angel on entering or leaving the house ...

How many young people, now men and women,
warmly remember the simple and exact explanation that
their mother or an older brother or sister gave them of the
real presence of Christ in the tabernacle, or the first time
they saw their mother ask for some urgent necessity, or
their father make a truly reverent genuflection! To pray as
a member of a family in which Christ is present should be
something natural, because He is one more in the home,
and one who should be loved above all things.

Precisely when the atmosphere is less favourable for
prayer and piety do we have to conserve as an inestimable
treasure those practices of piety that strengthen this
human love and bring us closer to our Father God.

---

6. *Conversations with Monsignor Escrivá*, 103

91.3 A family that prays together, stays together: the Rosary.

If we love one another, God abides in us[7] sings the liturgy of Maundy Thursday. When Christians meet to pray, there amongst us one finds Christ, who happily listens to this prayer founded in unity. This is what the apostles did too: *All these with one mind continued steadfastly in prayer with the women and Mary, the Mother of Jesus ...* [8] This was Christ's new family.

The family prayer 'par excellence' is the Holy Rosary. *The Christian family* – teaches Pope John Paul II – *finds and consolidates its identity in prayer. Make the daily effort to find a time to pray together, to talk with Our Lord and listen to his voice. How beautiful it is when the family prays in the evening, even though it be only a part of the Rosary.*

The family that prays together stays together; a family that prays is a family that is saved.

Act in such a way that your homes may be places of Christian faith and virtue through your praying together.[9]

When beginning to say the Rosary in the home, perhaps the parents will start out alone, but afterwards one of the children will join them, and the grandmother ... At times it can be prayed during a journey in the car or, even better, at a time previously agreed; perhaps in some countries it might be suitable before dinner, or right after it ... The Rosary and the Angelus, the Pope taught on another occasion, *should be for every Christian and even more so for Christian families, a spiritual oasis during the day from which to get courage and confidence.*[10] *How I wish that the beautiful custom of praying the family Rosary*

---

7. 1 John 4:12
8. Acts 1:14
9. John Paul II, *Address to families*, 24 March 1984
10. *idem*, Angelus in Otranto, 5 October 1980

would begin again.[11]

The Church has wanted to give many graces and indulgences when the family Rosary is prayed. Let us do what is necessary to encourage this prayer which is so pleasing to Our Lord and to his Most Holy Mother, and that is considered as *a great public and universal prayer in the face of the ordinary and extraordinary needs of the Church, of nations, and of the entire world.*[12] This is a good support upon which family unity can be based, and the best help for it to face up to its needs.

---

11. *idem, Homily,* 12 October 1980
12. John XXIII, *Address,* 29 September 1961

TWENTY-THIRD SUNDAY: YEAR B

92. LISTENING TO GOD AND SPEAKING TO HIM

92.1 The miraculous cure of a deaf mute.

The liturgy of this Sunday's Mass is a call to hope and absolute confidence in the Lord. In a moment of darkness the prophet Isaiah lifts up his voice to comfort the Chosen People who live in exile.[1] He announces the happy return to their homeland: *Say to those whose hearts are frightened: Be strong, fear not! Here is your God; He comes with vindication; with divine recompense He comes to save you.* And the prophet predicts wonders which will have their complete fulfilment with the coming of the Messiah: *Then will the eyes of the blind be opened, the ear of the deaf be unstopped; then will the lame leap like a stag, then the tongue of the dumb will sing. Streams will burst forth in the desert, and rivers in the dry land. The burning sands will become pools, and the thirsty ground springs of water.* With Christ, all mankind is healed, and the inexhaustible springs of grace convert the world into a new creation. The Lord has transformed everything, and especially men's souls.

The Gospel of the Mass narrates the cure of a deaf-mute.[2] The Lord brought him apart, placed his fingers in his ears and touched his tongue with spittle. Afterwards, Jesus raised his eyes to heaven *and said to him, 'Ephpheta!'* (*that is, 'Be opened!'*) *At once the man's ears*

---

1. Is 35:4-7
2. Mark 7:31-37

were opened; he was freed from the impediment, and began to speak plainly.

The fingers can signify a powerful divine action,[3] and saliva is thought to have a certain ability to heal wounds. Although it is the words of Christ that work the cure, He wished, as on other occasions, to use visible, material objects which in some way were intended to express the more profound action the sacraments were later going to work in souls.[4] Already in the first centuries, and throughout many generations,[5] the Church used these same gestures of the Lord at the moment of Baptism, while she prayed over the one to be baptized: *May the Lord Jesus, who made the deaf hear and the dumb speak, grant that at the proper time you may hear his Word and proclaim the Faith.*[6]

We can see in this cure which our Lord performs an image of his acting in souls: He frees man from sin, He opens his ears to hear the Word of God and loosens his tongue to praise and proclaim the marvellous works of God. At the moment of Baptism, the Holy Spirit, *digitus paternae dexterae*,[7] the finger of the right hand of God the Father, as the liturgy proclaims, freed our hearing to listen to the Word of God, and unloosed our tongue in order to announce it throughout the world; and this is continued during our whole life. Saint Augustine, in commenting on this passage of the Gospel, says that the tongue of someone united to God *will speak of the Good, will bring to agreement those who are divided, will console those who weep. God will be praised, Christ will be announced.*[8] These

---

3. cf Ex 8:19; Cant 8:4; Luke 11:20
4. cf M. Schmaus, *Dogmatic Theology*, VI, *The Sacraments*
5. cf A. G. Martimort, *The Church at Prayer*, Barcelona
6. cf *Ritual of Baptism*, Baptism of infants
7. cf Hymn, *Veni Creator*
8. St Augustine, *Sermon 311*, 11

things we will do if we have our hearing attentive to the continuous inspirations of the Holy Spirit and if we have our tongue ready to speak of God, uninhibited by human respect.

92.2 We should not be deaf in the presence of religious ignorance.

There is a deafness of soul which is worse than that of the body, since no one is more deaf than he who does not want to hear. There are many who have their ears closed to the Word of God, and many, too, who become more and more insensitive to the innumerable invitations of grace. An apostolate which is patient, tenacious, full of understanding, accompanied by prayer, will make many of our friends hear the voice of God and be themselves converted into new apostles who will speak of him everywhere. This is one of the missions which we receive in Baptism.[9]

We Christians cannot remain dumb when we must speak of God and transmit his message openly: parents to their children, teaching them their prayers and the basics of their faith from their infancy; a friend to his friend, when the opportune moment presents itself, and even making it arise if necessary; an office worker to his colleagues, offering them, by his word and example, a cheerful model to imitate; the student at the university, among those with whom he spends so many hours. We cannot remain silent during the countless opportunities the Lord places before us, in which we can show to everyone the path of sanctity in the middle of the world. There are even moments in which it would be unnatural for a good Christian not to say something supernatural: the death of a

---

9. cf Second Vatican Council, *Lumen gentium*, 33

loved one, a visit to a sick person (what broad horizons can be opened to those who suffer, if we ask them to offer their discomfort for some intention, for the Church or the Pope!), the conversation that touches upon some slanderous story in the news ... what opportunities to give good doctrine! People expect it of us and we cannot defraud them by remaining silent.

There are many reasons to speak of the beauty of our Faith, of the incomparable joy of having Christ. And, among others, there is the responsibility given in Baptism not to let anyone lose the Faith through the avalanche of ideas and doctrinal errors that leaves many defenceless. *The enemies of God and of his Church, manipulated by the devil's unremitting hatred, are relentless in their activities and organization. With 'exemplary' constancy they prepare their cadres, run their schools, appoint leaders and deploy agitators. In an undercover way – but very effectively – they spread their ideas and sow, in homes and places of work, a seed that is deliberately destructive of religion. What is there that we Christians should not be ready to do in order to serve our God, of course always with the truth?*[10] Are we perhaps content to remain passive? The mission we received on the day of our Baptism must be put into practice all our life, in all circumstances.

92.3 Speak with clarity and simplicity; this holds true, too, in spiritual direction.

As announced by the prophet Isaiah in the *First Reading*, the moment has arrived in which *the eyes of the blind will be opened, the ears of the deaf be unstopped; the lame will leap like the stag, the tongue of the dumb will sing* ... These wonders are accomplished in our time in a way

---

10. J. Escrivá, *The Forge*, 466

immensely more profound than that envisioned by the prophet; they take place in the soul docile to the Holy Spirit, who has been sent by the Lord. We ask for the Faith and for daring to announce clearly and openly the *magnalia Dei*,[11] the marvellous works of God we see around us, just as the Apostles did after Pentecost. Saint Augustine advises us: *If you love God, draw to you all those who gather around or live in your house, so that all will come to love him. If you love the Body of Christ, which is the unity of the Church, impel everyone to rejoice in God and tell them with David: 'Magnify with me the Lord, and let us together praise his holy name' (Prov 21:28); and in this do not be calculating or stingy, but rather win for the Lord all those you can by whatever means possible, according to your abilities: exhorting them, bearing them up, pleading with them, arguing with them and giving them the reasons for the things of faith, with all gentleness and tact.*[12] May we not remain silent when God wants to say so much through our words.

Saint Mark has preserved the Aramaic word used by our Lord, *'Ephpheta' - be opened*. Many times has the Holy Spirit made us aware, in different ways, of this imperative counsel in the depths of our soul. Our mouth has had to be opened and our tongue loosed in order to speak about the state of our own soul with clarity, being very sincere, explaining with simplicity what has occurred in our lives, our desires for holiness and the temptations of the enemy, our little victories and our setbacks, if there have been any. Our hearing has had to be cleared in order that we may be attentive to the many lessons and suggestions granted to us by the Master in spiritual direction.[13]

---

11. cf Acts 2:1
12. St Augustine, *Commentary on the Psalms*, 33:6-7
13. cf R. Garrigou-Lagrange, *The Three Ages of the Interior Life*, I, p. 295 etc

The difficult battle, if it is fought by one who is armed with sincerity and docility, will always be won; engaged in by someone equipped with deceit, in isolation, and with pride in his own opinion, it will invariably be lost. It is the Lord who cures and who chooses the means He will use – means that will always be disproportionate. Saint Vincent Ferrer affirmed that God *never gives his grace to one who, having available to him someone capable of instructing and directing him, chooses to despise this most efficacious means of sanctification, believing that he is sufficient unto himself and that by his efforts alone he can seek and find what is necessary for salvation ... Another who, having a director, elects to obey him without reserve and in everything, will arrive more easily than he would do if alone, although he might well possess a keen intelligence and have at hand knowledgeable books on spiritual matters ...* [14]

In the Most Blessed Virgin we find the perfect model of one who listens with attentive ear to what God is asking, in order to put it into practice from a standpoint of complete availability. *Indeed, at the Annunciation Mary entrusted herself to God completely, with 'full submission of intellect and will' (Dei Verbum, 5), manifesting 'the obedience of faith' to him who spoke to her through his messenger.* [15] We go to her, in finishing our prayer, asking her to teach us how to listen attentively to everything that comes from God, and to put it into practice.

---

14. St Vincent Ferrer, *Treatise on the Spiritual Life*, II, 1
15. John Paul II, Encyclical, *Redemptoris Mater*, 25 March 1987, 13

93. EXAMINATION OF CONSCIENCE

93.1 The following of Christ and self-knowledge. The examination of conscience.

In the Gospel of the Mass our Lord speaks to us of the requirements for following him, and since He has called each one of us, we must be attentive. He gives us a warning: *For which of you, desiring to build a tower, does not first sit down and count the cost, whether he has enough to complete it? Otherwise, when he has laid a foundation, and is not able to finish, all who see it begin to mock him ... Or what king, going to encounter another king in war, will not sit down first and take counsel whether he is able with ten thousand to meet him who comes against him with twenty thousand?*[1] When a person accepts a great undertaking, he needs to make an appraisal of the entire situation. He must consider various possibilities and look for the opportune means for bringing the work to a successful completion. The supreme undertaking which we are called to as disciples of Christ is that of following him faithfully in the midst of our daily activities. To do this and to do it well, we must know what means are available to us, and also how to use them. We have to be aware of what is lacking in order to ask our Lord for it with confidence. We need to put effort as well into removing obstacles. This is the purpose of the examination of conscience. If we do it well, in depth, it will help us to

---

1. Luke 14:28-32

know the truth with regard to our own life. *Knowledge of self is the first step the soul must take in order to arrive at the knowledge of God.*[2]

Good businessmen are in the habit of drawing up a balance-sheet on a daily basis. They examine profit and loss, and are concerned to know where improvements can be made. They try to detect quickly anything harmful and to apply a remedy before greater harm is done to their business. Our great business, a daily one, is corresponding to our Lord's call. There is nothing of more importance to us or more truly in our best interest than coming closer to Christ.

In the examination of conscience, we take a look at our behaviour, our daily response to his call, having in mind what God wants of us. We are brought to ask for forgiveness and to make frequent new beginnings. *The examination of conscience is the preparatory step and the daily point of departure which will enable us to become more fervently ablaze with a love of God which may be seen in deeds of self-giving.*[3] Making the effort to carry out our examination in depth *will make it difficult for the germs of lukewarmness to take root in our souls, and will facilitate keeping our distance from occasions of sin.*

If we truly intend to acquire cleanness of heart, which will bring us to see God in everything, we need to take the daily examination of our soul very seriously. Whoever settles for a routine and superficial glance ends up slipping backward along an inclined plane of negligence and spiritual laziness, leading him towards lukewarmness, that nearsightedness of soul which does not distinguish between good and evil, between what proceeds from God and what proceeds

2. St John of the Cross, *Spiritual Canticle*, 4, 1

3. A. del Portillo, *Pastoral Letter*, 8 December 1976, 8

from our own passions or from the devil.[4]

It is love which moves us to make the examination of conscience and which gives a particular keenness to the soul for detecting those aspects of our behaviour which are not pleasing to God. Let us make the resolution – one which we will try to keep every day of our life – of *making the examination of conscience conscientiously.*[5] We will see perhaps very quickly, how great a help it will be for us in making our way along the road which leads to Christ.

93.2 The spirit of examination. Humility. Conquering laziness through the use of this practice of piety.

In order to strike a balance at the end of the day, it will prove a great help to have fostered a spirit of examination throughout the day, like *the good banker who daily, towards evening, determines his debits and credits. But this cannot be done in detail unless he is continually recording his transactions. A glance at his ledger shows the situation for that whole day.*[6]

To construct the tower that God expects of us, and to face the battle against the enemies of the soul – following the examples that the Lord gives us in the Gospel – we ought to have in mind what resources we can count on and what help we need. We must be aware of the walls into which we have not placed the requisite defences, or the flanks we have left uncovered and exposed to the mercy of the enemy – all the defects, in fact, which are known to us and which we ought to correct. We may also be aware of inspirations for good undertakings and for a more joyful service to others which we have yet to act upon. We may have gone along with spiritual mediocrity by not

---

4. *ibidem*
5. *ibidem*
6. St John Climacus, *The Ladder to Paradise*, 4

responding with generosity in matters which require small personal sacrifices. We may be giving too much importance to material goods, or allowing ourselves to be ruled by a spirit of comfort, or be carrying out things that have to do with God in a half-hearted manner.

Self-knowledge is not easy, and we need to be on guard against *the mute devil.*[7] He will try to close the door on the truth in order that we may not see the imperfections and weaknesses that are rooted in our souls. He will tend to have us excuse in ourselves those lacks of love of God which are our sins and imperfections, and to encourage us to regard them as though they were details of little importance or simply due to external circumstances. In order to have a deeper and truer self-knowledge, it is helpful to ask ourselves frequently: To what is my heart attracted most often? Would it be my own self? ... my sorrows, my success, my possible failure, my work – which really ought to be an offering to God? How often do I turn to God during the day either to ask for his forgiveness and give him thanks or to seek his help? What are the motivations underlying my daily activities? Where do my thoughts go most often? Have I lived this day for myself or for God? Have I sought him, or have I been looking for myself?

To come to know ourselves truly and to appraise our strengths correctly, we need to ask for humility, because without this virtue we remain in the dark. Humility leads us to begin our examination of conscience with the profound awareness that we are sinners.

Another enemy of the examination of conscience is laziness, which, when it has to do with our dealings with God, is called lukewarmness. One of its first

---

7. cf J. Escrivá, *The Way*, 236

manifestations is precisely the meagre effort we put into making the examination of conscience. What occurs then in the soul is similar to what happens when a farmer leaves his land ploughed but unseeded and untended. Soon there appear in the soul the thistles of defects and the thorns of disordered passions that will smother the seed of grace. *I passed by the field of a sluggard, by the vineyard of a man without sense; and lo, it was all overgrown with thorns; the ground was covered with thistles, and its stone wall was broken down.*[8]

By making a diligent, deep, and humble examination of conscience, we discover the roots of our faults in the areas of charity, work, joy and piety. Our falls in these areas could perhaps be frequent. Recognising this we are able to struggle and to conquer with the help of grace.

93.3 The method and dispositions. Contrition. Resolutions.

The examination of conscience is not simply a retrospective reflection on one's own behaviour. It is a dialogue between the soul and God. At the beginning, therefore, we ought to place ourselves in the presence of our Lord, just as when we begin any other time of prayer. Sometimes it will be enough to say an aspiration or a short prayer. We may find helpful the words of that blind man of Jericho, Bartimaeus, who asked Jesus for light for those eyes of his that could not see: *Domine, ut videam!, Lord, that I may see!* [9] Give light to my soul so that I may realize what it is that still separates me from you and see what it is I ought to uproot and throw away. Help me to see where it is that I ought to improve, whether it be in my work, or my

8. Prov 24:30-31
9. cf Mark 10:51

character, or my presence of God, or my joyfulness, or my optimism, or my apostolate, or my concern to make the lives of those with whom I live more pleasant.

Once we have begun the examination of conscience it may be helpful to consider how our day will have appeared to our Lord's eyes. With the help of our guardian angel we can try to see it reflected in God as in a mirror, for *we will never come to know ourselves if we do not try to know God*.[10] Then it is a question of considering our behaviour towards God, our neighbour, and ourselves in a more detailed way. This may be done by briefly reviewing the day, proceeding either from hour to hour or by the various activities that make up our day. We should give special importance to the fulfilment of the plan established for our spiritual life, to the previous day's resolutions for improvement, and to the advice we have received in spiritual direction. This practice of piety is clearly a very personal one. However, through spiritual direction we can receive a good deal of help on how to do it effectively.

Contrition is the most important part of the examination of conscience, which usually is brief, lasting just a very few minutes. If it is sincere, our sorrow will lead to some resolutions which again ought to be few (often just one), specific and, perhaps, small. For example, we may conclude that we need to discover some way to turn more frequently to our guardian angel or to be more punctual for work or for Mass. We may note the need for us to have a smile even though we be tired or not feeling very well or to be more kind and considerate. We could perhaps be putting more intensity and struggle into our mental prayer. We may see the need to have recourse more frequently to the Virgin Mary or to Saint Joseph, or to Jesus present in

---

10. St Teresa, *Mansions*, 1, 2, 9

the Blessed Sacrament. We may want to finish a particular task well, without giving in to any tendency to take short-cuts. We may see how to fulfil some one of our small mortifications better, or how to add one at mealtimes or in the interests of a better personal order. We may decide not to let another day pass without inviting certain friends to attend a retreat ... We should foster a sorrow which is heartfelt even though the fault be slight, and along with it we must ask God's help to fulfil these resolutions. Otherwise, even the small resolutions will not be carried out.

We will also see the good deeds of our day, and these will lead us to be grateful to our Lord. With this in mind, we will be able to rest with our souls full of peace and joy, and will be desirous of setting out again tomorrow along this way of love of God and neighbour.

94. STRETCH OUT YOUR HAND

94.1 God does not ask for the impossible. He gives us the grace we need to be saints.

Jesus entered the synagogue one Sabbath day; there was a man there with *a withered hand.* Saint Luke gives the detail that it was his right hand.[1] The Scribes and Pharisees watched him to see whether he would heal on the Sabbath. The pharisaical interpretation of the Law allowed healing on the Sabbath only where there was danger of death. Such was not the case with this man, who had come to the synagogue with his hope placed in Jesus.

Jesus was well aware of the thought-processes and intrigues of those who were guided more by the letter of the law than by the spirit of the Law. He says to the sick man, *Come and stand here. And he rose and stood there.* And Jesus, looking up, fixed his gaze on them and said to the man, *Stretch out your hand.* In spite of previous experiences, the man made an effort to do as the Lord told him, *and his hand was restored.* Above all, the man was cured by the divine power of Christ's words, but it is also true that he was cured through his docility in exerting himself to carry out precisely what was asked of him. It is this way with miracles of grace: when confronted with deficiencies which seem insurmountable, or by apostolic goals which seem too lofty or difficult, the Lord asks of us a special kind of effort. On the one hand, this attitude

---

1. Luke 6:6-11

consists in confidence in him, shown by having recourse to the supernatural means available. On the other, it consists in doing what we can, listening to what He tells us in the intimacy of our prayer or through spiritual direction.

Some Fathers of the Church have seen in these words of the Lord, *Stretch out your hand,* the need to exercise the virtues. Saint Ambrose comments: *Stretch out your hand often by doing favours for your neighbour, by protecting from harm one who suffers under the weight of calumny; stretch out your hand to the poor man who begs from you; stretch out your hand to the Lord, asking pardon for your sins. This is how you stretch out your hand, and this is how you will be cured.*[2] We do this by performing small acts of the virtue we are seeking to acquire, taking small steps toward the goal we wish to reach. If we concentrate on what we are doing, God does wonders through our seemingly small efforts. If the man with the withered hand had placed his reliance on his own previous experience rather than on the word of the Lord, he might not have done the little our Lord asked of him, and perhaps would have spent the rest of his life with his disability uncured. Virtues are formed day by day. Sanctity is forged by being faithful in details, in everyday things, in actions which might seem irrelevant if not vivified by grace.

We need to smooth off the rough edges a little more each day – just as if we were working in stone or wood – and get rid of the defects in our own lives with a spirit of penance, with small mortifications ... Jesus Christ will later make up for whatever is still lacking.[3] It is really He who makes sanctity a reality; it is He who moves souls. However, He wishes to take into account our collaboration,

---

2. St Ambrose, *Commentary on St Luke's Gospel, in loc*
3. J. Escrivá, *The Forge*, 403

which we give by obeying in that which has been pointed out to us, even though it might seem insignificant, as would be the case in stretching out one's hand. All of this leads to a cheerful ascetical struggle in which we will never tire. Our power resides in what is small.

94.2 Struggle in little things, in what is within our reach, in the areas indicated to us in spiritual direction.

Stretch out your hand ... Push yourself in the area of those little things that constitute the fabric of your day. Often we do not achieve the goals we aim at because we are not interiorly convinced of the need for the divine grace which makes our small efforts effective.

Lukewarmness paralyses the exercise of the virtues, whereas love gives it wings. Love has been *the engine of the saints*. Lukewarmness makes the smallest effort seem too difficult (a letter we should write, a call we should make, a talk we should have, punctuality in carrying out our daily plan). A grain of sand becomes a mountain. The lukewarm person thinks that even though our Lord asks him to stretch out his hand, he cannot even do that much. As a result of this belief he does not stretch out his hand ... and he is not cured. Love, on the other hand, draws out an abundant supernatural effectiveness from the small acts of virtue we can perform from morning to night. This love forges virtues, eliminates defects and enkindles in us the desire for sanctity. Just as drops of water wear the rock smooth and eventually penetrate it, our repeated good deeds create habits, solid steps in virtue. They keep these virtues alive and increase them.[4] Charity is strengthened by acts which seem scarcely important – putting on a

---

4. cf R. Garrigou-Lagrange, *The Three Ages of the Interior Life*, vol. I, p. 532

good face, smiling, creating an agreeable climate around us even when we are tired, not speaking of things that annoy or create difficulties for others, not growing impatient in rush-hour traffic, helping a friend who is falling behind in his work, lending one's lecture-notes to someone who has been sick ...

Deeply-rooted defects (sloth, egoism, envy ...) are conquered by trying to relive this scene of the Gospel, recalling Christ's command to *stretch out your hand*. One improves if, with God's grace, one struggles in little things – getting up when we should and not later, having regard to care and order in our dress, in our books. We improve when we try to serve those who live with us without their noticing, when we try to think less about our health or personal worries. We should know how to make a good choice of television programmes, and should know how to turn the set off when we have made a bad choice.

Our Lord is always saying to us: *Stretch out your hand*. In spite of having failed on other occasions, we can overcome our incapacity by making the small efforts which come by means of the inspirations of the Holy Spirit, and through the suggestions received in spiritual direction.

Along with God's grace, which we can rely upon, holiness depends in large measure on ourselves, on our docility and unflagging effort. It is said of Saint Thomas Aquinas that he was a man of few words. One day his sister asked what was needed in order for her to be a saint. Without pause he answered: *To want it*. We ask our Lord that we might come to him each day, wanting to be holy, being obedient in our struggle to achieve the goals set out for us in spiritual direction.

94.3 Docility in what God asks of each of us.

The man with the withered hand was docile to Jesus' words. He got up in the midst of everyone as the Lord had asked him. He listened to his words telling him to stretch out his diseased hand. Spiritual direction is geared to the Holy Spirit's intimate action within the soul, unceasingly suggesting small conquests which dispose us to receive additional graces. When a Christian does all he can so that virtues develop in his soul (removing obstacles, distancing himself from occasions of sin, fighting resolutely and decisively at the first appearance of temptations) God then generously supplies new help to strengthen incipient virtues; He grants the gifts of the Holy Spirit which perfect the habits already formed by grace.

Our Lord wants us to have a true desire to be saints, a desire that is realised in specific deeds. In the interior life, general ideas are not enough. *Have you seen how that imposing building was constructed? One brick after another. Thousands. But one at a time, and bags and bags of cement, one by one. And stone upon stone, each of them insignificant compared with the massive whole. And beams of steel, and men working, hour after hour, day after day ...*

Did you see how that imposing building was constructed? ... By dint of little things! [5]

Frequently when people speak of sanctity they mention its more striking aspects – the great trials, the extraordinary circumstances, perhaps even the martyrdom – as if Christian life exercised with all its consequences necessarily consisted in these things and were meant for only a few exceptional persons, as if our Lord had decided to be satisfied with a second-class Christian life for the majority of people. The contrary is the truth. The Lord

---

5. J. Escrivá, *The Way*, 823

calls *everyone* to holiness – the very busy mother with children and hardly enough time to manage her household affairs, the businessman, the student, the clerk in the department store. The Holy Spirit says to all of us: *This is the Will of God – your sanctification.*[6] This Will is efficacious, since God takes into account the circumstances in our life through which we shall pass, and He gives us the grace needed for us to act in a holy manner.

To grow in virtue we must pay attention to what our Lord is saying to us, often through intermediaries, and we must put this advice into practice. *What a sublime example of this docility is given to all of us by the Most Holy Virgin, Mary of Nazareth. She pronounced her fiat of total availability to God's design, and the Spirit began in her the realization of the plan of salvation.*[7] We ask our Mother Mary to help us to be ever more docile to the Holy Spirit, growing in virtue by struggling to attain the little goals of each day.

---

6. 1 Thess 4:3
7. John Paul II, *Address*, 30 May 1981

95. THE PRAYER OF CHRIST
– OUR OWN PRAYER

95.1 From heaven, our Lord continuously intercedes for us. His prayer is always efficacious.

We read in the Gospel[1] that Christ *went up to the hills to pray, and all night He continued in prayer to God.* On the following day, He chose the twelve Apostles. It is the prayer of Christ for the incipient Church.

In many places in the Gospels we are shown Christ united with his heavenly Father in an intimate and confident prayer. It is fitting, too, that Jesus, perfect God and perfect man, should pray in order to give us an example of a prayer that is humble, confident, and persevering, since He commanded us to pray always, without losing heart,[2] without allowing ourselves to be overcome by tiredness, in the same way that one breathes unceasingly.

Jesus made petitions to his Father, and his prayer was always heard.[3] His disciples knew well how powerful was the prayer of the Lord. After the death of Lazarus, his sister Martha said to Jesus: *Lord, if you had been here, my brother would not have died; and even now I know that whatever you ask from God, God will give you.*[4] When Lazarus rose from the dead, Jesus raised his eyes to heaven and said: *Father, I thank you because you have*

---

1. Luke 6:12-19
2. cf Luke 18:1
3. cf St Thomas, *Summa Theologiae*, 3, q.21, a.4
4. John 11:21-22

heard me; I know that you always hear me.[5] Before his passion, he prayed for Peter: *Simon, Simon,* he warned him, *Satan demanded to have you, that he might sift you like wheat; but I have prayed for you that your faith may not fail, and when you have turned again, strengthen your brethren.*[6] And Peter turned back again after his fall. In the same way, he had prayed for the Apostles and for all the Christian faithful at the Last Supper: *I do not pray that you should take them out of the world, but that you should keep them from the evil one ... Sanctify them in the truth.*[7] Jesus knows the discouragement into which his disciples will fall a few hours later, but his prayer will sustain them; it will obtain for them the strength to be faithful even to the point of giving their lives for their Master.

In this priestly prayer of the Last Supper our Lord beseeches his Father for all those who are to believe in him throughout the centuries. The Lord prayed for us, and his grace will never fail us. *The living Christ continues loving us even until now, this very day, and He presents to us his heart as the source of our redemption: 'Semper vivens ad interpellandum pro nobis' (Heb 7:25). In every moment, all the world, including ourselves, is enveloped in the love of this heart which has loved men so much, and to which they have responded so little.*[8] For our own part, let us try to correspond better.

From heaven, Jesus Christ, *seated at the right hand of the Father,*[9] intercedes for us who are members of his Church, and *He remains always our advocate and our mediator.*[10] Saint Ambrose reminds us that Jesus always

---

5. John 11:41-42
6. Luke 22:31-32
7. cf John 17:15 ff
8. John Paul II, *Homily,* Paris, 1 June 1980
9. *Nicene-Constantinopolitan Creed*
10. St Gregory the Great, *Commentary on Psalm 5*

pleads our cause before his Father, and that his prayer cannot be refused.[11] He asks his Father that the merits He acquired during his earthly life be continuously applied to us.

What a joy to think that Christ, *always lives to make intercession for us!*[12] This is so that our prayers and our work can be united to his prayer and, together with it, assume an infinite value. On occasion, our prayer lacks the humility, the trust, and the perseverance it needs; then we bolster it with the prayer of Christ; we ask him to inspire us to pray as we ought, according to the divine intention, to make our prayer spring forth from our hearts and to present it to his Father, so that we may be one with him for all eternity.[13] Even further: we make our entire life an offering intimately united to that of Jesus, through his Blessed Mother. *Holy Father! Through the Immaculate Heart of Mary, I offer you Jesus, your dearly beloved Son, and I offer myself in him, with him, and through him, for all his intentions and in the name of all creatures.*[14] Thus, our prayer and all our actions, intimately united to those of Jesus, acquire a value that is infinite.

95.2 The fruits of prayer.

With his example, the Master taught us the need for prayer. He repeated over and over again that it is necessary to pray and not lose heart. When we too recollect ourselves for prayer we place ourselves at the source of living waters.[15] There we will find the peace and strength necessary in order to continue, with joy and optimism,

11. cf St Ambrose, *Commentary on the Epistle to the Romans*, 8:34
12. Heb 7:25
13. cf R. Garrigou-Lagrange, *The Saviour*, p. 351
14. P.M. Sulamitis, *Offering to the Merciful Love*
15. cf Ps 41:2

along this path of life.

How much good we do for the Church and for the world with our prayer, with these periods of time, as here and now, in which we are together with the Lord! It has been said that those who truly pray are like the *columns of the world*, the props and supports without which everything would collapse. Saint John of the Cross beautifully taught that *even if it seems that nothing is happening, a little of this pure love is more precious before God and the soul, and does greater good for the Church, than all other works put together,*[16] works that are worth little or nothing without Christ. Precisely because prayer makes us strong in the face of difficulties, it helps us to sanctify our work, to give good example in our deeds, and to deal cordially and appreciatively with those who live or work with us. In prayer we discover the urgency of bringing Christ into the environments in which we find ourselves, an urgency that is all the more pressing the further from God those around us happen to be.

Saint Teresa echoed the words of *a very learned man*, for whom *the souls who do not have a life of prayer are like a 'paralysed' or crippled body, which, although it has feet and hands, cannot use them.*[17] Prayer is necessary in order to love the Lord more and more, in order never to be separated from him; without it, the soul falls into lukewarmness, loses its joy and the strength to do good.

The intimate dialogue of Jesus with God the Father was continuous; it gave him the opportunity to ask, to praise, to thank him; in every circumstance, the Lord turned to his Father. We should also aspire to such a constant encounter, to deal with God always, and especially in

---

16. St John of the Cross, *Spiritual Canticle*, 29, 2 b
17. St Teresa of Avila, *Interior Castle, First Mansions*, I, 6

the moments which we dedicate specifically to speaking with him, as in the Holy Mass, and as here and now, in this time in which we are meeting him in considering these matters. Throughout the day, too, in the situations of which the tapestry of our day is woven, when we begin or end our work or study, while we wait for the lift, when we run into an acquaintance on the street. That invocation full of tenderness – *Abba, Father'* – was constantly on the lips of the Lord; with it he often began his acts of thanksgiving, his petitions, his praise. How much it will help our soul to accustom ourselves to call to God in this way, to address him as Father, with tenderness and trust, with love!

All the solemn moments in the life of the Lord were preceded by prayer. *The Evangelist tells us that it was precisely during the prayer of Jesus that he manifested the mystery of his Father's love and revealed the communion of the three divine Persons. It is in prayer that we learn the mystery of Christ and the wisdom of the Cross. In prayer we perceive, in all their dimensions, the real needs of our brothers and sisters throughout the world; in prayer we find the strength to face whatever lies before us; in prayer we obtain the strength for the mission which Christ shares with us.*[18]

The holy Curé d'Ars used to say that all the evils that oppress us on earth come precisely from not praying, or from not praying well.[19] Let us formulate the resolution of turning to God with love and trust through our mental prayer, through our vocal prayers, and through those brief formulae or aspirations that come so readily to mind, and let us have the joy of living our life close to God the Father, the only place where it is worth our while to live.

---

18. John Paul II, *Homily*, 13 January 1981
19. St Jean Vianney, (The Curé d'Ars), *Sermon on Prayer*

95.3 Vocal prayer.

The Holy Spirit teaches us to deal with Jesus in our mental prayer and through vocal prayer, perhaps also with those prayers that we learned from our mothers when we were little. Even though as God He was omniscient, our Lord as man had to learn from the lips of his Mother the formulae of many prayers that had been handed on from generation to generation among the Hebrew people, and He left us the example of his appreciation for vocal prayer. In his last prayer to his Father he used the words of a Psalm. And he taught us the prayer *par excellence*, the Our Father, which contains all that we should ask for. Vocal prayer is a manifestation of the piety of our heart and helps us to keep a lively presence of God throughout the day, and in those moments of mental prayer when we find ourselves dry and nothing occurs to us.

The texts of the vocal prayers, many with biblical roots, and of those in the liturgy as well as of others composed by the saints, have been useful to innumerable Christians for giving praise and thanks, for asking help, for making amends. When we have recourse to these prayers we are living the Communion of Saints in an intimate way, and are grounding our faith upon the faith of the Church.[20]

In order to pray better and to avoid routine, this advice can be helpful to us: *Try to say them with the same ardour with which a person who has just fallen in love speaks ... and as if it were the last chance you had to approach Our Lord.*[21]

20. cf G. Chevrot, *In Secret*, Madrid, 1960
21. cf J. Escriva, *The Forge*, 432

TWENTY-THIRD WEEK: WEDNESDAY

96. PEACE IN ADVERSITY

96.1 Near Christ sorrow turns to joy.

Our Lord announces on several occasions that anyone who truly aspires to follow him closely will come into confrontation with the deeds of those who show themselves to be enemies of God and also of those who, although Christians, do not live in accordance with their Faith. On his way towards sanctity the Christian will encounter at times a hostile climate that our Lord did not hesitate to name with the hard word *persecution*.[1] In the last of the Beatitudes collected by Saint Luke in the Gospel of the Mass,[2] Jesus tells us, *Blessed shall you be when men hate you, and when they shut you out, and reproach you, and reject your name as evil, because of the Son of Man.* And we should not think that this persecution in the different ways in which it can present itself is something exceptional, that it will happen in special times or only in determined places: *No disciple is above his teacher, nor is the servant above his master. If they have called the master of the house Beelzebub, how much more those of his household!*[3] And Saint Paul warned Timothy in this way: *And all who want to live piously in Christ Jesus will suffer persecution.*[4]

But persecution does not mean disgrace, but blessedness, joy and happiness because it is a sign of

---

1. cf J. Orlandis, *The Eight Beatitudes*, p. 141
2. Luke 6:20-26
3. Matt 10:24-25
4. 2 Tim 3:12

authenticity in the following of Christ, a clear indication that both persons and works are heading in the right direction. If sometimes God permits us to feel the pain of open persecution, calumny and defamation, or of something more hidden, employing, say, an irony that ridicules Christian values, or of the pressures of an environment that tries to intimidate those who dare to maintain Christian standards, lowering them instead in public esteem, we have to know that this is a circumstance permitted by God so that we can achieve good results, since, as one martyr said while on his way to death *the harder the struggle, the greater the prize.*[5] Then it is that we should thank our Lord for this confidence He has had in us, in considering us capable of suffering something, however little it might be, for his sake. We will imitate, even though it be at a long distance, the Apostles, who after having been whipped publicly for preaching the Good News, came joyfully away from the Sanhedrin, *because they had been counted worthy to suffer disgrace for the name of Jesus.*[6] They did not let up in their apostolate, but preached Jesus with more fervour and joy. Neither should we be silent in like circumstances: prayer then has to be more intense, and even greater our concern for souls. It is good to recall the words of the Lord, *Be glad on that day and rejoice, because your reward will be great in heaven.*

Near Christ, sorrow turns to joy. *It is better for me, Lord, to suffer tribulation, as long as you are with me, than to reign without you, rejoice without you, glory in myself without you. It is better for me, Lord, to embrace you in tribulation, to have you with me in the furnace of fire, than to be without you, even in heaven itself. What would heaven mean to me without you, and with you what would the earth matter?*[7]

---

5. St Ignatius of Antioch, *Letter to St Polycarp of Smyrna*
6. Acts 5:41
7. St Bernard, *Sermon 17*

96.2 The opposition from *the good*.

Also our Lord warns us in the Gospel of today's Mass: *Woe to you when all men speak well of you! In the self-same manner their fathers used to treat the prophets.* Faith, when it is authentic, *brings down into opposition with itself many selfish interests so as not to cause scandal.*[8] It is difficult, perhaps impossible, to be a good Christian and not find oneself in conflict with a bourgeois and comfortable atmosphere that is frequently pagan. We have to ask continually for peace in the Church and for Christians of every country, but we should not be surprised or frightened if there is resistance from our surroundings to the teaching of Christ that we want to spread, a resistance in the shape of defamation, calumnies, etc. God will help us to receive abundant results from these situations.

When Saint Paul arrived in Rome, the Jews living there said, referring to the infant Church: *We know that everywhere it is spoken against.*[9] At the end of twenty centuries we see, both in recent history as well as at the present moment, how in various countries thousands of good Christians, priests and lay persons, have suffered martyrdom on account of their faith or have been marginalized or discriminated against for their beliefs, or have been kept out of public offices or teaching positions on account of their Catholicism, or encounter difficulties in procuring for their children a Christian education. Alternatively, it is the same oppressive atmosphere that looks upon religion as archaic, while *modernity* and *progress* are conceived of as liberation from 'restrictive' religious ideas.

It is difficult to understand calumny or persecution – either open or veiled – in an era in which one hears so

---

8. G. Chevrot, *The Eight Beatitudes*, p. 234
9. Acts 28:22

much about tolerance, understanding, fellowship and peace. But the attacks are more difficult to understand when they come from *good* men, when Christian persecutes, no matter how, another Christian, or a brother his brother. Our Lord prepared his own for the inevitable times when those who would defame, calumniate, or undermine their apostolic work would not be pagans or enemies of Christ, but brothers in the Faith who would think that with these actions they would be doing *a service to God.*[10] This *opposition from the good*, an expression that the founder of Opus Dei coined to describe a phenomenon that he experienced so painfully in his own life, is a trial that God sometimes permits. It is particularly painful for the Christian to whom it happens. The motives of the calumniators are usually due to human passions that can distort good judgment and complicate the clear intention of men who profess the same faith as those they attack, and who make up the same People of God. There are at times jealousies that supervene, rather than zeal for souls, rash allegations that appear to derive from envy, and make it possible to consider as evil the good that is being done by others. There can also be a kind of blinkered dogmatism that refuses to recognize for others the right to think in a different way in matters left by God to the free judgement of men. The *opposition from the good* usually shows itself in antipathy towards some brothers in the Faith, in a more or less masked opposition to their work, and a criticism that is as destructive as it is ill-informed.[11]

In any case, the position of the Christian who wants above all to be faithful to Christ has to be one where he can pardon, make amends and act with rectitude of

---

10. cf John 16:2
11. J. Orlandis, *op cit*, p. 150

intention, all the time looking towards Christ. *Don't expect people's applause for your work. What is more, sometimes you mustn't even expect other people and institutions, who like you are working for Christ, to understand you. Seek only the glory of God and while loving everyone, don't worry if there are some who do not comprehend what it is you are doing.*[12]

96.3 Fruits from lack of understanding.

We have to benefit greatly from opposition. *Violent persecutions had broken out. And that priest prayed: Jesus, may every sacrilegious fire increase in me the fire of Love and Reparation.*[13] Not only should difficulties not make us lose our peace or be a cause of discouragement, but rather they have to help us to enrich our soul, to make gains in interior maturity, in fortitude, in charity, in spirit of reparation and amendment, and in understanding.

Now, and in the kind of difficult moments that without their being uninterrupted, can happen in our life, those patient and serene words Saint Peter wrote to the early Christians when they suffered calumnies and persecution will do us much good. *Better to suffer while doing good, if such is the will of God, than to suffer when doing evil.*[14]

The Lord will take advantage of our hours of sorrow in order to bring about good for other people. *Sometimes He makes his intervention by means of miracles, other times by punishment, other times again by the happy events of this world, and finally, in some cases, by adversity.*[15]

In every situation we will always have open to us motives for being happy and optimistic, with the optimism

---

12. J. Escrivá, *The Forge*, 255
13. *ibid*, 1026
14. 1 Pet 3:17
15. St Gregory the Great, *Homilies on the Gospels*, 36

born of faith and confident prayer. *Christianity has too often been in what appeared at the time to be fatal danger for us now to be frightened by yet another such test. The ways by which Providence ransoms and saves its elect are unforeseeable. At times, our enemy becomes a friend; at times he is despoiled of the capacity for evil that made him fearsome; at times he auto-destructs, or, without desiring it, produces beneficial effects and simply vanishes without leaving a trace. Generally, the Church does not have to do anything but persevere with peace and confidence in the fulfilment of its tasks, remain serene, and await salvation from God.*[16]

The moments in which we encounter opposition and difficulties without exaggerating them are particularly propitious for exercising a whole range of virtues: we should pray for those who do evil to us, even without our knowing it, so that they may leave off offending God; we can strive to make amends to the Lord, to be even more apostolic, and to protect with exquisite charity those weaker brothers in the faith who on account of their age, their lack of formation, or the special situations they find themselves in, could sustain a greater harm to their souls.

The Virgin, our Mother, who helps us in every moment, will hear us particularly in more difficult times. *Turn to our Lady, the Mother, Daughter, and Spouse of God, and our Mother, and ask her to obtain more graces for you from the Blessed Trinity – the grace of faith, of hope, of love and of contrition, so that when it seems that a harsh dry wind is blowing in your life, threatening to parch and blast the flowers of your soul, they will not wither, and neither will those of your brothers.*[17]

---

16. Cardinal J. H. Newman, *The Biglietto Speech*, 12 May 1879
17. J. Escrivá, *op cit*, 227

TWENTY-THIRD WEEK: THURSDAY

97. THE MERIT OF GOOD WORKS

97.1 The supernatural reward for good works.

Our Lord often speaks to us of the merit which even
the smallest of our deeds has if we do it for him. Not even
a cup of water offered for his sake will go unrewarded.[1] If
we are faithful to Christ, we will find treasure in heaven in
return for a life offered day by day to our Lord. Life is
truly a time in which to merit, for in heaven we can no
longer do so; there we only reap the reward. Nor do we
gain merit in Purgatory, where souls are purified of the
remains of their sins. This life is the only time in which we
can gain merit – the days remaining to us here on earth –
and perhaps they will be few.

In the Gospel of today's Mass our Lord teaches that
in order to obtain this supernatural reward the works of
the Christian have to be superior to those of the pagan. *If
you love those who love you, what credit is that to you? For
even sinners love those who love them. And if you do good
to those who do good to you, what credit is that to you?
... Even sinners lend to sinners, to receive as much again.*[2]
Charity must embrace all men: it should not be extended
only to those who do good to us, since then the help of
grace would be unnecessary. Even pagans love those who
love them. The deeds of a Christian must not only be
humanly good and exemplary, but be generously inspired
by the love of God in order to make them supernaturally

---

1. cf Matt 10:42
2. Luke 6:32-34

meritorious.

God has assured us through the prophet Isaiah: *Electi mei non laborabunt frustra*,[3] my chosen ones shall not labour in vain. Nothing done for God shall be fruitless. Much of what we have earned we will doubtless see here on earth. There will be blessings. The rest, perhaps the greater portion, we shall perceive only in God's heavenly presence. Saint Paul reminded the early Christians: *Each shall receive his wages according to his labour.*[4] *Each one shall receive good or evil, according to what he has done in the body.*[5] *Now* is the time for merit. Saint Ignatius of Antioch exhorts us: *Your good works should be your investments, from which you will one day receive interest.*[6] Even in this life God repays us bountifully.

97.2 The Merits of Christ and Mary.

Electi mei non laborabunt frustra. The deeds of each day – our work, each small act of service, all joy, pain, rest and fatigue graciously borne and offered to our Lord – are meritorious, thanks to the infinite merits that Christ himself gained for us during his earthly life. It is *from his fullness we have all received, grace upon grace.*[7] To some gifts others are added in the measure that we correspond with them; and all gifts come from Christ, who is their sole source, and whose fullness of grace is never exhausted. *Not by sharing with us does Christ possess the gift (of grace), but He himself is both fountain and root of all virtues. He himself is life, and light, and truth, not keeping within himself the wealth of these blessings, but pouring it*

---

3. Is 65:23
4. 1 Cor 3:8
5. 2 Cor 5:10; cf Rom 2:5-6
6. St Ignatius of Antioch, *Epistle to St Polycarp of Smyrna, I*
7. John 1:16

forth upon all others, and even after the outpourings still remaining full. He suffers loss in no way by giving his wealth to others, but, while always lavishly dispensing to and sharing these virtues with all men, he remains in the same state of perfection.[8]

The Church teaches that a single drop of Christ's blood would have been sufficient for the Redemption of all mankind. Saint Thomas expresses this in his hymn *Adoro te devote*, on which many Christians meditate to increase their love and devotion for the Blessed Eucharist: *Pie pellicane, Iesu Domine, me immundum munda tuo sanguine.*

> *O loving Pelican! O Jesu Lord!*
> *Unclean I am but cleanse me in Thy Blood;*
> *Of which a single drop for sinners spilt;*
> *Can purge the entire world from all its guilt.*

The smallest act of love performed by Jesus during his childhood, or in his life of work in Nazareth, or indeed in any moment of his earthly life, had an infinite value for mankind – past, present and future – in helping them to obtain sanctifying grace and eternal life.[9]

No one partook so fully of the merits of Christ as did the Blessed Virgin Mary, his Mother and our Mother. Her sinlessness made her merits greater and her actions more meritorious than those of any other. Because she was immune to the effects of concupiscence and was unhindered by other obstacles to grace, her freedom was greater, and freedom is the radical principle of merit. All the sacrifices she made, all the sorrows she bore, were meritorious – from the poverty of Bethlehem and the anxiety of the flight into Egypt to the sword that pierced her

---

8. St John Chrysostom, *Homilies on St John's Gospel*, 14:1
9. cf R. Garrigou-Lagrange, *The Saviour*, 365

heart on beholding her crucified Son. And meritorious, too, were all the joy and happiness that sprang from her immense faith and from a love that imbued and penetrated everything in her life. Indeed, it is not the difficulty involved in its carrying out that makes a deed meritorious, but rather the love with which it is done. As Saint Thomas Aquinas said: *The difficulty which is overcome in loving one's enemy is meritorious only to the degree that the perfection of love which triumphs over that difficulty is manifest in it.*[10] Such was Mary's love.

It should make us happy to consider frequently the infinite merits of Christ, who is the source of all our spiritual life. Our reflection on the graces which Mary has gained for us will also strengthen our hope and revive our spirit in times of weariness or discouragement, or when those we wish to bring to Christ seem unresponsive despite our continuing to realize the need of our meriting for them. *You said to me: "I seem not only unable to go ahead along my way, but also unable to be saved without a miracle of grace. Oh, my poor soul! I remain cold and, what is worse, almost indifferent. It is as though I were an outsider looking at 'a case' (mine) which had nothing to do with him. Will these days turn out to be completely futile?*

And nevertheless, my Mother is my Mother, and Jesus – dare I say it? – 'my' Jesus. And there are good and saintly souls, at this very moment, praying for me." Go on walking hand in hand with your Mother, I replied, and 'dare' to say to Jesus that He is yours. In his goodness He will bring clear light to your soul.[11]

---

10. St Thomas, *Disputed questions on charity*, q 8, ad 17
11. J. Escrivá, *The Forge*, 251

97.3 Offer God our ordinary life. Gain merit for others.

Electi mei non laborabunt frustra. Merit is the right to a reward because of the works we do, and literally all our works can be meritorious, enabling us to turn our whole life into a time of merit. Theology teaches us[12] that merit, in the proper sense (*de condigno*), is that by which a recompense is owed *in justice*, or at least by virtue of a promise. Thus, in the natural order, the worker merits his salary. There is also another kind of merit which is called *congruous* (*de congruo*), by which recompense is owed, not in strict justice, or as a consequence of a promise, but for reasons of friendship or esteem, or simply of liberality. Thus, in the natural order, the soldier who has distinguished himself by bravery in battle perhaps merits (*de congruo*) a decoration. Courage is required of him as a soldier; but if he could have yielded and did not, or if he could have limited himself to fulfilling his basic duty, but made, instead, an extraordinary effort, his Commander would be moved in honour to reward such action in a measure beyond what is normally stipulated.

In the supernatural order, our acts merit, by the Will of God, a recompense which far exceeds all the honour and glory which the world can offer. By fulfilling his duties in his ordinary life the Christian in the state of grace gains more grace in his soul and merits eternal life. *For this slight momentary affliction is preparing for us an eternal weight of glory beyond all comparison.*[13]

The works we do each day are meritorious if we do them well and with an upright intention, if we offer them to God at the beginning of the day and in the Holy Mass, when we with a right intention start some task as well as

---

12. cf R. Garrigou-Lagrange, *op cit*, 366
13. cf Luke 6:20-26

when we finish it. Our works will be especially meritorious
if we unite them to the merits of Christ and to those of our
Lady. In this way we gain possession of those graces of
infinite value which our Lord won for us, principally on
the Cross, and which our Lady also won for us, co-
redeeming with her Son in an exceptional manner. God
our Father then sees our works invested with a new and
infinite character, for we have become sharers in the merits of Christ.

Conscious of this supernatural reality, should we not
ask ourselves whether we are trying to offer everything to
our Lord – the ordinary things of each day, and the exceptional or difficult ones, such as sickness, persecution or
slander? It is especially in these most difficult times that
we should remember the words of yesterday's Gospel:[14]
*Rejoice in that day, and leap for joy, for behold, your reward
is great in heaven.* These then are the occasions for loving
our Lord more deeply and for uniting ourselves to him
more closely.

There is yet another thing that can help us carry out
our tasks more perfectly. This is the realization that
through them we can *congruously* merit – relying on our
friendship with our Lord – the conversion of a son, a
brother or a friend, so long as we ourselves are in the state
of grace and seek perfectly to carry out our work for
God's glory alone. This was the way of the saints.

Let us, therefore, take full advantage of every opportunity to help others along the path to heaven. And let us
act in this way with even greater fervour and tenacity in
the case of those whom God has placed near to us and of
those who are seen to be in greatest need of spiritual help.

---

14. Pet 3:17

TWENTY-THIRD WEEK: FRIDAY

98. DIVINE FILIATION

98.1 Generosity towards God, who has wished to make us his sons and daughters.

When Saint Paul writes to Timothy and confidently opens his heart, he recalls how our Lord trusted him and made him an Apostle, despite his having been a *blasphemer* and *persecutor* of Christians. *The grace of our Lord*, he says, *has abounded beyond measure in the faith and love that is in Christ Jesus.*[1] We, also, can acknowledge that God has poured forth his grace upon us in great measure. After creating us, God has wished freely to give us the greatest dignity – that of being his children and achieving the happiness proper to the *domestici Dei*, the members of his own family.[2]

Natural divine filiation belongs only to God the Son: *Jesus Christ, the Son of God, the only-begotten, born of the Father ...*, *begotten, not created, consubstantial with the Father.*[3] But God, by means of a new creation, has wanted to make us his adopted children, partakers of his only Son's filiation: *Behold what manner of love the Father has bestowed upon us, that we should be called children of God, and such we are.*[4] God wanted to give his grace to Christians so that they might share in the divine nature: *Divinae consortes naturae*, says Saint Peter in one of his

---

1. *First Reading*, Year 1: 1 Tim 1:12-14
2. Eph 2:19
3. Council of Nicea, 325, Denz-Sch. 125
4. 1 John 3:1

Epistles.[5] In human generation, the life once received by the children no longer belongs to their parents; in contrast, by means of sanctifying grace the life of God himself is given to men. Without destroying or distorting our human nature, we are admitted into the intimacy of the Blessed Trinity by way of filiation, which in God is given through the only-begotten Son of the Father.

Our whole life, our being and all our activity, is affected by the fact of our divine filiation.[6] Multiple practical consequences spring from it – prayer, for example, becomes the dialogue between a little child and his father, because beyond his necessary designation as the Supreme Being, Creator and Almighty, we discover that God is truly our Loving Father. Our interior life is no longer a lonely fight against our defects, or an exercise in *perfecting oneself,* but rather an abandonment into the strong arms of him whose children we now truly are. We conceive a lively and practical desire to please our Father, God, who loves us so much.

All Christians can truthfully say: *God has bestowed his grace upon me*; He has brought us forth into a new life in Christ Jesus.[7] By this life we come to resemble Christ our Brother, and as such we are sons and daughters of the Father. It is precisely the Paraclete who teaches us this magnificent reality, and who makes it real even without our notice. Through him we recognize Jesus as the Son of God; we recognize ourselves to be God's children, not strangers, and act accordingly. Saint Thomas Aquinas summarizes our relationship with the Blessed Trinity in these brief words: *Adoption, though common to the whole Trinity, is appropriated to the Father as its author; to the*

---

5. 2 Pet 1:4
6. cf F. Ocariz, *The Meaning of Divine Filiation*, Pamplona 1982
7. Gal 3:28

Son, as its exemplar; to the Holy Spirit, as imprinting on us the likeness of this exemplar.[8]

This reality imbues our life with firmness and gives it a specific way in which to face its challenges. *Draw strength from your divine filiation. God is a Father – your Father! – full of warmth and infinite love. Call him Father frequently and tell him, when you are alone, that you love him, that you feel proud and strong because you are his sons.*[9] God is the rest and strength we need.

98.2 Consequences of our divine filiation: abandonment in our Lord.

If being a son of God means identification with his Son, it also implies looking at all the events of our life with the Son's eyes, judging them with his judgment, and obeying like Christ, who made himself *obedient unto death.*[10] We should love and forgive as He did, always acting as children who know they are in the presence of their Father God,[11] always full of confidence and serenity, sure of being understood and continually urged to move ahead in our life.

He who knows himself to be a son of God knows no fear. God knows best what our real needs are; he is stronger than we are, and he is our Father.[12] We must react like the child who, in the middle of a storm, continued playing while the sailors feared for their lives: he was the captain's son. When after disembarking the child was asked how he was able to remain at ease, surrounded as

8. St Thomas, *Summa Theologiae*, 3, q. 23, a. 2, ad 3
9. J. Escrivá, *The Forge*, 331
10. cf Phil 2:8
11. cf Maria C. Calzona, *Divine filiation and Christian life in the middle of the world*, EUNSA, Pamplona 1987
12. cf V. Lehodey, *Holy Abandonment*

he had been by a roaring sea and a terrified crew, he answered: *Fear? Why? My father was at the helm.* When we try to identify our will with the Will of God, it is He who steers us with an expert hand towards a safe harbour. Our life is then in good hands, whether the seas are calm or when the storm rages.

When God permits it, a person seriously striving for holiness may find himself as if lost in the midst of difficulties, feeling hopeless and perplexed, not understanding what is happening despite his desire to belong completely to God. *There are moments when one feels confused about the Will of God, and one cries: Lord, how can you will this, if it is so evil, if it is abominable 'ab intrinsico' – such was the complaint of Christ's Humanity in the Garden of Gethsemane. There are moments when our senses reel and our heart breaks. If you ever feel as if you are falling into a bottomless pit, I offer to you a prayer that I repeated many times beside the tomb of a person I loved: 'Fiat, adimpleatur, laudetur atque in aeternum superexaltetur iustissima atque amabilissima Voluntas Dei ...* '[13] *May the most just and most lovable will of God be done, be fulfilled, be praised and eternally exalted above all things. Amen. Amen.*[14]

Then is the time to be very faithful to the Will of God, the time to be completely docile in spiritual direction, to let ourselves be helped and encouraged, whether we understand or not. He is our Father, and if He allows this situation, this state of darkness, He will also provide the necessary graces and help. Abandonment in the hands of God, without setting limits, will win for us unbreakable

---

13. *Postulation of the Cause of Beatification and Canonization of the Servant of God, Josemaría Escrivá, Priest, Founder of Opus Dei, Articles of the Postulator*, Rome 1979, 45, 2

14. J. Escrivá, *The Way*, 691

peace. And in the midst of the most absolute emptiness we will feel the arm of God – powerful, though gentle – sustaining us. Then, slowly and with a sweet taste in our mouth, we will also repeat that confident prayer: *May the most just and most lovable will of God be done, be fulfilled, be praised ...*

98.3 Fraternity: We must relate to all God's children as the children of God that we ourselves are.

Thou dost show me the path of life; in thy presence there is fullness of joy, in thy right hand are pleasures for evermore,[15] the Psalmist proclaims. There is no deeper joy than that of the child of God who abandons himself in the hands of his Father, even when he is surrounded by want and emptiness, because there is nothing comparable to the infinite richness of being a member of God's family, one of his children. This supernatural joy, closely linked to the Cross, is the *great secret of Christians.*[16] A child of God never loses his peace, not even in the darkest of moments; consciousness of his divine filiation frees him from interior tension, and moves him to return contritely and confidently to his Father's house if he has gone astray out of weakness.

Divine filiation is also the foundation of Christian fraternity, which lies far above the human bond of solidarity.[17] Knowing that we are sons and daughters of the only Father, we feel ourselves to be the brothers of other Christians, whom God our Father has wanted to join to us with the supernatural bond of charity. Our fraternity must have countless manifestations in our ordinary life – mutual respect, delicacy in dealing with others, a spirit of

---

15. *Responsorial Psalm*, Year 1: Ps 15:11
16. cf G. K. Chesterton, *Orthodoxy*,
17. Maria C. Calzona, *op cit*

service and mutual help on the way towards God. In the Gospel of today's Mass, God demands that his own people have a clear vision of their brothers. *Why dost thou see the speck in thy brother's eye, and yet dost not consider the beam in thy own eye? ... First cast out the beam from thine own eye, and then thou wilt see clearly to cast out the speck from thy brother's eye?* [18] The Master invites us to look at others without the prejudices that arise from our own faults, or from the pride which tends to magnify the weaknesses of others and diminish our own. *Our Lord exhorts us to look at others from deeper within, with a different kind of glance ... For that purpose it is necessary to remove the beam from our own eye. Sometimes we busy ourselves in the comparatively trivial task of trying to remove the speck from everybody else's eye, but what is necessary is to radically alter our way of looking at them,*[19] to behold them as brothers of ours for whom God feels a special love. *Consider the others, especially those who are at your side, as children of God, with all the dignity which that marvellous title entails.*

We have to behave as God's children towards all of God's sons and daughters. Our love has to be a dedicated love, practised every day and made up of a thousand little details of understanding, hidden sacrifice and unnoticed self-giving. This is the good 'fragrance of Christ' that made those who lived among our first brothers in the faith exclaim: 'See how they love one another!' [20]

We must relate to the children of God as the children of God that we are, looking at people with the same love and understanding with which Christ looks at them, and we must do so with those who are close to us and with

---

18. Luke 6:41-42
19. A. M. G. Dorronsoro, *God and his people*, Madrid 1974
20. J. Escrivá, *Christ is passing by*, 36

those who seem far away. Our fraternity extends to all people, for they are all children of God, all his creatures, and all invited without exception to the intimacy of the Father's household. This same fraternity will move us to do a wide-ranging apostolate, without neglecting any means to bring souls closer to God.

Following the broad way of divine filiation, we will go through life with serenity and peace, *doing good*[21] like Jesus Christ, who is the Model in whom we must see ourselves constantly, in whom we learn how to be children of God and to behave as such. The Blessed Virgin, Mother of God and Mother of us all, will teach us to abandon ourselves in God, like the small and needy children we are. If we call upon her, Mary will never leave us unaided.

---

21. cf Acts 10:38

TWENTY-THIRD WEEK: SATURDAY

99. FULL OF GRACE

99.1 Mary's soul was filled with grace by the Holy Spirit.

No good tree bears bad fruit, nor again does a bad tree bear good fruit; each tree is known by its own fruit. For figs are not gathered from thorns, nor are grapes picked from a bramble bush. The good man out of the good treasure of his heart produces good, and the evil man out of his evil treasure produces evil; for out of the abundance of the heart his mouth speaks.[1]

By means of this double comparison – of the tree giving forth good or bad fruits, and of the man speaking from the depth of his heart – Jesus teaches us that sanctity cannot be feigned or substituted for by anything else: a man simply gives what is in him, no more and no less. Saint Bede elaborates on that idea: *The treasure of a soul is the same as the root of a tree. A person with a treasure of patience and charity in his soul produces beautiful fruits: he loves his neighbour, and possesses other qualities that Jesus recommends; he loves his enemies, does good to those who hate him, blesses those who curse him, and prays for the one who slanders him. But the man who has a source of evil in his soul does the exact opposite; he hates his friends, speaks badly of the one who loves him, and does all the other things condemned by the Lord.*[2]

Our Blessed Mother's heart was filled with graces by the Holy Spirit. Except for Christ's life, no life ever gave

---

1. Luke 6:43-49
2. St Bede, *Commentary on St Luke's Gospel*, 2:6

or will give forth such sweet fruit as the life of our Lady
has done. All graces come to us and keep coming to us
through her; above all, Jesus himself comes to us, the
blessed fruit of her most pure womb. From her lips have
poured forth the greatest, most pleasing, and most tender
praises of God. From her we have all received the best
advice: *Do whatever he tells you.*[3] It is advice that she
repeats silently in the intimacy of our hearts.

The Virgin Mary received the Angel's message in
Nazareth, the message by which she learned what had
been God's will for her from all eternity: that she should
be the Mother of his Son, the Saviour of the human race.
*For the messenger greets Mary as 'full of grace'; he calls her
thus as if it were her real name. He does not call her by her
proper earthly name, Miryam (Mary), but by this new name
– 'full of grace'. What does this name mean? Why does the
archangel address the Virgin of Nazareth in this way?*

*When we read that the messenger addresses Mary as
'full of grace', the Gospel context, which mingles revelations
and ancient promises, enables us to understand that among
all the 'spiritual blessings in Christ' this is a special 'blessing'. In the mystery of Christ she is present even 'before the
creation of the world', as the one whom the Father 'has
chosen' as Mother of his Son in the Incarnation. And, what
is more, together with the Father, the Son has chosen her,
entrusting her eternally to the Spirit of holiness.*[4]

Mary's dignity flows from the initial grace that she
received, preparing her to be the Mother of God; this
grace places her in a realm distinct from that of the angels
and saints. As the Second Vatican Council states, Mary is
the *Mother of the Son of God; and therefore she is also the*

---

3. John 2:5
4. John Paul II, Encyclical, *Redemptoris Mater*, 25 March 1987, 8

beloved daughter of the Father and the temple of the Holy Spirit. Because of this gift of sublime grace she far surpasses all creatures, both in heaven and on earth.[5]

All goodness, all beauty, all majesty, all loveliness, all grace adorn our Mother. Doesn't it make you fall in love, to have a Mother like that?[6]

99.2 Mary's plenitude of grace is an immense gift for us. Gratitude to God for this Marian privilege.

Saint Thomas states that the goodness of one grace is greater than the natural goodness of the entire universe.[7] The smallest amount of sanctifying grace within the soul of a child after his or her baptism is worth more than the natural goods of the entire universe, more than all of created nature, including the angels. Grace is a participation in God's inner life, which is greater than all miracles. What would Mary's soul be like, when God encompassed her with all possible splendour and with his infinite love?

God was pleased with Mary in the eternity of his being. *From always, in a continuous present, God delights in the the thought of his Mother, Daughter, and Spouse. It is not chance or caprice that the Church in her Liturgy has applied to our Lady those words of Scripture whose direct meaning refers to Uncreated Wisdom.*[8] And so we read in the Book of Proverbs: *Ages ago I was set up, at the first, before the beginning of the earth. When there were no depths I was brought forth, when there were no springs abounding with water. Before the mountains had been shaped, before the hills, I was brought forth; before he had made the earth with its fields, or the first of the dust of the world. When he*

---

5. Second Vatican Council, *Lumen gentium*, 53
6. J. Escrivá, *The Forge*, 491
7. cf St Thomas, *Summa Theologiae*, 1-2, q.113, a.9
8. C. Lopez Pardo, *The Ave Maria*, Madrid 1975

*established the heavens, I was there, when he drew a circle
on the face of the deep, when he made firm the skies above,
when he established the fountains of the deep, when he
assigned to the sea its limits, that the waters might not
transgress his command, when he marked out the foundations of the earth, then I was beside him, like a master workman; and I was daily his delight, rejoicing before him
always, rejoicing in his inhabited world and delighting in the
sons of men. And now, my sons, listen to me: happy are
those who keep my ways.*[9]

Our Lady is the throne of grace, in a very profound
way. To her we can apply these words from the epistle to
the Hebrews: *Let us then with confidence draw near to the
throne of grace, that we may receive mercy and find grace to
help in time of need.*[10] The throne is a symbol of the
authority which belongs to Christ, who is the King of the
living and the dead. But the throne is a throne of grace
and mercy,[11] and we can apply it to Mary according to
ancient liturgical texts;[12] through her all graces come to us.
Mary's protection is *like a spiritual river which has been
pouring down upon all men for nearly two thousand years.*[13]
It is a tree that keeps giving fruit, a tree that God willed to
plant with so much love. It is the immense treasure of
Mary who is constantly caring for her children. What
better way to obtain divine mercy than by having recourse
to the Mother of God, who is also our Mother?

The plenitude of grace with which God wished to fill
her soul is also an immense gift for us. Let us give thanks
to God for having given us his Mother as our own, for

---

9. Prov 8:23-32
10. Heb 4:16
11. cf *The Navarre Bible*, Epistle to the Hebrews, *in loc*
12. cf *Introit*, Mass of 22 August, before modification.
13. R. Garrigou Lagrange, *The Mother of the Saviour*

having made her so exquisitely beautiful in her whole being. And the best way to thank him is to love her very much, to deal with her throughout each day, to learn to imitate her in her love for her Son – and in her complete availability for whatever refers to God.

We say to her: *'Hail, full of grace'* ... and we are captivated by so much greatness and so much beauty, as the Archangel Gabriel must have been when he appeared before her. *Your name, Mother of God, your name! You are all my love!*[14]

99.3 Mary's most faithful correspondence with all graces.

Our Lady had the plenitude of grace which corresponded to her at every moment, and this grace grew and increased day by day, since graces and supernatural gifts do not limit the capacity of the one receiving them, but rather increase and expand that capacity for new gifts. The more we love God, the more our soul is enabled to love him further and to receive more grace. By loving we obtain new powers to love; whoever loves more has a greater desire to love and a greater capacity for loving. Grace invites more grace, and a plenitude of grace calls for an ever greater plenitude.

Mary's soul, at the first instant of its creation, received an immense treasure of graces. At that moment the words that the Angel spoke to her on the day of the Annunciation were already fulfilled: 'Hail, full of grace.[15] From the beginning Mary has been loved by God above all creatures, because the Lord was fully pleased with her and filled her with supernatural graces, *more than all the angelic spirits and more than all the saints.*[16] Many saints

---

14. St Alphonsus Liguori, *The Glories of Mary*
15. Luke 1:28
16. cf Pius IX, *Ineffabilis Deus*, 8 December 1854

and doctors of the Church consider that the initial grace in Mary was greater than the final grace of all other beings. Of our Lady, Saint Thomas states that *her dignity is in a certain sense infinite.*[17] This grace was given to Mary on account of her divine Motherhood.

What is more, because of her physical and spiritual contact with the Sacred Humanity of Christ – as his Mother – she is able to grow in grace in a continual and inexhaustible way. *In an entirely special and exceptional manner Mary is united to Christ, and similarly she is eternally loved in this 'beloved Son', this Son who is of one being with the Father, in whom is concentrated all the 'glory of grace.'*[18] The fruits of her maternity were extraordinarily great, according to the principle which Saint Thomas expresses as follows: the closer the recipient is to the source, the more he or she participates in its effects.[19] No other creature was ever so close to God. The continuous increase of our Mother's fullness of grace was more intense at certain specific moments of her life: at the Incarnation, at the Nativity, at the Cross, at Pentecost, when our Lady received the Holy Eucharist ...

Fullness of grace and fullness of freedom went together in our Lady, since one is more free in so far as one is more holy. As a result, she gave a most faithful response to these gifts of God, and through that response she obtained abundant merits. Let us, who are her children and who have such great need of her help, go to her now.

---

17. St Thomas, *op cit* 1, q.25, a.6 ad.4
18. John Paul II, *op cit* 8
19. cf St Thomas, *op cit* 3, q.7, a.1

Index to Quotations from the Fathers, Popes and the Saints

Note: References are to **Volume**/Chapter.Section

SUBJECT INDEX

Note: References are to **Volume**/Chapter.Section